lonely planet

ITALY

TOP SIGHTS, AUTHENTIC EXPERIENCES

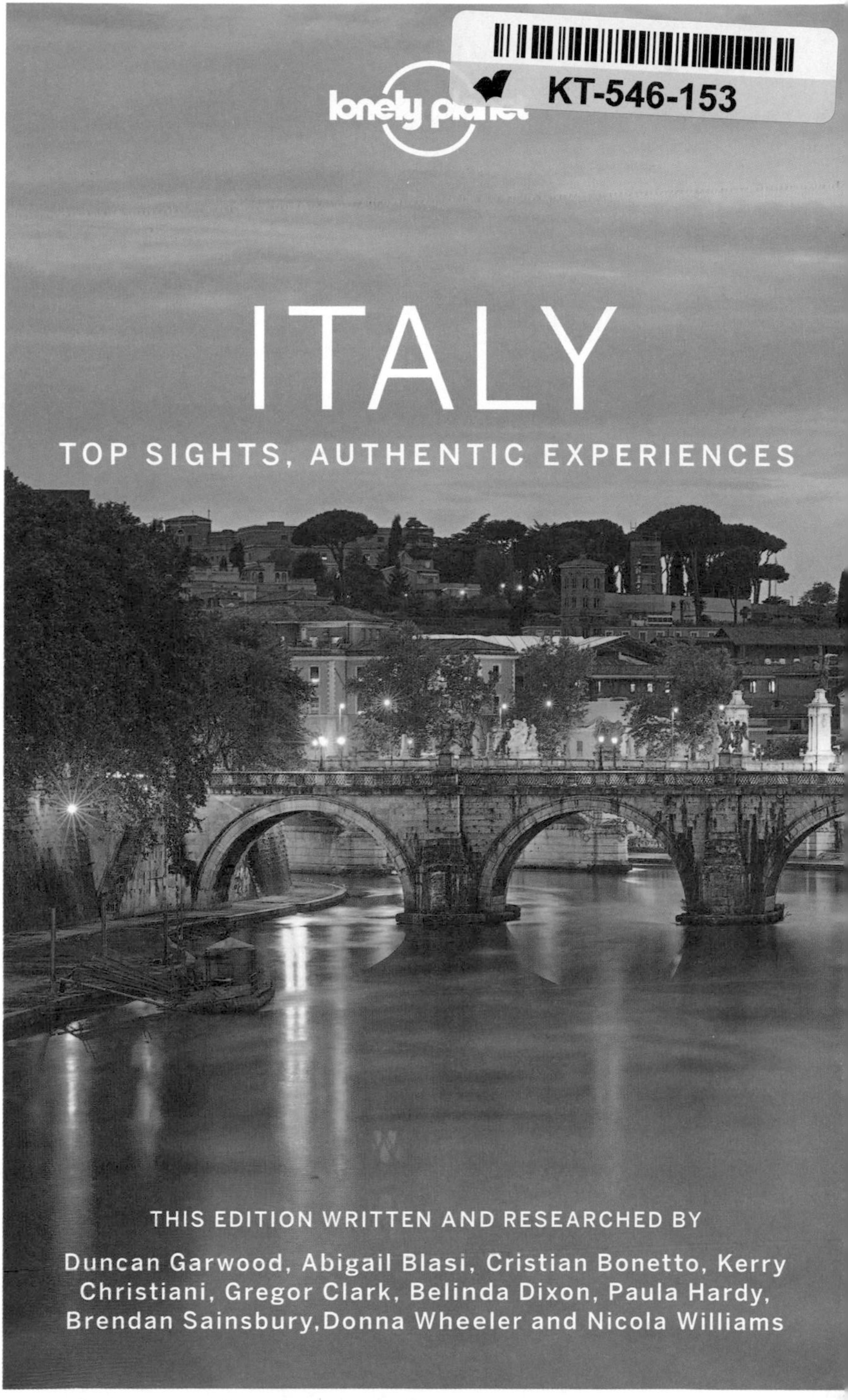

THIS EDITION WRITTEN AND RESEARCHED BY

Duncan Garwood, Abigail Blasi, Cristian Bonetto, Kerry Christiani, Gregor Clark, Belinda Dixon, Paula Hardy, Brendan Sainsbury,Donna Wheeler and Nicola Williams

Welcome to Italy

Epicentre of the Roman Empire and birthplace of the Renaissance, this sun-kissed virtuoso groans under the weight of its cultural cachet: it's here that you'll stand in the presence of Michelangelo's David *and Sistine Chapel frescoes, Botticelli's* Birth of Venus *and* Primavera *and da Vinci's* The Last Supper. *In fact, Italy has more Unesco World Heritage cultural sites than any other country on Earth.*

In few places do art and life intermingle so effortlessly. This may be the land of Dante, Titian and Verdi, but it's also the home of Prada, chef Gualtiero Marchesi and architect Renzo Piano. Beauty, style and flair furnish every aspect of daily life, from those immaculately knotted ties and perfect espressos to the flirtatious smiles of striking strangers. The root of Italian psychology is a dedication to living life well and, effortless as it may seem, driving that dedication is a reverence for the finer things. So slow down, take note and indulge in a little *bella vita*.

Italy's fortes extend beyond its galleries, plates and wardrobes. The country is one of Mother Nature's masterpieces, its geography offering extraordinary natural diversity. From the north's icy Alps and glacial lakes to the south's volcanic craters and turquoise grottoes, this is a place for doing as well as seeing.

> *beauty, style and flair furnish every aspect of daily life*

St Peter's Basilica (p42) and the River Tiber

SWITZERLAND
ITALIAN LAKES p218
Bolzano
Geneva
Lago Maggiore
Lago di Como
Trento
Aosta
Lake di Garda
VALLE D'AOSTA
PIEDMONT
Brescia
Padua
Verona
MILAN p198
Turin
FRANCE
Mantua
VENETO
EMILIA-ROMAGNA
Genoa
Bologna
CINQUE TERRE p144
FLORENCE p94
LIGURIA
MONACO
Pisa
San Gimignano
Arezz
Siena
Perugia
TUSCANY p126
CORSICA (FRANCE)
Viterbo
Ligurian Sea
ROME p34
Sassari
Oristano
SARDINIA
Cagliari
MEDITERRANEAN SEA
Trap
ALGERIA
TUNISIA
TUNIS

From left: Grand Canal (p170), Venice; Positano (p270), Amalfi Coast; Duomo (p133), Siena
MATTEO COLOMBO/GETTY IMAGES ©; ROBERT HARDING/GETTY IMAGES ©; ARTHERNG/GETTY IMAGES ©

Week 2

Naples to Sicily

Continue south for a two-day stopover in **Naples** (p232). Explore its highly charged streets and wonderful museums, and fill up on pizza.

35 minutes; 30 minutes

Take a day trip from Naples to discover the ruins of ancient **Pompeii** (p254).

to Sorrento 70 minutes, then to Positano 40 minutes; 1¾ hours

Leave Naples and take some time out on the **Amalfi Coast** (p266). Enjoy two days of breathtaking scenery in Positano, Amalfi and Ravello. If you have time, try for a trip over to Capri.

12 hours; 1 hour

Scoot back to Naples, then spend three days in **Sicily** (p280): one venturing up Mt Etna, one visiting the Valley of the Temples, and one in the island's hot-blooded capital, Palermo.

1¼ hours, then 3¼ hours

Staying Longer

Assisi to the Italian Lakes

Fly back to Rome and then take a bus up to **Assisi** (p156), the Umbrian birthplace of St Francis.

to Siena via Perugia 2 hours; 1¾ hours

From Assisi, push on to Tuscany. Spend three days here, one exploring medieval **Siena** (p132), one visiting **San Gimignano** (p130), then over to **Pisa** (p139) to see the legendary Leaning Tower.

via La Spezia 1¾ hours; 1½ hours

Next head up to the **Cinque Terre** (p144) for some stunning coastal walking.

via Genoa Piazza Principe 3¾ to 4½ hours; 3½ hours

Jump on a train and steer northwards for a blast of urban life in **Milan** (p198).

30 minutes to 1 hour; 1¼ hours

Finally, hotfoot it over to **Lago di Como** (p228), a relaxing spot to end your tour.

Contents

In Focus

Survival Guide

Plan Your Trip
Italy's Top 12

Rome

Rome was legendarily spawned by a wolf-suckled boy, grew to be Western Europe's first superpower, became the spiritual centrepiece of the Christian world and is now the repository of over two millennia of European art and architecture. From the Pantheon and the Colosseum to Michelangelo's Sistine Chapel and countless works by Caravaggio, there's simply too much to see in one visit. So, do as countless others have done before you: toss a coin into the Trevi Fountain and promise to return. From left: Street view in Trastevere (p74); Trevi Fountain (p67)

1

GONZALO AZUMENDI/GETTY IMAGES ©

Florence

According to Unesco, Florence contains 'the greatest concentration of universally renowned works of art in the world'. Florence is where the Renaissance kicked off and giants such as Brunelleschi, Michelangelo and Botticelli rewrote the rules of creative expression. The result is a city laden with artistic treasures, blockbuster museums and jewel-box churches. Its flawless medieval streets teem with wine bars, trattorias and elegant boutiques.

Top: Duomo (p98); Bottom: Ponte Vecchio (p115)

2

Tuscany

Italy's most romanticised region, Tuscany is tailor-made for aesthetes with its fabled landscape of vine-clad slopes, cypress trees and stone villas. Dotting this undulating wonderland are a string of urban masterpieces, from Gothic Siena to Manhattan-esque San Gimignano, and Pisa, home of Italy's iconic Leaning Tower. Wine lovers are in the right place, too, for Tuscany is home to some of the country's greatest wines.

3

4

Cinque Terre

For the sinful inhabitants of the Cinque Terre's five sherbert-coloured villages – Monterosso, Vernazza, Corniglia, Manarola and Riomaggiore – penance involved a hike up the vertiginous cliffside to the sanctuary to appeal for forgiveness. Scale the same trails today through terraced vineyards, and as the heavenly views unfurl, it's hard to think of a more benign punishment. For those seeking less exertion, hop from one village to the next on the train.

Riomaggiore (p154)

Assisi

Follow in the footsteps of St Francis to his home town of Assisi. Incredibly, this Umbrian hilltop centre seems to have changed little since the peace-loving saint and his friend St Clare lived here in the 12th century, and it's a thrilling experience to walk its narrow medieval lanes to the Basilica di San Francesco. This, the town's great landmark church, is one of Italy's most revered religious sites, a serene Gothic basilica adorned with a breathtaking series of frescoes.

MICHAL KRAKOWIAK/GETTY IMAGES ©

JUERGEN RICHTER/GETTY IMAGES ©

RASPU/GETTY IMAGES ©

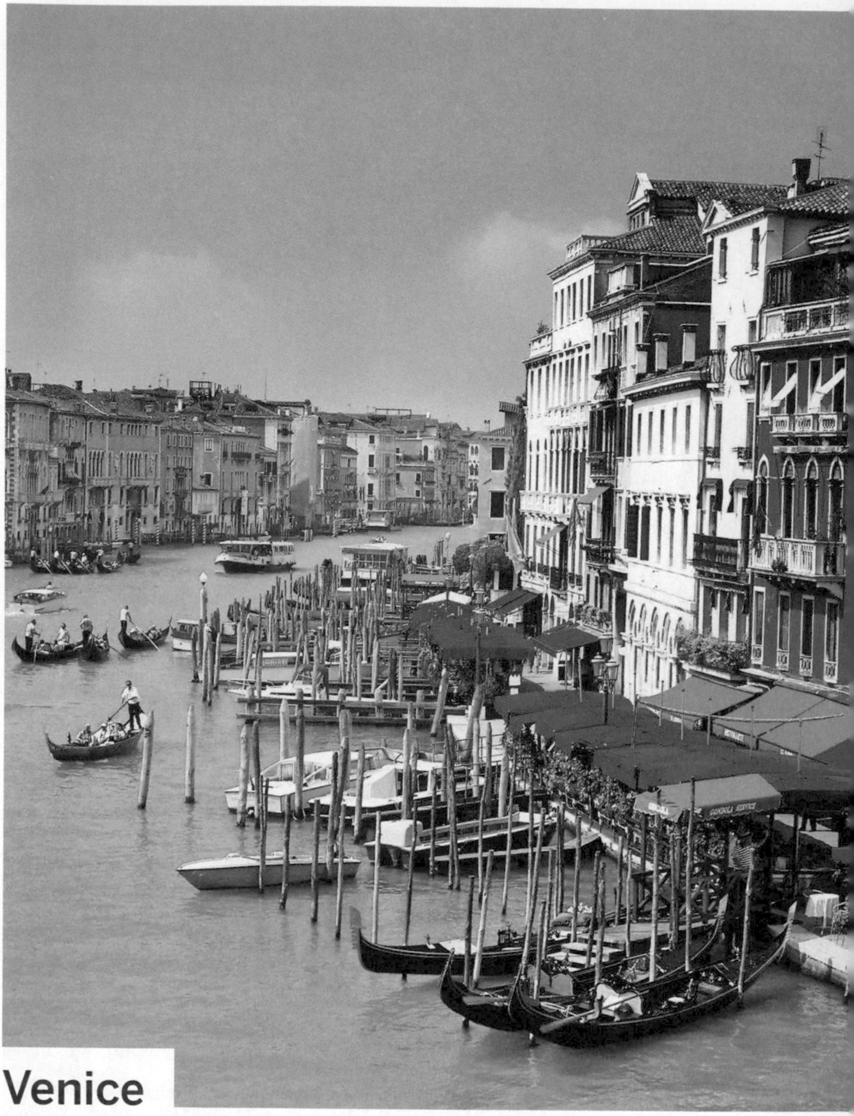

Venice

Venice isn't only beautiful; over the past millennium, the dazzling lagoon city has become musically gifted, exceptionally handy with molten glass and a single oar, and wickedly funny. The Grand Canal, the Basilica di San Marco and the Palazzo Ducale focus visitors' attention, but to savour the charms of *La Serenissima* (Venice's nickname, meaning 'the most serene') get lost in the crooked *calli* (backstreets), pause for a bubbly prosecco and tasty *cicheti* (Venetian bar snacks). Grand Canal (p170)

6

Milan

Italy's financial and fashion capital wows with its cosmopolitan, can-do atmosphere, vibrant cultural scene and sophisticated shopping. The city's legendary boutiques, contemporary galleries and dedication to cutting-edge design make for a stylish, forward-looking city. But Milan is not all about models and money; see historic sights including Leonardo da Vinci's *The Last Supper*, the immense Duomo and La Scala opera house. Duomo (p204)

7

Italian Lakes

If it's good enough for George Clooney, it's good enough for mere mortals. Nestled in the shadow of the Rhaetian Alps, dazzling Lago di Como is the most spectacular of the northern lakes, its art-nouveau villas home to movie moguls, fashion royalty and Arab sheikhs. Over the regional border in Piedmont, Lago Maggiore has been seducing visitors since its heyday as a fashionable belle époque retreat and Ernest Hemingway found inspiration for his WWI romance, *A Farewell to Arms*.

Lago di Como (p228)

BORIS STROUJKO/SHUTTERSTOCK ©

ANGELAFOTO/GETTY IMAGES ©

9

Naples

Nowhere else in Italy are people as conscious of their role in the theatre of everyday life as in Naples. And in no other Italian city does daily life radiate such drama and intensity. Naples' ancient streets are a stage, so to savour the flavour dive into the city's rough-and-tumble Porta Nolana market, a loud, lavish opera of hawking fruit vendors, wriggling seafood and the irresistible aroma of just-baked *sfogliatelle* (sweetened ricotta pastries).

From left: Naples Porta Norlana market; *sfogliatelle* pastries

REIDL/SHUTTERSTOCK ©

MICHELE FALZONE/GETTY IMAGES ©

EDELLA/GETTY IMAGES ©

Pompeii

Frozen in its death throes, the sprawling, time-warped ruins of Pompeii hurtle you back 2000 years. Wander through chariot-grooved Roman streets, lavishly frescoed villas, markets, theatres and even an ancient brothel. With one eye on ominous Mt Vesuvius, ponder Pliny the Younger's terrifying account of the town's final hours: 'Darkness came on again, again ashes, thick and heavy. We got up repeatedly to shake these off; otherwise we would have been buried and crushed by the weight'.

10

Amalfi Coast

Italy's most celebrated coastline blends superlative beauty and gripping geology: coastal mountains plunge into creamy blue sea in a scene of precipitous crags, sun-bleached villages and lush forests. Between sea and sky, mountain-top hiking trails deliver Tyrrhenian panoramas fit for a god. American writer John Steinbeck described the coast as a 'dream place that isn't quite real when you are there and...beckoningly real after you have gone'. Amalfi (p276)

Sicily

Sour, spicy and sweet, the flavours of Sicily reflect millennia of cross-cultural influences: Greek, Arab, Spanish and French. Tuck into golden *panelle* (chickpea fritters), fragrant couscous and chilli-spiked chocolate. From Palermo's Mercato di Ballarò to Catania's Pescheria, market stalls burst with local delicacies: Bronte pistachios, briny olives, glistening swordfish and nutty Canestrato cheese. Just leave room for a slice of sweet Sicilian *cassata* and *cannoli*.

12

…ve-Day Itinerary

A Slice of the South

Sample the best of Italy's sun-kissed south on this five-day trip from Naples to Sicily. Naples' fiery streets and majestic sights will warm you up for the road ahead, which takes in amazing ancient ruins and brooding volcanoes, as well as sublime food at every turn.

❶ Naples (p232)

Begin your southern getaway with two days in hyperactive Naples. The city's *centro storico* (historic centre) is home to baroque splendour galore, from the **Duomo** to the **Certosa di San Martino** (aloof above the city, with stunning views), the unparalleled **Museo Archeologico Nazionale** and the ultra-hip **MADRE** museum of contemporary art. Take a trip to **Mt Vesuvius** and wonder at the preservation of **Pompeii**. In between explorations, graze at myriad delicious restaurants, and decide whether Neapolitan pizza is the best in the world at **Pizzeria Gino Sorbillo**.

Naples to Catania

12 hours One daily departure

❷ Mt Etna (p284)

Having docked in Catania, dedicate your first day in Sicily to scaling **Mt Etna**, the island's legendary, and very active, volcano. Take the daily bus from Catania to the Rifugio Sapienza and then the cable car up to

From left: View over Naples (p233) to Mt Vesuvius; Fontana Aretusa (p300), Syracuse

2500m. From there either continue on foot or on a tour bus to the crater zone. Once back safely, spend the evening feasting on seafood and strolling Catania's Unesco-listed baroque centre. With more time, both **Syracuse** and **Taormina** are within striking distance of the city.

Catania to Agrigento

3 hours Hourly departures

❸ Valley of the Temples, Agrigento (p286)

Sicily's single most popular attraction more than merits the three-hour bus ride through the island's scorched interior to get to it. Centred on a series of fantastically preserved Greek temples, the ruins of the ancient city of Akragas are a truly unforgettable sight – the star of the show is the **Tempio della Concordia** in the eastern zone. Afterwards, overnight in Agrigento's historic centre.

Agrigento to Palermo

2½ hours Up to 11 daily departures

❹ Palermo (p288)

Spend your last day getting to grips with Palermo's highly charged streets and magnificent hybrid architecture. Must-sees include the mosaic-clad **Cappella Palatina** in the **Palazzo dei Normanni**, the **Cattedrale**, and the exquisite domed churches of **La Martorana** and **San Cataldo**. Before you leave, make sure to try one of the city's spectacular *arancini* (fried rice balls).

…en-Day Itinerary

PIERRE OGERON/GETTY IMAGES ©

Rome to the Lakes

This 10-day jaunt through central and northern Italy offers a vivid snapshot of the country's beauty. From Rome's ancient wonders to Tuscan treasures, a spectacular stretch of coastline and romantic lakes, it's a spellbinding trip.

❶ Rome (p34)

Spend your first two days in Rome. After experiencing Michelangelo's **Sistine Chapel**, summit **St Peter's Basilica**, then hit the historic centre for **Piazza Navona** and the **Pantheon**. Toss a coin into the **Trevi Fountain** and thrill at the sight of the **Colosseum**.

Rome to Assisi

3¼ hours Two daily departures

❷ Assisi (p156)

Follow the pilgrims to Assisi, the Unesco-listed home town of St Francis. Navigate your way to the **Basilica di San Francesco**, where you can see the saint's life unfold in a technicolour fresco cycle by Giotto.

Assisi to Florence

2½ hours Departures every two hours

❸ Florence (p94)

Continue northwest to Florence to go face to face with celebrated masterpieces: Brunelleschi's **Duomo** cupola, Botticelli's *Birth of Venus* in the **Galleria degli Uffizi** and Michelangelo's *David* in the **Galleria dell'Accademia**.

Florence to Lucca

1¼ to 1¾ hours Hourly departures

❹ Lucca (p138)

From Florence, head to the charming walled city of Lucca. Check out the striking **Cattedrale di San Martino** and join the locals for a *passeggiata* (evening stroll) on the monumental walls.

Lucca to Pisa

30 minutes Half-hourly departures

From left: Leaning Tower of Pisa and Pisa's Duomo (p139); Manarola (p153), Cinque Terre

FRANCESCO RICCA IACOMINO/GETTY IMAGES ©

❺ Pisa (p139)

Pisa is a must on anyone's Tuscan itinerary. Make a beeline for the **Piazza dei Miracoli**, where you'll find the **Leaning Tower** alongside Pisa's magnificent Duomo and cup-cake Battistero.

Pisa to Cinque Terre (Riomaggiore)

1¼ to 1¾ hours Via La Spezia; up to 15 daily departures

❻ Cinque Terre (p144)

Italy's coastal scenery is a sight to behold on the Cinque Terre, a glorious stretch of coastline punctuated by five picturesque villages. This is the place to get in some serious walking.

Riomaggiore to Milan

3¾ to 4½ hours Via Genoa Piazza Principe; hourly departures

❼ Milan (p198)

Suitably recharged, head across to high-octane Milan, home of the outlandishly Gothic **Duomo** and legendary opera house **Teatro alla Scala** (La Scala). Make sure you're booked to see Leonardo da Vinci's *The Last Supper*.

Milan to the Italian Lakes

To Como **30 minutes to 1 hour** at least hourly; to Stresa (Lago Maggiore) **1¼ hours** hourly departures

❽ Italian Lakes (p218)

See out your trip with a couple of days lakeside. Take your pick between the belle èpoque charms of **Lago Maggiore**, or scenic **Lago di Como**, hang-out of Hollywood stars and Midas-rich sheiks.

…wo-Week Itinerary

Classic Cities

Taking in much of the boot, this two-week tour of Italy's greatest hits leads from Milan to the Amalfi Coast by way of the country's headline cities. On the way you'll encounter artistic masterpieces, inspiring cityscapes and stunning natural scenery.

❶ Milan (p198)

Kick off with a day in Italy's great northern metropolis. Marvel at the awe-inspiring **Duomo** and Leonardo da Vinci's *The Last Supper*, browse designer boutiques in the **Quadrilatero d'Oro** and bar-hop in the Navigli canal district.

Milan to Venice

2½ to 3½ hours Departures two or three times hourly

❷ Venice (p166)

Spend the next couple of days basking in Venice's haunting beauty. Check off must-sees such as the **Basilica di San Marco**, **Palazzo Ducale** and the **Grand Canal**, and toast your travels with a glass of local *prosecco* wine.

Venice to Florence

2¼ hours Fast trains leave hourly throughout the day

❸ Florence (p94)

Next up is a three-day Tuscan interlude. Spend the first couple of days marvelling at Florence's Renaissance treasures: the **Duomo**, the **Galleria degli Uffizi** and the **Galleria dell'Accademia**. On day three, take a day trip to **Pisa** to visit the **Leaning Tower**.

Florence to Siena

1¼ hours Departures at least hourly

From left: Bridge of Sighs, Venice (p167); Interior of St Peter's Basilica (p42), Rome

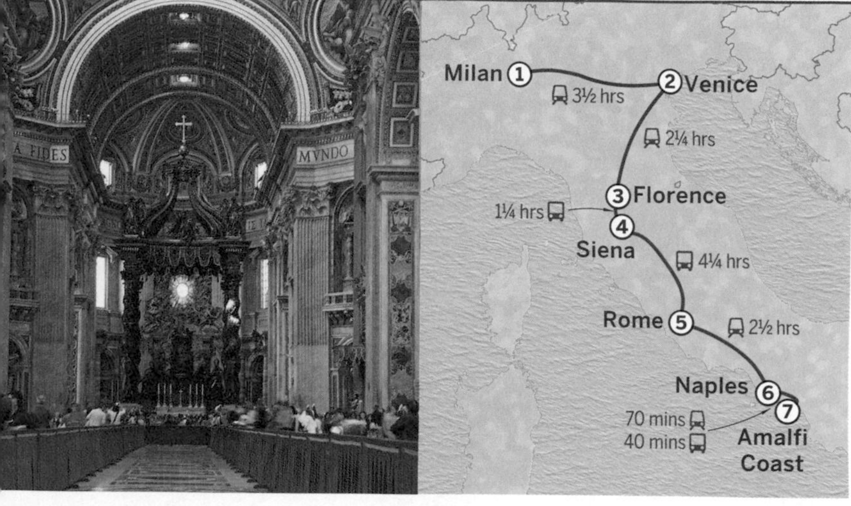

❹ Siena (p132)

Continue south to the magnificent medieval city of Siena. Kick off with a cappuccino in **Piazza del Campo** (Il Campo), then visit the **Museo Civico** and the city's astonishing landmark **Duomo**.

Siena to Rome

3¾ hours To Fiumicino Airport twice daily, then **30 minutes** into central Rome

❺ Rome (p34)

The beginning of week two opens with three days in the Eternal City. That's not much time, but move quickly and you can take in top sights such as the **Colosseum**, **Roman Forum**, **Pantheon** and Vatican, home to **St Peter's Basilica** and the **Vatican Museums**.

Rome to Naples

2 to 2½ hours Frequent daily departures

❻ Naples (p232)

Head south for a couple of days in Naples. Take in the **Museo Archeologico Nazionale** and the Dickensian streets of the *centro storico*, stopping off at the **Cappella Sansevero** and **Complesso Monumentale di Santa Chiara**. Dedicate the second day to **Pompeii**.

Naples to Positano/Amalfi

70 minutes Circumvesuviana train to Sorrento, then **40 minutes** to Positano

❼ Amalfi Coast (p266)

After two weeks on the road, Italy's most spectacular stretch of coastline makes the ideal finale. Revel in spectacular views from lofty **Ravello**, browse chintzy boutiques in **Positano** and lap up the holiday vibe in medieval **Amalfi**.

f You Like...

Masterpieces

Sistine Chapel More than just Michelangelo's show-stealing ceiling, this world-famous chapel in Rome also features work by Botticelli and Ghirlandaio. (p41)

Galleria degli Uffizi Cimabue, Botticelli, da Vinci, Raphael, Titian: Florence's blockbuster art museum delivers a who's who of artistic deities. (p104)

Museo e Galleria Borg hese A perfectly sized serve of Renaissance and baroque masterpieces in an elegant villa in Rome. (p50)

Basilica di San Fran cesco See just how Giotto revolutionised art with his masterly works in this church in Assisi. (p160)

Museo del Novecento Modigliani, de Chirico, Kandinsky, Picasso, Fontana: a first-class 20th-century art museum in modernist Milan. (p208)

Villa dei Misteri, Pompeii The Dionysiac Frieze in the dining room of this grand villa is one of the world's largest ancient frescoes. (p264)

Palazzo Grassi The exceptional contemporary collection of French billionaire François Pinault is showcased against Tadao Ando interior sets in Venice. (p171)

Museo Archeologico Nazionale Naples' premier museum showcases one of the world's finest collections of ancient Greek and Roman art. (p236)

Fabulous Food

Seafood So fresh you can eat it raw in Venice and Sicily.

Pizza Italy's most famous export, but who makes the best: Naples or Rome?

Tuscan T-bone Carnivores drool over Florence's *bistecca alla fiorentina* (T-bone steak), hailing from Tuscany's prized Val di Chiana.

Sicilian specialities Buxom eggplants, juicy raisins, fragrant couscous and velvety marzipan – cross-cultural Sicily puts the fusion in Italian cuisine.

Gelato Innovative flavours ready for licking at Rome's gelaterie artigianale.

Cicheti Venice's answer to tapas.

From left: Selection of fish *cicheti*, Venice; Galleria Doria Pamphilj (p83), Rome

PHOTOGOLFER/SHUTTERSTOCK ©

Villas, Palaces & Gardens

In Rome don't miss **Galleria Doria Pamphilj** (p83), **Palazzo Farnese** (p67) and **Palazzo Barberini**. (p71)

Palazzo Ducale The doge's Venetian palace comes with a golden staircase and interrogation rooms. (p174)

Palazzo Reale di Capodimonte Naples' colossal Bourbon palace houses masterpieces by Botticelli, Caravaggio, Titian and Andy Warhol. (p247)

The Italian Lakes Fringed with fabulous gardens such as those at **Isola Madre** (p225), **Villa Serbelloni** (p222) and **Villa Taranto** (p228).

Villa Romana del Casale The remains of a decadent Roman villa decorated with the finest Roman floor mosaics in existence. (p298)

Villa Rufolo Stroll among a Scotsman's romantic 19th-century gardens in atmospheric Ravello. (p278)

Giardini Pubblici Venice's first green space and the home of the celebrated Biennale with its avant-garde pavilions. (p185)

Markets

Porta Nolana Elbow your way past fragrant bakeries and bootleg CD stalls for a slice of Neapolitan street theatre.

Mercato di Ballarò Fruit, fish, meat and veg stalls packed under striped awnings down cobbled alleys: Palermo's market is more African bazaar than Italian market. (p289)

Porta Portese A modern commedia dell'arte takes place every Sunday between vendors and bargain hunters at Rome's mile-long flea market. (p79)

Mercato Centrale Crammed with fresh produce, Florence's oldest and largest food market also houses a bookshop, cook school, bar and food stalls. (p120)

Mercato Metropolitano Housed in a former railway station, Milan's newest food market whets the appetite. (p213)

Plan Your Trip
Month by Month

OLEG ZNAMENSKIY/SHUTTERSTOCK ©

January

Regata della Befana

Witches in Venice don't ride brooms: they row boats. Venice celebrates Epiphany on 6 January with the Regatta of the Witches, complete with a fleet of brawny men dressed in their finest *befana* (witch) drag.

February

Carnevale

In the period leading up to Ash Wednesday, many Italian towns stage pre-Lenten carnivals, with whimsical costumes, confetti and special festive treats. Venice's Carnevale (www.carnevale.venezia.it) is the most famous.

March

Taste

For three days in March, gourmands flock to Florence for Taste (www.pittimmagine.com), a bustling food fair held inside industrial-sleek Stazione Leopolda. The program includes culinary-themed talks, cooking demonstrations and the chance to sample food, coffee and liquor from more than 300 Italian artisan producers.

Settimana Santa

On Good Friday, the Pope leads a candlelit procession to the Colosseum and on Easter Sunday he gives his blessing in St Peter's Sq, while in Florence, a cartful of fireworks explodes in Piazza del Duomo.

April

Salone Internazionale del Mobile

Held annually in Milan, the world's most prestigious furniture fair (salonemilano.it) is joined in alternate years by lighting, accessories, office, kitchen and bathroom shows too.

Maggio Musicale Fiorentino

Established in 1933, Italy's oldest art festival (www.operadifirenze.it) brings world-class performances of theatre, classical music, jazz and dance to Florence's

From left: Carnevale, Venice; Parade during Il Palio celebrations (p28), Siena

DARIO MITIDIERI/GETTY IMAGES ©

sparkling new opera house and other venues across the city. Events run from late April to June.

Settimana del Tulipano

Tulips erupt in spectacular bloom during the Week of the Tulip, held at Lake Maggiore's Villa Taranto; the dahlia path and dogwood are also in bloom in one of Europe's finest botanical gardens.

May

Maggio dei Monumenti

As the weather warms up, Naples rolls out a mammoth, month-long program of art exhibitions, concerts, performances and tours around the city. Many historical and architectural treasures usually offlimits to the public are open and free to visit.

Ciclo di Rappresentazioni Classiche

Classical intrigue in an evocative Sicilian setting, the Festival of Greek Theatre (www.indafondazione.org), held from mid-May to mid-June, brings Syracuse's 5th-century-BC amphitheatre to life with performances from Italy's acting greats.

Wine & The City

A two-week celebration of regional vino in Naples (www.wineandthecity.it), with free wine degustations, *aperitivo* sessions, theatre, music and exhibitions. Venues span museums, castles and galleries to restaurants, shops and yachts.

June

Napoli Teatro Festival Italia

For three weeks in June, Naples celebrates all things performative with the Napoli Teatro Festival Italia (www.napoliteatrofestival.it). Using both conventional and unconventional venues, the program ranges from classic works to specially commissioned pieces from both local and international acts.

La Biennale di Venezia
Held in odd-numbered years, the Venice Biennale (www.labiennale.org) is one of the art world's most prestigious events. Exhibitions are held in venues around the city from June to October.

Ravello Festival
Perched high above the Amalfi Coast, Ravello draws world-renowned artists during its summer-long Ravello Festival (www.ravellofestival.com). Covering everything from music and dance to film and art exhibitions, several events take place in the exquisite Villa Rufolo gardens from late June to early September.

Giostra del Saracino
This medieval jousting tournament sees the four *quartieri* (quarters) of Arezzo put forward a team of knights to battle on one of Tuscany's most beautiful and unusual city squares, Piazza Grande; third Saturday in June and first Sunday in September.

July

Il Palio di Siena
Daredevils in tights thrill the crowds with this chaotic bareback horse race around the piazza in Siena. Preceding the race is a dashing medieval-costume parade. Held on 2 July and 16 August.

August

Ferragosto
After Christmas and Easter, Ferragosto, on 15 August, is Italy's biggest holiday. It marks the Feast of the Assumption, but even before Christianity the Romans honoured their gods on Feriae Augusti. Naples celebrates with particular fervour.

Mostra Internazionale d'Arte Cinematografica
The Venice International Film Festival (www.labiennale.org/en/cinema) is one of the world's most prestigious silver-screen events. Held at the Lido from late August to early September, it draws the international film glitterati with its red-carpet premieres and paparazzi glamour.

September

Regata Storica
On the first Sunday in September, gondoliers in period dress work those biceps in Venice's Historic Regatta. Period boats are followed by gondola and other boat races along the Grand Canal.

Chianti Classico Wine Fair
There is no finer opportunity to taste Tuscany's Chianti Classico than at Greve in Chianti's annual Chianti Classico Expo (www.expochianticlassico.com), the second weekend in September.

October

Romaeuropa Festival
From late September to early December, top international artists take to the stage for Rome's premier festival of theatre, opera and dance (romaeuropa.net).

November

Ognissanti
All Saints' Day on 1 November commemorates the Saint Martyrs, while All Souls' Day, on 2 November, is set aside to honour the deceased.

Opera Season
Italy is home to four of the world's great opera houses: La Scala in Milan, La Fenice in Venice, Teatro San Carlo in Naples and Teatro Massimo in Palermo. The season traditionally runs from mid-October to March, although La Scala opens later on St Ambrose Day, 7 December.

December

Natale
The weeks preceding Christmas are studded with religious events. Many churches set up nativity scenes known as *presepi*. Naples is especially famous for these. On Christmas Eve the Pope serves midnight mass in St Peter's Sq.

Plan Your Trip
Get Inspired

MATTEO COLOMBO/GETTY IMAGES ©

Barcaccia fountain, Piazza di Spagna (p67), Rome

Read

History (Elsa Morante; 1974) War, sexual violence and a mother's struggles define this controversial novel.

The Baron in the Trees (Italo Calvino; 1957) This tragicomic fable is a metaphor for Italy's postwar reinvention.

The Snack Thief (Andrea Camilleri; 2000) A maverick cop on his toes stars in this whodunit.

The Leopard (Giuseppe di Lampedusa; 1958) An epic tale of Sicily's Independence upheavals; it's Italy's all-time best seller.

My Brilliant Friend (Elena Ferrante; 2012) The first of an exquisite quartet of Neopolitan novels.

Watch

La Dolce Vita (1960) Federico Fellini's tale of hedonism, celebrity and suicide in 1950s Rome.

Bicycle Thieves (1958) Vittorio di Sica's poignant tale of an honest man trying to provide for his son in postwar Rome.

Il Postino (1994) Massimo Troisi plays Italy's most adorable postman.

Gomorra (2008) In-your-face mafia exposé based on Roberto Saviano's best seller.

Videocracy (2009) Chilling documentary about Italy's celebrity and television-infused culture.

La Grande Bellezza (2013) Set in Rome, Paolo Sorrentino's wonderful Fellini-esque peer into modern Italy's psyche.

Listen

La Traviata (1955) Diva Maria Callas embodies Verdi's fallen woman in La Scala's production by film-maker Luchino Visconti.

Crêuza de mä (Fabrizio de André) Bob Dylan–style poetry in Genovese dialect.

Mina (Mina) Best-selling album from Italy's foremost female rocker.

Stato di Necessità (Carmen Consoli) Guitar riffs and soulful lyrics from Sicily's favourite singer-songwriter.

Suburb ('A67) Neapolitan rock-crossover group 'A67 collaborate with anti-Mafia activists.

Plan Your Trip
Family Travel

DAVID SOANES PHOTOGRAPHY/GETTY IMAGES ©

Kids love Italy: pizza and ice cream as a staple diet; white-sand beaches for bucket-and-spade magic; ancient Roman ruins for roaming around; mountains for skiing down, lakes for splashing and boating. Gladiators, volcanoes, gondolas... it's a story book come true. Not only that, but the feeling's mutual – Italy loves kids. You can feel relaxed eating out, there'll be no raised eyebrows if kids are out past their bedtime and the welcome is warm – babies will be particularly adored.

Inspiration

How do you get kids to go along with holiday plans, and let them think it's their idea? Italy makes it easy, with sights and activities that appeal to kids and grown-ups alike. Sprawling ancient Roman sites give kids a chance to run around, and let adults daydream about what life was like thousands of years ago. Caves and catacombs are worthy dares, though the latter are cramped and spooky enough only to be good for older kids. Grand villa estates have gardens for picnics and playtime, and art for contemplation and downtime. *Agriturismi* (farmhouse stays) are money-savers that may include rustic meals, sometimes a pool and farm animals.

Everyone's a winner with Italian island beach vacations, and across Italy there is gelato and a place to run about on every major piazza. For more information and ideas, see Lonely Planet's *Travel with Children* and *Not For Parents Rome*, and the superb Italy-focused website www.italiakids.com.

Planning

Italians love children, but there are few special amenities. In this guide, look for the family-friendly icon 👪 highlighting places that are especially welcoming to families. Book accommodation in advance, and ask about extra beds. Reserve train

From left: Marina Grande, Capri (p272); Grand Canal (p170), Venice

ALEXANDER HAASE/EYEEM/GETTY IMAGES ©

seats when-ever possible to avoid finding yourselves standing.

Need to Know

Baby formula and sterilising solution Available at pharmacies.

Disposable nappies (diapers) Available at supermarkets and pharmacies.

High chairs Available at many restaurants.

Change facilities Rare outside airports and more state-of-the-art museums.

Cots Request ahead at hotels.

Strollers Bring your own.

Infant car seats Reserve at car-rental firms.

Budgeting

Sights Admission to many tourist attractions is free or heavily discounted for children under 18 (listed as 'reduced' in this guide).

Best Destinations for Kids

Sicily (p280)

Venice (p166)

Capri (p272)

Rome (p34)

Amalfi Coast (p266)

Transport Discounts are often available for children under age 12.

Hotels and agriturismi Many offer special rates on room and board for kids. Check the handy website www.booking.com, which details the 'kid policy' for every hotel it lists, including what extra charges apply to kids' breakfasts and extra beds.

Restaurants Kids' menus are uncommon, but you can ask for a mezzo piatto (half-plate), usually at half-price.

Plan Your Trip
Need to Know

When to Go

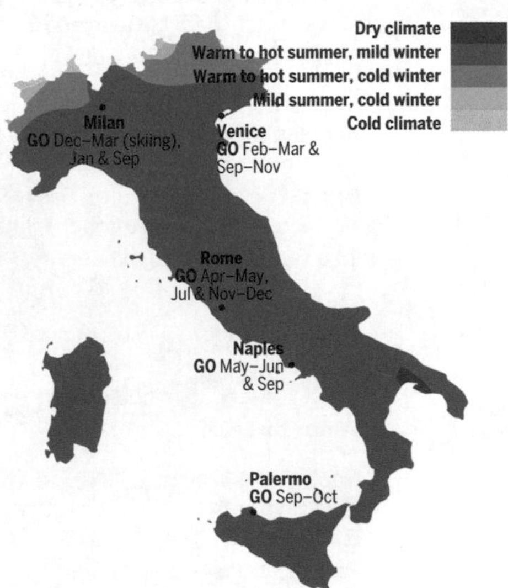

High Season (Jul–Aug)

- Queues at sights and on the road, especially in August.
- Prices also rocket for Christmas, New Year and Easter.
- Late December to March is high season for skiing.

Shoulder (Apr–Jun & Sep–Oct)

- Good deals on accommodation, especially in the south.
- Spring is best for festivals, flowers and local produce.
- Autumn provides warm weather and the grape harvest.

Low Season (Nov–Mar)

- Prices up to 30% less than in high season.
- Many sights and hotels closed in country areas.
- A good period for cultural events in large cities.

Currency

Euro (€)

Language

Italian

Visas

Generally not required for stays of up to 90 days (or at all for EU nationals); some nationalities need a Schengen visa.

Money

ATMs at every airport, most train stations and widely available in towns and cities. Credit cards accepted in most hotels and restaurants.

Mobile Phones

Local SIM cards can be used in European, Australian and some unlocked US phones. Other phones must be set to roaming.

Time

Central European Time (GMT/UTC plus one hour)

Room Tax

Visitors may be charged an extra €1 to €7 per night 'room occupancy tax'.

Daily Costs

Budget: Less than €100

- Dorm bed: €15–30; double room in a budget hotel: €50–110
- Pizza or pasta: €6–12

Midrange: €100–250

- Double room in a hotel: €110–200
- Local restaurant dinner: €25–50
- Admission to museum: €4–15

Top End: More than €250

- Double room in a four- or five-star hotel: €200–450
- Top restaurant dinner: €50–150
- Opera ticket: €40–200

Websites

Lonely Planet (www.lonelyplanet.com/italy) Destination information, hotel bookings, traveller forum and more.
Trenitalia (www.trenitalia.com) Italian railways website.
Agriturismi (www.agriturismi.it) Guide to farm accommodation.
Enit Italia (www.italia.it) Official Italian-government tourism website.
The Local (www.thelocal.it) English-language news from Italy, including travel-related stories.

Opening Hours

We've provided high-season opening hours. 'Summer' times generally refer to April to September or October, while 'winter' times are from October or November to March.

Banks 8.30am–1.30pm & 2.45–3.45pm or 4.30pm Monday to Friday

Restaurants Noon–2.30pm & 7.30–11pm or midnight

Cafes 7.30am–8pm

Bars and clubs 10pm–4am or 5am

Shops 9am–1pm & 4–8pm Monday to Saturday, some also open Sunday

Arriving in Italy

The following local transport options will get you from the airport to the city centre.

Fiumicino airport, Rome (p91)

Express train €14; every 30 minutes, 6.23am to 11.23pm

Bus €5 to €7; 5am, 10.55am, noon, 3.30pm, 7pm (Sunday only), plus night services at 1.15am, 2.15am and 3.30am

Taxi €48 set fare; 45 minutes

Malpensa airport, Milan (p216)

Express train €12; every 30 minutes, 6.53am to 9.53pm

Bus €10; every 20 minutes, 5am to 10.30pm, then hourly through night

Taxi €90 set fare; 50 minutes

Marco Polo airport, Venice (p195)

Ferry €15; every 30 to 60 minutes, 6.15am to 1.15am

Bus €6; every 30 minutes, 8am to midnight

Water taxi €110; 30 minutes

Capodichino airport, Naples (p251)

Shuttle bus €3 to €4; every 20 minutes, 6.30am to 11.40pm

Taxi €19 set fare; 30 minutes

Getting Around

Train Reasonably priced, with extensive coverage and frequent departures. High-speed trains connect major cities.
Car Handy for travelling at your own pace, or for visiting regions with minimal public transport. Not a good idea for travelling within major urban areas.
Bus Cheaper and slower than trains. Useful for more remote villages not serviced by trains.

For more, see the **Survival Guide** (p333)

Colosseum (p46)

ROME

PETER M. WILSON/DESIGN PICS/GETTY IMAGES ©

JOACHIM MESSERSCHMIDT/GETTY IMAGES ©

NIKADA/GETTY IMAGES ©

Discover More
www.lonelyplanet.com/italy/rome

Clockwise from top left:
Trevi Fountain (p67);
Piazza della Rotonda (p60);
Ponte Sant'Angelo and Castel Sant'Angelo (p76);
Barcaccia fountain in the Piazza di Spagna, and the Spanish Steps (p67);
St Peter's Sq (p75)

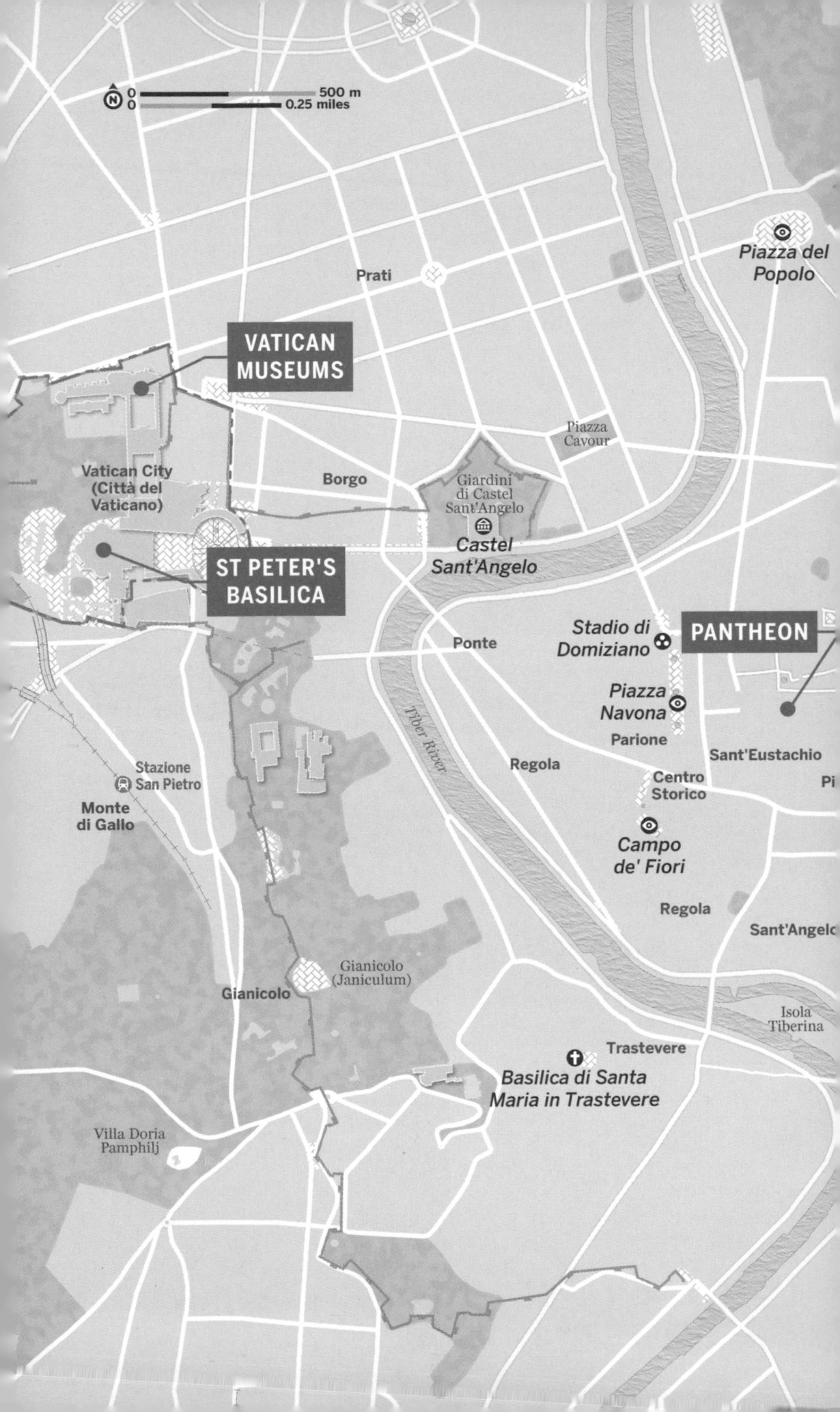
0 500 m
0 0.25 miles
Prati
Piazza del Popolo
VATICAN MUSEUMS
Piazza Cavour
Vatican City (Città del Vaticano)
Borgo
Giardini di Castel Sant'Angelo
Castel Sant'Angelo
ST PETER'S BASILICA
Stadio di Domiziano
PANTHEON
Ponte
Piazza Navona
Parione
Tiber River
Sant'Eustachio
Stazione San Pietro
Regola
Centro Storico
Monte di Gallo
Campo de' Fiori
Regola
Sant'Angelo
Gianicolo (Janiculum)
Gianicolo
Isola Tiberina
Trastevere
Basilica di Santa Maria in Trastevere
Villa Doria Pamphilj

St Peter's Basilica (p42)

Planning Ahead

☑ When to Go

In spring and early autumn there's good weather and many festivals and outdoor events.

What's On

Easter At noon on Easter Sunday the pope blesses the crowds in St Peter's Square.

Natale di Roma Rome celebrates its birthday on 21 April with music, historical re-enactments and fireworks.

Lungo il Tevere (www.lungoiltevereroma.it) A summer-long festival with music, films and bars on the banks of the Tiber.

Festa del Cinema di Roma (www.romacinemafest.it) Rome's October film festival at the Auditorium Parco della Musica.

➡ Rome in Two Days

Start early at the **Colosseum** (p46), then the **Palatino** (p62) and **Roman Forum** (p52). Spend the afternoon and evening in the *centro storico*, exploring **Piazza Navona** (p66) and the **Pantheon** (p44). On day two, hit the **Vatican Museums** (p38) and **St Peter's Basilica** (p42). Afterwards, check out the **Spanish Steps** (p67) and **Trevi Fountain** (p67). Round the day off in the **Campo de' Fiori** (p67).

➡ Rome in Four Days

Spend day three investigating **Villa Borghese** (p76) – make sure to book for the **Museo e Galleria Borghese** (p50) – and **Piazza del Popolo** (p70). End the day with dinner in **Trastevere** (p84). Next day, admire classical art at the **Capitoline Museums** (p62) before checking out the basilicas on the **Esquiline** (p71). See the evening out in boho **Monti** (p89).

From left: Pizza; Stazione Termini; Colosseum (p46); Villa Borghese (p76)

Vatican Museums

Founded in the early 16th century, the Vatican Museums boast one of the world's greatest art collections. Highlights include spectacular classical statuary, a suite of rooms frescoed by Raphael, and Michelangelo's painted Sistine Chapel.

Great For...

☑ Don't Miss

Two of the world's most famous works of art: Michelangelo's frescoes and the *Last Judgment*.

Housing the museums are the lavishly decorated halls and galleries of the Palazzo Apostolico Vaticano. This vast 5.5-hectare complex consists of two palaces – the Vatican palace (nearer to St Peter's) and the Belvedere Palace – joined by two long galleries. On the inside are three courtyards: the Cortile della Pigna, the Cortile della Biblioteca and, to the south, the Cortile del Belvedere.

Pinacoteca

Often overlooked by visitors, the papal picture gallery contains Raphael's last work, *La Trasfigurazione* (Transfiguration; 1517– 20), and paintings by Giotto, Fra Angelico, Filippo Lippi, Perugino, Titian, Guido Reni, Guercino, Pietro da Cortona, Caravaggio and Leonardo da Vinci, whose haunting *San Gerolamo* (St Jerome; c 1480) was never finished.

WIBOWO RUSLI/GETTY IMAGES ©

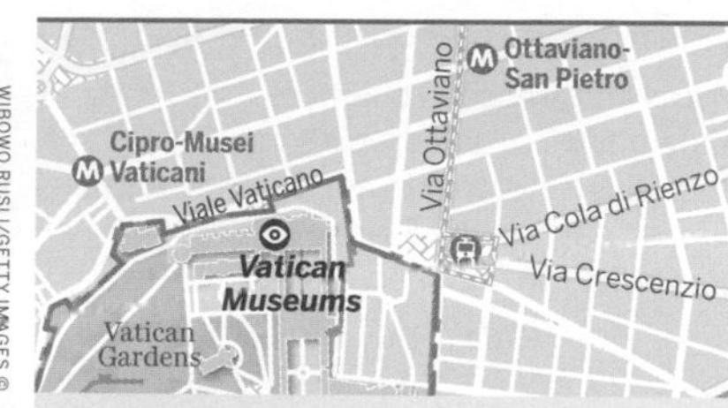

Need to Know

Musei Vaticani; ☎06 6988 4676; http://mv.vatican.va; Viale Vaticano; adult/reduced €16/8, last Sun of month free; ⏰9am-4pm Mon-Sat, 9am-12.30pm last Sun of month; Ⓜ Ottaviano-San Pietro

Take a Break

Head out to **Pizzarium** (p85) for some of Rome's best sliced pizza.

★ Top Tip

Avoid queues by booking tickets online at http://biglietteriamusei.vatican.va/musei/tickets/do (plus €4 booking fee).

Museo Pio-Clementino

This stunning museum contains some of the Vatican Museums' finest classical statuary. To the left as you enter the Cortile Ottagono (Octagonal Courtyard), the *Apollo Belvedere* is a 2nd-century Roman copy of a 4th-century-BC Greek bronze. A beautifully proportioned representation of the sun god Apollo, it's considered one of the great masterpieces of classical sculpture. Nearby, the 1st-century *Laocoön* depicts a muscular Trojan priest and his two sons in mortal struggle with two sea serpents.

Back inside, the Sala degli Animali is filled with sculpted creatures and some magnificent 4th-century mosaics. Continuing on, you come to the Sala delle Muse, centred on the *Torso Belvedere*, a fragment of a muscular 1st-century-BC Greek sculpture used by Michelangelo as a model for his *ignudi* (male nudes) in the Sistine Chapel. It's currently undergoing restoration.

The next room, the Sala Rotonda, contains a number of colossal statues, including a gilded-bronze *Ercole* (Hercules) and an exquisite floor mosaic. The enormous basin in the centre of the room was found at Nero's Domus Aurea and is made out of a single piece of red porphyry stone.

Galleria delle Carte Geografiche (Map Gallery)

The last of three galleries – the other two are the Galleria dei Candelabri (Gallery of the Candelabra) and the Galleria degli Arazzi (Tapestry Gallery) – this 120m-long corridor is hung with 40 16th-century topographical maps of Italy.

Stanze di Raffaello (Raphael Rooms)

These four frescoed chambers, currently undergoing partial restoration, were part of Pope Julius II's private apartments. Raphael himself painted the Stanza della Segnatura (1508–11) and the Stanza d'Eliodoro (1512–14), while the Stanza dell'Incendio (1514–17) and Sala di Costantino (1517–24) were decorated by students following his designs.

The first room you come to is the Sala di Costantino, which features a huge fresco depicting Constantine's defeat of Maxentius at the battle of Milvian Bridge.

The Stanza d'Eliodoro, which was used for private audiences, takes its name from the *Cacciata d'Eliodoro* (Expulsion of Heliodorus from the Temple), an allegorical work reflecting Pope Julius II's policy of forcing foreign powers off Church lands. To its right, the *Messa di Bolsena* (Mass of Bolsena) shows Julius paying homage to the relic of a 13th-century miracle at the lakeside town of Bolsena. Next is the *Incontro di Leone Magno con Attila* (Encounter of Leo the Great with Attila) by Raphael and his school, and, on the fourth wall, the *Liberazione di San Pietro* (Liberation of St Peter), a brilliant work illustrating Raphael's masterful ability to depict light.

The Stanza della Segnatura, Julius' study and library, was the first room that Raphael painted, and it's here that you'll find his great masterpiece, *La Scuola di Atene* (The School of Athens), featuring philosophers and scholars gathered around Plato and Aristotle.

The most famous work in the Stanza dell'Incendio di Borgo is the *Incendio di Borgo* (Fire in the Borgo), which depicts

Galleria delle Carte Geografiche (p39)

Pope Leo IV extinguishing a fire by making the sign of the cross. The ceiling was painted by Raphael's master, Perugino.

Sistine Chapel (Capella Sistina)

The museums' grand finale, the Sistine Chapel is home to two of the world's most famous works of art: Michelangelo's ceiling frescoes (1508–1512) and his *Giudizio Universale* (Last Judgment; 1535–1541).

Michelangelo's ceiling design, best viewed from the far east wall, covers the entire 800-sq-metre surface. With painted architectural features and a cast of colourful biblical characters, it's centred on nine panels depicting scenes from the Creation, the story of Adam and Eve, the Fall, and the plight of Noah.

As you look up from the east wall, the first panel is the *Drunkenness of Noah*, followed by *The Flood*, and the *Sacrifice of Noah*. Next, *Original Sin and Banishment from the Garden of Eden* depicts Adam and Eve being sent packing after accepting the forbidden fruit from Satan, represented by a snake with the body of a woman coiled around a tree. The *Creation of Eve* is then followed by the *Creation of Adam*. This, one of the most famous images in Western art, shows a bearded God pointing his finger at Adam, thus bringing him to life. Completing the sequence are the *Separation of Land from Sea*; the *Creation of the Sun, Moon and Plants*; and the *Separation of Light from Darkness*, featuring a fearsome God reaching out to touch the sun. Set around the central panels are 20 athletic male nudes, known as *ignudi*.

Opposite on the west wall, is Michelangelo's mesmeric *Giudizio Universale*, showing Christ – in the centre near the top – passing sentence over the souls of the dead as they are torn from their graves to face him. The saved get to stay up in heaven (in the upper right), the damned are sent down to face the demons in hell (in the bottom right).

The chapel's walls also boast superb frescoes. Painted in 1481–82 by a crack team of Renaissance artists, including Botticelli, Ghirlandaio, Pinturicchio, Perugino and Luca Signorelli, they represent events in the lives of Moses (to the left looking at the *Giudizio Universale*) and Christ (to the right).

When to Go

Tuesdays and Thursdays are quietest; Wednesday mornings are good as everyone is at the pope's weekly audience.

Guides

On the whole, exhibits are not well labelled, so consider hiring an audio guide (€7) or buying the excellent *Guide to the Vatican Museums & City* (€14).

St Peter's Basilica overlooking St Peter's Sq

St Peter's Basilica

In this city of outstanding churches, none hold a candle to St Peter's Basilica, Italy's largest and most spectacular basilica. Its lavish interior contains three of Italy's most celebrated masterpieces: Michelangelo's Pietà, *his soaring dome, and Bernini's 29m-high baldachin.*

Great For...

☑ Don't Miss

The *Pietà* is a hauntingly sad depiction of a youthful Mary, cradling the body of Jesus after the crucifixion.

Facade

Built between 1608 and 1612, Carlo Maderno's immense facade is 48m high and 118.6m wide. Eight 27m-high columns support the upper attic on which 13 statues stand representing Christ the Redeemer, St John the Baptist and the 11 Apostles. The central balcony is known as the Loggia della Benedizione, and it's from here that the pope delivers his *Urbi et Orbi* blessing at Christmas and Easter.

Interior

The cavernous interior contains many artistic masterpieces, including Michelangelo's hauntingly beautiful *Pietà* at the head of the right nave. Sculpted when he was only 25, it is the only work he ever signed – his signature is etched into the sash across the Madonna's breast.

Interior of St Peter's Basilica

WIBOWO RUSLI/GETTY IMAGES ©

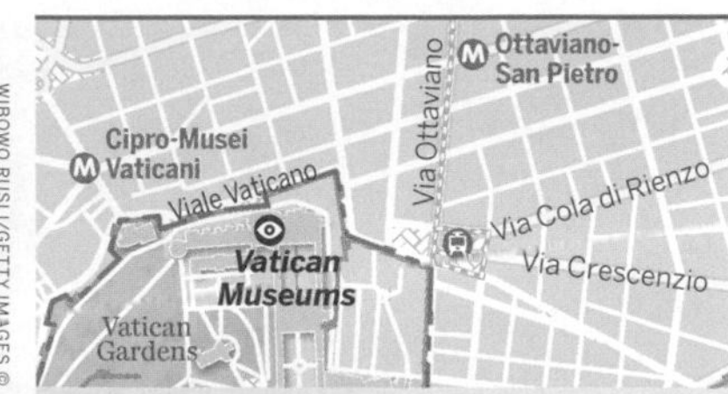

Need to Know

Basilica di San Pietro; www.vatican.va; St Peter's Sq; 7am-7pm summer, to 6.30pm winter; M Ottaviano-San Pietro; FREE

Take a Break

Search out **Fa-Bìo** (p85) for a freshly made sandwich or a healthy salad.

★ Top Tip

Strict dress codes are enforced, so no shorts, miniskirts or bare shoulders.

Nearby, a red floor disk marks the spot where Charlemagne and later Holy Roman Emperors were crowned by the pope.

Dominating the centre of the basilica is Bernini's famous baldachin. It stands over the high altar, which itself sits on the site of St Peter's grave.

Above, Michelangelo's dome soars to a height of 119m. Based on Brunelleschi's design for the Duomo in Florence, the towering cupola is supported by four stone piers named after the saints whose statues adorn their Bernini-designed niches: Longinus, Helena, Veronica and Andrew. At the base of the Pier of St Longinus is Arnolfo di Cambio's much-loved 13th-century statue of St Peter, whose right foot has been worn down by centuries of caresses.

Dome

From the **dome** (with/without lift €7/5; 8am-5.45pm summer, to 4.45pm winter) entrance on the right of the basilica's main portico, you can walk the 551 steps to the top or take a small lift halfway and then follow on foot for the last 320 steps. It's a long, steep climb. But make it to the top, and you're rewarded with stunning rooftop views.

Museo Storico Artistico

The **Museo Storico Artistico** (Tesoro; adult/reduced €7/5; 9am-6.15pm summer, to 5.15pm winter) sparkles with sacred relics, including a tabernacle by Donatello and the 6th-century Crux Vaticana, a jewel-studded cross that was a gift of the emperor Justinian II.

Vatican Grottoes

Extending beneath the basilica, the **Vatican Grottoes** (9am-6pm summer, to 5pm winter) contain the tombs and sarcophagi of numerous popes, as well as several huge columns from the original 4th-century basilica.

Pantheon

A striking 2000-year-old temple, now a church, the Pantheon is the best preserved of Rome's ancient monuments and one of the most influential buildings in the Western world.

Great For...

☑ Don't Miss

The entrance doors – once covered in gold, these 7m bronze doors are still fit for a giant.

Built by Hadrian over Marcus Agrippa's earlier 27 BC temple, the Pantheon has stood since around AD 125, and although its greying exterior looks its age, it's still a unique and exhilarating experience to pass through its vast bronze doors and gaze up at the largest unreinforced concrete dome ever built.

For centuries the inscription under the pediment – 'M:AGRIPPA.L.F.COS.TERTIUM. FECIT' ('Marcus Agrippa, son of Lucius, consul for the third time built this') – led scholars to think that the current building was Agrippa's original temple. However, 19th-century excavations revealed traces of an earlier temple and historians realised that Hadrian had simply kept Agrippa's original inscription.

Hadrian's temple was dedicated to the classical gods – hence Pantheon, a deriva-

Oculus in the dome of the Pantheon

JULIAN ELLIOTT PHOTOCRAPHY/GETTY IMAGES ©

tion of the Greek words *pan* (all) and *theos* (god) – but in AD 608 it was consecrated as a Christian church and it's now officially known as the Basilica di Santa Maria ad Martyres.

Thanks to this consecration, it was spared the worst of the medieval plundering that reduced many of Rome's ancient buildings to near dereliction. But it didn't escape entirely unscathed: its gilded-bronze roof tiles were removed and bronze from the portico was used by Bernini for his baldachin at St Peter's Basilica. These days the exterior is somewhat the worse for wear, but it's still an imposing sight with 16 Corinthian columns supporting a triangular pediment. Rivets and holes in the brickwork indicate where the original marble-veneer panels were removed.

During the Renaissance, the building was much studied – Brunelleschi used it as inspiration for his cupola in Florence – and it became an important burial chamber. In the cavernous marble-clad interior, you'll find the tomb of the artist Raphael alongside those of kings Vittorio Emanuele II and Umberto I.

Need to Know

Map p64; Piazza della Rotonda; 8.30am-7.30pm Mon-Sat, 9am-6pm Sun; Largo di Torre Argentina; FREE

Take a Break

For an uplifting coffee try **La Casa del Caffè Tazza d'Oro** (p88).

★ Top Tip

Mass is celebrated at the Pantheon at 5pm on Saturdays and 10.30am on Sundays.

Dome

The real fascination of the Pantheon lies in its massive dimensions and awe-inspiring dome. Considered the ancient Romans' greatest architectural achievement, this was the largest cupola in the world until the 15th century and is still the largest unreinforced concrete dome in existence. Its harmonious appearance is due to a precisely calibrated symmetry – its diameter is equal to the building's interior height of 43.3m. At its centre, the 8.7m-diameter oculus, which symbolically connected the temple with the gods, plays a vital structural role by absorbing and redistributing the dome's huge tensile forces. Rainwater enters but drains away through 22 almost-invisible holes in the sloping marble floor.

Colosseum

A monument to raw, merciless power, the Colosseum is the most thrilling of Rome's ancient sights. It was here that gladiators met in mortal combat and condemned prisoners fought off wild beasts in front of baying, bloodthirsty crowds. Two thousand years on and it's Italy's top tourist attraction, drawing more than five million visitors a year.

Great For...

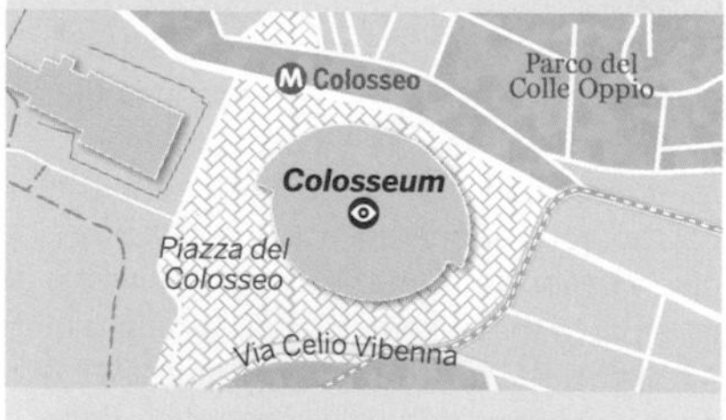

Need to Know

Map p68; Colosseo; www.coopculture.it; Piazza del Colosseo; 8.30am-1hr before sunset adult/reduced incl Roman Forum & Palatino €12/7.50; M Colosseo

★ Top Tip

Beat the queues by getting your ticket at the Palatino at Via di San Gregorio 30.

EVAN REINHEIMER/GETTY IMAGES ©

Built by Vespasian (r AD 69–79) in the grounds of Nero's vast Domus Aurea complex, the Colosseum was inaugurated in AD 80, eight years after it had been commissioned. To mark the occasion, Vespasian's son and successor Titus (r AD 79–81) staged games that lasted 100 days and nights, during which 5000 animals were slaughtered. Trajan (r AD 98–117) later topped this, holding a marathon 117-day killing spree involving 9000 gladiators and 10,000 animals.

The 50,000-seat arena was originally known as the Flavian Amphitheatre, and although it was Rome's most fearsome arena it wasn't the biggest – the Circo Massimo could hold up to 250,000 people. The name Colosseum, when introduced in medieval times, was not a reference to its size but to the Colosso di Nerone, a giant statue of Nero that stood nearby.

With the fall of the Roman Empire in the 5th century, the Colosseum was abandoned and gradually became overgrown. In the Middle Ages it served as a fortress for two of the city's warrior families, the Frangipani and the Annibaldi. Later, during the Renaissance and baroque periods, it was plundered of its precious travertine, and marble stripped from it was used to make huge palaces such as Palazzo Venezia, Palazzo Barberini and Palazzo Cancelleria.

More recently, pollution and vibrations caused by traffic and the metro have taken their toll. It is currently undergoing a €25-million clean-up, the first in its two thousand year history, which is due for completion in 2016.

Interior of the Colosseum

Exterior

The outer walls have three levels of arches, framed by Ionic, Doric and Corinthian columns. These were originally covered in travertine, and marble statues filled the niches on the 2nd and 3rd storeys. The upper level, punctuated with windows and slender Corinthian pilasters, had supports for 240 masts that held up a huge canvas awning over the arena, shielding the spectators from sun and rain. The 80 entrance arches, known as *vomitoria*, allowed the spectators to enter and be seated in a matter of minutes.

☑ Don't Miss

The hypogeum – imagine gladiators waiting for combat, caged wild animals, and boats surging through flooded tunnels up to the arena.

DEVASAHAYAM CHANDRA DHAS/GETTY IMAGES ©

Arena

The arena originally had a wooden floor covered in sand to prevent the combatants from slipping and to soak up the blood. It could also be flooded for mock sea battles. Trapdoors led down to the hypogeum, a subterranean complex of corridors, cages and lifts beneath the arena floor.

Stands

The cavea, for spectator seating, was divided into three tiers: magistrates and senior officials sat in the lowest tier, wealthy citizens in the middle and the plebs in the highest tier. Women (except for Vestal Virgins) were relegated to the cheapest sections at the top. And as in modern stadiums, tickets were numbered and spectators were assigned a precise seat in a specific sector – in 2015 restorers uncovered traces of red numerals on the arches, indicating how the sectors were numbered. The podium, a broad terrace in front of the tiers of seats, was reserved for the emperor, senators and VIPs.

Hypogeum

The hypogeum served as the stadium's backstage area. Sets for the various battle scenes were prepared here and hoisted up to the arena by a complicated system of pulleys. Caged animals were kept here and gladiators would gather here before showtime, having come in through an underground corridor from the nearby Ludus Magnus (gladiator school).

The hypogeum, and top tier, are open to the public by guided tour only. Visits, which cost €9 on top of the normal Colosseum ticket, require advance booking.

✂ Take a Break

Head to **Cavour 313** (p87) for a post-arena glass of wine.

Museo e Galleria Borghese

Housing what's often referred to as the 'queen of all private art collections', the magnificent Museo e Galleria Borghese boasts paintings by Caravaggio, Raphael and Titian, as well as a series of sculptures by Bernini.

Great For...

☑ **Don't Miss**

Ratto di Proserpina – an amazing contrast of of tenderness and cruelty.

The museum's collection was formed by Cardinal Scipione Borghese (1579–1633), the most knowledgable and ruthless art collector of his day. It was originally housed in the cardinal's residence near St Peter's but in the 1620s he had it transferred to his new villa just outside Porta Pinciana. And it's here, in the villa's central building, the Casino Borghese, that you'll see it today.

Entrance & Ground Floor

Things get off to a cracking start in the entrance hall, decorated with 4th-century floor mosaics of fighting gladiators and a 2nd-century *Satiro Combattente* (Fighting Satyr). High on the wall is a gravity-defying bas-relief of a horse and rider falling into the void (*Marco Curzio a Cavallo*) by Pietro Bernini (Gian Lorenzo's father).

Sala I is centred on Antonio Canova's daring depiction of Napoleon's sister,

Museo e Galleria Borghese
Vialle dell'Uccelliera
Via Pinciana
Viale del Museo Borghese
Piazzale del Museo Borghese

Need to Know

www.galleriaborghese.it; Piazzale del Museo Borghese 5; 9am-7pm Tue-Sun; adult/reduced €11/6.50; Via Pinciana

Take a Break

There's a bar in the basement entrance area, behind the bookshop.

★ Top Tip

Remember to pre-book your ticket, and take ID when you go to pick it up.

Paolina Bonaparte Borghese, reclining topless as *Venere vincitrice* (1805–08). But it's Gian Lorenzo Bernini's spectacular sculptures – flamboyant depictions of pagan myths – that really steal the show. Just look at Daphne's hands morphing into leaves in the swirling *Apollo e Dafne* (1622–25) in Sala III, or Pluto's hand pressing into the seemingly soft flesh of Persephone's thigh in the *Ratto di Proserpina* (1621–22) in Sala IV.

Caravaggio dominates Sala VIII. There's a dissipated-looking *Bacchino malato* (Young Sick Bacchus; 1592–95), the strangely beautiful *La Madonna dei Palafenieri* (Madonna with Serpent; 1605–06), and *San Giovanni Battista* (St John the Baptist; 1609–10), probably Caravaggio's last work. There's also the much-loved *Ragazzo con Canestro di Frutta* (Boy with a Basket of Fruit; 1593–95), and the dramatic *Davide con la Testa di Golia* (David with the Head of Goliath; 1609–10) – Goliath's severed head is said to be a self-portrait.

First Floor

Upstairs, the pinacoteca (picture gallery) offers a wonderful snapshot of Renaissance art. Don't miss Raphael's extraordinary *La Deposizione di Cristo* (The Deposition; 1507) in Sala IX, and his *Dama con Liocorno* (Lady with a Unicorn; 1506). In the same room is Fra Bartolomeo's superb *Adorazione del Bambino* (Adoration of the Christ Child; 1495) and Perugino's *Madonna con Bambino* (Madonna and Child; first quarter of the 16th century).

Other highlights include Correggio's erotic *Danae* (1530–31) in Sala X, Bernini's self-portraits in Sala XIV, and Titian's early masterpiece, *Amor Sacro e Amor Profano* (Sacred and Profane Love; 1514) in Sala XX.

Tempio di Saturno (p55)

Roman Forum

The Roman Forum was ancient Rome's showpiece centre, a grandiose district of temples, basilicas and vibrant public spaces. Nowadays, it's a collection of impressive, if badly labelled, ruins that can leave you drained and confused. But if you can get your imagination going, there's something wonderfully compelling about walking in the footsteps of Julius Caesar and other legendary figures of Roman history.

Great For...

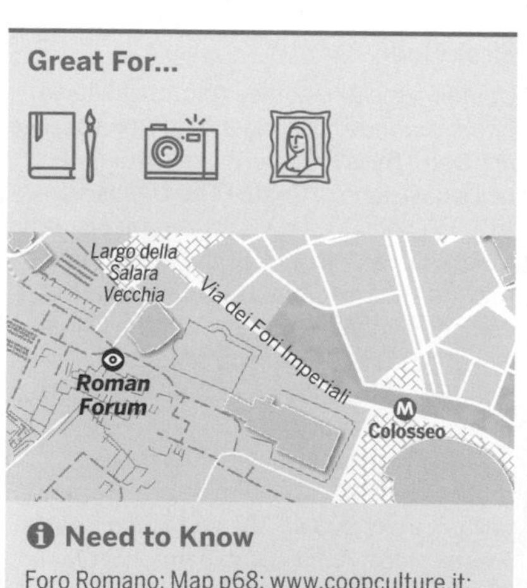

Need to Know

Foro Romano; Map p68; www.coopculture.it; Largo della Salara Vecchia & Via Sacra; adult/reduced incl Colosseum & Palatino €12/7.50; 8.30am-1hr before sunset; Via dei Fori Imperiali

Did You Know

Vestal Virgins served a term of 30 years as attendants in the Tempio di Vesta.

AFRIANDI/GETTY IMAGES ©

Originally an Etruscan burial ground, the Forum was first developed in the 7th century BC, growing over time to become the social, political and commercial hub of the Roman Empire. In the Middle Ages it was reduced to pasture land and extensively plundered for its marble. The area was systematically excavated in the 18th and 19th centuries and work continues to this day.

Via Sacra Towards Campidoglio

Entering the Forum from Largo della Salara Vecchia – you can also enter from the Palatino or via an entrance near the Arco di Tito – you'll see the **Tempio di Antonino e Faustina** ahead to your left. Erected in AD 141, this was later transformed into a church, the **Chiesa di San Lorenzo in Miranda**. To your right, the 179 BC **Basilica Fulvia Aemilia** was a 100m-long public hall with a two-storey porticoed facade.

At the end of the path, you'll come to **Via Sacra**, the Forum's main thoroughfare, and the **Tempio di Giulio Cesare** (aka the Tempio del Divo Giulio). Built by Augustus in 29 BC, this marks the spot where Julius Caesar was cremated. Heading right up Via Sacra brings you to the **Curia**, the original seat of the Roman Senate. This barn-like construction was rebuilt on various occasions and what you see today is a 1937 reconstruction of how it looked in the reign of Diocletian (r 284–305).

In front of the Curia, and hidden by scaffolding, is the **Lapis Niger**, a large piece of black marble that's said to cover the tomb of Romulus.

At the end of Via Sacra, the 23m-high **Arco di Settimio Severo** (Arch of

Statues on the Arco di Tito

Septimius Severus) is dedicated to the eponymous emperor and his sons, Caracalla and Geta. Close by are the remains of the **Rostrum**, an elaborate podium where Shakespeare had Mark Antony make his famous 'Friends, Romans, countrymen...' speech. Facing this, the **Colonna di Foca** (Column of Phocus) rises above what was once the Forum's main square, Piazza del Foro.

The eight granite columns that rise behind the Colonna are all that survive of the **Tempio di Saturno** (Temple of Saturn), an important temple that doubled as the state treasury. Behind it are (from north to south): the ruins of the **Tempio della Concordia** (Temple of Concord), the **Tempio di Vespasiano** (Temple of Vespasian and Titus) and the **Portico degli Dei Consenti**.

☑ Don't Miss

At the Tempio di Saturno the translation of the motto on the pediment is 'The Senate and People of Rome have restored what fire consumed'.

RENATA SEDMAKOVA/SHUTTERSTOCK ©

Tempio di Castore e Polluce & Casa delle Vestali

From the path that runs parallel to Via Sacra, you'll pass the stubby ruins of the **Basilica Giulia**, which was begun by Caesar and finished by Augustus. At the end of the basilica, three columns remain from the 5th-century-BC **Tempio di Castore e Polluce** (Temple of Castor and Pollux). Nearby, the 6th-century **Chiesa di Santa Maria Antiqua** is the oldest Christian church in the Forum.

Back towards Via Sacra is the **Casa delle Vestali** (House of the Vestal Virgins; currently off limits), home of the virgins who tended the flame in the adjoining **Tempio di Vesta**.

Via Sacra Towards the Colosseum

Heading up Via Sacra past the **Tempio di Romolo** (Temple of Romulus), you'll come to the **Basilica di Massenzio**, the largest building on the forum. Started by Maxentius and finished by Constantine in 315 – it's also known as the Basilica di Costantino – it originally measured approximately 100m by 65m. It's currently out of bounds due to construction work on a new metro line.

Beyond the basilica, the **Arco di Tito** (Arch of Titus) was built in AD 81 to celebrate Vespasian and Titus' victories against rebels in Jerusalem.

Take a Break

The best spot for a picnic is the **Vigna Barberini** (Barberini Vineyard), near the Orti Farnesiani, in the Palatino. A grassy area with several benches, it's signposted off the path to the Roman Forum.

Roman Forum

In ancient times, a forum was a market place, civic centre and religious complex all rolled into one, and the greatest of all was the Roman Forum (Foro Romano). Situated between the Palatino (Palatine Hill), ancient Rome's most exclusive neighbourhood, and the Campidoglio (Capitoline Hill), it was the city's busy, bustling centre. On any given day it teemed with activity. Senators debated affairs of state in the **Curia** ❶, shoppers thronged the squares and traffic-free streets, crowds gathered under the **Colonna di Foca** ❷ to listen to politicians holding forth from the **Rostrum** ❷. Elsewhere, lawyers worked the courts in basilicas including the **Basilica di Massenzio** ❸, while the Vestal Virgins quietly went about their business in the **Casa delle Vestali** ❹.

Special occasions were also celebrated in the Forum: religious holidays were marked with ceremonies at temples such as **Tempio di Saturno** ❺ and **Tempio di Castore e Polluce** ❻, and military victories were honoured with dramatic processions up Via Sacra and the building of monumental arches like **Arco di Settimio Severo** ❼ and **Arco di Tito** ❽.

The ruins you see today are impressive but they can be confusing without a clear picture of what the Forum once looked like. This spread shows the Forum in its heyday, complete with temples, civic buildings and towering monuments to heroes of the Roman Empire.

TOP TIPS

» Get grandstand views of the Forum from the Palatino and Campidoglio.

» Visit first thing in the morning or late afternoon; crowds are worst between 11am and 2pm.

» In summer it gets hot in the Forum and there's little shade, so take a hat and plenty of water.

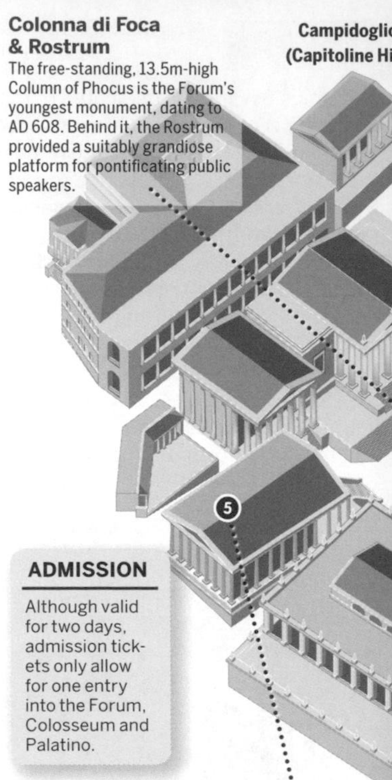

ADMISSION

Although valid for two days, admission tickets only allow for one entry into the Forum, Colosseum and Palatino.

Tempio di Saturno
Ancient Rome's Fort Knox, the Temple of Saturn was the city treasury. In Caesar's day it housed 13 tonnes o gold, 114 tonnes of silver and 30 million sestertii worth

JONATHAN SMITH/GETTY IMAGES©

LONELY PLANET/GETTY IMAGES©

Tempio di Castore e Poll
Only three columns the Temple of Casto and Pollux remain. temple was dedicat to the Heavenly Twi after they suppose led the Romans to victory over the Lat League in 496 BC.

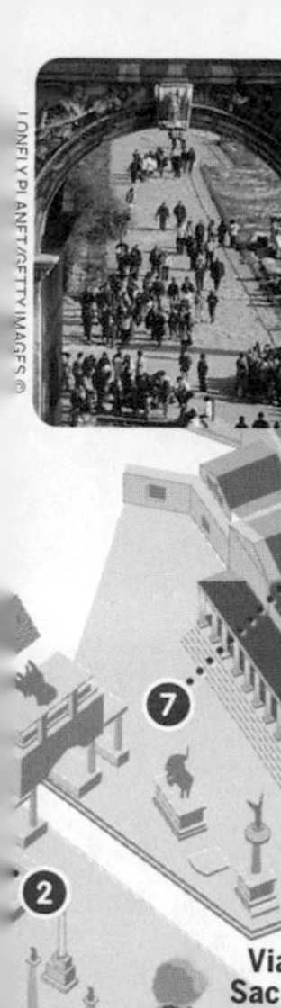

LONELY PLANET/GETTY IMAGES ©

Arco di Settimio Severo
One of the Forum's signature monuments, this imposing triumphal arch commemorates the military victories of Septimius Severus. Relief panels depict his campaigns against the Parthians.

Curia
This big barn-like building was the official seat of the Roman Senate. Most of what you see is a reconstruction, but the interior marble floor dates to the 3rd-century reign of Diocletian.

THEJIPEN/GETTY IMAGES ©

Basilica di Massenzio
Marvel at the scale of this vast 4th-century basilica. In its original form the central hall was divided into enormous naves; now only part of the northern nave survives.

JULIUS CAESAR
Julius Caesar was cremated on the site where the Tempio di Giulio Cesare now stands.

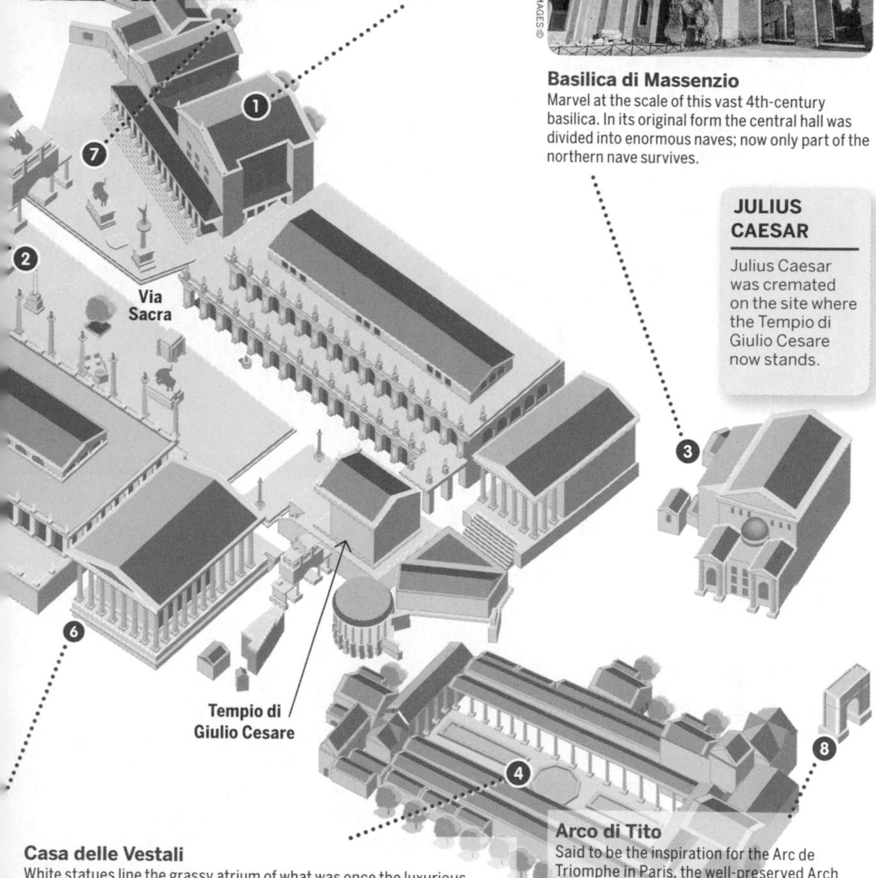

Casa delle Vestali
White statues line the grassy atrium of what was once the luxurious 50-room home of the Vestal Virgins. The virgins played an important role in Roman religion, serving the goddess Vesta.

Arco di Tito
Said to be the inspiration for the Arc de Triomphe in Paris, the well-preserved Arch of Titus was built by the emperor Domitian to honour his elder brother Titus.

MANAKIN/GETTY IMAGES ©

Palatino

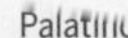

Walking Tour: Emperors' Footsteps

Follow in the footsteps of Rome's legendary emperors on this walk around the best of the city's ancient treasures.

Distance: 1.5km
Duration: 3 hours

Take a Break

Hidden away in the Capitoline Museums but accessible by its own entrance, the Caffè Capitolino is a refined spot for a restorative coffee.

Start Colosseum MColosseo

1 Colosseum

More than any other monument of the ancient city, it's the Colosseum (p46) that symbolises the power and glory of ancient Rome. A spectacular feat of engineering, the 50,000-seat stadium was inaugurated by Emperor Titus in AD 80 with a bloodthirsty bout of games that lasted 100 days and nights.

2 Palatino

A short walk from the Colosseum, past the Arco di Costantino, the Palatino (p62) was ancient Rome's most sought-after neighbourhood, site of the emperor's palace and home to the cream of imperial society. The evocative ruins are confusing but their grandeur gives some sense of the luxury in which the ancient VIPs liked to live.

3 Roman Forum

Coming down from the Palatino you'll enter the Roman Forum (p52) near the Arco di Tito (p55), one of Rome's great triumphal arches. In imperial times, the Forum was the empire's nerve centre, a teeming hive of law courts, temples, piazzas and shops. The Vestal Virgins lived here and senators debated matters of state in the Curia (p54).

4 Piazza del Campidoglio

Leave the Forum and climb up to the Michelangelo-designed Piazza del Campidoglio (p62). This striking piazza, one of Rome's most beautiful, sits atop the

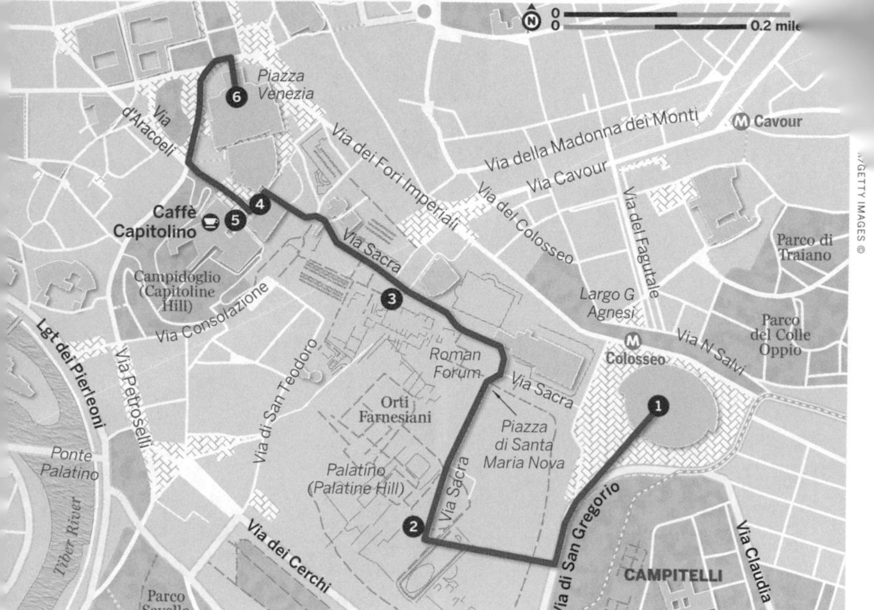

Campidoglio (Capitoline Hill), one of the seven hills on which Rome was founded. In ancient times this was the spiritual heart of the city, home to two of the city's most important temples.

5 Capitoline Museums

Flanking Piazza del Campidoglio are two stately *palazzi* (mansions) that together house the Capitoline Museums (p62). These, the world's oldest public museums, boast an important picture gallery and a superb collection of classical sculpture that includes an iconic Etruscan bronze of a wolf, the *Lupa capitolina*, standing over Romulus and Remus.

6 Il Vittoriano

From the Campidoglio, pop next door to the massive mountain of white marble that is Il Vittoriano (p63). No emperor ever walked here, but it's worth stopping off to take the panoramic lift to the top, from where you can see the whole of Rome laid out beneath you

Finish Il Vittoriano 🚍 Piazza Venezia

Walking Tour: Piazzas of Rome

Rome's tightly packed historic centre boasts some of the city's most celebrated piazzas, and several beautiful but lesser known squares.

Distance: 1.5km
Duration: 2 to 3 hours

Take a Break

Between the Pantheon and Piazza Navona, Caffè Sant'Eustachio (p88) is a good bet for a quick pit stop. Its coffee is reckoned by many to be the best in Rome.

Campo de' Fiori market

Start Largo di Torre Argentina Largo di Torre Argentina

1 Largo di Torre Argentina

Start off in Largo di Torre Argentina, set around the ruins of four Republic-era temples. On the piazza's western flank, the Teatro Argentina, Rome's premier theatre, sits near the site where Julius Caesar was assassinated.

2 Piazza della Minerva

Head along Via dei Cestari until you come to Piazza della Minerva and the Elefantino, a sculpture of a puzzled elephant carrying an Egyptian obelisk. Flanking the square, the Gothic Basilica di Santa Maria Sopra Minerva (p66) boasts Renaissance frescoes and a minor Michelangelo.

3 Piazza di Sant'Ignazio Loyola

Next, strike off down Via Santa Caterina da Siena, then take Via del Piè di Marmo and Via di Sant'Ignazio in order to reach the exquisite 18th-century Piazza di Sant'Ignazio Loyola. Overlooking the piazza, the Chiesa di Sant'Ignazio di Loyola features a magical *trompe l'œil* ceiling fresco.

4 Piazza della Rotonda

A short stroll down Via del Seminario brings you to the bustling Piazza della Rotonda, where the Pantheon (p44) needs no introduction. Rome's best-preserved ancient building is one of the city's iconic sights with its epic portico and dome.

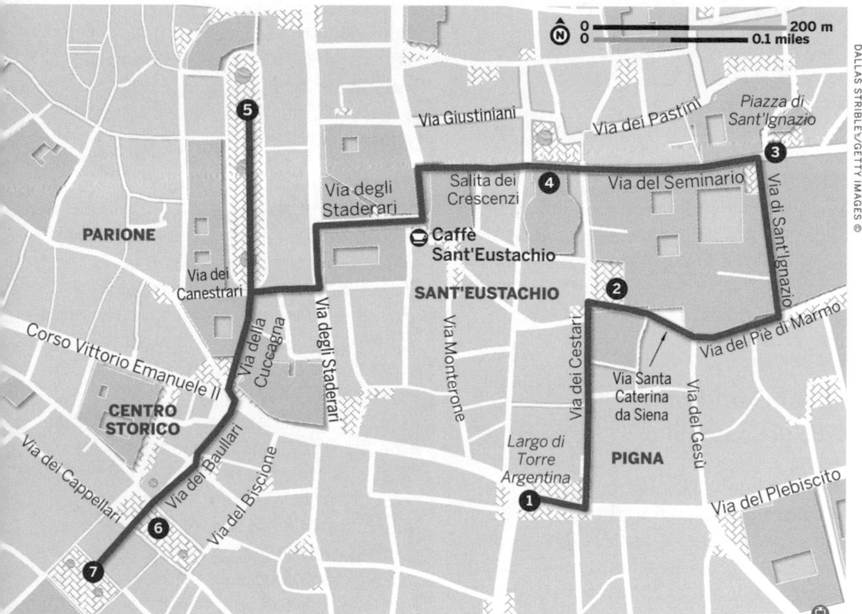

❺ Piazza Navona

From the Pantheon, follow the signs to Piazza Navona (p66), central Rome's great showpiece square. Here, among the street artists, tourists and pigeons, you can compare the two giants of Roman baroque: Gian Lorenzo Bernini, creator of the Fontana dei Quattro Fiumi, and Francesco Borromini, author of the Chiesa di Sant'Agnese in Agone.

❻ Campo de' Fiori

On the other side of Corso Vittorio Emanuele II, the busy road that bisects the *centro storico* (historic centre), life is focused on Campo de' Fiori (p67). By day, this noisy square stages a colourful market, at night it transforms into a raucous open-air pub.

❼ Piazza Farnese

Just beyond the Campo, Piazza Farnese is a refined square overlooked by the Renaissance Palazzo Farnese (p67). This magnificent *palazzo*, now home to the French embassy, boasts some superb frescoes, said by some to rival those of the Sistine Chapel.

Finish Piazza Farnese 🚌 Largo di Torre Argentina

SIGHTS

They say that a lifetime's not enough for Rome *(Roma, non basta una vita!)*. There's simply too much to see. So the best plan is to choose selectively, and leave the rest for next time.

Note that many of Rome's major museums and monuments, including the Capitoline Museums and all four seats of the Museo Nazionale Romano, host regular exhibitions. When these are on, ticket prices are increased slightly, typically by about €3.

Ancient Rome

Arco di Costantino Monument

On the western side of the Colosseum, this monumental triple arch was built in AD 315 to celebrate the emperor Constantine's victory over his rival Maxentius at the Battle of the Milvian Bridge (AD 312). Rising to a height of 25m, it's the largest of Rome's surviving triumphal arches. (Map p68; M Colosseo)

Palatino Archaeological Site

Sandwiched between the Roman Forum and the Circo Massimo, the Palatino (Palatine Hill) is an atmospheric area of towering pine trees, majestic ruins and memorable views. It was here that Romulus supposedly founded the city in 753 BC and Rome's emperors lived in unabashed luxury. Look out for the **stadio** (stadium), the ruins of the **Domus Flavia** (imperial palace), and grandstand views over the Roman Forum from the **Orti Farnesiani** (Map p68; Palatine Hill; 06 3996 7700; www.coopculture.it; Via di San Gregorio 30 & Via Sacra; adult/reduced incl Colosseum & Roman Forum €12/7.50; 8.30am-1hr before sunset; M Colosseo)

Imperial Forums Archaeological Site

The forums of Trajan, Augustus, Nerva and Caesar are known collectively as the Imperial Forums. These were largely buried when Mussolini bulldozed Via dei Fori Imperiali through the area in 1933, but excavations have since unearthed much of them. The standout sights are the **Mercati di Traiano** (Trajan's Markets), accessible through the Museo dei Fori Imperiali (p62), and the landmark **Colonna di Traiano** (Trajan's Column; Map p68; Via dei Fori Imperiali). (Fori Imperiali; Via dei Fori Imperiali; Via dei Fori Imperiali)

Mercati di Traiano Museo dei Fori Imperiali Museum

This striking museum brings to life the Mercati di Traiano, emperor Trajan's great 2nd-century market complex, while also providing a fascinating introduction to the Imperial Forums with multimedia displays, explanatory panels and a smattering of archaeological artefacts.

Sculptures, friezes and the occasional bust are set out in rooms opening onto what was once the market's Great Hall. But more than the exhibits, the real highlight here is the chance to explore the echoing ruins of the vast complex. The three-storey hemicycle that housed the markets is in remarkably good shape and it doesn't take a huge leap of imagination to picture it full of traders selling everything from oil and vegetables to flowers, silks and spices. Rising above the markets is the **Torre delle Milizie** (Militia Tower), a 13th-century red-brick tower. (Map p68; 06 06 08; www.mercatiditraiano.it; Via IV Novembre 94; adult/reduced €11.50/9.50; 9.30am-7.30pm, last admission 6.30pm; Via IV Novembre)

Piazza del Campidoglio Piazza

This hilltop piazza, designed by Michelangelo in 1538, is one of Rome's most beautiful squares. You can reach it from the Roman Forum, but the most dramatic approach is via the graceful **Cordonata** (Map p68) staircase up from Piazza d'Ara Coeli. The piazza is flanked by Palazzo Nuovo and Palazzo dei Conservatori, together home to the Capitoline Museums, and Palazzo Senatorio, seat of Rome city council. In the centre is a copy of an equestrian statue of Marcus Aurelius. (Map p68; Piazza Venezia)

Capitoline Museums Museum

Dating to 1471, the Capitoline Museums are the world's oldest public museums. Their

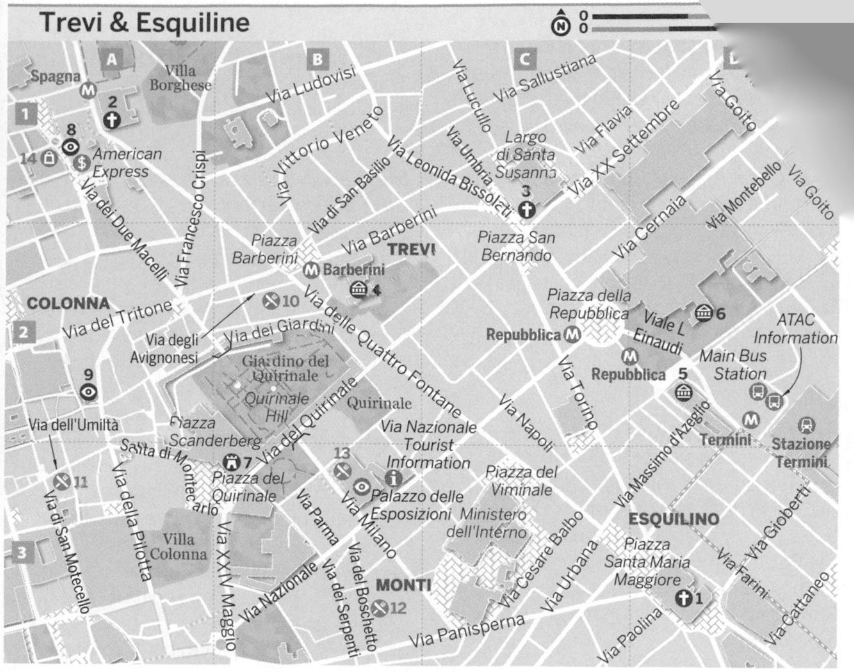

Trevi & Esquiline

Sights

1 Basilica di Santa Maria Maggiore............. D3
2 Chiesa della Trinità dei Monti..................... A1
3 Chiesa di Santa Maria della Vittoria.......... C1
4 Galleria Nazionale d'Arte Antica: Palazzo Barberini.......................................B2
Keats–Shelley House.........................(see 8)
5 Museo Nazionale Romano: Palazzo Massimo alle Terme D2
6 Museo Nazionale Romano: Terme di Diocleziano D2
7 Palazzo del Quirinale..................................B3
8 Piazza di Spagna & the Spanish Steps..A1
9 Trevi Fountain... A2

Eating

10 Colline Emiliane.. B2
11 Da Michele... A3
12 L'Asino d'Oro B3
13 Open Colonna.. B3

Shopping

14 Sermoneta A1

collection of classical sculpture is one of Italy's finest, including crowd-pleasers such as the iconic *Lupa capitolina* (Capitoline Wolf), a sculpture of Romulus and Remus under a wolf, and the *Galata morente* (Dying Gaul), a moving depiction of a dying Gaul warrior. There's also a formidable picture gallery with masterpieces by the likes of Titian, Tintoretto, Rubens and Caravaggio. Note that ticket prices go up when there's a temporary exhibition on. (Map p68; Musei Capitolini; ☎06 06 08; www.museicapitolini.org; Piazza del Campidoglio 1; adult/reduced €11.50/9.50; ⏲9.30am-7.30pm, last admission 6.30pm; 🚌Piazza Venezia)

Il Vittoriano Monument

Love it or loathe it, as most locals do, you can't ignore Il Vittoriano (aka the Altare della Patria; Altar of the Fatherland), the

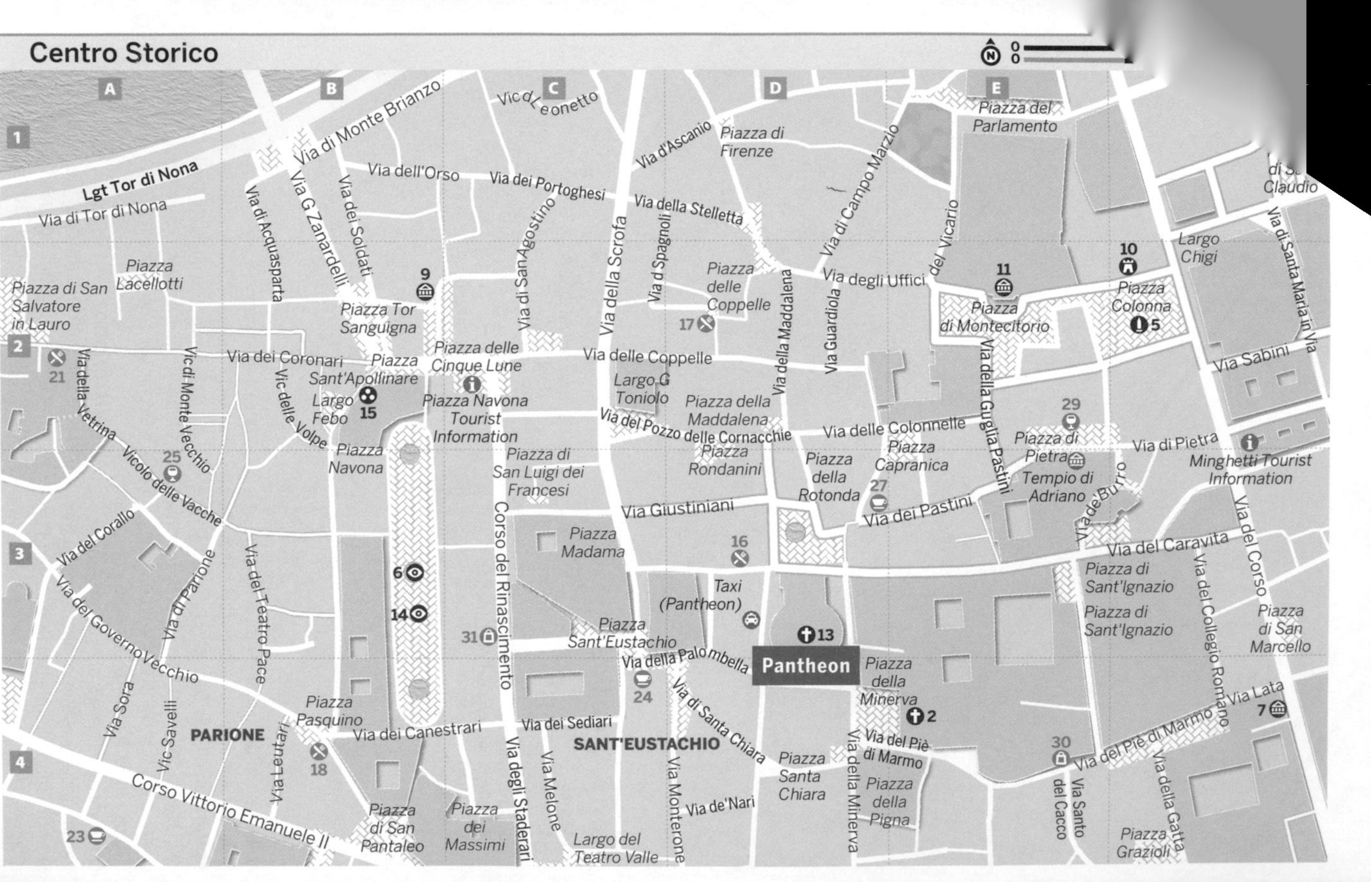
Centro Storico
A
B
C
D
E
1
2
3
4
Lgt Tor di Nona
Via di Tor di Nona
Piazza di San Salvatore in Lauro
Piazza Lacellotti
Via di Monte Brianzo
Vic d Leonetto
Via dell'Orso
Via dei Portoghesi
Via d'Ascanio
Piazza di Firenze
Via di Campo Marzio
Piazza del Parlamento
Via di Acquasparta
Via G Zanardelli
Via dei Soldati
Via di San Agostino
Via della Scrofa
Via della Stelletta
Via d Spagnoli
Piazza delle Coppelle
Via della Maddalena
Via Guardiola
Via degli Uffici
del Vicario
Piazza di Montecitorio
Piazza Colonna
Largo Chigi
Via di Santa Maria in Via
Claudio
Piazza Tor Sanguigna
Via dei Coronari
Piazza Sant'Apollinare
Piazza delle Cinque Lune
Via delle Coppelle
Largo G Toniolo
Piazza della Maddalena
Via della Guglia Pastini
Via Sabini
Vic di Monte Vecchio
Vic delle Volpe
Largo Febo
Piazza Navona Tourist Information
Via del Pozzo delle Cornacchie
Piazza Rondanini
Via delle Colonnelle
Piazza Capranica
Piazza di Pietra
Via di Pietra
Minghetti Tourist Information
Via della Vetrina
Vicolo delle Vacche
Piazza Navona
Piazza di San Luigi dei Francesi
Piazza della Rotonda
Tempio di Adriano
Via de Burrò
Via dei Pastini
Via Giustiniani
Via del Corallo
Via di Parione
Via del Teatro Pace
Corso del Rinascimento
Piazza Madama
Via del Caravita
Via del Corso
Piazza di Sant'Ignazio
Piazza di Sant'Ignazio
Via del Collegio Romano
Piazza di San Marcello
Via del Governo Vecchio
Taxi (Pantheon)
Piazza Sant'Eustachio
Via della Palombella
Pantheon
Piazza della Minerva
Via Lata
Piazza Pasquino
Via dei Canestrari
Via dei Sediari
Via di Santa Chiara
Via Sora
Vic Savelli
PARIONE
SANT'EUSTACHIO
Via del Piè di Marmo
Via del Piè di Marmo
Via Leutari
Piazza Santa Chiara
Via della Minerva
Piazza della Pigna
Via Santo del Cacco
Via della Gatta
Corso Vittorio Emanuele II
Piazza di San Pantaleo
Piazza dei Massimi
Via degli Staderari
Via Melone
Largo del Teatro Valle
Via Monterone
Via de'Nari
Piazza Grazioli
1
2
5
6
7
9
10
11
13
14
15
16
17
18
21
23
24
25
27
29
30
31

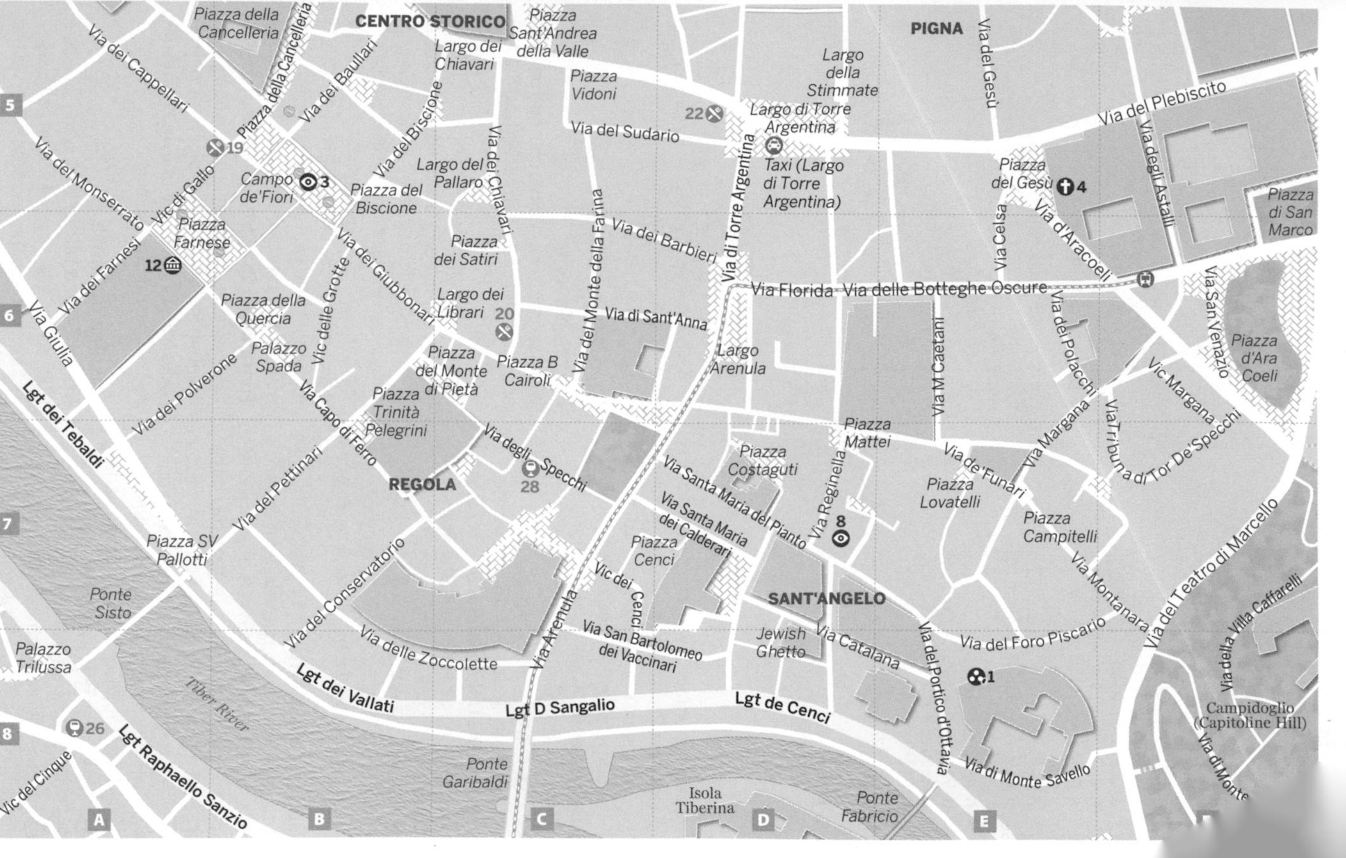

CENTRO STORICO
PIGNA
REGOLA
SANT'ANGELO
Piazza della Cancelleria
Via dei Cappellari
Piazza della Cancelleria
Via dei Baullari
Via del Biscione
Largo dei Chiavari
Piazza Sant'Andrea della Valle
Piazza Vidoni
Largo della Stimmate
Via del Gesù
Via del Plebiscito
Via degli Astalli
Piazza di San Marco
Largo di Torre Argentina
Taxi (Largo di Torre Argentina)
Via del Sudario
Via del Monserrato
Vic di Gallo
Campo de'Fiori
Piazza del Biscione
Largo del Pallaro
Via dei Chiavari
Piazza del Gesù
Via Celsa
Via d'Aracoeli
Piazza Farnese
Via dei Farnesi
Piazza dei Satiri
Via del Monte della Farina
Via dei Barbieri
Via di Torre Argentina
Via Florida
Via delle Botteghe Oscure
Via San Venazio
Piazza d'Ara Coeli
Via Giulia
Piazza della Quercia
Vic delle Grotte
Via dei Giubbonari
Largo dei Librari
Via di Sant'Anna
Largo Arenula
Via M Caetani
Via dei Polacchi
Vic Margana
Palazzo Spada
Via dei Polverone
Piazza del Monte di Pietà
Piazza B Cairoli
Piazza Trinità Pelegrini
Via Capo di Ferro
Via degli Specchi
Piazza Mattei
Via Margana
Via Tribuna di Tor De'Specchi
Lgt dei Tebaldi
Via dei Pettinari
Piazza Costaguti
Via Santa Maria del Pianto
Via Reginella
Via de'Funari
Piazza Lovatelli
Piazza Campitelli
Via del Teatro di Marcello
Piazza SV Pallotti
Via Santa Maria dei Calderari
Piazza Cenci
Vic dei Cenci
Via Montanara
Via della Villa Caffarelli
Ponte Sisto
Via del Conservatorio
Via Arenula
Via San Bartolomeo dei Vaccinari
Jewish Ghetto
Via Catalana
Via del Portico d'Ottavia
Via del Foro Piscario
Palazzo Trilussa
Tiber River
Via delle Zoccolette
Lgt dei Vallati
Lgt D Sangalio
Lgt de Cenci
Campidoglio (Capitoline Hill)
Via di Monte
Via di Monte Savello
Lgt Raphaello Sanzio
Vic del Cinque
Ponte Garibaldi
Isola Tiberina
Ponte Fabricio
A
B
C
D
E
5
6
7
8

ntro Storico

Sights

1 Area Archeologica del Teatro di Marcello e del Portico d'Ottavia.............E8
2 Basilica di Santa Maria Sopra Minerva.....E4
3 Campo de' Fiori...B5
4 Chiesa del Gesù E5
5 Colonna di Marco Aurelio F2
6 Fontana dei Quattro Fiumi..........................B3
7 Galleria Doria Pamphilj...............................F4
8 Jewish Ghetto..D7
9 Museo Nazionale Romano: Palazzo Altemps..B2
10 Palazzo Chigi F2
11 Palazzo di Montecitorio E2
12 Palazzo Farnese..A6
13 Pantheon... D3
14 Piazza Navona...B3
15 Stadio di Domiziano B2

Eating

16 Armando al Pantheon D3
17 Casa Coppelle.. D2
18 Cul de Sac B4
19 Forno di Campo de' Fiori........................... B5
20 Forno Roscioli..C6
21 Gelateria del Teatro A2
22 Vice D5

Drinking & Nightlife

23 Barnum Cafe.. A4
24 Caffè Sant'Eustachio C4
25 Etablì A3
26 Freni e Frizioni A8
27 La Casa del Caffè Tazza d'Oro D3
28 Open Baladin C7
29 Salotto 42.. E2

Shopping

30 Confetteria Moriondo & Gariglio............... E4
31 Officina Profumo Farmaceutica di Santa Maria Novella................................ C3

massive mountain of white marble that towers over Piazza Venezia. Begun in 1885 to honour Italy's first king, Victor Emmanuel II, it incorporates the **Museo Centrale del Risorgimento** (Map p68; www.risorgimento.it; adult/reduced €5/2.50; 9.30am-6.30pm, closed 1st Mon of month), a small museum documenting Italian unification, and the **Tomb of the Unknown Soldier**. For Rome's best 360-degree views, take the **Roma dal Cielo lift** (Map p68; adult/reduced €7/3.50; 9.30am-6.30pm Mon-Thu, to 7.30pm Fri-Sun) to the top. (Piazza Venezia; 9.30am-5.30pm summer, to 4.30pm winter; Piazza Venezia) FREE

Bocca della Verità Monument

A bearded face carved into a giant marble disc, the *Bocca della Verità* is one of Rome's most popular curiosities. Legend has it that if you put your hand in the mouth and tell a lie, the Bocca will slam shut and bite your hand off. The mouth, which was originally part of a fountain, or possibly an ancient manhole cover, now lives in the portico of the Chiesa di Santa Maria in Cosmedin, a handsome medieval church. (Mouth of Truth; Piazza Bocca della Verità 18; donation €0.50; 9.30am-5.50pm summer, to 4.50pm winter; Piazza Bocca della Verità)

Centro Storico

Piazza Navona Piazza

With its ornate fountains, baroque *palazzi* and colourful cast of street artists, hawkers and tourists, Piazza Navona is central Rome's elegant showcase square. Built over the 1st-century **Stadio di Domiziano** (Domitian's Stadium; Map p64; www.stadiodomiziano.com; Via di Tor Sanguigna 3; adult/reduced €8/6; 10am-7pm Sun-Fri, to 8pm Sat), it was paved over in the 15th century and for almost 300 years hosted the city's main market. Its grand centrepiece is Bernini's **Fontana dei Quattro Fiumi** (Fountain of the Four Rivers; Map p64), an ornate, showy fountain featuring personifications of the rivers Nile, Ganges, Danube and Plate. (Map p64; Corso del Rinascimento)

Basilica di Santa Maria Sopra Minerva Basilica

Built on the site of three pagan temples, including one to the goddess Minerva, the

Dominican Basilica di Santa Maria Sopra Minerva is Rome's only Gothic church. However, little remains of the original 13th-century structure and these days the main drawcard is a minor Michelangelo sculpture and the colourful, art-rich interior. (Map p64; www.santamariasopraminerva.it; Piazza della Minerva 42; 6.45am-7pm Mon-Fri, 6.45am-12.30pm & 3.30-7pm Sat, 8am-12.30pm & 3.30-7pm Sun; Largo di Torre Argentina)

Campo de' Fiori Piazza

Noisy, colourful 'Il Campo' is a major focus of Roman life: by day it hosts one of Rome's best-known markets, while at night it morphs into a raucous open-air pub. For centuries the square was the site of public executions, and it was here that the philosopher Giordano Bruno was burned at the stake for heresy in 1600. The spot is marked by a sinister statue of the hooded monk, created by Ettore Ferrari and unveiled in 1889. (Map p64; Corso Vittorio Emanuele II)

Palazzo Farnese Historic Building

Home of the French embassy, this formidable Renaissance *palazzo,* one of Rome's finest, was started in 1514 by Antonio da Sangallo the Younger, continued by Michelangelo and finished by Giacomo della Porta. Inside, it boasts a series of frecsoes by Annibale Carracci that are said by some to rival Michelangelo's in the Sistine Chapel. The highlight, painted between 1597 and 1608, is the monumental ceiling fresco *Amori degli Dei* (The Loves of the Gods) in the recently restored Galleria dei Carracci. (Map p64; www.inventerrome.com; Piazza Farnese; admission €5; guided tours 3pm, 4pm & 5pm Mon, Wed & Fri; Corso Vittorio Emanuele II)

Jewish Ghetto Neighbourhood

Centred on lively Via Portico d'Ottavia, the Jewish Ghetto is a wonderfully atmospheric area studded with artisans' studios, vintage clothes shops, kosher bakeries and popular trattorias. (Map p64; Lungotevere de' Cenci)

Chiesa del Gesù

An imposing example of the archi[tecture] of the Counter-Reformation, Rome['s most] important Jesuit church is a treasure [trove] of baroque art. Headline works include [a] swirling vault fresco by Giovanni Battista Gaulli (aka Il Baciccia), and Andrea del Pozzo's opulent tomb for Jesuit founder Ignatius Loyola. The Spanish saint lived in the church from 1544 until his death in 1556 and you can visit his private rooms to the right of the main building. (Map p64; www.chiesadelgesu.org; Piazza del Gesù; 7am-12.30pm & 4-7.45pm, St Ignatius rooms 4-6pm Mon-Sat, 10am-noon Sun; Largo di Torre Argentina)

Tridente, Trevi & the Quirinale

Trevi Fountain Fountain

The *Fontana di Trevi* (Trevi Fountain) scene of Anita Ekberg's dip in *La Dolce Vita,* is a flamboyant baroque ensemble of mythical figures and wild horses. It takes up the entire side of the 17th-century Palazzo Poli. A Fendi-sponsored restoration finished in 2015, and the fountain now gleams brighter than it has for years.The tradition is to toss a coin into the water, thus ensuring that you'll return to Rome. (Map p63; Fontana di Trevi; Piazza di Trevi; M Barberini)

Piazza di Spagna & the Spanish Steps Piazza

A magnet for visitors since the 18th century, the Spanish Steps (Scalinata della Trinità dei Monti) provide a perfect people-watching perch and you'll almost certainly find yourself taking stock here at some point. Piazza di Spagna was named after the Spanish embassy to the Holy See, although the staircase, designed by the Italian Francesco de Sanctis and built in 1725 with a legacy from the French, leads to the French **Chiesa della Trinità dei Monti**. This landmark church, which was commissioned by King Louis XII of France and consecrated in 1585, commands memorable views and boasts some wonderful frescoes by Daniele da Volterra, including

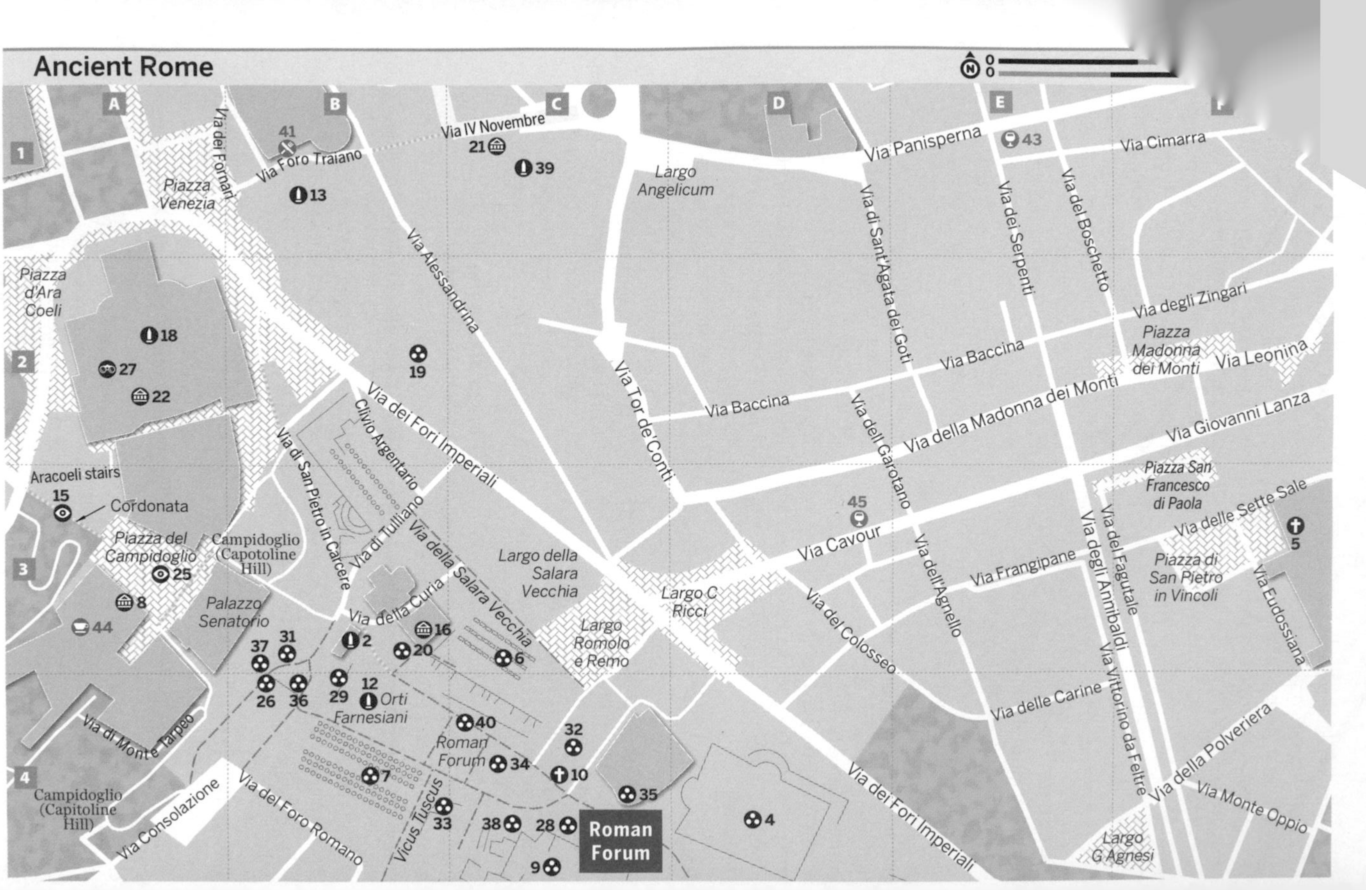

Ancient Rome
A
B
C
D
E
1
2
3
4
Via dei Fornari
Piazza Venezia
Via Foro Traiano
41
13
Via IV Novembre
21
39
Largo Angelicum
Via Panisperna
43
Via Cimarra
Piazza d'Ara Coeli
18
27
22
Via Alessandrina
19
Via di Sant'Agata dei Goti
Via dei Serpenti
Via del Boschetto
Via degli Zingari
Piazza Madonna dei Monti
Via Leonina
Via Baccina
Via della Madonna dei Monti
Via Giovanni Lanza
Via Tor de'Conti
Via dell'Garotano
Via dei Fori Imperiali
Clivio Argentario
Via di San Pietro in Carcere
Aracoeli stairs
15
Cordonata
Piazza del Campidoglio
Campidoglio (Capotoline Hill)
25
8
44
Palazzo Senatorio
Via di Tulliano
Via della Salara Vecchia
Largo della Salara Vecchia
Via della Curia
16
20
2
6
37
31
26
36
29
12
Orti Farnesiani
40
Roman Forum
34
7
Largo Romolo e Remo
Largo C Ricci
45
Via Cavour
Piazza San Francesco di Paola
Via delle Sette Sale
5
Via Frangipane
Via dell'Agnello
Via del Colosseo
Via degli Annibaldi
Via del Fagutale
Piazza di San Pietro in Vincoli
Via Eudossiana
Via delle Carine
Via Vittorino da Feltre
Via della Polveriera
Via Monte Oppio
Largo G Agnesi
Via di Monte Tarpeo
Campidoglio (Capitoline Hill)
Via Consolazione
Via del Foro Romano
Vicus Tuscus
32
10
35
33
38
28
9
Roman Forum
4

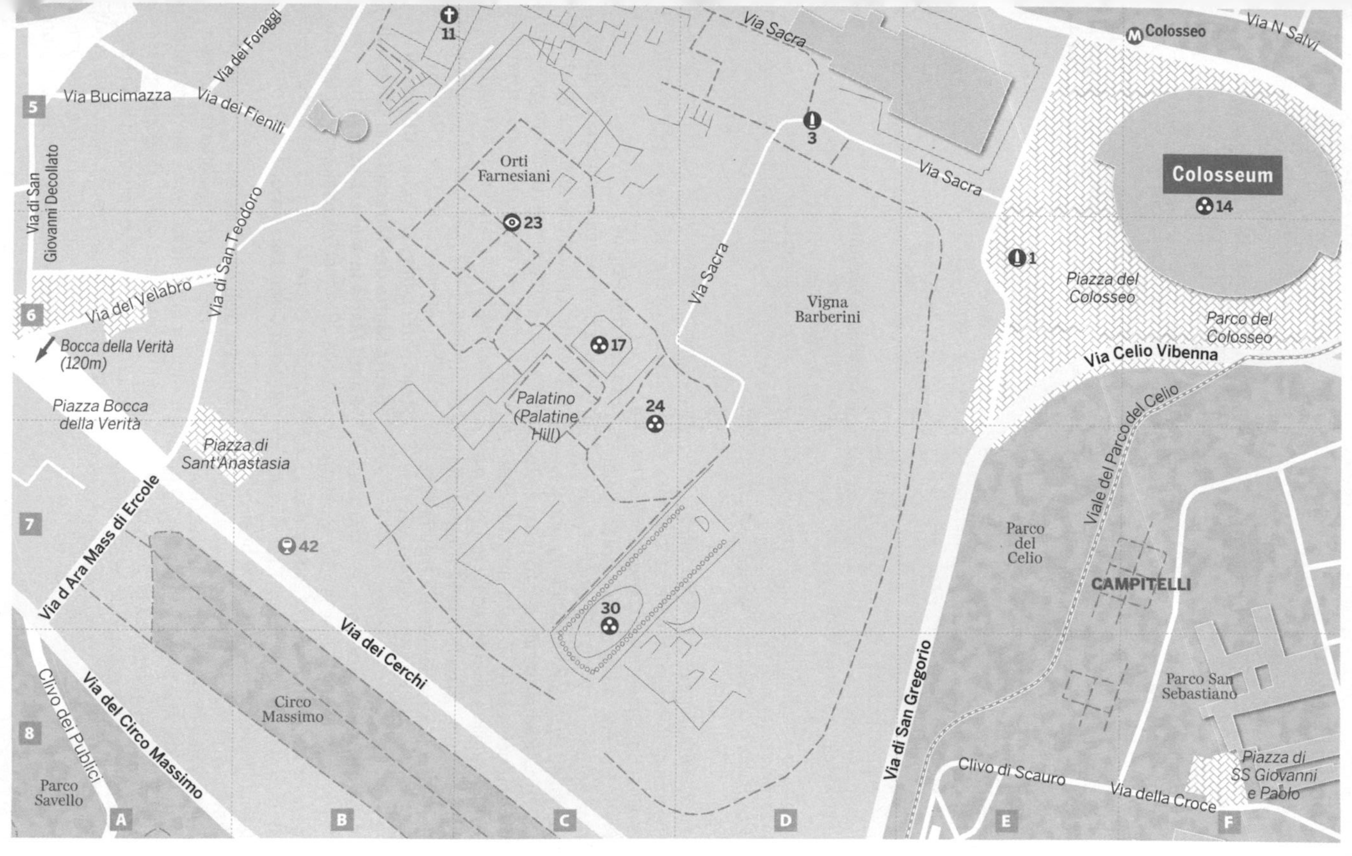
Via Bucimazza
Via dei Foraggi
Via dei Fienili
11
Via Sacra
Colosseo
Via N Salvi
Colosseum
14
3
Via Sacra
Orti Farnesiani
23
Via di San Giovanni Decollato
Via di San Teodoro
Via del Velabro
Bocca della Verità (120m)
Piazza Bocca della Verità
Piazza di Sant'Anastasia
Via Sacra
Vigna Barberini
1
Piazza del Colosseo
Parco del Colosseo
Via Celio Vibenna
17
Palatino (Palatine Hill)
24
Viale del Parco del Celio
Parco del Celio
CAMPITELLI
42
Via d Ara Mass di Ercole
30
Via dei Cerchi
Circo Massimo
Via del Circo Massimo
Clivo dei Publici
Parco Savello
Via di San Gregorio
Parco San Sebastiano
Clivo di Scauro
Via della Croce
Piazza di SS Giovanni e Paolo
A
B
C
D
E
F
5
6
7
8

Ancient Rome

Sights

1 Arco di Costantino ... E6
2 Arco di Settimio Severo ... B3
3 Arco di Tito ... D5
4 Basilica di Massenzio ... D4
5 Basilica di San Pietro in Vincoli ... F3
6 Basilica Fulvia Aemilia ... C3
7 Basilica Giulia ... B4
8 Capitoline Museums ... A3
9 Casa delle Vestali ... C4
10 Chiesa di San Lorenzo in Miranda ... C4
11 Chiesa di Santa Maria Antiqua ... B5
12 Colonna di Foca ... B4
13 Colonna di Traiano ... B1
14 Colosseum ... F5
15 Cordonata ... A3
16 Curia ... B3
17 Domus Flavia ... C6
18 Il Vittoriano ... A2
19 Imperial Forums ... B2
20 Lapis Niger ... B3
21 Mercati di Traiano Museo dei Fori Imperiali ... C1
22 Museo Centrale del Risorgimento ... A2
23 Orti Farnesiani ... C6
24 Palatino ... C6
25 Piazza del Campidoglio ... A3
26 Portico degli Dei Consenti ... B4
27 Roma dal Cielo ... A2
28 Roman Forum ... C4
29 Rostrum ... B4
30 Stadio ... C7
31 Tempio della Concordia ... B3
32 Tempio di Antonino e Faustina ... C4
33 Tempio di Castore e Polluce ... B4
34 Tempio di Giulio Cesare ... C4
35 Tempio di Romolo ... C4
36 Tempio di Saturno ... B4
37 Tempio di Vespasiano ... B3
38 Tempio di Vesta ... C4
39 Torre delle Milizie ... C1
40 Via Sacra ... C4

Eating

41 Terre e Domus ... B1

Drinking & Nightlife

42 0,75 ... B7
43 Ai Tre Scalini ... E1
44 Caffè Capitolino ... A3
45 Cavour 313 ... D3

a masterful Deposizione (Deposition). At the foot of the steps, the Barcaccia (the 'sinking boat' fountain) is believed to be by Pietro Bernini, father of the more famous Gian Lorenzo. In 2015 the fountain was damaged by Dutch football fans, and the Dutch subsequently offered to repair it. To the southeast of the piazza, adjacent Piazza Mignanelli is dominated by the Colonna dell'Immacolata, built in 1857 to celebrate Pope Pius IX's declaration of the Immaculate Conception. (Map p63; M Spagna)

Keats-Shelley House — Museum

The Keats-Shelley House is where Romantic poet John Keats died of tuberculosis at the age of 25, in February 1821. A year later, fellow poet Percy Bysshe Shelley drowned off the coast of Tuscany. The small apartment evokes the impoverished lives of the poets, and is now a small museum crammed with memorabilia, from faded letters to death masks. (Map p63; ☎06 678 42 35; www.keats-shelley-house.org; Piazza di Spagna 26; adult/reduced €5/4, ticket gives discount for Casa di Goethe; ⏰10am-1pm & 2-6pm Mon-Fri, 11am-2pm & 3-6pm Sat; M Spagna)

Piazza del Popolo — Piazza

This dazzling piazza was laid out in 1538 to provide a grandiose entrance to what was then Rome's main northern gateway. Piazza del Popolo has since been remodelled several times, most recently by Giuseppe Valadier in 1823. Guarding its southern approach are Carlo Rainaldi's twin 17th-century churches, **Chiesa di Santa Maria dei Miracoli** and **Chiesa di Santa Maria in Montesanto**. In the centre, the 36m-high **obelisk** was brought by Augustus from ancient Egypt and originally stood in **Circo Massimo**.

Museo dell'Ara Pacis — Museum

The first modern construction in Rome's historic centre since WWII, Richard Meier's controversial and widely detested glass-and-marble pavilion houses the *Ara Pacis Augustae* (Altar of Peace), Augustus' great monument to peace. One of the most important works of ancient Roman sculpture, the vast marble altar – measuring 11.6m by 10.6m by 3.6m – was completed in 13 BC. (06 06 08; www.arapacis.it; Lungotevere in Auga; adult/reduced €10.50/8.50, audio guide €4; 9am-7pm, last admission 6pm; M Flaminio)

Galleria Nazionale d'Arte Antica: Palazzo Barberini — Gallery

Commissioned to celebrate the Barberini family's rise to papal power, Palazzo Barberini is a sumptuous baroque palace that impresses even before you go inside and start on the breathtaking art. Many high-profile architects worked on it, including rivals Bernini and Borromini: the former contributed a large squared staircase, the latter a helicoidal one.

Amid the masterpieces, don't miss Pietro da Cortona's *Il Trionfo della Divina Provvidenza* (Triumph of Divine Providence; 1632–39), the most spectacular of the palazzo's ceiling frescoes in the 1st-floor main salon. Other must-sees include Hans Holbein's famous portrait of a pugnacious Henry VIII (c 1540), Filippo Lippi's luminous *Annunciazione e due devoti* (Annunciation with two Kneeling Donors) and Raphael's *La Fornarina* (The Baker's Girl), a portrait of his mistress who worked in a bakery in Trastevere. Works by Caravaggio include *San Francesco d'Assisi in meditazione* (St Francis in Meditation), *Narciso* (Narcissus; 1571–1610) and the mesmerisingly horrific *Giuditta e Oloferne* (Judith Beheading Holophernes; c 1597–1600). (Map p63; 06 3 28 10; www.galleriabarberini.benicultural.it; Via delle Quattro Fontane 13; adult/reduced €7/3.50, incl Palazzo Corsini, valid 3 days €9/4.50; 8.30am-7pm Tue-Sun; M Barberini)

Palazzo del Quirinale — Palace

Overlooking Piazza del Quirinale, this immense palace is the official residence of Italy's head of state, the Presidente della Repubblica. For almost three centuries it was the pope's summer residence, but in 1870 Pope Pius IX begrudgingly handed the keys over to Italy's new king. Later, in 1948, it was given to the Italian state.

You can visit by booking at least five days ahead; the shorter tour visits the sumptuous reception rooms, while the longer tour includes the interiors as well as the gardens and the carriages. (Map p63; 06 4 69 91; www.quirinale.it; Piazza del Quirinale; admission €10, 30mins tour €1.50, 2½hr tour €10; 9.30am-4pm Tue, Wed & Fri-Sun, closed Aug; M Barberini)

Monti, Esquiline & San Lorenzo

Chiesa di Santa Maria della Vittoria — Church

This modest church is an unlikely setting for an extraordinary work of art – Bernini's extravagant and sexually charged *Santa Teresa trafitta dall'amore di Dio* (Ecstasy of St Teresa). This daring sculpture depicts Teresa, engulfed in the folds of a flowing cloak, floating in ecstasy on a cloud while a teasing angel pierces her repeatedly with a golden arrow. (Map p63; Via XX Settembre 17; 8.30am-noon & 3.30-6pm; M Repubblica)

Basilica di Santa Maria Maggiore — Basilica

One of Rome's four patriarchal basilicas, this monumental 5th-century church stands on the summit of the Esquiline Hill, on the spot where snow is said to have miraculously fallen in the summer of AD 358. Much altered over the centuries, it's something of an architectural hybrid, with a 14th-century Romanesque belfry, an 18th-century baroque facade, a largely baroque interior, and a series of glorious 5th-century mosaics. (Map p63; Piazza Santa Maria Maggiore; basilica/museum/loggia/archaeological site free/€3/5/5; 7am-7pm, museum & loggia 9am-5.30pm; Piazza Santa Maria Maggiore)

Basilica di San Pietro in Vincoli — Basilica

Pilgrims and art lovers flock to this 5th-century basilica for two reasons: to marvel at Michelangelo's colossal *Moses* (1505) sculpture and to see the chains that supposedly bound St Peter when he was imprisoned in the Carcere Mamertino (near the Roman Forum). Access to the church is via a flight of steps through a low arch that leads up from Via Cavour. (Map p68; Piazza di San Pietro in Vincoli 4a; 8am-12.20pm & 3-7pm summer, to 6pm winter; M Cavour)

Museo Nazionale Romano: Palazzo Massimo alle Terme Museum

One of Rome's great unheralded museums, this is a fabulous treasure trove of classical art. The ground and 1st floors are devoted to sculpture with some breathtaking pieces: check out the *Pugile* (Boxer), a 2nd-century-BC Greek bronze; the graceful 2nd-century-BC *Ermafrodite dormiente* (Sleeping Hermaphrodite); and the idealised *Il discobolo* (Discus Thrower). It's the magnificent and vibrantly coloured frescoes on the 2nd floor, however, that are the undisputed highlight. (Map p63; 06 3996 7700; www.coopculture.it; Largo di Villa Peretti 1; adult/reduced €7/3.50; 9am-7.45pm Tue-Sun; M Termini)

Domus Aurea Archaeological Site

Nero had his Domus Aurea constructed after the fire of AD 64 (which it's rumoured he had started to clear the area). Named after the gold that lined its facade and interiors, it was a huge complex covering up to a third of the city. The excavated part of the site has been repeatedly closed due to flooding, but opened for weekend guided tours from late 2014; check the website for current opening status. (Golden House; 06 3996 7700; www.coopculture.it; Viale della Domus Aurea; admission/with online booking fee €10/12; guided tours Sat & Sun; M Colosseo)

Celian Hill & San Giovanni

Basilica di San Clemente Basilica

Nowhere better illustrates the various stages of Rome's turbulent past than this fascinating multi-layered church. The ground-level 12th-century basilica sits atop a 4th-century church, which, in turn, stands over a 2nd-century pagan temple and a 1st-century Roman house. Beneath everything are foundations dating from the Roman Republic. (www.basilicasanclemente.com; Via di San Giovanni in Laterano; excavations adult/reduced €10/5; 9am-12.30pm & 3-6pm Mon-Sat, 12.15-6pm Sun; Via Labicana)

Basilica di San Giovanni in Laterano

Basilica di San Giovanni in Laterano — Basilica

For a thousand years this monumental cathedral was the most important church in Christendom. Commissioned by Constantine and consecrated in AD 324, it was the first Christian basilica built in the city and, until the late 14th century, was the pope's main place of worship. It's still Rome's official cathedral and the pope's seat as the bishop of Rome. The basilica has been revamped several times, most notably by Borromini in the 17th century, and by Alessandro Galilei, who added the immense white facade in 1735. (Piazza di San Giovanni in Laterano 4; basilica/cloister free/€5; ⏲7am-6.30pm, cloister 9am-6pm; Ⓜ San Giovanni)

Santuario della Scala Santa & Sancta Sanctorum — Chapel

The Scala Sancta, said to be the staircase that Jesus walked up in Pontius Pilate's Jerusalem palace, was brought to Rome by St Helena in the 4th century. Pilgrims consider it sacred and climb it on their knees, saying a prayer on each of the 28 steps. At the top, the richly frescoed Sancta Sanctorum (Holy of Holies) was formerly the pope's private chapel. (www.scala-santa.it; Piazza di San Giovanni in Laterano 14; admission Scala free, Sancta with/without audio guide €5/3.50; ⏲Scala 6am-1pm & 3-7pm summer, to 6.30pm winter, Sancta Sanctorum 9.30am-12.40pm & 3-5.10pm Mon-Sat; Ⓜ San Giovanni)

Southern Rome

Basilica di San Paolo Fuori le Mura — Basilica

The largest church in Rome after St Peter's (and the world's third largest), this magnificent basilica stands on the site where St Paul was buried after being decapitated in AD 67. Built by Constantine in the 4th century, it was largely destroyed by fire in 1823 and much of what you see is a 19th-century reconstruction. (www.abbaziasanpaolo.net; Via Ostiense 190; cloisters €4, archaeological walk €4, audioguide €5; ⏲7am-6.30pm; Ⓜ San Paolo)

Ancient Rome

If you're fascinated by Ancient Rome, seek out these sights that will illuminate Imperial life.

Area Archeologica del Teatro di Marcello e del Portico d'Ottavia (Map p64; entrances Via del Teatro di Marcello 44 & Via Portico d'Ottavia 29; ⏲9am-7pm summer, to 6pm winter; 🚌Via del Teatro di Marcello) FREE To the east of the Jewish Ghetto, the **Teatro di Marcello** (Theatre of Marcellus) is the star turn of this dusty archaeological area. This 20,000-seat mini-Colosseum was planned by Julius Caesar and completed in 11 BC by Augustus.

Museo Nazionale Romano: Terme di Diocleziano (Map p63; www.coopculture.it; Viale Enrico de Nicola 78; adult/reduced €7/3.50; ⏲9am-7.30pm Tue-Sun; Ⓜ Termini) Ancient Rome's largest bath complex, covering about 13 hectares and with a capacity for 3000 people. Today its ruins give a fascinating insight into Roman life through memorial inscriptions and other artefacts. Outside, the vast, elegant cloister was constructed from drawings by Michelangelo.

Museo Nazionale Romano: Palazzo Altemps (Map p64; www.coopculture.it; Piazza Sant'Apollinare 44; adult/reduced €7/3.50; ⏲9am-7.45pm Tue-Sun; 🚌Corso del Rinascimento) Just north of Piazza Navona, Palazzo Altemps is a beautiful late-15th-century *palazzo,* housing a formidable collection of classical sculpture.

Terme di Caracalla (www.coopculture.it; Viale delle Terme di Caracalla 52; adult/reduced €6/3; ⏲9am-1hr before sunset Tue-Sun, 9am-2pm Mon; 🚌Viale delle Terme di Caracalla)The remains of the emperor Caracalla's vast baths complex are among Rome's most awe-inspiring ruins. Inaugurated in 216, the original 10-hectare site, which comprised baths, gyms, libraries, shops and gardens, was used by up to 8000 people daily.

Understanding Rome's Catacombs

Built as communal burial grounds, the catacombs were the early Christians' solution to the problem of what to do with their dead. Belief in the Resurrection meant that they couldn't cremate their corpses, as was the custom at the time, and Roman law forbade burial within the city walls. Furthermore, as a persecuted minority they didn't have their own cemeteries. So, in the 2nd century they began to dig beneath Via Appia Antica, where a number of Christians already had family tombs.

Over time, as Christianity became more popular, competition for burial space became fierce and a cut-throat trade in tomb real estate developed. However, by the late 4th century, Christianity had been legalised and the Christians had begun to bury their dead near the basilicas that were springing up within the city walls. By the Middle Ages the catacombs had been all but abandoned.

More than 30 catacombs have been uncovered in the Rome area since scholars started researching them in the 19th century.

Via Appia Antica Historic Site

Named after consul Appius Claudius Caecus who laid the first 90km section in 312 BC, ancient Rome's *regina viarum* (queen of roads) was extended in 190 BC to reach Brindisi on Italy's southern Adriatic coast. Via Appia Antica has long been one of Rome's most exclusive addresses, a beautiful cobbled thoroughfare flanked by grassy fields, Roman structures and towering pine trees. Most splendid of the ancient houses was Villa dei Quintilli, so desirable that emperor Commodus murdered its owners and took it for himself. (Appian Way; 06 513 53 16; www.parcoappiaantica.it; bike hire hr/day €3/15; Info Point 9.30am-1pm & 2-5.30pm Mon-Fri, 9.30am-6.30pm Sat & Sun, to 5pm winter; Via Appia Antica)

Chiesa del Domine Quo Vadis? Church

This pint-sized church marks the spot where St Peter, fleeing Rome, met a vision of Jesus going the other way. When Peter asked: '*Domine, quo vadis?*' (Lord, where are you going?), Jesus replied, '*Venio Roman iterum crucifigi*' (I am coming to Rome to be crucified again). Reluctantly deciding to join him, Peter tramped back into town where he was arrested and executed. (Via Appia Antica 51; 8am-6.30pm Mon-Fri, 8.15am-6.45pm Sat & Sun winter, to 7.30pm summer; Via Appia Antica)

Catacombe di San Callisto Catacomb

These are the largest and busiest of Rome's catacombs. Founded at the end of the 2nd century and named after Pope Calixtus I, they became the official cemetery of the newly established Roman Church. In the 20km of tunnels explored to date, archaeologists have found the tombs of 500,000 people and seven popes who were martyred in the 3rd century. (06 513 01 51; www.catacombe.roma.it; Via Appia Antica 110 & 126; adult/reduced €8/5; 9am-noon & 2-5pm, closed Wed & Feb; Via Appia Antica)

Trastevere & Gianicolo

Standing atop **Gianicolo** (Via del Gianicolo; Via del Gianicolo) hill, you'll experience the city's best views, the closest you can get to soaring like a bird.

Piazza Santa Maria in Trastevere Piazza

Trastevere's focal square is a prime people-watching spot. By day it's full of mums with strollers, chatting locals and guidebook-toting tourists; by night it's the domain of foreign students, young Romans and out-of-towners, all out for a good time. The fountain in the centre of the square is of Roman origin and was restored by Carlo Fontana in 1692. (Viale di Trastevere, Viale di Trastevere)

Basilica di Santa Maria in Trastevere — Basilica

Nestled in a quiet corner of Trastevere's focal square, this is said to be the oldest church dedicated to the Virgin Mary in Rome. In its original form it dates to the early 3rd century, but a major 12th-century makeover saw the addition of a Romanesque bell tower and glittering facade. The portico came later, added by Carlo Fontana in 1702. Inside, the 12th-century mosaics are the headline feature. (Piazza Santa Maria in Trastevere; 7.30am-9pm; Viale di Trastevere, Viale di Trastevere)

Tempietto di Bramante & Chiesa di San Pietro in Montorio — Church

Considered the first great building of the High Renaissance, Bramante's sublime Tempietto (Little Temple; 1508) is a perfect surprise, squeezed into the courtyard of the Chiesa di San Pietro in Montorio, on the spot where St Peter is said to have been crucified. It's small, but perfectly formed; its classically inspired design and ideal proportions epitomise the Renaissance zeitgeist. (www.sanpietroinmontorio.it; Piazza San Pietro in Montorio 2; Chiesa 8.30am-
& 3-4pm Mon-Fri, Tempietto 9.30am-12.30pm
2-4.30pm Tue-Fri, 9am-3pm Sat; Via Garibal

Vatican City, Borgo & Prati

St Peter's Square — Piazza

Overlooked by St Peter's Basilica, the Vatican's central square was laid out between 1656 and 1667 to a design by Gian Lorenzo Bernini. Seen from above, it resembles a giant keyhole with two semicircular colonnades, each consisting of four rows of Doric columns, encircling a giant ellipse that straightens out to funnel believers into the basilica. The effect was deliberate – Bernini described the colonnades as representing 'the motherly arms of the church'.

The scale of the piazza is dazzling: at its largest it measures 340m by 240m. There are 284 columns and, atop the colonnades, 140 saints. The 25m obelisk in the centre was brought to Rome by Caligula from Heliopolis in Egypt, and later used by Nero as a turning post for the chariot races in his circus. (Piazza San Pietro; M Ottaviano-San Pietro)

Ponte Sant'Angelo and Castel Sant'Angelo (p76)

Top Five Film Locations

iazza Navona (p66)

Trevi Fountain (p67)

Bocca della Verità (p66)

Spanish Steps (p67)

Pantheon (p44)

From left: Spanish Steps (p67); Fontana del Moro, Piazza Navona (p66); Trevi Fountain (p67)

THOMAS STANKIEWICZ/LOOK-FOTO/GETTY IMAGES ©

Castel Sant'Angelo Museum, Castle
With its chunky round keep, this castle is an instantly recognisable landmark. Built as a mausoleum for the emperor Hadrian, it was converted into a papal fortress in the 6th century and named after an angelic vision that Pope Gregory the Great had in 590. Nowadays, it houses the Museo Nazionale di Castel Sant'Angelo and its eclectic collection of paintings, sculpture, military memorabilia and medieval firearms. (06 681 91 11; www.castelsantangelo.beniculturali.it; Lungotevere Castello 50; adult/reduced €7/3.50; 9am-7.30pm Tue-Sun; Piazza Pia)

Ponte Sant'Angelo Bridge
The emperor Hadrian built the Ponte Sant'Angelo in 136 to provide an approach to his mausoleum, but it was Bernini who brought it to life, designing the angel sculptures in 1668. The three central arches of the bridge are part of the original structure; the end arches were restored and enlarged in 1892–94 during the construction of the Lungotevere embankments. (Piazza Pia)

Villa Borghese & Northern Rome

Villa Borghese Park
Locals, lovers, tourists, joggers – no one can resist the lure of Rome's most celebrated park. Originally the 17th-century estate of Cardinal Scipione Borghese, it covers about 80 hectares of wooded glades, gardens and grassy banks. Among its attractions are several excellent museums and the landscaped **Giardino del Lago**. (entrances at Piazzale San Paolo del Brasile, Piazzale Flaminio, Via Pinciana, Via Raimondo, Largo Pablo Picasso; dawn-dusk; Porta Pinciana)

Museo Nazionale Etrusco di Villa Giulia Museum
Pope Julius III's 16th-century villa provides the charming setting for Italy's finest collection of Etruscan and pre-Roman treasures. Exhibits, many of which came from burial tombs in the surrounding Lazio region, range from bronze figurines and black *bucchero* tableware to temple decorations, terracotta vases and a dazzling display of sophisticated jewellery. (www.

villagiulia.beniculturali.it; Piazzale di Villa Giulia; adult/reduced €8/4; 8.30am-7.30pm Tue-Sun; Via delle Belle Arti)

Galleria Nazionale d'Arte Moderna e Contemporanea — Gallery

Housed in a vast belle époque palace, this oft-overlooked gallery is an unsung gem. Its superlative collection runs the gamut from neoclassical sculpture to abstract expressionism, with works by many important exponents of 19th- and 20th-century art. (06 3229 8221; www.gnam.beniculturali.it; Viale delle Belle Arti 131, disabled entrance Via Gramsci 73; adult/reduced €8/4; 8.30am-7.30pm Tue-Sun; Piazza Thorvaldsen)

TOURS

A Friend in Rome — Tour

Silvia Prosperi organises private tailor-made tours (on foot, by bike or scooter) to suit your interests. Rates are €50 per hour, with a minimum of three hours for most tours. She can also arrange kid-friendly tours, cooking classes, vintage car tours and more. (340 501 92 01; www.afriendinrome.it)

SHOPPING

Confetteria Moriondo & Gariglio — Food

Roman poet Trilussa was so smitten with this historic chocolate shop – established by the Torinese confectioners to the royal house of Savoy – that he dedicated several sonnets to it. And we agree, it's a gem. Many of the bonbons and handmade chocolates laid out in ceremonial splendour in the glass cabinets are still prepared according to original 19th-century recipes. (Map p64; Via del Piè di Marmo 21-22; 9am-7.30pm Mon-Sat; Via del Corso)

Officina Profumo Farmaceutica di Santa Maria Novella — Beauty

This, the Roman branch of one of Italy's oldest pharmacies, stocks natural perfumes and cosmetics as well as herbal infusions, teas and pot pourri, all shelved in wooden, glass-fronted cabinets under a Murano chandelier. The original pharmacy nded in Florence in 1612 by the ican monks of Santa Maria Novella, many of its cosmetics are based on -century herbal recipes. (Map p64; vw.smnovella.it; Corso del Rinascimento 47; 10am-7.30pm Mon-Sat; Corso del Rinascimento)

Vertecchi Art Arts

Ideal for last-minute gift buying, this large paperware and art shop has beautiful printed paper, cards and envelopes that will inspire you to bring back the art of letter writing, plus an amazing choice of notebooks, art stuff and trinkets. It's not far from the Spanish Steps. (Via della Croce 70; 3.30-7.30pm Mon, 10am-7.30pm Tue-Sat; M Spagna)

C.U.C.I.N.A. Homewares

If you need a foodie gadget, C.U.C.I.N.A. is the place. Make your own *cucina* (kitchen) look the part with the designerware from this famous shop, with myriad devices you'll decide you simply must have, from jelly moulds to garlic presses. (06 679 12 75; Via Mario de' Fiori 65; 3.30-7.30pm Mon, 10am-7.30pm Tue-Fri, 10.30am-7.30pm Sat; M Spagna)

Sermoneta Accessories

Buying leather gloves in Rome is a rite of passage for some, and its most famous glove-seller is the place to do it. Choose from a kaleidoscopic range of quality leather and suede gloves lined with silk and cashmere. An expert assistant will size up your hand in a glance. Just don't expect them to crack a smile. (Map p63; 06 679 19 60; www.sermonetagloves.com; Piazza di Spagna 61; 9.30am-8pm Mon-Sat, 10am-7pm Sun; M Spagna)

Volpetti Food & Drink

In Testaccio, this superstocked deli, considered by many the best in town, is a treasure trove of gourmet delicacies. Helpful staff will guide you through the extensive selection of smelly cheeses, homemade pastas, olive oils, vinegars, cured meats, veggie pies, wines and grappas. It also serves excellent sliced pizza. (www.volpetti.com; Via Marmorata 47; 8am-2pm & 5-8.15pm Mon-Sat; Via Marmorata)

Flea market, Trastevere

Porta Portese Market Market

To see another side of Rome, head to Trastevere to this mammoth flea market. With thousands of stalls selling everything from rare books and fell-off-a-lorry bikes to Peruvian shawls and MP3 players, it's crazily busy and a lot of fun. Keep your valuables safe and wear your haggling hat. (Piazza Porta Portese; 6am-2pm Sun; Viale di Trastevere, Viale di Trastevere)

ENTERTAINMENT

Watching the world go by in Rome is often entertainment enough, but don't overlook the local arts and sports scene. As well as gigs and concerts in every genre, there are fantastic arts festivals (especially in summer) performances with Roman ruins as a backdrop, and football games that split the city asunder.

Auditorium Parco della Musica Concert Venue

The hub of Rome's thriving cultural scene, the Auditorium is the capital's premier concert venue and one of Europe's most popular arts centres. Its three concert halls offer superb acoustics and, together with a 3000-seat open-air arena, stage everything from classical-music concerts to jazz gigs, public lectures and film screenings. The Auditorium is also home to Rome's world-class Orchestra dell' Accademia Nazionale di Santa Cecilia (www.santacecilia.it). (06 8024 1281; www.auditorium.com; Viale Pietro de Coubertin 30; Viale Tiziano)

EATING

Rome teems with trattorias, *ristoranti*, pizzerias, *enoteche* (wine bars serving food) and gelaterie. Excellent places dot the *centro storico*, Trastevere, Prati, Testaccio and San Lorenzo. Be warned that the area around Termini has quite a few substandard restaurants, as does the Vatican, which is packed with tourist traps.

PLANET/GETTY IMAGES ©

Rome's Best Gelato

Gelato is as much a part of Roman life as traffic jams, and the city has some superb *gelaterie artigianale* (artisanal ice-cream shops). To gauge the quality, check out the pistachio flavour: if it's a pale olive green it's good; if it's bright green, go elsewhere. Our road-tested top gelaterie:

Fatamorgana (www.gelateriafatamorgana.it; Via Bettolo 7; gelato from €2; noon-11pm; M Ottaviano–San Pietro) Try the mouthwatering *agrumi* (citrus fruit) and *basilico, miele e noci* (basil, honey and hazelnuts).

Gelateria del Teatro (Map p64; Via dei Coronari 65; gelato from €2.50; 11.30am-midnight; Corso del Rinascimento) Does a great turn in Sicilian *pistacchio* (pistachio) and *mandorle* (almonds).

Vice (Map p64; www.viceitalia.it; Corso Vittorio Emanuele II 96; gelato from €2.50; 11am-1am; Largo di Torre Argentina) A contemporary outfit serving traditional and modern flavours such as blueberry cheesecake.

Il Caruso (Via Collina 15; noon-9pm; M Repubblica) Top your gelato with *zabaglione* (egg and marsala custard) mixed with *panna* (whipped cream).

Many restaurants close for several weeks during the traditional summer holiday month of August.

Authentic Roman Cooking

The hallmark of an authentic Roman menu is the presence of offal. The Roman love of nose-to-tail eating arose in Testaccio around the city abattoir, and many of the neighbourhood's trattorias still serve traditional offal-based dishes. So whether you want to avoid it or try it, look out for *pajata* (veal's intestines), *trippa* (tripe), *coda alla vaccinara* (oxtail), *coratella* (heart, lung and liver), *animelle* (sweetbreads), *testarella* (head), *lingua* (tongue) and *zampe* (trotters).

Ancient Rome

Terre e Domus Lazio Cuisine **€€**

This modern white-and-glass restaurant is the best option in the touristy Forum area. Overlooking the Colonna di Traiano, it serves a menu of traditional staples, all made with ingredients sourced from the surrounding Lazio region, and a thoughtful selection of regional wines. Lunchtime can be busy but it quietens down in the evening. (Map p68; 06 6994 0273; Via Foro Traiano 82-4; meals €30; 7.30am-12.30am Mon-Sat; Via dei Fori Imperiali)

Centro Storico

Forno Roscioli Pizza, Bakery **€**

This is one of Rome's top bakeries, much loved by lunching locals who crowd here for luscious sliced pizza, prize pastries and hunger-sating *supplì*. There's also a counter serving hot pastas and vegetable side dishes. (Map p64; Via dei Chiavari 34; pizza slices from €2, snacks from €1.50; 7am-7.30pm Mon-Sat; Via Arenula)

Forno di Campo de' Fiori Pizza, Bakery **€**

This buzzing bakery on Campo de' Fiori does a roaring trade in *panini* and delicious fresh-from-the-oven *pizza al taglio* (by the slice). Aficionados swear by the *pizza bianca* ('white' pizza with olive oil, rosemary and salt), but the *panini* and *pizza rossa* ('red' pizza, with olive oil, tomato and oregano) taste plenty good, too. (Map p64; Campo de' Fiori 22; pizza slices about €3; 7.30am-2.30pm & 4.45-8pm Mon-Sat; Corso Vittorio Emanuele II)

Casa Coppelle Ristorante **€€**

Exposed brick walls, flowers and subdued lighting set the stage for creative Italian- and French-inspired food at this intimate, romantic restaurant. There's a full range of starters and pastas, but the real tour de force are the deliciously tender steaks and rich meat dishes. Service is attentive and the setting, on a small piazza near the Pantheon, memorable. Book ahead. (Map p64; 06 6889 1707; www.casacoppelle.it; Piazza delle Coppelle 49; meals €35-40; 12-3.30pm & 6.30-11.30pm; Corso del Rinascimento)

Armando al Pantheon Trattoria **€€**

An institution in these parts, Armando al Pantheon is a rare find – a genuine family-run trattoria in the touristy Pantheon area. It's been on the go for more than 50 years and has served its fair share of celebs, but it hasn't let fame go to its head and it remains one of the best bets for earthy Roman cuisine. Reservations essential. (Map p64; 06 6880 3034; www.armandoalpantheon.it; Salita dei Crescenzi 31; meals €40; 12.30-3pm & 7-11pm Mon-Fri, 12.30-3pm Sat; Largo di Torre Argentina)

Cul de Sac Wine Bar, Trattoria **€€**

A perennially popular wine bar just off Piazza Navona, with an always-busy terrace and narrow, bottle-lined interior. Choose your tipple first – the encyclopaedic wine list boasts about 1500 labels – and then pick what to go with it from the ample menu of no-nonsense Roman staples, Gallic-inspired cold cuts, pâtés, and cheeses. Book ahead for the evening. (Map p64; 06 6880 1094; www.enotecaculdesacroma.it; Piazza Pasquino 73; meals €30; noon-12.30am; Corso Vittorio Emanuele II)

Villa Borghese (p76)

> *locals, lovers, tourists – no one can resist the lure of Rome's most celebrated park*

Tridente, Trevi & the uirinale

a Michele Pizza €

handy address in Spagna district: buy ur fresh, light and crispy *pizza al taglio* y the slice), and you'll have a delicious st lunch. It's all kosher, so meat and eese is not mixed. (Map p63; ☎349 25347; Via dell'Umiltà 31; pizza slices from €3; 8am-6pm Mon-Fri, to 10pm summer; Via l Corso)

astificio Fast Food €

great find in this pricey 'hood. Pasticcio a pasta shop that serves up two choices pasta at lunchtime. It's fast food, Italianyle: freshly cooked (if you time it right) asta, with wine and water included. It's no isurely lunch: there's not much room so u'll have to nab a chair while you can and at quickly. This is better than taking away, owever, as if you do, you'll miss out on ur drink and your pasta will get cold. (Via lla Croce 8; pasta, wine & water €4; lunch 3pm Mon-Sat; M Spagna)

Colline Emiliane Italian €€

This welcoming, tucked-away restaurant just off Piazza Barberini flies the flag for Emilia-Romagna, the well-fed Italian province that has blessed the world with Parmesan, balsamic vinegar, bolognese sauce and Parma ham. This is a consistently excellent place to eat; there are delicious meats, homemade pasta and rich *ragù*. Try to save room for dessert too. (Map p63; ☎06 481 75 38; Via degli Avignonesi 22; meals €50; 12.45-2.45pm Tue-Sun & 7.30-10.45pm Tue-Sat, closed Aug; M Barberini)

Matricianella Trattoria €€

With its gingham tablecloths, chintzy murals and fading prints, Matricianella is an archetypal trattoria, much loved for its traditional Roman cuisine. Its loyal clientele go crazy for ever-green crowd-pleasers like battered vegetables, artichoke *alla giudia* (fried, Jewish-style) and *saltimbocca* (veal cutlet with ham and sage). Booking is

Esedra di Marco Aurelia, Capitoline Museums (p62)

essential. (☎06 683 21 00; www.matricianella.it; Via del Leone 2/4; meals €40; 🕒12.30-3pm & 7.30-11pm Mon-Sat; 🚌Via del Corso)

Enoteca Regionale Palatium Ristorante, Wine Bar **€€€**

A rich showcase of regional bounty, run by the Lazio Regional Food Authority, this sleek wine bar serves excellent local specialities, such as *porchetta* (pork roasted with herbs) or *gnocchi alla Romana con crema da zucca* (potato dumplings Roman-style with cream of pumpkin), as well as an impressive array of Lazio wines (try lesser-known drops such as Aleatico). *Aperitivo* is a good bet too. (☎06 692 02 132; Via Frattina 94; meals €55; 🕒11am-11pm Mon-Sat, closed Aug; 🚌Via del Corso)

Monti, Esquiline & San Lorenzo

Panella l'Arte del Pane Bakery, Cafe **€**

With a magnificent array of *pizza al taglio, arancini*, focaccia, fried croquettes and pastries, this smart bakery-cum-cafe is good any time of the day. The outside tables are ideal for a leisurely breakfast or chilled evening drink, or you can perch on a high stool and lunch on something from the sumptuous counter display. (☎06 487 24 35; Via Merulana 54; snacks about €3.50; 🕒8am-11pm Mon-Thu, to midnight Fri & Sat, 8.30am-4pm Sun; Ⓜ Vittorio Emanuele)

Roscioli Pizza, Bakery **€**

Off-the-track branch of this splendid deli-bakery-pizzeria, with delish *pizza al taglio*, pasta dishes and other goodies that make it ideal for a swift lunch or picnic stock-up. It's on a road leading off Piazza Vittorio Emanuele II. (Via Buonarroti 48; pizza slices €3.50; 🕒7am-8pm Mon-Sat; Ⓜ Vittorio Emanuele)

L'Asino d'Oro Italian **€€**

This fabulous restaurant was transplanted from Orvieto and its Umbrian origins resonate in Lucio Sforza's delicious, exceptional cooking. It's unfussy yet innovative, with dishes featuring lots of flavourful contrasts, such as lamb meatballs with pear and blue cheese. Save room for the amazing desserts. For such excellent food, this intimate, informal yet classy place is one of

Rome's best deals. Hours are changeable so call ahead. (Map p63; 06 4891 3832; Via del Boschetto 73; meals €45; 12.30-2.30pm Sat, 7.30-11pm Tue-Sat; M Cavour)

Trattoria Monti Ristorante **€€**

The Camerucci family runs this elegant brick-arched place, proffering top-notch traditional cooking from the Marches region. There are wonderful *fritti* (fried things), delicate pastas and ingredients such as *pecorino di fossa* (sheep's cheese aged in caves), goose, swordfish and truffles. Try the egg-yolk *tortelli* pasta. Desserts are delectable, including apple pie with *zabaglione*. Word has spread, so be sure to book ahead. (06 446 65 73; Via di San Vito 13a; meals €45; 12.45-2.45pm Tue-Sun, 7.45-11pm Tue-Sat, closed Aug; M Vittorio Emanuele)

Open Colonna Italian **€€€**

Spectacularly set at the back of Palazzo delle Esposizioni, superchef Antonello Colonna's superb restaurant is tucked onto a mezzanine floor under an extraordinary glass roof. The cuisine is new Roman: innovative takes on traditional dishes, cooked with wit and flair. The best thing? There's a more basic but still delectable fixed two-course lunch for €16, and Saturday and Sunday brunch is €30, served in the dramatic, glass-ceilinged hall, with a terrace for sunny days. (Map p63; 06 4782 2641; www.antonellocolonna.it; Via Milano 9a; meals €20-80; 12.30-3.30pm Tue-Sun, 8-11.30pm Tue-Sat; Via Nazionale)

 Celian Hill & San Giovanni

Li Rioni Pizza **€**

Locals swear by Li Rioni, arriving for the second sitting around 9pm after the tourists have left. A classic neighbourhood pizzeria, it buzzes most nights as diners squeeze into the kitschy interior – set up as a Roman street scene – and tuck into wood-fired thin-crust pizzas and crispy fried starters. (06 7045 0605; Via dei Santissimi Quattro Coronati 24; meals €15-20; 7pm-midnight Thu-Tue, closed Aug; Via di San Giovanni in Laterano)

 Art & Politics on Via del Corso

On Via del Corso, the arrow-straight road that links Piazza Venezia to Piazza del Popolo, you'll find one of Rome's finest private art galleries. The **Galleria Doria Pamphilj** (Map p64; www.dopart.it; 06 679 73 23; Via del Corso 305; adult/reduced €11/7.50; 9am-7pm, last admission 6pm; Via del Corso) which houses an extraordinary collection of works by the likes of Raphael, Tintoretto, Brueghel, Titian, Caravaggio, Bernini and Velázquez. Masterpieces abound, but the undisputed star is Velázquez' portrait of Pope Innocent X.

A short walk to the north of the gallery, the 30m-high **Colonna di Marco Aurelio** (Map p64; Piazza Colonna; Via del Corso) heralds the presence of **Palazzo Chigi** (Map p64; www.governo.it; Piazza Colonna 370; guided visits 9am-1pm Sat Oct-May, bookings required; Via del Corso) FREE, the official residence of the Italian prime minister. Next door, on Piazza di Montecitorio, the Bernini-designed **Palazzo di Montecitorio** (Map p64; 800 012955; www.camera.it; Piazza di Montecitorio; guided visits noon-2.30pm 1st Sun of month; Via del Corso) FREE is home to Italy's Chamber of Deputies.

Galleria Doria Pamphilj

e & Testaccio

Fast Food €

t-size joint is the birthplace of zzino, a kind of hybrid sandwich by stuffing a small cone of doughy a with fillers like *polpette al sugo* eatballs in tomato sauce) or *pollo alla acciatore* (stewed chicken). They're messy to eat but quite delicious. (www.trapizzino.it; Via Branca 88; trapizzini from €3.50; noon-1am Tue-Sun; Via Marmorata)

Flavio al Velavevodetto Trattoria €€

Housed in a rustic Pompeian-red villa, this welcoming eatery specialises in earthy, no-nonsense *cucina romana* (Roman cuisine). Expect antipasti of cheeses and cured meats, huge helpings of homemade pastas, and uncomplicated meat dishes. (06 574 41 94; www.ristorantevelavevodetto.it; Via di Monte Testaccio 97-99; meals €30-35; 12.30-3pm & 7.45-11pm; Via Galvani)

Trastevere & Gianicolo

Sisini Pizza €

Locals love this fast-food takeaway joint (the sign outside says 'Supplì'), serving up fresh *pizza al taglio* and different pasta and risotto dishes served in plastic boxes. It's also worth sampling the *supplì* (fried rice balls), and roast chicken. (Via di San Francesco a Ripa 137; pizza & pasta from €3, supplì €1.20; 9am-10.30pm Mon-Sat, closed Aug; Viale di Trastevere, Viale di Trastevere)

Da Augusto Trattoria €

For a Trastevere feast, plonk yourself at one of Augusto's rickety tables, either inside or out on the small piazza, and prepare to enjoy some mamma-style cooking. The gruff waiters dish out hearty platefuls of *rigatoni all'amatriciana* and *stracciatella* (clear broth with egg and Parmesan) among a host of Roman classics. Be prepared to queue. Cash only. (06 580 37 98; Piazza de' Renzi 15; meals €25; 12.30-3pm & 8-11pm; Viale di Trastevere, Viale di Trastevere)

Pizzeria Ivo Pizza €

One of Trastevere's most famous pizzerias, Ivo's has been slinging pizzas for some 40 years, and still the hungry come. With the TV on in the corner and the tables full (a few outside on the cobbled street), Ivo is a noisy and vibrant place, and the waiters fit the gruff-and-fast stereotype. (☎06 581 70 82; Via di San Francesco a Ripa 158; pizzas from €7; ⏰7pm-midnight Wed-Mon; 🚌Viale di Trastevere, 🚋Viale di Trastevere)

La Gensola Sicilian €€

This tranquil, classy yet unpretentious trattoria thrills foodies with delicious food that has a Sicilian slant and emphasis on seafood, including an excellent tuna tartare, linguine with fresh anchovies and divine *zuccherini* (tiny fish) with fresh mint. (☎06 581 63 12; Piazza della Gensola 15; meals €45; ⏰12.30-3pm & 7.30-11.30pm, closed Sun mid-Jun–mid-Sep; 🚌Viale di Trastevere, 🚋Viale di Trastevere)

Glass Hostaria Italian €€€

Trastevere's foremost foodie address, the Glass is a modernist-styled, sophisticated setting decorated in warm wood and contemporary gold, with fabulous coo to match. Chef Cristina Bowerman cre inventive, delicate dishes that combine with fresh ingredients and traditional elements to delight and surprise the palate. Glass Hostaria offers tasting menus at €75, €80 and €100. (☎06 5833 5903; Vicolo del Cinque 58; meals €90; ⏰7.30-11.30pm Tue-Sun; 🚌Piazza Trilussa)

Vatican City, Borgo & Prati

Pizzarium Pizza €

Pizzarium, or 'Bonci pizza rustica #pizzarium', as it has recently rebranded itself, serves some of Rome's best sliced pizza. Scissor-cut squares of meticulously crafted dough are topped with original combinations of seasonal ingredients and served on paper trays for immediate consumption. There's also a daily selection of freshly fried *supplì* (crunchy rice croquettes). (Via della Meloria 43; pizza slices from €3; ⏰11am-10pm; Ⓜ Cipro-Musei Vaticani)

Fa-Bìo Sandwiches €

Sandwiches, salads and smoothies are all prepared with speed, skill and fresh

JAVARMAN3/GETTY IMAGES ©

★ Top Five Bars & Cafes

- Barnum Cafe (p87)
- Ma Che Siete Venuti a Fà (p89)
- La Casa del Caffè Tazza d'Oro (p88)
- Caffè Sant'Eustachio (p88)
- Ai Tre Scalini (p89)

From left: Il Vittoriano (p63); Elefantino statue in Piazza della Minerva (p60); Piazza della Rotonda and the Pantheon (p44)

VISIONS OF OUR LAND/GETTY IMAGES ©

…c ingredients at this tiny takeaway. …s and in-the-know visitors come to …o a quick lunchtime bite, and if you can …queeze in the door you'd do well to follow …uit. (06 6452 5810; www.fa-bio.com; Via Germanico 43; sandwiches €5; 10am-5.30pm Mon-Fri, to 4pm Sat)

Romeo Pizza, Ristorante **€€**

This chic, contemporary outfit is part bakery, part deli, part takeaway and part restaurant. For a quick bite, there's delicious sliced pizza or you can have a *panino* made up at the deli counter; for a full restaurant meal, the à la carte menu offers a mix of traditional Italian dishes and forward-looking international creations. (06 3211 0120; www.romeo.roma.it; Via Silla 26a; pizza slices €2.50, meals €45; 9am-midnight; M Ottaviano-San Pietro)

Velavevodetto Ai Quiriti Lazio Cuisine **€€**

This welcoming restaurant continues to win diners over with its unpretentious, earthy food and honest prices. The menu reads like a directory of Roman staples, and while it's all pretty good, standout choices include *fettuccine con asparagi, guanciale e pecorino* (pasta ribbons with asparagus, guanciale and pecorino cheese) and *polpette di bollito* (fried meat balls). (06 3600 0009; www.ristorantevelavevodetto.it; Piazza dei Quiriti 5; meals €35; 12.30-2.30pm & 7.30-11.30pm; M Lepanto)

Osteria dell'Angelo Trattoria **€€**

With rugby paraphernalia on the walls and basic wooden tables, this laid-back neighbourhood trattoria is a popular spot for genuine local cuisine. The fixed-price menu features a mixed antipasti, a robust Roman-style pasta and a choice of hearty mains with a side dish. To finish off, spiced biscuits are served with sweet dessert wine. Reservations recommended. (06 372 94 70; Via Bettolo 24; fixed-price menu €25-35; 12.30-2.30pm Tue-Fri, 8.30-11pm Mon-Sat; M Ottaviano–San Pietro)

Settembrini Ristorante **€€€**

All labels, suits and media gossip, this fashionable restaurant is part of the ever-growing Settembrini empire. Next door is a stylish all-day cafe, while over the way, Libri & Cucina is a laid-back bookshop

Dining in the Jewish Ghetto

eatery, and L'Officina an upscale food store. At the casually chic main restaurant expect contemporary Italian cuisine and quality wine to match. (☎06 323 26 17; www.viasettembrini.it; Via Settembrini 25; menus lunch €28-38, dinner €48-65; ⏰12.30-3pm Mon-Fri, 8-11pm Mon-Sat; 🚌Piazza Giuseppe Mazzini)

Southern Rome

Eataly Italian €

Eataly is an enormous, mall-like complex, a glittering, gleaming, somewhat confusing department store, entirely devoted to Italian food. As well as foodstuffs from all over the country, books and cookery implements, the store is also home to 19 cafes and restaurants, including excellent pizzas, pasta dishes, ice cream and more. (☎06 9027 9201; www.eataly.net/it_en; Air Terminal Ostiense, Piazzale XII Ottobre 1492; ⏰shop 10am-midnight, restaurants noon-11.30pm; Ⓜ Piramide)

Trattoria Priscilla Trattoria €€

Set in a 16th-century former stable, this intimate family-run trattoria has been feeding hungry travellers along the Appian Way for more than a hundred years, serving up traditional *cucina Romana*, so think carbonara, *amatriciana* and *cacio e pepe*. The tiramisu wins plaudits. (☎06 513 63 79; Via Appia Antica 68; meals €30; ⏰1-3pm daily, 8-11pm Mon-Sat; 🚌Via Appia Antica)

DRINKING & NIGHTLIFE

Rome has plenty of drinking venues, ranging from traditional *enoteche* (wine bars) and streetside cafes to dressy lounge bars, pubs (trendy by virtue of their novelty) and counter-culture hang-outs.

Ancient Rome

Cavour 313 Wine Bar

Close to the Forum, wood-panelled Cavour 313 attracts everyone from tourists to actors and politicians. It serves a daily food menu and a selection of salads, cold cuts and cheeses (€8 to €12), but the headline act is the wine. And with more than 1200 labels to choose from, you're sure to find something to tickle your palate. (Map p68; ☎06 678 54 96; www.cavour313.it; Via Cavour 313; ⏰12.30-2.45pm & 7.30pm-12.30am, closed Sun summer; Ⓜ Cavour)

Trevi Coins

On an average day around €3000 is thrown into the Trevi Fountain. This is collected daily and handed over to the Catholic charity Caritas. The fountain's yield has increased noticeably since 2012 when city authorities clamped down on thieves helping themselves and introduced legislation making it illegal to remove coins from the water.

Caffè Capitolino Cafe

The Capitoline Museums' charming terrace cafe is a good place to relax over a drink or light snack (*panini*, salads and pizza) and enjoy wonderful views across the city's rooftops. Although part of the museum complex, you don't need a ticket to come here as it's accessible via an independent entrance on Piazzale Caffarelli. (Map p68; Piazzale Caffarelli 4; ⏰9am-7.30pm Tue-Sun; 🚌Piazza Venezia)

0,75 Bar

This welcoming bar on the Circo Massimo is good for a lingering drink, an *aperitivo* (6.30pm onwards) or a light meal (mains €6 to €13.50, salads €5.50 to €7.50). It's a friendly place with a laid-back vibe, an attractive exposed-brick look and cool tunes. (Map p68; www.075roma.com; Via dei Cerchi 65; ⏰11am-2am; 📶; 🚌Via dei Cerchi)

Centro Storico

Barnum Cafe Cafe

A relaxed, friendly spot to check your email over a freshly squeezed orange juice or spend a pleasant hour reading a newspaper on one of the tatty old armchairs in the white bare-brick interior. Come evenings and the scene is cocktails, smooth tunes and coolly dressed-down locals. (Map p64;

Views on the Aventine

Head up to the Aventine Hill for one of Rome's most celebrated views. Flanking the Piazza dei Cavalieri di Malta, the **Priorato dei Cavalieri di Malta** (Piazza dei Cavalieri di Malta; closed to the public; Lungotevere Aventino) is the Roman headquarters of the Cavalieri di Malta (Knights of Malta). The building is closed to the public, but look through its keyhole and you'll see the dome of St Peter's Basilica perfectly aligned at the end of a hedge-lined avenue.

Just down from the piazza, there are more gorgeous views to be had at **Parco Savello** (Via di Santa Sabina; 7am-8pm)

View over Rome from Parco Savello
JULIAN ELLIOTT PHOTOGRAPHY/GETTY IMAGES ©

www.barnumcafe.com; Via del Pellegrino 87; 9am-10pm Mon, 8.30am-2am Tue-Sat; ; Corso Vittorio Emanuele II)

La Casa del Caffè Tazza d'Oro Cafe

A busy, stand-up cafe with burnished 1940s fittings, this is one of Rome's best coffee houses. Its espresso hits the mark nicely and there's a range of delicious coffee concoctions, including a cooling *granita di caffè,* a crushed-ice coffee drink served with whipped cream. There's also a small shop and, outside, a coffee *bancomat* for those out-of-hours caffeine emergencies. (Map p64; www.tazzadorocoffeeshop.com; Via degli Orfani 84-86; 7am-8pm Mon-Sat, 10.30am-7.30pm Sun; Via del Corso)

Caffè Sant'Eustachio Cafe

This small, unassuming cafe, generally three deep at the bar, is reckoned by many to serve the best coffee in town. Created by beating the first drops of espresso and several teaspoons of sugar into a frothy paste, then adding the rest of the coffee, it's superbly smooth and guaranteed to put some zing into your sightseeing. (Map p64; www.santeustachioilcaffe.it; Piazza Sant'Eustachio 82; 8.30am-1am Sun-Thu, to 1.30am Fri, to 2am Sat; Corso del Rinascimento)

Etablì Bar, Ristorante

Housed in a lofty 16th-century *palazzo,* Etablì is a rustic-chic lounge-bar-restaurant where you can drop by for a morning coffee, have a light lunch or chat over an *aperitivo*. It's laid-back and good-looking, with original French-inspired country decor – think leather armchairs, rough wooden tables and a crackling fireplace. It also serves weekend brunch, full restaurant dinners (€45) and the occasional jam session. (Map p64; 06 9761 6694; www.etabli.it; Vicolo delle Vacche 9a; 11am-2am, closed Mon in winter, Sun in summer; ; Corso del Rinascimento)

Open Baladin Bar

A hip, shabby-chic lounge bar near Campo de' Fiori, Open Baladin is a leading light in Rome's craft-beer scene, with more than 40 beers on tap and up to 100 bottled brews, many from Italian artisanal microbreweries. There's also a decent food menu with *panini,* gourmet burgers and daily specials. (Map p64; www.openbaladinroma.it; Via degli Specchi 6; noon-2am; ; Via Arenula)

Salotto 42 Bar

On a picturesque piazza, facing the columns of the Temple of Hadrian, this is a glamorous lounge bar, complete with subdued lighting, vintage 1950s armchairs, Murano lamps and a collection of heavyweight design books. Come for the daily lunch buffet or to hang out with the 'see-and-be-seen' crowd over an evening cocktail. (Map p64; www.salotto42.it; Piazza di Pietra 42; 10.30am-2am Tue-Sun; Via del Corso)

Tridente, Trevi & the Quirinale

La Scena Bar

Part of the art deco Hotel Locarno, this bar has a faded Agatha Christie–era feel, and a greenery-shaded outdoor terrace bedecked in wrought-iron furniture. Cocktails cost €13 to €15, or you can partake of afternoon tea from 3pm to 6pm and *aperitivo* from 7pm to 10pm. (Via della Penna 22; 7am-1am; M Flaminio)

Stravinskij Bar – Hotel de Russie Bar

Can't afford to stay at the celeb-magnet Hotel de Russie? Then splash out on a drink at its swish bar. There are sofas inside, but best is a drink in the sunny courtyard, with sunshaded tables overlooked by terraced gardens. Impossibly romantic in the best *dolce vita* style, it's perfect for a cocktail (from €20) or beer (€13) and some posh snacks. (06 328 88 70; Via del Babuino 9; 9am-1am; M Flaminio)

Monti, Esquiline & San Lorenzo

Ai Tre Scalini Wine Bar

The 'Three Steps' is always packed, with crowds spilling out into the street. Apart from a tasty choice of wines, it sells the damn fine Menabrea beer, brewed in northern Italy. You can also tuck into a heart-warming array of cheeses, salami and dishes such as *polpette al sugo* (meatballs with sauce; €7.50). (Map p68; Via Panisperna 251; 12.30pm-1am; M Cavour)

Trastevere & Gianicolo

Ma Che Siete Venuti a Fà Pub

Named after a football chant, which translates politely as 'What did you come here for?', this pint-sized Trastevere pub is a beer-buff's paradise, packing in at least 13 international craft beers on tap and even more by the bottle. (www.football-pub.com; Via Benedetta 25; 11am-2am; Piazza Trilussa)

Auditorium Parco della Musica (p79), by architect Renzo Piano

Chiesa del Gesù (p67)

Bar San Calisto Cafe

Those in the know head to the down-at-heel 'Sanca' for its basic, stuck-in-time atmosphere and cheap prices (beer €1.50). It attracts everyone from intellectuals to keeping-it-real Romans, alcoholics and American students. It's famous for its chocolate – hot with cream in winter, ice cream in summer. Try the *Sambuca con la Mosca* ('with flies' – raw coffee beans). Expect occasional late-night jam sessions. (☎06 589 56 78; Piazza San Calisto 3-5; ⏲6am-1.45am Mon-Sat; 🚌Viale di Trastevere, 🚋Viale di Trastevere)

Freni e Frizioni Bar

This perennially cool Trastevere bar is housed in a former mechanic's workshop – hence its name (Brakes and Clutches). It draws a young *spritz*-loving crowd that swells onto the small piazza outside to sip well-priced cocktails (from €7) and to snack on the daily *aperitivo* (€6 to €10, 7pm to 10pm). (Map p64; ☎06 4549 7499; www.freniefrizioni.com; Via del Politeama 4-6; ⏲6.30pm-2am; 🚌Piazza Trilussa)

Ombre Rosse Bar

A seminal Trastevere hang-out; grab a table on the terrace and watch the world go by amid a clientele ranging from elderly Italian wide boys to wide-eyed tourists. Tunes are slinky and there's live music (jazz, blues, world) on Thursday evenings from September to April. (☎06 588 41 55; Piazza Sant'Egidio 12; ⏲8am-2am Mon-Sat, 11am-2am Sun; 🚌Piazza Trilussa)

INFORMATION

MEDICAL SERVICES

For problems that don't require hospital treatment, call the **Guardia Medica Turistica** (☎06 8840113; Via Mantova 44; ⏲24 hr).

For emergency treatment, go to the *pronto soccorso* (casualty) section of an *ospedale* (hospital).

MONEY

ATMs are liberally scattered around the city. There are money-exchange booths at Stazione Termini and Fiumicino and Ciampino airports.

In the centre, there are numerous bureaux de change, including the American Express office (06 6 76 41; Piazza di Spagna 38; 9am-5.30pm Mon-Fri, 9am-12.30pm Sat).

TOURIST INFORMATION

For phone enquiries, the Comune di Roma runs a free multilingual **tourist information line** (06 06 08; 9am-9pm).

There are tourist information points at Rome's two international airports – **Fiumicino** (Terminal 3, International Arrivals; 8am-7.30pm) and **Ciampino** (International Arrivals, baggage claim area; 9am-6.30pm) – and at the following locations across the city:

Castel Sant'Angelo Tourist Information (Piazza Pia; 9.30am-7.15pm)

Fori Imperiali Tourist Information (Map p68; Via dei Fori Imperiali; 9.30am-7pm)

Piazza delle Cinque Lune Tourist Information (Map p64; 9.30am-7.15pm) Near Piazza Navona.

Stazione Termini Tourist Information (8am-7.45pm) In the hall that runs parallel to platform 24.

Trevi Fountain Tourist Information (Map p64; Via Marco Minghetti; 9.30am-7.15pm) Near the Trevi Fountain.

Via Nazionale Tourist Information (Via Nazionale; 9.30am-7.15pm)

For information about the Vatican, contact the **Centro Servizi Pellegrini e Turisti** (06 6988 1662; St Peter's Sq; 8.30am-6pm Mon-Sat).

GETTING THERE & AWAY

AIR

Rome's main international airport Leonardo da Vinci, better known as Fiumicino, is on the coast 30km west of the city.

The much smaller **Ciampino Airport** (06 6 59 51; www.adr.it/ciampino), 15km southeast of the city centre, is the hub for European low-cost carrier Ryanair.

TRAIN

Almost all trains serve **Stazione Termini** (Piazza dei Cinquecento; M Termini), Rome's main train station and principal transport hub. There are regular connections to other European countries, all major Italian cities and many smaller towns.

GETTING AROUND

TO/FROM THE AIRPORT

FIUMICINO/LEONARDO DA VINCI

The easiest way to get to/from Fiumicino is by train, but there are also buses and private shuttle services.

Taxi The set fare to/from the city centre is €48, which is valid for up to four passengers with luggage. Taxis registered in Fiumicino charge more, so make sure you catch a Comune di Roma taxi – they are white with the words *Roma capitale* on the side and the driver's ID number.

Leonardo Express (one way €14) Runs to/from Stazione Termini. There are departures from the airport every 30 minutes between 6.23am and 11.23pm; from Termini between 5.35am and 10.35pm. Journey time is 30 minutes.

FR1 Train (one way €8) Connects to Trastevere, Ostiense and Tiburtina stations, but not Termini. There are departures from the airport every 15 minutes (half-hourly on Sundays and public holidays) between 5.57am and 10.42pm; from Tiburtina every 15 minutes between 5.46am and 7.31pm, then half-hourly to 10.02pm.

Airport Shuttle (www.airportshuttle.it) Offers transfers to/from your hotel for €25 for one person, then €5 for each additional passenger up to a maximum of eight.

Cotral (www.cotralspa.it; one way €5, if bought on the bus €7) Runs to/from Fiumicino from Stazione Tiburtina via Termini. There are eight daily departures including night services from the airport at 1.15am, 2.15am, 3.30am and 5am, and from Tiburtina at 12.30am, 1.15am, 2.30am and 3.45am. Journey time is one hour.

CIAMPINO

To get into town, the best bet is to take one of the dedicated bus services. You can also take a bus to Ciampino station and pick up a train to Stazione Termini. By taxi, the set fare to/from the airport is €30.

Atral (www.atral-lazio.com) Runs buses to/from Anagnina metro station (€1.20) and Ciampino train station (€1.20), where you can get a train to Termini (€1.30).

SIT Bus (06 591 68 26; www.sitbusshuttle.com; from/to airport €4/6) Regular departures from the airport to Via Marsala outside Stazione Termini between 7.45am and 11.15pm; from Termini between 4.30am and 9.30pm. Get tickets on the bus. Journey time is 45 minutes.

Terravision Bus (www.terravision.eu; one way €6, online €4) Twice hourly departures to/from Via Marsala outside Stazione Termini. From the airport services are between 8.15am and 12.15am; from Via Marsala between 4.30am and 9.20pm. Buy tickets at Terracafè in front of the Via Marsala bus stop. Journey time is 40 minutes.

PUBLIC TRANSPORT

Public transport is cheap and reasonably efficient. Buy a 24-/48-/72-hour pass to save time and money. For information see www.atac.roma.it.

BUS & TRAM

Bus is the the best bet for the centro storico. Rome's buses and trams are run by **ATAC** (06 5 70 03; www.atac.roma.it). The main bus station (Piazza dei Cinquecento) is in front of Stazione Termini on Piazza dei Cinquecento, where there's an information booth (7.30am-8pm). Other important hubs are at Largo di Torre Argentina and Piazza Venezia. Buses generally run from about 5.30am until midnight, with limited services throughout the night.

METRO

Rome has two main metro lines, A (orange) and B (blue), which cross at Termini. A branch line, 'B1', serves the northern suburbs, and a line C runs through the southeastern outskirts, but you're unlikely to need these. Trains run between 5.30am and 11.30pm (to 1.30am on Friday and Saturday).

TICKETS

Public-transport tickets are valid on all of Rome's bus, tram and metro lines, except for routes to Fiumicino airport. They come in various forms:

BIT (*biglietto integrato a tempo*, a single ticket valid for 100 minutes and one metro ride) €1.50

Roma 24h (valid for 24 hours) €7

Roma 48h (valid for 48 hours) €12.50

Roma 72h (valid for 72 hours) €18

CIS (*carta integrata settimanale*, weekly) €24

Abbonamento mensile (a monthly pass) A pass restricted to a single user €35; a pass that can be used by anyone €53

Buy tickets at *tabaccaio*, newsstands and from vending machines at main bus stops and metro stations. They must be purchased before you start your journey and validated in the machines on buses, at the entrance gates to the metro or at train stations. Ticketless riders risk an on-the spot €50 fine. Children under 10 travel free. The Roma Pass (two-/three days €28/36) comes with a two/three-day travel pass valid within the city boundaries.

TAXI

Taxis are useful late at night when bus services are slow and the metro has closed.

Official licensed taxis are white with an ID number and *Roma capitale* written on the sides.

Always go with the metered fare, never an arranged price (the set fares to and from the airports are exceptions). In town (within the ring road) flag fall is €3 between 6am and 10pm on weekdays, €4.50 on Sundays and holidays, and €6.50 between 10pm and 7am. Then it's €1.10 per kilometre. Official rates are posted in taxis and on www.viviromaintaxi.eu. You can hail a taxi, but it's often easier to wait at a rank or phone for one. There are taxi ranks at the airports, Stazione Termini, the Colosseum, Largo di Torre Argentina, Piazza San Silvestro, Piazza della Repubblica, Piazza Belli in Trastevere and in the Vatican at Piazza del Pio XII and Piazza del Risorgimento.

You can book a taxi by phoning the Comune di Roma's automated taxi line on 06 06 09, or calling a taxi company direct.

Note that when you call for a cab, the meter is switched on immediately and you pay for the cost of the journey from wherever the driver receives the call.

La Capitale (06 49 94)

Pronto Taxi (06 66 45)

Where to Stay

Rome doesn't really have a low season as such but most hotels drop prices from November to March (excluding Christmas and New Year) and from mid-July through August. Always try to book ahead.

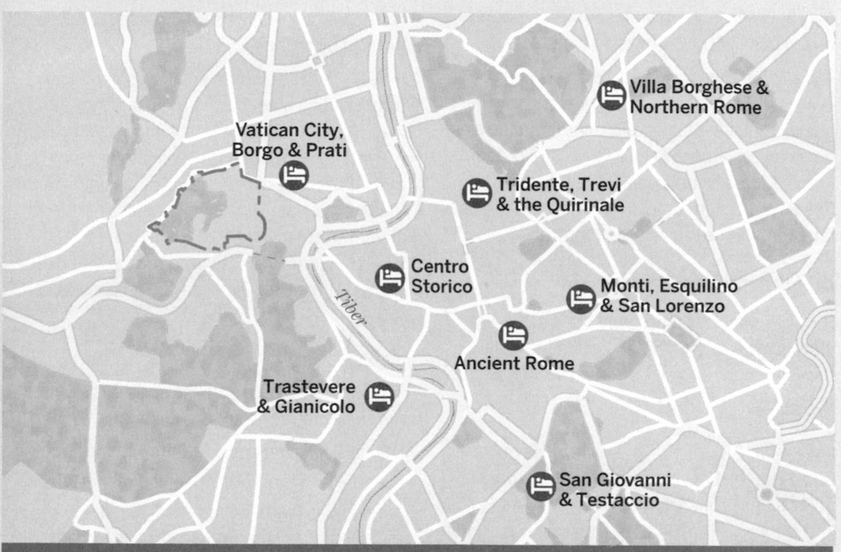

Neighbourhood	Atmosphere
Ancient Rome	Close to major sights such as Colosseum, Roman Forum and Capitoline Museums; quiet at night. Few budget options; touristy.
Centro Storico	Atmospheric area with everything on your doorstep: sights, restaurants, bars, shops. Most expensive part of town; can be noisy.
Tridente, Trevi & the Quirinale	Good for designer shopping; excellent midrange to top-end options; good transport links. Not cheap; subdued after dark.
Monti, Esquilino & San Lorenzo	Lots of budget accommodation around Stazione Termini; top eating options and good nightlife. Some dodgy streets in Termini area.
San Giovanni & Testaccio	Authentic atmosphere with good eating and drinking options; Aventino a quiet, romantic area; Testaccio a top food and nightlife district. Few options available; not many big sights.
Trastevere & Gianicolo	Gorgeous, atmospheric area; hundreds of bars, cafes and restaurants; some interesting sights. Very noisy; expensive.
Vatican City, Borgo & Prati	Decent range; some excellent shops and restaurants. Not much nightlife; sells out quickly for religious holidays.
Villa Borghese & Northern Rome	Largely residential area good for the Auditorium and some top museums; quiet after dark. Out of the centre; few budget choices.

Duomo (p98)

FLORENCE

Florence

Return time and again to Florence and you still won't see it all. Surprisingly small as it is, this riverside city looms large on the world's 'must-see' list. Cradle of the Renaissance and of tourist masses that flock here to feast on world-class art, Florence (Firenze) is magnetic, romantic and busy. Its urban fabric has hardly changed since the Renaissance, its narrow streets evoke a thousand tales, and its food and wine are so wonderful the tag 'Fiorentina' has become an international label of quality assurance.

Fashion designers parade on Via de' Tornabuoni. Gucci was born here, as was Roberto Cavalli, who, like many a smart Florentine these days, hangs out in the wine-rich hills around Florence. After a while in this absorbing city, you might want to do the same.

☑ In This Section

Arriving in Florence

Pisa International Airport Tuscany's main international airport. Buses run to Stazione di Santa Maria Novella. Buy tickets (one way €5) online, on board or at the desk in the arrivals hall.

Florence Airport Also known as Amerigo Vespucci. ATAF operates a half-hourly Volainbus shuttle (one way €6) to Florence bus station. A taxi costs €20.

Stazione di Santa Maria Novella A 10-minute walk from the historic centre. Florence's main train station is on the main Rome–Milan line.

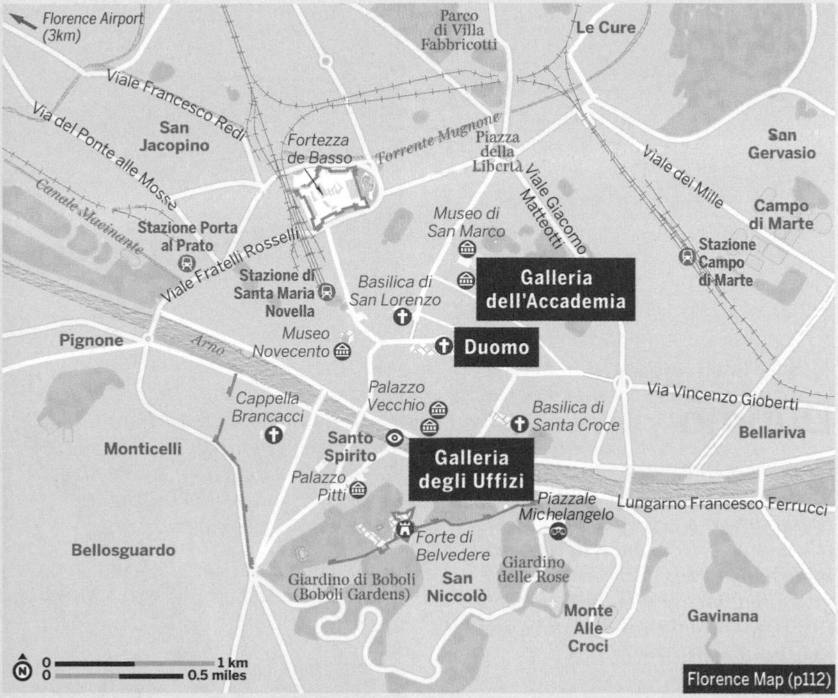

Florence Airport (3km)
Parco di Villa Fabbricotti
Le Cure
Viale Francesco Redi
Via del Ponte alle Mosse
San Jacopino
Fortezza de Basso
Torrente Mugnone
Piazza della Libertà
Viale Giacomo Matteotti
Viale dei Mille
San Gervasio
Campo di Marte
Canale Macinante
Stazione Porta al Prato
Viale Fratelli Rosselli
Museo di San Marco
Stazione Campo di Marte
Stazione di Santa Maria Novella
Basilica di San Lorenzo
Galleria dell'Accademia
Pignone
Arno
Museo Novecento
Duomo
Via Vincenzo Gioberti
Palazzo Vecchio
Cappella Brancacci
Basilica di Santa Croce
Bellariva
Monticelli
Santo Spirito
Galleria degli Uffizi
Palazzo Pitti
Piazzale Michelangelo
Lungarno Francesco Ferrucci
Forte di Belvedere
Bellosguardo
Giardino di Boboli (Boboli Gardens)
San Niccolò
Giardino delle Rose
Monte Alle Croci
Gavinana
0 1 km
0 0.5 miles
Florence Map (p112)

➡ Florence in Two Days

Start with a coffee on Piazza della Repubblica before hitting the **Uffizi** (p104). After lunch visit the **Duomo** (p98), **baptistry** (p110) and the **Grande Museo del Duomo** (p110). Next day visit the **Galleria dell'Accademia** (p102) and **Museo di San Marco** (p115). Later, venture across to the Oltrarno, stopping to admire the view from **Ponte Vecchio** (p115) and **Piazzale Michelangelo** (p116).

➡ Florence in Four Days

On day three, explore **Palazzo Pitti** (p115) and the **Giardino di Boboli** (p116). Alternatively, visit the city's major basilicas: **San Lorenzo** (p114), **Santa Croce** (p115) and **Santa Maria Novella** (p114). For dinner, enjoy good food and entertainment at **Il Teatro del Sale** (p121). On day four, take a guided tour of **Palazzo Vecchio** (p110)then explore the city's artisanal **shops** (p118).

From left: View of the Duomo (p98); Stazione di Santa Maria Novella; Museo di San Marco; Giardino di Boboli

Duomo

Florence's Duomo is the city's most iconic landmark. Capped by Filippo Brunelleschi's red-tiled cupola, it's a staggering construction and its breathtaking pink, white and green marble facade and graceful campanile *(bell tower) dominate the medieval cityscape.*

Great For...

Need to Know

Cattedrale di Santa Maria del Fiore; www.operaduomo.firenze.it; Piazza del Duomo; 10am-5pm Mon-Wed & Fri, to 4.30pm Thu, to 4.45pm Sat, 1.30-4.45pm Sun FREE

★ Top Tip

Buy tickets from the Duomo ticket office at Piazza San Giovanni 7, opposite the baptistry's northern entrance.

LEE YOU TUNG/SHUTTERSTOCK ©

Sienese architect Arnolfo di Cambio began work on the Duomo in 1296, but construction took almost 150 years and it wasn't consecrated until 1436.

Facade

The neo-Gothic facade was designed in the 19th century by architect Emilio de Fabris to replace the uncompleted original, torn down in the 16th century. The oldest and most clearly Gothic part of the cathedral is its south flank, pierced by the Porta dei Canonici (Canons' Door), a mid-14th-century High Gothic creation (you enter here to climb up inside the dome).

Dome

One of the finest masterpieces of the Renaissance, the **cupola** (Brunelleschi's Dome; www.operaduomo.firenze.it; adult/child incl campanile & baptistry €15/3; 8.30am-7pm Mon-Fri, to 5.40pm Sat) is a feat of engineering that cannot be fully appreciated without climbing its 463 interior stone steps. It was built between 1420 and 1436 to a design by Filippo Brunelleschi, and is a staggering 91m high and 45.5m wide.

Taking his inspiration from Rome's Pantheon, Brunelleschi arrived at an innovative engineering solution of a distinctive octagonal shape of inner and outer concentric domes resting on the drum of the cathedral rather than the roof itself, allowing artisans to build from the ground up without needing a wooden support frame. Over four million bricks were used in the construction, all of them laid in consecutive rings in horizontal courses using a vertical herringbone pattern.

Frescoes decorating the dome of the Duomo

The climb up the spiral staircase is relatively steep. Make sure to pause when you reach the balustrade at the base of the dome, which gives an aerial view of the octagonal *coro* (choir) in the cathedral below and the seven round stained-glass windows (by Donatello, Andrea del Castagno, Paolo Uccello and Lorenzo Ghiberti) that pierce the octagonal drum.

Interior

After the visual wham-bam of the facade, the sparse decoration of the cathedral's vast interior, 155m long and 90m wide, comes as a surprise – most of its artistic treasures have been removed over the centuries according to the vagaries of ecclesiastical fashion, and many will be on show in the sparkling new Grande Museo del Duomo (p110). The interior is also unexpectedly secular in places (a reflection of the sizeable chunk of the cathedral not paid for by the church): down the left aisle two immense frescoes of equestrian statues portray two *condottieri* (mercenaries) – on the left Niccolò da Tolentino by Andrea del Castagno (1456), and on the right Sir John Hawkwood (who fought in the service of Florence in the 14th century) by Uccello (1436).

Between the left (north) arm of the transept and the apse is the Sagrestia delle Messe (Mass Sacristy), its panelling a marvel of inlaid wood carved by Benedetto and Giuliano da Maiano. The fine bronze doors were executed by Luca della Robbia – his only known work in the material. Above the doorway is his glazed terracotta *Resurrezione* (Resurrection).

A stairway near the main entrance of the cathedral leads down to the Cripta Santa Reparata (crypt), where excavations between 1965 and 1974 unearthed parts of the 5th-century Chiesa di Santa Reparata that originally stood on the site.

Campanile

The 414-step climb up the cathedral's 85m-tall campanile begun by Giotto in 1334, rewards with a staggering city panorama. The first tier of bas-reliefs around the base of its elaborate Gothic facade are copies of those carved by Pisano depicting the Creation of Man and the *attività umane* (arts and industries). Those on the second tier depict the planets, the cardinal virtues, the arts and the seven sacraments. The sculpted Prophets and Sibyls in the upper-storey niches are copies of works by Donatello and others.

☑ Don't Miss

The flamboyant dome frescoes by Giorgio Vasari and Federico Zuccari,

RICHARD I'ANSON/GETTY IMAGES ©

Take a Break

Take time out over a taste of Tuscan wine at stylish **Coquinarius** (p122).

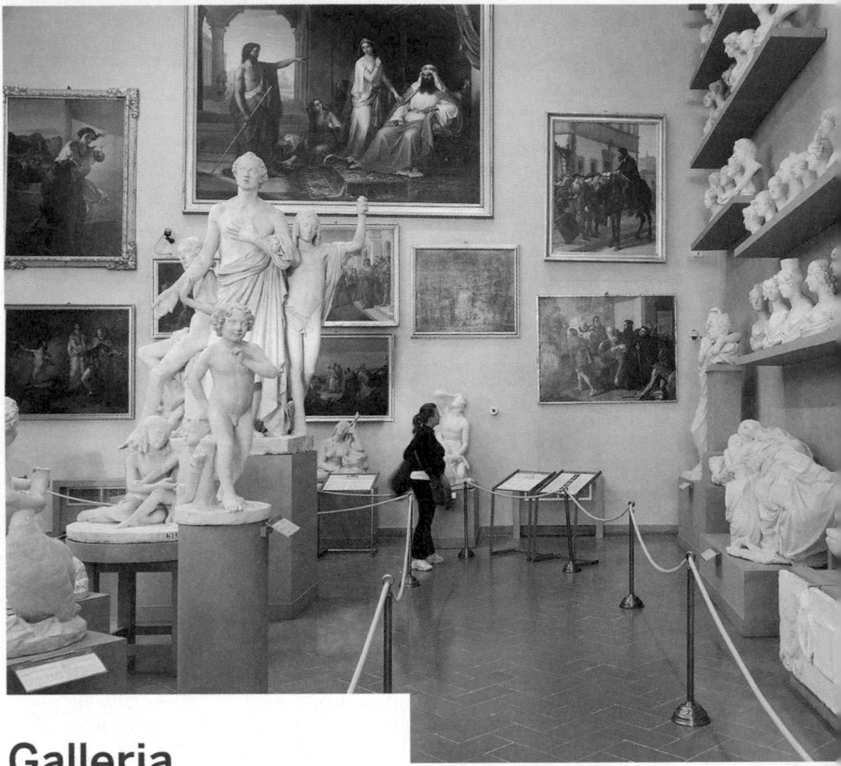

Galleria dell'Accademia

A lengthy queue marks the door to the Galleria dell'Accademia, the late-18th-century gallery that's home to one of the Renaissance's most iconic masterpieces, Michelangelo's David.

Great For...

☑ Don't Miss

David: There are two pale lines visible on his lower left arm where it was broken in 1527.

David

Fortunately, the world's most famous statue is worth the wait. Standing at over 5m tall and weighing in at 19 tonnes, it's a formidable sight. But it's not just its scale that impresses, it's also the subtle detail – the veins in *David*'s sinewy arms, the muscles in his legs, the change in expression as you move around him. Carved from a single block of marble, Michelangelo's most famous work was also his most challenging – he didn't choose the marble himself, it was veined, and its larger than life dimensions were already decided.

When the statue of the boy-warrior, depicted for the first time as a man in the prime of life rather than a young boy, assumed its pedestal in front of Palazzo Vecchio on Piazza della Signoria in 1504,

Michelangelo's *David*

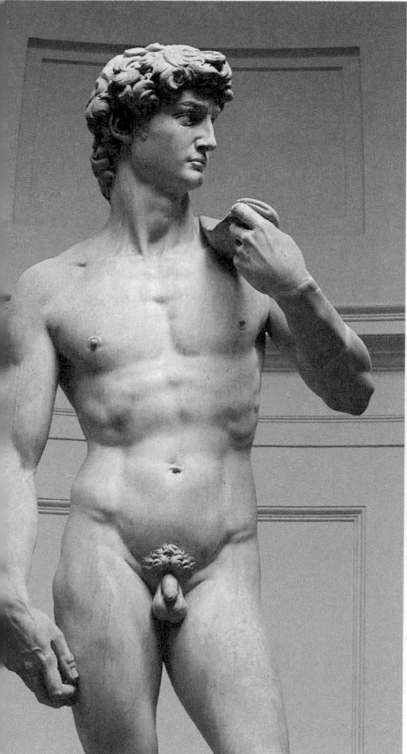

MARVIN E. NEWMAN/GETTY IMAGES ©

Florentines immediately adopted it as a powerful emblem of Florentine power, liberty and civic pride. It stayed in the piazza until 1873, when it was moved to its current purpose-built tribune in the Galleria.

Other Works

Michelangelo was also the master behind the unfinished *San Matteo* (St Matthew; 1504–08) and four *Prigioni* ('Prisoners' or 'Slaves'; 1521–30), also displayed in the gallery. The Prisoners seem to be writhing and struggling to free themselves from the marble; they were meant for the tomb of Pope Julius II, itself never completed.

Adjacent rooms contain paintings by Andrea Orcagna, Taddeo Gaddi, Domenico Ghirlandaio, Filippino Lippi and Sandro Botticelli.

Need to Know

www.polomuseale.firenze.it; Via Ricasoli 60; adult/reduced €8/4; 8.15am-6.50pm Tue-Sun)

Take a Break

Grab a pizza slice at the much-loved **Pugi** (p120), a stone's throw from the Galleria.

Top Tip

Skip the queues by booking online at www.b-ticket.com/b-ticket/uffizi (plus €4 booking fee).

What's Nearby

To the east of the Galleria, Giambologna's equestrian statue of Grand Duke Ferdinando I de' Medici lords it over **Piazza della Santissima Annunziata**, a majestic square dominated by the facades of the **Chiesa della Santissima Annunziata**, built in 1250 then rebuilt by Michelozzo et al in the mid-15th century, and the **Ospedale degli Innocenti** (Hospital of the Innocents; Piazza della SS Annunziata 12), Europe's first orphanage founded in 1421. Look up to admire Brunelleschi's classically influenced portico, decorated by Andrea della Robbia (1435–1525) with terracotta medallions of babies in swaddling clothes

About 200m southeast of the piazza is the **Museo Archeologico** (Piazza Santissima Annunziata 9b; adult/reduced €4/2; 8.30am-7pm Tue-Fri, to 2pm Sat-Mon); its rich collection of finds, including most of the Medici hoard of antiquities, plunges you deep into the past and offers an alternative to Renaissance splendour.

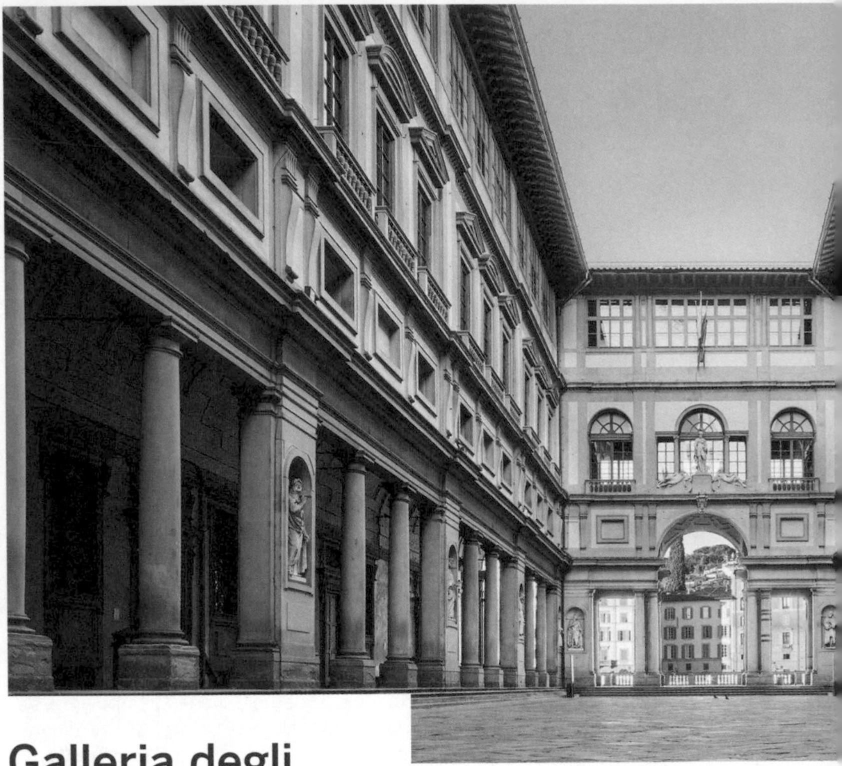

Galleria degli Uffizi

Home to the world's greatest collection of Italian Renaissance art, the Galleria degli Uffizi boasts some of Italy's best-known paintings, including Sandro Botticelli's celebrated masterpiece La nascita di Venere *(The Birth of Venus).*

Great For...

☑ Don't Miss

The reverse side of *The Duke and Duchess of Urbino* features the duke and duchess depicted with the Virtues.

Florence's premier gallery occupies Palazzo degli Uffizi, a vast U-shaped palace built between 1560 and 1580 to house government offices. Nowadays it showcases the colossal art collection that the Medici family bequeathed to the city in 1743 on condition that it never leave Florence.

The gallery is currently undergoing a €65-million refurbishment that will eventually see the doubling of exhibition space. A number of revamped rooms are open, but until the project is completed (date unknown) expect some halls to be closed and the contents of others changed.

Tuscan Masters: 13th to 14th Centuries

Arriving in the Primo Corridoio (First Corridor) on the 2nd floor, the first seven rooms – closed for renovation at the time of writing – are dedicated to pre-Renaissance

Need to Know

Uffizi Gallery; www.uffizi.firenze.it; Piazzale degli Uffizi 6; adult/reduced €8/4, incl temporary exhibition €12.50/6.25; 8.15am-6.50pm Tue-Sun

Take a Break

To clear your head of art overload, stop by the gallery's rooftop cafe.

Top Tip

Save money and visit on the first Sunday of the month – admission is free.

Tuscan art. Among the 13th-century Sienese works displayed are three large altarpieces from Florentine churches by Duccio di Buoninsegna, Cimabue and Giotto.

Moving into Siena in the 14th century, the highlight is Simone Martini's shimmering *Annunciazione* (1333), painted with Lippo Memmi and setting the Madonna in a sea of gold. Also of note is the *Madonna in trono con il Bambino in trono e otto angeli* (Madonna with Child and Saints; 1340) by Pietro Lorenzetti, which demonstrates a realism similar to Giotto's.

Masters in 14th-century Florence paid as much attention to detail as their Sienese counterparts: savour the realism and and extraordinary gold-leaf work of the *Pietà di San Remigio* (1360–65) by gifted Giotto pupil, Giottino.

Renaissance Pioneers

In Room 8, Piero della Francesca's famous profile portraits (1465) of the crooked-nosed, red-robed duke and duchess of Urbino are wholly humanist in spirit: the former painted from the left side as he'd lost his right eye in a jousting accident, and the latter painted a deathly stone-white, reflecting the fact the portrait was painted posthumously.

Carmelite monk Fra' Filippo Lippi had an unfortunate soft spot for earthly pleasures, scandalously marrying a nun from Prato. Search out his self-portrait as a podgy friar in *Incoronazione Maringhi* (Coronation of the Virgin; 1439–47) and don't miss his later *Madonna con Bambino e due angeli* (Madonna and Child with Two Angels; 1460–65), an exquisite work that clearly influenced his pupil, Sandro Botticelli.

Another related pair, brothers Antonio and Piero del Pollaiolo, fill Room 9, where their seven cardinal and theological values of 15th-century Florence radiate energy. More restrained is Piero's *Portrait of Galeazzo Maria Sforza* (1471).

The only canvas in the theological and cardinal virtues series not painted by the Pollaiolos is *Fortitude* (1470), the first documented work by Botticelli.

Botticelli Room

The spectacular Sala del Botticelli, numbered as Rooms 10 to 14, but in fact one large hall, is one of the Uffizi's hot spots and is always packed. Of the 15 works by the Renaissance master known for his ethereal figures, the best known are: *La nascita di Venere* (The Birth of Venus; c 1485); *Primavera* (Spring; c 1482); the deeply spiritual *Annunciazione di Cestello* (Cestello Annunciation; 1489–90); the *Adorazione dei Magi* (Adoration of the Magi; 1475) featuring the artist's self-portrait (look for the blond-haired guy, extreme right, dressed in yellow); and the *Madonna del Magnificat* (Madonna of the Magnificat; 1483). True aficionados rate his twin set of miniatures depicting a sword-bearing Judith returning from the camp of Holofernes and the discovery of the decapitated Holofernes in his tent (1495–1500) as being among his finest works.

Leonardo Room

Room 15 displays three early Florentine works by Leonardo da Vinci: the incomplete *Adorazione dei Magi* (Adoration of the Magi; 1481–82), drawn in red earth pigment (removed for restoration at the time of writing); his *Annunciazione* (c 1475–80); and *The Baptism of Christ* (1470-75).

La Tribuna

The Medici clan stashed away their most precious masterpieces in this exquisite octagonal-shaped treasure trove (Room 18), created by Francesco I between 1581 and 1586. Designed to amaze and perfectly restored to its original exquisite state, its walls are upholstered in crimson silk and adorned by a small collection of classical statues and paintings. The domed ceiling is encrusted with 6000 mother-of-pearl shells painted with crimson varnish.

★ Top Tip

The Uffizi Gallery presents works in chronological order, giving viewers the opportunity to see the whole panoply of Renaissance art in the manner it developed.

JUERGEN RICHTER/LOOK-FOTO/GETTY IMAGES ©

High Renaissance to Mannerism

Passing through the loggia or Secondo Corridoio (Second Corridor), visitors enjoy wonderful views of Florence before entering the Terzo Corridoio (Third Corridor).

Michelangelo dazzles with the *Doni Tondo*, a depiction of the Holy Family that steals the High Renaissance show in Room 35. The composition is unusual – Joseph holding an exuberant Jesus on his muscled mother's shoulder as she twists round to gaze at him, the colours as vibrant as when they were first applied in 1506–08. It was painted for wealthy Florentine merchant Agnolo Doni (who hung it above his bed) and bought by the Medici for Palazzo Pitti in 1594.

First-Floor Galleries

Head downstairs to the 1st-floor galleries where Rooms 46 to 55 display the Uffizi's collection of 16th- to 18th-century works by foreign artists, including Rembrandt (room 49); Rubens and Van Dyck share room 55. The next 10 rooms give to a nod to antique sculpture, before moving back into the 16th century with Andrea del Sarto (Rooms 57 and 58) and Raphael (Room 66), whose *Madonna del cardellino* (Madonna of the Goldfinch; 1505–06) steals the show.

Rooms 90 to 94 feature works by Caravaggio, deemed vulgar at the time for his direct interpretation of reality. The *Head of Medusa* (1598–99), commissioned for a ceremonial shield, is supposedly a self-portrait of the young artist, who died at the age of 39. The biblical drama of an angel steadying the hand of Abraham as he holds a knife to his son Isaac's throat in Caravaggio's *Sacrifice of Isaac* (1601–02) is glorious in its intensity.

Did You Know

In 1966 flood waters threatened to destroy the Uffizi Gallery. Locals and tourists rushed to the gallery to help rescue the artworks, and these saviours became known as 'mud angels'.

Walking Tour: Heart of the City

Every visitor to Florence spends time navigating the cobbled medieval lanes that run between Via de' Tornabuoni and Via del Proconsolo but few explore them thoroughly.

Distance: 2km
Duration: 2 hours

Take a Break

Fashionable Via de' Tornabuoni is the heart of Florence's cafe society. Try Procacci (www.procacci1885.it; Via de' Tornabuoni 64r; h10am-9pm Mon-Sat, 11am-8pm Sun).

Piazza della Repubblica

Start Piazza della Repubblica

1 Piazza della Repubblica

Start with a coffee at one of the historic cafes on this handsome 19th-century square. Its construction entailed the demolition of a Jewish ghetto and produce market, and the relocation of nearly 6000 residents.

2 Chiesa e Museo di Orsanmichele

Take Via Calimala then Via Orsanmichele to reach the unique **Chiesa e Museo di Orsanmichele** (Via dell'Arte della Lana; church 10am-5pm, museum 10am-5pm Mon), created in the 14th century when the arcades of a century-old grain market were walled in and two storeys added.

3 Mercato Nuovo

Back at Via Calimala, continue walking south until you see the 16th-century **New Market** (Loggia Mercato Nuovo; 8.30am-7pm Mon-Sat). Florentines call the bronze statue of a wild boar on its southern side 'Il Porcellino' (The Piglet) – rub its snout to ensure your return to Florence!

4 Museo di Palazzo Davanzati

On Via Porta Rossa is the **Museo di Palazzo Davanzati** (Via Porta Rossa 13; 8.15am-1.50pm, closed 1st, 3rd & 5th Mon, 2nd & 4th Sun of month; adult/reduced €2/1), a 14th-century warehouse residence with studded doors and central loggia. A few doors down, next to the Slowly bar, peep through the sturdy iron gate and up to see the ancient brick vaults.

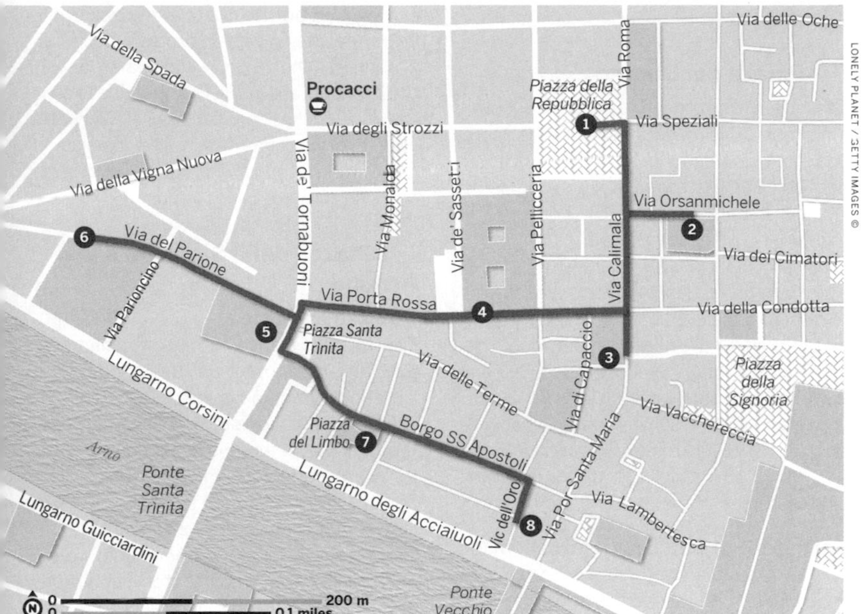

❺ Chiesa di Santa Trinìta

Continue to Via de' Tornabuoni, the city's most famous shopping strip. Cross Piazza Santa Trinìta, looking up to admire 13th-century Palazzo Spini-Feroni, home of Salvatore Ferragamo's flagship store. Then enter the **Chiesa di Santa Trinita** (8am-noon & 4-5.45pm Mon-Sat, 8-10.45am & 4-5.45pm Sun) to admire its frescoed chapels.

❻ Via del Parione

Wander down this narrow street filled with old mansions (now apartments) and artisan's workshops. Pop into paper marbler **Alberto Cozzi** (Via del Parione 35r; 9am-1pm & 2.30-7pm Mon-Fri, 3-7pm Sat) and puppet maker **Letizia Fiorini** (Via del Parione 60r; 10am-7pm Tue-Sat) to see them at work.

❼ Chiesa dei Santissimi Apostoli

Back to Via de' Tornabuoni, veer into Borgo SS Apostoli for this Romanesque church set in a sunken square once used as a cemetery for unbaptised babies. Onwards, find Tuscan olive-oil products in **La Bottega dell'Olio** (Piazza del Limbo 2r; 2.30-6.30pm Mon, 10am-1pm & 2-6.30pm Tue-Sat) and resin jewellery at **Angela Caputi** (www.angelacaputi.com; Borgo SS Apostoli 42-46; 10am-1pm & 3.30-7.30pm Mon-Sat).

❽ Hotel Continental

Continue around to the Hotel Continental. Finish your walk at its rooftop bar La Terrazza (p122), which has a spectacular view of the Ponte Vecchio.

Finish La Terrazza bar

SIGHTS

Piazza del Duomo

Grande Museo del Duomo Museum
This impressive museum safeguards sacred and liturgical treasures from the Duomo, baptistry and bell tower. Inspiring highlights include Ghiberti's original 15th-century masterpiece, Porta del Paradiso (Gates of Paradise) – gloriously golden, 16m-tall gilded bronze doors designed for the eastern entrance to the Baptistry – as well as those he sculpted for the northern entrance. The best-known work is Michelangelo's *La Pietà*, a work he sculpted when he was almost 80 and intended for his own tomb. (Cathedral Museum; www.ilgrandemuseodelduomo.it; Piazza del Duomo 9; adult/child incl cathedral bell tower, cupola & baptistry €15/3; 9am-7pm)

Battistero di San Giovanni Landmark
This 11th-century baptistry is a Romanesque, octagonal, striped structure of white and green marble with three sets of doors conceived as panels on which to tell the story of humanity and the Redemption. Most celebrated of all are Lorenzo Ghiberti's gilded bronze doors at the eastern entrance, the *Porta del Paradiso* (Gates of Paradise). What you see today are copies; the originals are in the Grande Museo del Duomo. (Baptistry; Piazza di San Giovanni; adult/child incl cupola, campanile & museum €15/3; 8.15-10.15am & 11.15am-7pm Mon-Sat, 8.30am-2pm Sun & 1st Sat of month)

Piazza della Signoria & Around

Palazzo Vecchio Museum
This fortress palace, with its crenellations and 94m-high tower, was designed by Arnolfo di Cambio between 1298 and 1314 for the *signoria* (city government). It remains the seat of the city's power, home to the mayor's office and the municipal council. From the top of the Torre d'Arnolfo (tower), you can revel in unforgettable rooftop views. Inside, Michelangelo's *Genio della Vittoria* (Genius of Victory) sculpture graces the Salone dei Cinquecento, a magnificent painted hall created for the city's 15th-century ruling Consiglio dei Cinquecento (Council of 500). (055 276

Battistero di San Giovanni

82 24; www.musefirenze.it; Piazza della Signoria; museum adult/reduced €10/8, tower €10/8, archaeology tour €2, museum & tower €14/12; museum 9am-midnight Fri-Wed, to 2pm Thu summer, 9am-7pm Fri-Wed, to 2pm Thu winter, tower 9am-9pm Fri-Wed, to 2pm Thu summer, 10am-5pm Fri-Wed, to 2pm Thu winter)

Gucci Museo Museum

Strut through the chic cafe and icon store to reach this museum. It tells the tale of the Gucci fashion house, from the first luggage pieces in Gucci's signature beige fabric emblazoned with the interlocking 'GG' logo to the 1950s red-and-green stripe and beyond. Don't miss the 1979 Cadillac Seville with gold Gs on the hubcaps and Gucci fabric upholstery. Displays continue to present day. In the final room exhibiting men's loafers, look in the mirrors (to admire your own feet and inferior footwear). (www.gucci.com; Piazza della Signoria 10; adult/child €7/free, after 5pm €5; 10am-8pm, to 11pm Thu)

Museo del Bargello Museum

It was behind the stark walls of Palazzo del Bargello, Florence's earliest public building, that the *podestà* meted out justice from the late 13th century until 1502. Today the building safeguards Italy's most comprehensive collection of Tuscan Renaissance sculpture, with some of Michelangelo's best early works and a hall full of Donatello's. Michelangelo was just 21 when a cardinal commissioned him to create the drunken, grape-adorned *Bacchus* (1496–97), displayed in Bargello's Sala di Michelangelo. (www.polomuseale.firenze.it; Via del Proconsolo 4; adult/reduced €4/2; 8.15am-4.50pm summer, to 1.50pm winter, closed 1st, 3rd & 5th Sun & 2nd & 4th Mon of month)

Santa Maria Novella

Museo Novecento Museum

Don't allow the Renaissance to distract from Florence's fantastic modern-art museum, in a 13th-century palazzo previously used as a pilgrim shelter, hospital and school. A well-articulated itinerary guides visitors through modern Italian painting and sculpture from the early 20th century to the late 1980s. Installation art makes effective use of the outside space on the 1st-floor loggia. Fashion and theatre get a nod on the 2nd floor, and the itinerary ends with a 20-minute cinematic montage of the best films set in Florence. (Museum of the 20th Century; 055 28 61 32; www.museonovecento.it; Piazza di Santa Maria Novella 10; adult/reduced €8.50/4; 10am-6pm Mon-Wed, to 2pm Thu, to 9pm Fri, to 8pm Sat & Sun)

Museum Passes

The Firenze Card (www.firenzecard.it; €72) is valid for 72 hours and covers admission to some 70 museums, villas and gardens in Florence as well as unlimited use of public transport and free wi-fi across the city. Its biggest advantage is reducing queueing time in high season – museums have separate queues for card-holders. Buy it online (and collect upon arrival in Florence) or in Florence at tourist offices, the ticketing desks of the Uffizi (Entrance 2), Palazzo Pitti, Palazzo Vecchio, Museo del Bargello, Cappella Brancacci, Museo di Santa Maria Novella and Giardini Bardini. If you're an EU citizen, your card also covers under-18s travelling with you.

Skip the Queues

In July, August and other busy periods such as Easter, unbelievably long queues are a fact of life at Florence's key museums – if you haven't pre-booked your ticket, you could well end up standing in line queuing for hours.

To cut waiting time you can book tickets for the Uffizi and Galleria dell'Accademia, as well as several other museums through **Firenze Musei** (Florence Museums; 055 29 48 83; www.firenzemusei.it), with ticketing desks (open 8.30am to 7pm Tuesday to Sunday) at the Uffizi and Palazzo Pitti.

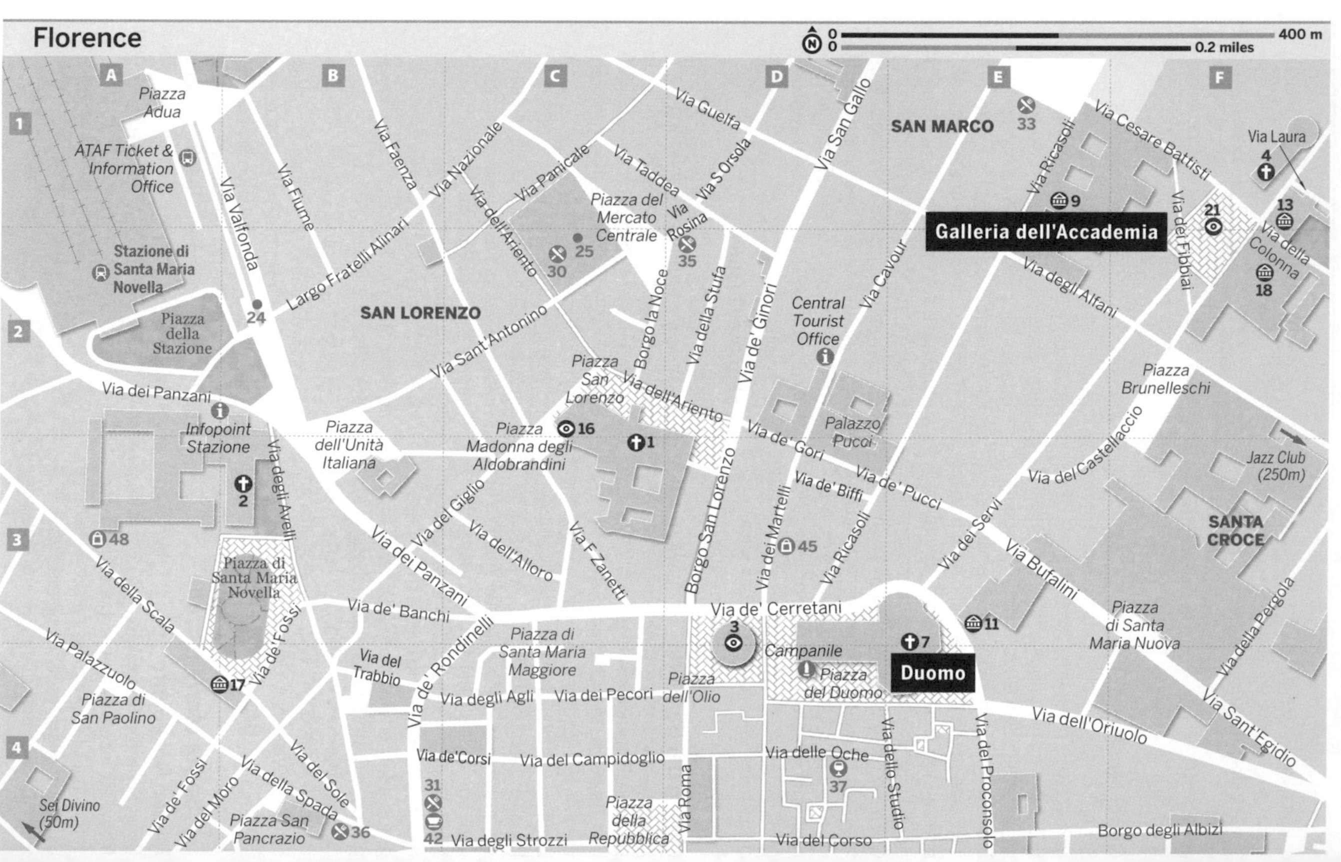
Florence
0.2 miles
400 m
A
B
C
D
E
F
1
2
3
4
Piazza Adua
ATAF Ticket & Information Office
Stazione di Santa Maria Novella
Piazza della Stazione
Via Valfonda
24
Via Fiume
Via Faenza
Largo Fratelli Alinari
Via Nazionale
Via dell'Ariento
Via Panicale
Piazza del Mercato Centrale
25
30
Via Taddea
Via Rosina
35
Via Guelfa
Via S Orsola
Via della Stufa
Borgo la Noce
SAN LORENZO
Via Sant'Antonino
Piazza San Lorenzo
Via dell'Ariento
16
1
Piazza Madonna degli Aldobrandini
Piazza dell'Unità Italiana
Via degli Avelli
Infopoint Stazione
2
Via dei Panzani
48
Via della Scala
Via Palazzuolo
Piazza di San Paolino
Sei Divino (50m)
Piazza di Santa Maria Novella
17
Via de' Fossi
Via del Moro
Via della Spada
Piazza San Pancrazio
Via del Sole
36
Via del Giglio
Via dell'Alloro
Via F Zanetti
Via dei Panzani
Via de' Banchi
Via del Trabbio
Via de' Rondinelli
Piazza di Santa Maria Maggiore
Via degli Agli
Via de'Corsi
31
42
Via degli Strozzi
Via del Campidoglio
Piazza della Repubblica
Via Roma
Via dei Pecori
Piazza dell'Olio
Via de' Cerretani
3
Borgo San Lorenzo
Via de' Ginori
Via San Gallo
Via de' Gori
Via dei Martelli
45
Campanile
Piazza del Duomo
Via delle Oche
37
Via del Corso
Via dello Studio
Duomo
7
Via Ricasoli
Via de' Biffi
Via de' Pucci
Palazzo Pucci
Central Tourist Office
Via Cavour
SAN MARCO
Galleria dell'Accademia
Via dei Servi
11
Via del Proconsolo
Via dell'Oriuolo
Borgo degli Albizi
Via Bufalini
Piazza di Santa Maria Nuova
Via Sant'Egidio
Via del Castellaccio
Via degli Alfani
Piazza Brunelleschi
SANTA CROCE
Jazz Club (250m)
Via della Pergola
Via Ricasoli
33
9
Via Cesare Battisti
Via dei Fibbiai
21
Via Laura
4
13
Via della Colonna
18

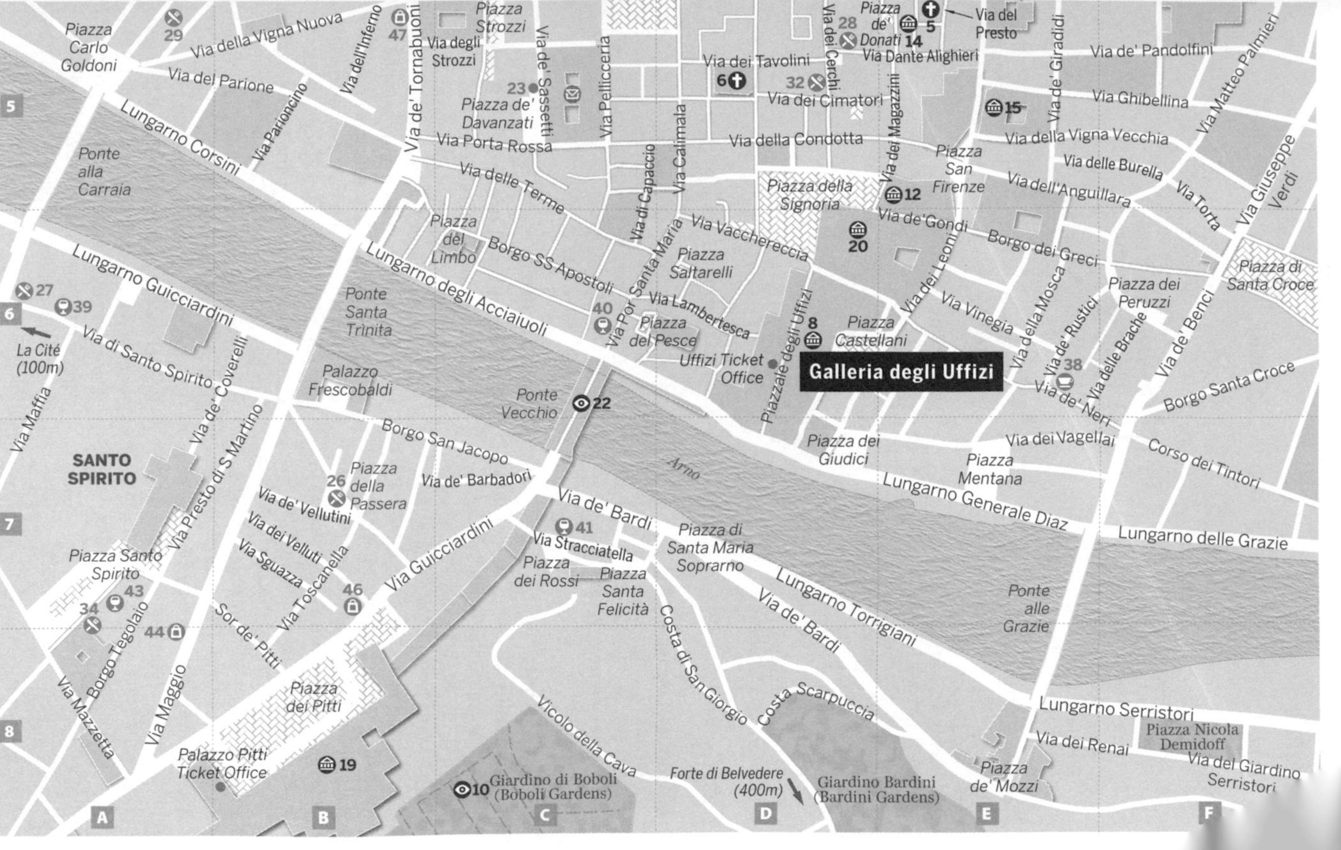
Piazza Carlo Goldoni
Via della Vigna Nuova
Via dell'Inferno
Via de' Tornabuoni
Piazza Strozzi
Via degli Strozzi
Via de' Sassetti
Via Pellicceria
Via dei Tavolini
Via dei Cerchi
Piazza de' Donati
Via Dante Alighieri
Via del Presto
Via de' Pandolfini
Via Matteo Palmieri
Via del Parione
Via Parioncino
Piazza de' Davanzati
Via dei Cimatori
Via Ghibellina
Via de' Giraldi
Lungarno Corsini
Via Porta Rossa
Via Calimala
Via della Condotta
Via dei Magazzini
Via della Vigna Vecchia
Via Giuseppe Verdi
Ponte alla Carraia
Via delle Terme
Via di Capaccio
Piazza della Signoria
Piazza San Firenze
Via delle Burella
Via dell'Anguillara
Via Torta
Via de' Gondi
Piazza del Limbo
Borgo SS Apostoli
Via Por Santa Maria
Via Vacchereccia
Borgo dei Greci
Piazza Saltarelli
Piazza di Santa Croce
Lungarno Guicciardini
Lungarno degli Acciaiuoli
Via dei Leoni
Piazza dei Peruzzi
Ponte Santa Trinita
Via Lambertesca
Piazzale degli Uffizi
Piazza Castellani
Via Vinegia
Via della Mosca
Via de' Rustici
Via delle Brache
Via de' Benci
La Cité (100m)
Via di Santo Spirito
Piazza del Pesce
Uffizi Ticket Office
Galleria degli Uffizi
Borgo Santa Croce
Via de' Coverelli
Palazzo Frescobaldi
Via de' Neri
Via Maffia
Ponte Vecchio
Via Presto di S Martino
Borgo San Jacopo
Piazza dei Giudici
Via dei Vagellai
Corso dei Tintori
SANTO SPIRITO
Arno
Piazza della Passera
Piazza Mentana
Via de' Barbadori
Lungarno Generale Diaz
Via de' Vellutini
Via de' Bardi
Piazza di Santa Maria Soprarno
Lungarno delle Grazie
Via dei Velluti
Via Stracciatella
Via Guicciardini
Piazza Santo Spirito
Piazza dei Rossi
Piazza Santa Felicità
Via Sguazza
Via Toscanella
Lungarno Torrigiani
Ponte alle Grazie
Sdr de' Pitti
Borgo Tegolaio
Costa di San Giorgio
Via de' Bardi
Via Maggio
Piazza dei Pitti
Costa Scarpuccia
Lungarno Serristori
Via Mazzetta
Vicolo della Cava
Piazza Nicola Demidoff
Via dei Renai
Palazzo Pitti Ticket Office
Forte di Belvedere (400m)
Via del Giardino Serristori
Giardino di Boboli (Boboli Gardens)
Giardino Bardini (Bardini Gardens)
Piazza de' Mozzi

…rence

Sights
1 Basilica di San Lorenzo ... C3
2 Basilica di Santa Maria Novella ... B3
3 Battistero di San Giovanni ... D3
4 Chiesa della Santissima Annunziata ... F1
5 Chiesa di Santa Margherita ... E5
6 Chiesa e Museo di Orsanmichele ... D5
7 Duomo ... E3
8 Galleria degli Uffizi ... D6
9 Galleria dell'Accademia ... E1
10 Giardino di Boboli ... C8
11 Grande Museo del Duomo ... E3
12 Gucci Museo ... E5
13 Museo Archeologico ... F1
14 Museo Casa di Dante ... E5
15 Museo del Bargello ... E5
16 Museo delle Cappelle Medicee ... C2
17 Museo Novecento ... B4
18 Ospedale degli Innocenti ... F2
19 Palazzo Pitti ... B8
20 Palazzo Vecchio ... D6
21 Piazza della Santissima Annunziata ... F1
22 Ponte Vecchio ... C6

Activities, Courses & Tours
23 ArtViva ... C5
24 City Sightseeing Firenze ... B2
25 Cucina Lorenzo de' Medici ... C2

Eating
26 5 e Cinque ... B7
Da Vinattieri ... (see 5)
27 Il Santo Bevitore ... A6
28 L'Antico Trippaio ... D5
29 L'Osteria di Giovanni ... A5
30 Mercato Centrale ... C2
31 Obicà ... B4
32 Osteria Il Buongustai ... D5
33 Pugi ... E1
34 Tamerò ... A7
35 Trattoria Mario ... D2
36 Trattoria Marione ... B4

Drinking & Nightlife
37 Coquinarius ... D4
38 Ditta Artigianale ... E6
39 Il Santino ... A6
40 La Terrazza ... C6
41 Le Volpi e l'Uva ... C7
42 Procacci ... B4
43 Volume ... A7

Shopping
44 & Company ... A8
45 Eataly ... D3
46 Giulio Giannini e Figlio ... B7
47 Gucci ... B5
48 Officina Profumo-Farmaceutica di Santa Maria Novella ... A3

Basilica di Santa Maria Novella — Church

The striking green-and-white marble facade of 13th- to 15th-century Basilica di Santa Maria Novella fronts an entire monastical complex, comprising romantic church cloisters and a frescoed chapel. The basilica itself is a treasure chest of artistic masterpieces, climaxing with frescoes by Domenico Ghirlandaio. The lower section of the basilica's striped marbled facade is transitional from Romanesque to Gothic; the upper section and the main doorway (1456–70) were designed by Leon Battista Alberti. (www.chiesasantamarianovella.it; Piazza di Santa Maria Novella 18; adult/reduced €5/3.50; 9am-5.30pm Mon-Thu, 11am-5.30pm Fri, 9am-5pm Sat, 1-5pm Sun)

San Lorenzo

Basilica di San Lorenzo — Basilica

Considered one of Florence's most harmonious examples of Renaissance architecture, this unfinished basilica was the Medici parish church and mausoleum. It was designed by Brunelleschi in 1425 for Cosimo the Elder and built over an earlier 4th-century church. Michelangelo was commissioned to design the facade in 1518, but his design in white Carrara marble was never executed, hence the building's rough unfinished appearance.

In the solemn interior look out for Brunelleschi's austerely beautiful *Sagrestia Vecchia* (Old Sacristy) with its sculptural decoration by Donatello. Columns of *pietra serena* (soft grey stone) crowned with Corinthian capitals separate the nave from the two aisles. Donatello, who was still sculpting the two bronze pulpits (1460–67) adorned with panels of the Crucifixion when he died, is buried in the chapel featuring Fra' Filippo Lippi's *Annunciation* (c 1450). (Piazza San Lorenzo; admission €4.50, incl Biblioteca Medicea Laurenziana €7; 10am-5.30pm Mon-Sat, plus 1.30-5pm Sun winter)

Museo delle Cappelle Medicee Mausoleum

Nowhere is Medici conceit expressed so explicitly as in the Medici Chapels. Adorned with granite, marble, semiprecious stones and some of Michelangelo's most beautiful sculptures, it is the burial place of 49 dynasty members. Francesco I lies in the dark, imposing Cappella dei Principi (Princes' Chapel) alongside Ferdinando I and II and Cosimo I, II and III. Lorenzo il Magnifico is buried in the graceful Sagrestia Nuova (New Sacristy), which was Michelangelo's first architectural work. (Medici Chapels; 055 29 48 83; www.polomuseale.firenze.it; Piazza Madonna degli Aldobrandini; adult/reduced €6/3; 8.15am-1.50pm, closed 2nd & 4th Sun & 1st, 3rd & 5th Mon of month)

San Marco

Museo di San Marco Museum

At the heart of Florence's university area sits Chiesa di San Marco and the adjoining 15th-century Dominican monastery where both gifted painter Fra' Angelico (c 1395–1455) and the sharp-tongued Savonarola piously served God. Today the monastery, aka one of Florence's most spiritually uplifting museums, showcases the work of Fra' Angelico. After centuries of being known as 'Il Beato Angelico' (literally 'The Blessed Angelic One') or simply 'Il Beato' (The Blessed), the Renaissance's most blessed religious painter was made a saint by Pope John Paul II in 1984. (www.polomuseale.firenze.it; Piazza San Marco 1; adult/reduced €4/2; 8.15am-1.50pm Mon-Fri, to 4.50pm Sat & Sun, closed 1st, 3rd & 5th Sun & 2nd & 4th Mon of month)

Santa Croce

Basilica di Santa Croce Church, M

The austere interior of this Francisc basilica is a shock after the magnific neo-Gothic facade enlivened by varying shades of coloured marble. Most visitors come to see the tombs of Michelangelo, Galileo and Ghiberti inside this church, but frescoes by Giotto in the chapels right of the altar are the real highlights. The basilica was designed by Arnolfo di Cambio between 1294 and 1385 and owes its name to a splinter of the Holy Cross donated by King Louis of France in 1258. (www.santacroceopera.it; Piazza di Santa Croce; adult/reduced €6/4; 9.30am-5.30pm Mon-Sat, 2-5.30pm Sun)

The Oltrarno

Ponte Vecchio Bridge

Dating to 1345, Ponte Vecchio was the only Florentine bridge to survive destruction at the hands of retreating German forces in 1944. Above the jewellers' shops on the eastern side, the Corridoio Vasariano (Vasari Corridor) is a 16th-century passageway between the Uffizi and Palazzo Pitti that runs around, rather than through, the medieval Torre dei Mannelli at the bridge's southern end. The first documentation of a stone bridge here, at the narrowest crossing point along the entire length of the Arno, dates from 972.

Palazzo Pitti Museum

Commissioned by banker Luca Pitta and designed by Brunelleschi in 1457, this vast Renaissance palace was later bought by the Medici family. Over the centuries, it served as the residence of the city's rulers until the Savoys donated it to the state in 1919. Nowadays it houses an impressive silver museum, a couple of art museums and a series of rooms re-creating life in the palace during House of Savoy times. (www.polomuseale.firenze.it; Piazza dei Pitti; 8.15am-6.50pm Tue-Sun, reduced hours winter)

…nte, …aly's Supreme Poet

…Sommo Poeta (Supreme Poet) …born in 1265 in a wee house down …arrow lane in the backstreets of …lorence. Tragic romance made him tick and there's no better place to unravel the medieval life and times of Dante Alighieri than the **Museo Casa di Dante** (055 21 94 16; Via Santa Margherita 1; adult/reduced €4/2; 10am-5pm Tue-Sun).

When Dante was just 12 he was promised in marriage to Gemma Donati. But it was another Florentine, Beatrice Portinari (1266–90), who was the love of his life (despite only ever meeting her twice). In the *Divina Commedia* (Divine Comedy) Dante broke with tradition by using Italian, not formal Latin, to describe travelling through the circles of hell in search of his beloved Beatrice.

Beatrice, who wed a banker and died a couple of years later aged just 24, is buried in 11th-century **Chiesa di Santa Margherita** (Via Santa Margherita 4) near Dante's house. This chapel was also where the poet married Gemma in 1295. Dimly lit, it remains much as it was in medieval Florence. No wonder novelist Dan Brown chose to set a scene here in his Dante-themed thriller, *Inferno* (2013), that takes place in Florence.

Cappella Brancacci Chapel

Fire in the 18th century all but destroyed 13th-century Basilica di Santa Maria del Carmine, but fortunately it spared the magnificent frescoes in this chapel – a treasure of paintings by Masolino da Panicale, Masaccio and Filippino Lippi commissioned by rich merchant Felice Brancacci upon his return from Egypt in 1423. The entrance to the chapel is to the right of the main church entrance. Only 30 people are allowed in at any one time and visits are limited to 30 minutes in high season. (055 276 82 24; http://museicivici fiorentini.comune.fi.it; Piazza del Carmine 14; adult/reduced €6/4.50; 10am-5pm Wed-Sat & Mon, 1-5pm Sun)

Piazzale Michelangelo Viewpoint

Turn your back on the bevy of ticky-tacky souvenir stalls flogging *David* statues and boxer shorts and take in the spectacular city panorama from this vast square, pierced by one of Florence's two *David* copies. Sunset here is particularly dramatic. It's a 10-minute uphill walk along the serpentine road, paths and steps that scale the hillside from the Arno and Piazza Giuseppe Poggi; from Piazza San Niccolò walk uphill and bear left up the long flight of steps signposted Viale Michelangelo. Or take bus 13 from Stazione di Santa Maria Novella.

Forte di Belvedere Fortress, Gallery

Forte di Belvedere is a rambling fort designed by Bernardo Buontalenti for Grand Duke Ferdinando I at the end of the 16th century. From the massive bulwark soldiers kept watch on four fronts – as much for internal security as to protect the Palazzo Pitti as against foreign attack. Today the fort hosts seasonal art exhibitions, well worth a peek if only to revel in the sweeping city panorama that can be had from the fort. (www.museicivicifiorentini.comune.fi.it; Via di San Leonardo 1; adult/reduced €5/3; variable)

Giardino di Boboli Gardens

Behind Palazzo Pitti, the Boboli Gardens were laid out in the mid-16th century to a design by architect Niccolò Pericoli. At the upper, southern limit, beyond the box-hedged rose garden and Museo delle Porcellane, fantastic views over the Florentine countryside unfold. (Piazza dei Pitti; adult/reduced incl Museo degli Argenti, Museo delle Porcellane & Galleria del Costume €7/3.50; 8.15am-7.30pm summer, reduced hours winter)

TOURS

City Sightseeing Firenze Bus Tour

Explore Florence by red open-top bus, hopping on and off at 15 bus stops around the city. Tickets, sold by the driver, are valid for 24 hours. (055 29 04 51; www.firenze.city-sightseeing.it; Piazza della Stazione 1; adult 1/2/3 days €20/25/30)

500 Touring Club Driving Tour

Hook up with Florence's 500 Touring Club for a guided tour in a vintage motor – with you behind the wheel! Every car has a name in this outfit's fleet of gorgeous vintage Fiat 500s from the 1960s (Giacomo is the playboy, Anna the feminist girl and so on). Motoring tours are guided – hop in your car and follow the leader – and themed – families love the picnic trip, couples wine tasting. (www.500touringclub.com; Via Gherardo Silvani 149a)

ArtViva Walking Tour

One- to three-hour city walks led by historians or art-history graduates: tours include the Uffizi, the Original David tour and an adult-only 'Sex, Drugs & the Re-naissance' art tour. (055 264 50 33; ww italy.artviva.com; Via de' Sassetti 1; per person from €25)

SHOPPING

If there is one Italian city that screams fashion, it's Florence, birthplace of Gucci, Emilio Pucci, Roberto Cavalli and a bevy of lesser-known designers. Legendary Via de' Tornabuoni, a glittering catwalk of designer boutiques, is the place to start. Nearby, Via della Vigna Nuova – the street where icon of Florence fashion **Gucci** (055 26 40 11; www.gucci.com; Via de' Tornabuoni 73-81r; 10am-7.30pm) started out as a tiny saddlery shop in 1921 – is another fashion hot street. Local designers to look for include Michele Negri, Enrico Coveri, Patrizia Pepe and Ermanno Daelli.

> *Via de' Tornabuoni is a glittering catwalk of designer boutiques*

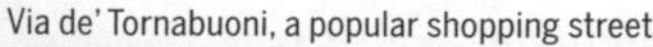

Via de' Tornabuoni, a popular shopping street

MAREMAGNUM/GETTY IMAGES ©

Palazzo Vecchio (p110)

Officina Profumo-Farmaceutica di Santa Maria Novella Beauty, Gifts

In business since 1612, this perfumery-pharmacy began life when the Dominican friars of Santa Maria Novella began to concoct cures and sweet-smelling unguents using medicinal herbs cultivated in the monastery garden. The shop today sells a wide range of fragrances, skin-care products, ancient herbal remedies and preparations alongside teas, herbal infusions, liqueurs, scented candles, organic olive oil, chocolate, honey and cookies. (www.smnovella.it; Via della Scala 16; ⌚9.30am-7.30pm)

& Company Arts, Crafts

This mesmerisming Pandora's box of beautiful objects and paper creations is the love child of Florence-born, British-raised callligrapher and graphic designer Betty Soldi and her vintage-loving husband, Matteo Perduca. Together the pair have created an extraordinary boutique showcasing their own customised cards and upcycled homewares alongside work by other designers. Souvenir shopping at its best! (http://andcompanyshop.tumblr.com/; Via Maggio 60r; ⌚10.30am-1pm & 3-6.30pm Mon-Sat)

Giulio Giannini e Figlio Handicrafts

This quaint old shopfront has watched Palazzo Pitti turn pink with the evening sun since 1856. One of Florence's oldest artisan families, the Gianninis – bookbinders by trade – make and sell marbled paper, beautifully bound books, stationery and so on. Don't miss the workshop upstairs. (www.giuliogiannini.it; Piazza dei Pitti 37r; ⌚10am-7pm Mon-Sat, 11am-6.30pm Sun)

✪ ENTERTAINMENT

La Cité Live Music

A hip cafe-bookshop with an eclectic choice of vintage seating, La Cité makes a wonderful, intimate venue for live music – jazz, swing, world music – and book readings. (www.lacitelibreria.info; Borgo San Frediano 20r; ⌚8am-2am Mon-Sat, 3pm-2am Sun; 📶)

Jazz Club Jazz
Catch salsa, blues, Dixieland and world music as well as jazz at Florence's top jazz venue. (Via Nuovo de' Caccini 3; 10.30pm-2am Tue-Sat, closed Jul & Aug)

EATING

Around Piazza del Duomo & Piazza della Signoria

Osteria Il Buongustai Osteria €
Run with breathtaking speed and grace by Laura and Lucia, this place is unmissable. Lunchtimes heave with locals who work nearby and savvy students who flock here to fill up on tasty Tuscan home cooking at a snip of other restaurant prices. The place is brilliantly no frills – expect to share a table and pay in cash; no credit cards. (Via dei Cerchi 15r; meals €15; 11.30am-3.30pm Mon-Sat)

Trattoria Marione Trattoria €
For the quintessential 'Italian dining' experience, Marione is gold. It's busy, it's noisy, it's 99.9% local and the cuisine is right out Nonna's Tuscan kitchen. No one appears to speak English so go for Italian – the tasty, excellent-value traditional fare is worth it. If you don't get a complimentary *limoncello* with the bill you clearly failed the language test. (055 21 47 56; Via della Spada 27; meals €25; noon-3pm & 7-11pm)

Obicà Italian €€
Given its exclusive location in Palazzo Tornabuoni, this designer address is naturally ubertrendy – even the table mats are upcycled from organic products. Taste different mozzarella cheeses in the cathedral-like interior or snuggle beneath heaters on sofa seating in the elegant, star-topped courtyard. At *aperitivo* hour nibble on *taglierini* (tasting boards loaded with cheeses, salami, deep-fried vegetables and so on). (055 277 35 26; www.obica.com; Via de' Tornabuoni 16; 1/2/3 mozzarella €13/20/30, pizzas €9.50-17, taglierini €4.50-19.50; noon-4pm & 6.30-11.30pm Mon-Fri, noon-11pm Sat & Sun)

Gastronomy

If you not only enjoy eating, but also like learning to cook, tasting wine and seeking out the finest products, then try these on for size.

Cucina Lorenzo de' Medici A shiny new state-of-the-art cooking school with 16 work stations in the fabulously bustling food mall above Florence's central food market; there are cooking classes (€90 to €130, three hours) and cooking demonstrations with tastings (€38, 1½ hours) around the chef's table. Sign up online or in situ at the information desk in the food mall. (www.cucinaldm.com; Via dell'Ariento, Piazza del Mercato Centrale)

Eataly Eataly shops are as much about learning about food as shopping for it, and the Florence branch is no exception. Grab a free audio guide at the information desk (near the exit) and peruse aisles laden with coffee, biscuits, conserved vegetables, pasta, rice, olive oil et al while listening to Renaissance tales. Many products are local and/or organic; most are by small producers. (055 015 36 01; Via de' Martelli 22r; 10am-10.30pm)

Accidental Tourist Become an Accidental Tourist (membership €10), then sign up for a wine tour (€60), cooking class (€70), gourmet picnic (€35) and so on; tours happen in and around Florence. (055 69 93 76; www.accidentaltourist.com)

Curious Appetite Private or group food and wine tastings led by Italian-American Coral Lelah. Tastings last 3½ hours, cost from €65 per person (minimum four people) and are themed: at the market, craft cocktails and *aperitivi*, Italian food-and-wine pairings, artisan gelato. (www.curiousappetitetravel.com)

…eria di …vanni Tuscan €€€

…sine at this smart neighbourhood …atery is sumptuously Tuscan. Imagine …ruffles, tender steaks and pastas such as *pici al sugo di salsicccia e cavolo nero* (thick spaghetti with a sauce of sausage and black cabbage). Throw in a complimentary glass of *prosecco* and you'll want to return time and again. (☎055 28 48 97; www.osteriadigiovanni.it; Via del Moro 22; meals €50; ⏰7-10pm Mon-Fri, noon-3pm & 7-10pm Sat & Sun)

 San Lorenzo & San Marco

Trattoria Mario Tuscan €

Arrive by noon to ensure a stool around a shared table at this noisy, busy, brilliant trattoria – a legend that retains its soul (and allure with locals) despite being in every guidebook. Charming Fabio, whose grandfather opened the place in 1953, is front of house while big brother Romeo and nephew Francesco cook with speed in the kitchen. (www.trattoria-mario.com; Via Rosina 2; meals €20; ⏰noon-3.30pm Mon-Sat, closed 3 weeks Aug)

Mercato Centrale Market €

Meander the maze of stalls rammed with fresh produce at Florence's oldest and largest food market, on the ground of a 19th-century iron-and-glass structure. Then head up to the shiny new 1st floor – a vibrant food fair with dedicated bookshop, cookery school, bar and stalls cooking up steaks, grilled burgers, vegetarian dishes, pizza, gelato, pastries and pasta. Load up and find a free table. (☎055 239 97 98; www.mercatocentrale.it; Piazza del Mercato Centrale 4; dishes €7-15; ⏰10am-1am, food stalls noon-3pm & 7pm-midnight; 📶)

Pugi Bakery €

The inevitable line outside the door says it all. This bakery is a Florentine favourite for pizza slices and chunks of *schiacciata* (Tuscan flatbread) baked up plain, spiked with salt and rosemary, or topped or stuffed with whatever delicious edible goodie's in season. Grab a number, drool over the savoury (and

WESTEND61/GETTY IMAGES ©

sweet) treats demanding to be devoured, and wait for your number to be called.

Should you be queueing to see *David*, Pugi is a perfect two-minute hop from the Galleria dell'Accademia. (www.focacceria-pugi.it; Piazza San Marco 9b; ⌚7.45am-8pm Mon-Sat, closed 2 weeks mid-Aug)

Santa Croce

Il Teatro del Sale Tuscan **€€**

Florentine chef Fabio Picchi is one of Florence's living treasures who steals the Sant' Ambrogio show with this eccentric, good-value members-only club (everyone welcome, annual membership €7) inside an old theatre. He cooks up weekend brunch, lunch and dinner, culminating at 9.30pm in a live performance of drama, music or comedy arranged by his wife, artistic director and comic actress Maria Cassi. (☎055 200 14 92; www.teatrodelsale.com; Via dei Macci 111r; lunch/dinner/weekend brunch €15/20/30; ⌚11am-3pm & 7.30-11pm Tue-Sat, 11am-3pm Sun, closed Aug)

The Oltrarno

5 e Cinque Vegetarian **€**

The hard work and passion of a photography and antique dealer is behind this highly creative, intimate eating space adored by every savvy local. Cuisine is vegetarian with its roots in Genova's kitchen: '5 e Cinque' (meaning '5 and 5') is a chickpea sandwich from Livorno, and the restaurant's *cecina* (traditinal Ligurian flat bread made from chickpea flour) is legendary.

Find 5 e Cinque sitting sweet on one of Florence's cutest old-world squares, pedestrian to boot. (☎055 274 15 83; Piazza della Passera 1; meals €25; ⌚10am-10pm Tue-Sun; 🖉)

Tamerò Italian **€**

A happening address on Florence's hippest square: admire pasta cooks at work in the open kitchen while you wait for a table – the chances are you'll have to. A buoyant, party-loving crowd flocks here to fill up on imaginative fresh pasta, giant salads and copious cheese/salami platters. Decor is

SYLVAIN SONNET/GETTY IMAGES ©

★ Top Five Eateries

Osteria Il Buongustai (p119)
Trattoria Mario (p120)
Il Teatro del Sale (p121)
Mercato Centrale (p120)
Il Santo Bevitore (p122)

From left: River Arno and the Ponte Vecchio (p115); Frescoes in the Cappella Brancacci (p116); Palazzo Pitti (p115)

Florentine Tripe

When Florentines fancy a fast munch-on-the-move, they flit by a *trippaio* – a cart on wheels or mobile stand – for a tripe *panini* (sandwich). Think cow's stomach chopped up, boiled, sliced, seasoned and bunged between bread.

Those great bastions of Florentine tradition still going strong include the cart on the southwest corner of Mercato Nuovo, **L'Antico Trippaio** (Piazza dei Cimatori; variable), and hole-in-the-wall **Da Vinattieri** (Via Santa Margherita 4; panini €4.50; 10am-7.30pm Mon-Fri, to 8pm Sat & Sun), tucked down an alley next to Dante's Chiesa di Santa Margherita. Pay between €3.50 and €4.50 for a *panini* with tripe doused in *salsa verde* (pea-green sauce of smashed parsley, garlic, capers and anchovies) or garnished with salt, pepper and ground chilli.

trendy industrial and weekend DJs spin sets from 10pm. (055 28 25 96; www.tamero.it; Piazza Santo Spirito 11r; meals €20; noon-3pm & 7pm-2am Tue-Sun)

Gnam Burgers €

Bread arrives at the table in a brown paper bag and fries are served in a miniature copper cauldron at this green, artisanal burger joint in San Frediano. Ingredients are seasonal, locally sourced and organic – and there are vegetarian and gluten-free burgers as well as the traditional beefy variety. Delicous homemade soups also, to eat in or take away. (055 22 39 52; www.gnamfirenze.it; Via di Camaldoli 2r; meals from €10; noon-3pm & 6pm-midnight)

Il Santo Bevitore Tuscan €€

Reserve or arrive dot-on 7.30pm to snag the last table at this ever-popular address, an ode to stylish dining where gastronomes dine by candlelight in a vaulted, white-washed, bottle-lined interior. The menu is a creative reinvention of seasonal classics, different for lunch and dinner: purple cabbage soup with mozzarella cream and anchovy syrup, acacia honey *bavarese* (firm, creamy mousse) with Vin Santo–marinated dried fruits. (055 21 12 64; www.ilsantobevitore.com; Via di Santo Spirito 64-66r; meals €40; 12.30-2.30pm & 7.30-11pm, closed Aug)

DRINKING & NIGHTLIFE

La Terrazza Bar

This rooftop bar with wooden-decking terrace accessible from the 5th floor of the Ferragamo-owned Hotel Continentale is as chic as one would expect of a fashion-house hotel. Its *aperitivo* buffet is a modest affair, but who cares with that fabulous, drop-dead-gorgeous panorama of one of Europe's most beautiful cities. Dress the part or feel out of place. (www.continentale.it; Vicolo dell' Oro 6r; 2.30-11.30pm Apr-Sep)

Coquinarius Wine Bar

With its old stone vaults, scrubbed wooden tables and refreshingly modern air, this *enoteca* (wine bar) run by the dynamic and charismatic Nicolas is spacious and stylish. The wine list features bags of Tuscan greats and unknowns, and outstanding crostini and *carpacci* (cold sliced meats) ensure you don't leave hungry. (www.coquinarius.com; Via delle Oche 11r; crostini & carpacci €4, meals €35; noon-10.30pm)

Ditta Artigianale Cafe, Bar

With industrial decor and welcoming laid-back vibe, ingenious coffee roastery–cafe-bar Ditta Artigianale rocks. Behind the bar is well-travelled Florentine barrista Francesco Sanapo and gin queen Cecilia who together shake and mix what the city's most compelling hybrid is famed for – first-class coffee and outstanding gin cocktails. (055 274 15 41; www.dittaartigianale.it; Via dei Neri 32r; 8am-10pm Mon-Thu, 8am-midnight Fri, 9.30am-midnight Sat, 9.30am-10pm Sun;)

Wine bar, Florence

Sei Divino Wine Bar

This stylish wine bar tucked beneath a red-brick vaulted ceiling is privy to one of Florence's most happening *aperitivo* scenes. It plays music, hosts occasional exhibitions and in summertime the pavement action kicks in. *Aperitivi* 'hour' (with copious banquet) runs 7pm to 10pm. (Borgo d'Ognissanti 42r; ⏲6pm-2am Wed-Mon)

Il Santino Wine Bar

This pocket-sized wine bar is packed every evening. Inside, squat modern stools contrast with old brick walls, but the real action is outside, from around 9pm, when the buoyant wine-loving crowd spills onto the street. (Via di Santo Spirito 60r; ⏲12.30-11pm)

Volume Bar

Armchairs, recycled and upcycled vintage furniture, books to read, jukebox, crêpes and a tasty choice of nibbles with coffee or a light lunch give this hybrid cafe-bar-gallery real appeal – all in an old hat-making workshop with tools and wooden moulds strewn around. Watch for various music, art and DJ events and happenings.

> *most of the city's bars offer* aperitivi *in some form or other*

(www.volumefirenze.com; Piazza Santo Spirito 3r; ⏲9am-1.30am)

Le Volpi e l'Uva Wine Bar

This unassuming wine bar hidden away by Chiesa di Santa Felicità remains as appealing as the day it opened over a decade ago. Its food and wine pairings are first-class: taste and buy boutique wines by 150 small producers from all over Italy, matched perfectly with cheeses, cold meats and the best crostini in town. Wine-tasting classes too. (www.levolpieluva.com; Piazza dei Rossi 1; ⏲11am-9pm Mon-Sat)

Le Murate Caffè Letterario Cafe, Bar

Florence's old city jail (1883–1985) and 15th-century nunnery behind the Mercato di Sant'Ambrogio is one of the city's most interesting cultural spaces. Arranged around an interior courtyard, the historic red-brick complex is, in itself, compelling: there's absolutely no mistaking the thick sturdy doors leading to the old prison cells, many of which now open onto a bookshop, wine bar, art gallery and so on. The pièce de résistance is this artsy cafe-bar in the heart of the complex that hosts everything from readings and interviews with authors – Florentine, Italian and international – to film screenings, debates, live music and art exhibitions. (☎055 234 68 72; www.lemurate.it; Piazza delle Murate Firenze; ⏰9am-1am)

 INFORMATION

There are several places in the city to get information, including the following:

Airport tourist office (☎055 31 58 74; www.firenzeturismo.it; Via del Termine, Aeroporto Vespucci; ⏰9am-7pm Mon-Sat, to 2pm Sun)

Central tourist office (☎055 29 08 32; www.firenzeturismo.it; Via Cavour 1r; ⏰9am-6pm Mon-Sat)

Infopoint Stazione (☎055 21 22 45; www.firenzeturismo.it; Piazza della Stazione 5; ⏰9am-7pm Mon-Sat, to 2pm Sun)

 GETTING THERE & AWAY

AIR

Florence Airport (Aeroport Vespucci; ☎055 306 13 00; www.aeroporto.firenze.it; Via del Termine) Also known as Amerigo Vespucci or Peretola airport, 5km northwest of the city centre; domestic and European flights.

Pisa International Airport (Galileo Galilei Airport; ☎050 84 93 00; www.pisa-airport.com) Tuscany's main international airport, a 10-minute drive south of Pisa; flights to most major European cities.

TRAIN

Florence's central train station is **Stazione di Santa Maria Novella** (Piazza della Stazione). The **left-luggage counter** (Deposito Bagagliamano; Stazione di Santa Maria Novella; first 5hr €6, then per hr €0.90; ⏰6am-11pm) is located on platform 16.

Florence is on the Rome–Milan line. Services include travel to Lucca (€7.20, 1½ hours to 1¾ hours, half-hourly), Pisa (€8, 45 minutes to one hour, half-hourly), Rome (€43 to €52, 1¾ hours

Oltrarno and Forte di Belvedere (p116)

to 4¼ hours), Bologna (€24, one hour to 1¾ hours), Milan (€29.50 to €53, 2¼ hours to 3½ hours) and Venice (€50 to 60, 2¾ hours to 4½ hours).

GETTING AROUND

TO/FROM THE AIRPORT

BUS

A shuttle (single/return €6/8, 25 minutes) travels between Florence airport and Florence's Stazione di Santa Maria Novella train station every 30 minutes between 6am and 8pm, then hourly from 8.30pm until 11.30pm (from 5.30am to 12.30am from airport).

Terravision (www.terravision.eu; one way €4.99, 70 minutes) and **Autostradale** (www.airportbusexpress.it; one way €5, 80 minutes, hourly) run daily services between the bus stop outside Florence's Stazione di Santa Maria Novella on Via Alamanni (under the station's digital clock) and Pisa International Airport: buy tickets online or on board.

TAXI

A taxi between Florence Airport and town costs a flat rate of €20 (€23 on Sunday and holidays) plus €1 per bag.

TRAIN

Regular trains link Florence's Stazione di Santa Maria Novella with the central train station in Pisa, Pisa Centrale (€8, 1½ hours, at least hourly from 4.30am to 10.25pm), from where the Pisa Mover shuttle bus (€1.30, 8 minutes) continues to Pisa International Airport.

Where to Stay

Florence is unexpectedly small, rendering almost anywhere in the centre convenient.

Budget hotels are clustered around the Santa Maria Novella train station and Mercato Centrale in neighbouring San Lorenzo.

Hip Santa Croce and the Oltrarno are packed with great dining addresses.

Book months ahead, especially if travelling on holiday weekends, in summer or during local festivals.

PUBLIC TRANSPORT

Buses, electric *bussini* (minibuses) and trams run by ATAF serve the city. Most buses start and terminate at the bus stops opposite the southeastern exit of Stazione di Santa Maria Novella.

Tickets valid for 90 minutes (no return journeys) cost €1.20 (€2 on board; drivers don't give change) and are sold at kiosks, tobacconists and the ATAF ticket and information office inside the main ticketing hall at Stazione di Santa Maria Novella.

A travel pass valid for 1/3/7 days is €5/12/18. Upon boarding time-stamp your ticket (punch on board) or risk a fine.

TAXI

Taxis can't be hailed in the street. Pick one up at the train station or call ☎055 42 42.

TUSCANY

Tuscany

With its lyrical landscapes, world-class art and superb cucina contadina *(food from the farmer's kitchen), the Tuscan experience is perfectly in symbiosis with the land.*

And oh, the art! During the medieval and Renaissance periods, Tuscany's painters, sculptors and architects created world-class masterpieces. Squirrelled away and safeguarded today in churches, museums and galleries all over the region, art in Tuscany is truly unmatched.

No land is more caught up with the fruits of its fertile earth than Tuscany, a gourmet destination where locality, seasonality and sustainability are revered. Buon appetito!

☑ In This Section

ℹ Arriving in Tuscany

Tuscany's principal international gateway is Pisa International Airport. From there, buses run to Pisa and direct to Florence.

Florence also has its own, much smaller, airport serving flights from Italian and European destinations.

Regular fast trains run to Florence, which is on the main Rome–Milan rail line. Its main station, Stazione di Santa Maria Novella, is the region's biggest and busiest.

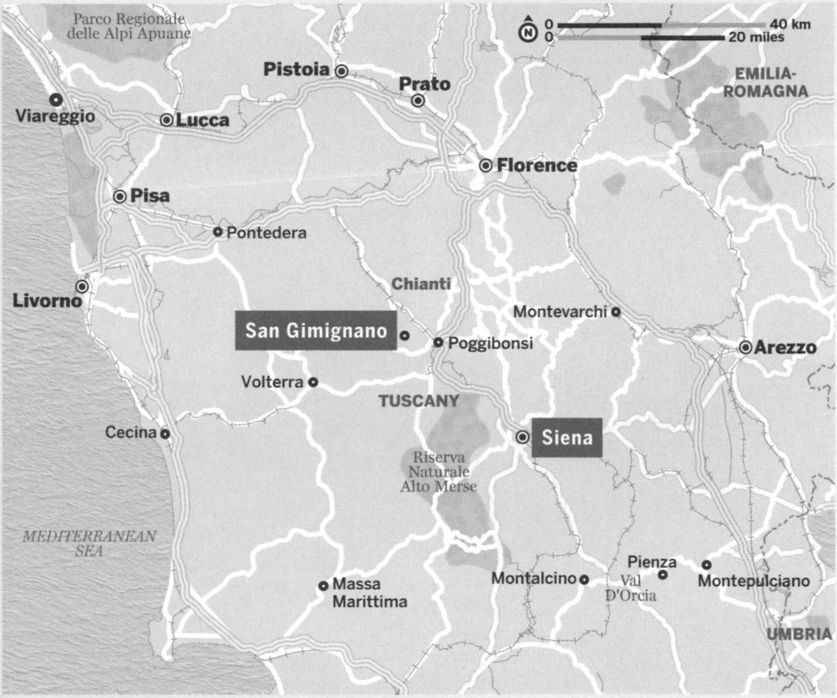

From left: Piazza dell' Anfiteatro, Lucca (p138); Grapevines; Tuscan countryside, near Siena

CARLOS SANCHEZ PEREYRA/GETTY IMAGES ©; WESTEND61/GETTY IMAGES ©; WEERAKARN SATITNIRAMAI/GETTY IMAGES ©

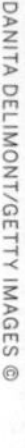
DANITA DELIMONT/GETTY IMAGES ©

Towers of San Gimignano

San Gimignano, known as the 'medieval Manhattan', features 15 11th-century towers that soar above its hilltop centro storico *(historic centre).*

Great For...

☑ Don't Miss

Galleria Continua (www.galleria continua.com; Via del Castello 11) One of the best contemporary art galleries in Europe.

Originally an Etruscan village, the town was named after the bishop of Modena, San Gimignano, who is said to have saved it from Attila the Hun. It became a comune in 1199 and quickly flourished, thanks in no small part to its position on the Via Francigena. Up to 72 towers were built as the town's prosperous burghers sought to outdo their neighbours and flaunt their wealth.

Collegiata

San Gimignano's Romanesque cathedral, the **Collegiata** (Duomo or Basilica di Santa Maria Assunta; Piazza del Duomo; adult/reduced €4/2; ⏲10am-7pm Mon-Fri, to 5pm Sat, 12.30-7pm Sun summer, to 4.30pm daily winter), is named after the college of priests who originally managed it. Parts of the building were built in the second half of the 11th century,

ENZODEBERNARDO/GETTY IMAGES ©

but its remarkably vivid frescoes date from the 14th century.

Entry is via the side stairs and through a loggia that originally functioned as the baptistry. Once in the main space, face the altar and look to your left (north). On the wall are scenes from Genesis and the Old Testament by Bartolo di Fredi, dating from around 1367. On the right (south) wall are scenes from the New Testament by the workshop of Simone Martini, which were completed in 1336. On the inside of the front facade is Taddeo di Bartolo's striking depiction of the *Last Judgment*: on the upper-left side is a fresco depicting *Paradiso* (Heaven) and on the upper-right *Inferno* (Hell).

Need to Know

Frequent buses run to/from Florence (€7, 1¼ to 2 hours) and Siena (€6, one to 1½ hours).

Take a Break

Stop by for some earthy local fare at **Locanda Sant'Agostino** (0577 94 31 41; www.locandasantagostino.net; Piazza Sant'Agostino 15; meals €30; 12.30-2.30pm & 7-10pm Thu-Tue).

★ Top Tip

San Gimignano's helpful tourist office (0577 94 00 08; www.sangimignano.com; Piazza del Duomo 1; 9am-1pm & 3-7pm summer, 9am-1pm & 2-6pm winter) **organises a range of English-language tours.**

Palazzo Comunale

The 12th-century **Palazzo Comunale** (Museo Civico; 0577 99 03 12; Piazza del Duomo 2; adult/reduced €6/5; 9am-6.30pm summer, 11am-5pm winter) has always been the centre of local government – its **Sala di Dante** is where the great poet addressed the town's council in 1299, urging it to support the Guelph cause. The room (also known as the Sala del Consiglio) is home to Lippo Memmi's early-14th-century *Maestà*, which portrays the enthroned Virgin and Child surrounded by angels, saints and local dignitaries.

Upstairs, the **pinacoteca** has a charming collection of paintings from the Sienese and Florentine schools of the 12th to 15th centuries.

In the **Camera del Podestà** is a meticulously restored cycle of frescoes by Memmo di Filippuccio, illustrating a moral history – the rewards of marriage are shown in the scenes of a husband and wife naked in a bath and in bed.

After you've enjoyed the art, be sure to climb the 218 steps of the palazzo's 54m-tall **Torre Grossa** for spectacular views of the town and surrounding countryside.

Maestà fresco by Simone Martini, Museo Civico

OLIVIER CIRENDINI/GETTY IMAGES ©

Siena

A must on any Tuscan tour, Siena is one of Italy's most enchanting medieval cities. Its historic centre, compact and easily strolled in a day, is a photogenic warren of dark lanes and stunning Gothic buildings.

Great For...

☑ Don't Miss

The Fonte Gaia in the upper part of the Piazza del Campo.

SIGHTS

Piazza del Campo Piazza

This sloping piazza, popularly known as Il Campo, has been Siena's civic and social centre since the mid-12th century. It's in Il Campo where the colourful Palio pagaents are held in July and August, the piazza converted into a temporary dirt racetrack. Ten horses and their bareback riders career three times around the track at ferocious speeds; the whole thing taking scarcely one exhilarating minute. The festival dates from the Middle Ages, and ten of Siena's 17 *contrade* (town districts) compete for the coveted *palio* (silk banner). Each *contrada* has its own traditions, symbol and colours plus its own church and *palio* museum.

For the rest of the year Il Campo is the undoubted heart of the city. Its magnificent

Palazzo Comunale and the Piazza del Campo

pavement acts as a carpet on which students and tourists picnic and relax, and the cafes around the perimeter are the most popular *aperitivo* spots in town.

Palazzo Comunale — Building

The restrained, 14th-century Palazzo Comunale serves as the grand centrepiece of the square in which it sits – notice how its concave facade mirrors the opposing convex curve. From the palazzo soars a graceful bell tower, the **Torre del Mangia** (Palazzo Comunale, Piazza del Campo; admission €10; ⏲10am-7pm summer, to 4pm winter), 102m high and with 500-odd steps. The views from the top are magnificent.

Museo Civico — Museum

Siena's most famous museum occupies rooms richly frescoed by artists of the Sienese school. Commissioned by the governing body of the city, rather than by the Church, many – unusually – depict secular subjects. The highlight is Simone Martini's celebrated *Maestà* (Virgin Mary in Majesty; 1315). It features the Madonna beneath a canopy surrounded by saints and angels, and is Martini's first known work. (Palazzo Comunale, Piazza del Campo; adult/reduced €9/8; ⏲10am-7pm summer, to 6pm winter)

Need to Know

Tourist office (☎0577 28 05 51; www.terresiena.it; Piazza del Duomo 1; ⏲9am-6pm daily summer, 10am-5pm Mon-Sat, to 1pm Sun winter)

Take a Break

Morbidi offersthe classiest cheap feed in Siena, set in the stylish basement of Morbidi's deli (www.morbidi.com; Via Banchi di Sopra 75; lunch buffet €12; ⏲8am-8pm Mon-Thu, to 9pm Fri & Sat).

★ Top Tip

During the Palio, hotels raise their rates between 10% and a staggering 50%, with a strict minimum-stay requirement.

Duomo — Church

Siena's 13th-century Duomo is a triumph of Romanesque-Gothic architecture with its banded facade and stunning interior. Inside, walls and pillars continue the exterior's striped theme, while the vaults are painted blue with gold stars. The intricate floor is inlaid with 56 panels depicting historical and biblical scenes executed by about 40 artists over 200 years from the 14th century on. (www.operaduomo.siena.it; Piazza del Duomo; summer/winter €4/free, when floor displayed €7)

Museo dell'Opera del Duomo — Museum

The collection at the Museo dell'Opera del Duomo showcases artworks that formerly adorned the cathedral, including 12 statues

of prophets and philosophers by Giovanni Pisano that originally stood on the facade. Many of the statues were designed to be viewed from ground level, which is why they look so distorted as they crane uncomfortably forward. The museum's highlight is Duccio di Buoninsegna's striking *Maestà* (1311), which was painted on both sides as a screen for the duomo's high altar. (www.operaduomo.siena.it; Piazza del Duomo 8; admission €7; 10.30am-7pm summer, to 5.30pm winter)

Casa Santuario di Santa Caterina — Religious Site

An air of serenity pervades this pilgrimage site which is the former home of the eponymous saint, her parents and 24 siblings. The rooms were converted into small chapels in the 15th century. The lower-level bedroom, frescoed in 1893 by Alessandro Franchi, includes her untouched, nearly bare cell. (Costa di Sant'Antonio 6; 9am-6.30pm Mar-Nov, 10am-6pm Dec-Feb) FREE

Chiesa di San Domenico — Church

St Catherine was welcomed into the Dominican fold within this imposing church, and its **Cappella di Santa Caterina** is adorned with frescoes by Il Sodoma depicting events in her life. Catherine died in Rome but her head was returned to Siena – it's clearly visible in a 15th-century tabernacle above the altar in a signed chapel near the gift shop. Also here are her desiccated thumb (in a small window box on the chapel's right) and a nasty-looking chain that the saint is said to have flagellated herself with. (Piazza San Domenico; 9am-12.30pm & 3-7pm) FREE

Duomo (p133)

GETTING THERE & AWAY

Siena isn't on a major train line so buses are generally a better alternative. **Siena Mobilità** (www.sienamobilita.it), part of the Tiemme network, runs services between Siena and other parts of Tuscany. It has a **ticket office** (0577 20 42 25; www.tiemmespa.it; Piazza Gramsci, 6.30am-7.30pm Mon-Fri, 7am-7.30pm Sat & Sun) underneath the main bus station in Piazza Gramsci; there's also a left-luggage office here (per 24 hours €5.50).

A Siena Mobilità bus travels between Pisa airport and Siena (one way/return €13/26, two hours), leaving Siena at 7.10am and Pisa at 11.45am. Tickets should be purchased at least one day in advance from the bus station or online.

Regional destinations include Florence (€8, 1¼ hours, frequent), San Gimignano (€6, one to 1½ hours, 10 daily), Montalcino (€5, 1½ hours, six daily) and Montepulciano (€6.60, 1½ hours, two daily).

Sena (www.sena.it) also has a ticket office (0861 1991900; Piazza Gramsci; 8.30am-7.45pm Mon-Sat) underneath the Piazza Gramsci bus station. Routes include Milan (€25, 4¼ hours, three daily), Perugia (€15, 1½ hours, two daily), Rome (€20, 3½ hours, nine daily), Turin (€20, 7¼ hours, two daily) and Venice (€20, 5½ hours, two daily).

Don't Miss

Try panforte by Lorenzo Rossi, Siena's best baker, at Panificio Il Magnifico (Via dei Pellegrini 27; 7.30am-7.30pm Mon-Sat).

JULIAN ELLIOTT PHOTOGRAPHY/GETTY IMAGES ©

Take a Break

Enoteca I Terzi is a favourite for many locals who head to this historic *enoteca* to linger over lunch or *aperitivi*. Casual dinners feature top-notch Tuscan salumi (cured meats), delicate handmade pasta and wonderful wines. (0577 4 43 29; www.enotecaiterzi.it; Via dei Termini 7; meals €35-40; 11am-1am summer 11am-4pm & 6.30pm-midnight winter, closed Sun)

Grotta Santa Caterina da Bagoga is where you'll find Pierino Fagnani ('Bagogoga'), one of Siena's most famous Palio jockeys, who swapped his saddle for an apron in 1973 and has been operating his much-loved restaurant ever since. Traditional Tuscan palate-pleasers feature on the menu, and are perhaps best showcased in the four-course *tipico* (€35) or *degustazione* (€50 with wine) menus. (0577 28 22 08; www.bagoga.it; Via della Galluzza 26; meals €35; noon-3pm & 7-10pm Tue-Sat, 12-3pm Sun).

Driving Tour: Tuscany

Taking in Tuscany's two great medieval rivals, Florence and Siena, the wine-rich hills of Chianti, and the Unesco-listed Val d'Orcia, this drive through the region's southern reaches offers a taste of artistic masterpieces, soul-stirring scenery and captivating Renaissance towns.

Distance: 185km
Duration: 4 days

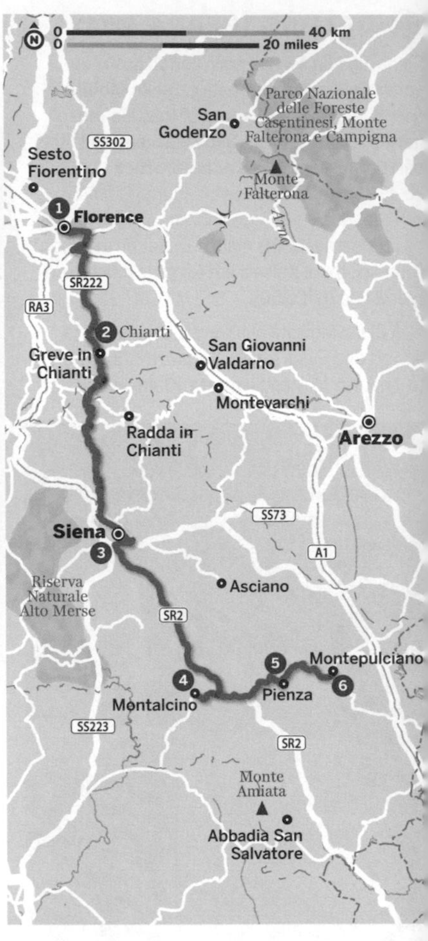

Start Florence

❶ Florence

Cradle of the Renaissance and home to some of the world's most recognisable artworks, Florence gets things off with a bang. Scale Brunelleschi's dome atop the landmark Duomo and go face to face with sculptures on Piazza della Signoria. Nearby, the Galleria degli Uffizi harbours innumerable treasures including Botticelli's show-stopping *La nascita di Venere* (The Birth of Venus). To the north, Michelangelo's *David* stars at the Galleria dell'Accademia.

❷ Chianti

From Florence pick up the SR222, the Via Chiantigiana, and head south to the Chianti wine country. Stop off in Greve, a wine centre for centuries, en route to Badia Passignano. Encircled by cypress trees and surrounded by swaths of olive groves and vineyards, this 11th-century abbey sits at the heart of a historic wine estate. Enjoy a meal at the **Osteria di Passignano** (www.osteriadipassignano.com) before pushing on south toward Siena.

❸ Siena

Siena's medieval cityscape is one of Italy's most captivating. At its heart, the city's majestic Duomo is an awe-inspiring sight with its intricate facade, striped exterior and glorious interior design. From there,

THIERRYHENNET/GETTY IMAGES ©

Pienza

it's a short walk down to Piazza del Campo, the city's signature square, and Palazzo Comunale, the graceful Gothic building that houses the city's finest art museum, the Museo Civico.

❹ Montalcino

About 45km south of Siena (take the SR2, Via Cassia), Montalcino is known to wine buffs around the world for its celebrated local drop, Brunello. You can stock up at the many *enoteche* (wine cellars) in the hilltop centre, including in the Fortezza, the 14th-century fortress that dominates the town's skyline.

❺ Pienza

Laden with red wine, turn your sights east to the Val d'Orcia and Pienza. This is one of the trip's most beautiful stretches, offering open views over undulating fields peppered with stone farmhouses and rows of elegant cypresses. Pretty Pienza is a true one-off. This once-sleepy hamlet was transformed when, in 1459, Pope Pius II began turning his home village into an ideal Renaissance town. The result is magnificent: the church, papal palace, town hall and accompanying buildings in and around Piazza Pio II went up in just four years and haven't been remodelled since. Make sure to check out Piazza Pio II and the splendid Duomo.

❻ Montepulciano

The last leg leads on to Montepulciano, a steeply stacked hill town harbouring a wealth of palazzi and fine buildings, as well as offering grandstand views over the Val di Chiana and Val d'Orcia. For some of the best panoramas, search out the terrace of the Palazzo Comunale on Piazza Grande. Round off your trip with a glass or two of the local Vino Nobile.

Finish Montepulciano

Lucca

This beautiful old city elicits love at first sight with its rich history, handsome churches and excellent restaurants. Hidden behind imposing Renaissance walls, it is an essential stopover on any Tuscan tour and a perfect base for exploring the Apuane Alps.

SIGHTS

City Wall Historic Site

Lucca's monumental *mura* (wall) was built around the old city in the 16th and 17th centuries and remains in almost-perfect condition. It superceded two previous walls, the first built from travertine stone blocks as early as the 2nd century BC. Twelve metres high and 4.2km long, today's ramparts are crowned with a tree-lined footpath looking down on the *centro storico* and out towards the Apuane Alps. This path is a favourite location for the locals' daily *passeggiata* (traditional evening stroll).

Cattedrale di San Martino Cathedral

Lucca's predominantly Romanesque cathedral dates to the 11th century. Its stunning facade was constructed in the prevailing Lucca-Pisan style and designed to accommodate the pre-existing *campanile* (bell tower). The reliefs over the left doorway of the portico are believed to be by Nicola Pisano, while inside, treasures include the **Volto Santo** (literally, Holy Countenance) crucifix sculpture and a wonderful 15th-century tomb in the **sacristy**. The cathedral interior was rebuilt in the 14th and 15th centuries with a Gothic flourish. (www.museocattedralelucca.it; Piazza San Martino; adult/reduced €3/2, with museum & Chiesa e Battistero dei SS Giovanni & Reparata €7/5; 9.30am-5pm Mon-Fri, to 6pm Sat, 11.30am-5pm Sun)

Torre Guinigi Tower

The bird's-eye view from the top of this medieval, 45m-tall red-brick tower adjoining 14th-century **Palazzo Guinigi** is predictably magnificent. But what

Lucca's city walls

impresses even more are the seven oak trees planted in a U-shaped flower bed at the top of the tower. Legend has it that upon the death of powerful Lucchese ruler Paolo Guinigi (1372–1432) all the leaves fell off the trees. Count 230 steps to the top. (Via Guinigi; adult/reduced €4/3; 9.30am-6.30pm summer, 10.30am-4.30pm winter)

Palazzo Pfanner Palace

Fire the romantic in you with a stroll around this beautiful 17th-century palace where parts of *Portrait of a Lady* (1996) starring Nicole Kidman and John Malkovich were shot. Its baroque-styled garden – the only one of substance within the city walls – enchants with ornamental pond, lemon house and 18th-century statues of Greek gods posing between potted lemon trees. Summertime chamber music concerts hosted here are absolutely wonderful. (www.palazzopfanner.it; Via degli Asili 33; palace or garden adult/reduced €4.50/4, both €6/5; 10am-6pm Apr-Nov)

EATING

Grom Gelateria €

Natural and organic is the philosophy of this master ice-cream maker. Join the line of locals for a tub of caramel and pink Himalayan salt, yoghurt, tiramisu or seasonal fruit sorbet. (www.grom.it; Via Fillungo 56; cones €2.20-3.30; 11.30am-10pm Sun-Thu, to 11pm or midnight Fri & Sat)

Da Felice Pizza €

This buzzing spot behind Piazza San Michele is where the locals come for wood-fired pizza, *cecina* (salted chickpea pizza) and *castagnacci* (chestnut cakes). Eat in or take away, *castagnaccio* comes wrapped in crisp white paper, and my it's good with a chilled bottle of Moretti beer. (www.pizzeriadafelice.it; Via Buia 12; focaccias €1-3, pizza slices €1.30; 10am-8.30pm)

Port Ellen Clan Tuscan €€

'Ristorante, Enoteca, Design Ideas' is the strapline of this romantic candlelit space named after the town in the Scottish Hebrides where the owner holidays. Cuisine is imaginative with homemade *tortelli* stuffed with stewed oxtail, and pork tenderloin with fennel mash jostling for attention on the creative menu. Excellent artisan beer and whisky list. (0583 49 39 52;

MARTIN RUEGNER/GETTY IMAGES ©

Pisa's Leaning Tower

One of Italy's signature sights, the Leaning Tower (Torre Pendente; www.opapisa.it; Piazza dei Miracoli; admission €18; 9am-8pm summer, 10am-5pm winter) truly lives up to its name, leaning a startling 3.9 degrees off the vertical. The 56m-high tower, officially the Duomo's *campanile* (bell tower), took almost 200 years to build, but was already listing when it was unveiled in 1372. Over time, the tilt, caused by a layer of weak subsoil, steadily worsened until it was finally halted by a major stabilisation project in the 1990s.

Access to the Leaning Tower is limited to 40 people at a time; children under eight are not allowed and those aged eight to 10 years must hold an adult's hand. To avoid disappointment, book in advance online or go straight to a ticket office when you arrive in Pisa to book a slot for later in the day. Visits last 30 minutes and involve a steep climb up 300-odd occasionally slippery steps. All bags must be deposited at the free left-luggage desk next to the central ticket office – cameras are about the only thing you can take up. Regular trains run to Pisa from Florence's Stazione di Santa Maria Novella (€8, 45 minutes to one hour, half-hourly).

Tuscan Wineries

Stripe upon stripe of vines over undulating, sun-drenched Tuscan hills: try these local wineries to sample some of Italy's finest tipples.

Antinori nel Chianti Classico
Visiting this cellar complex is a James Bond–esque experience. Get cleared at the gated, guarded entrance, approach a sculptural main building that's set into the hillside, then explore an exquisitely designed winery full of architectural flourishes and state-of-the-art equipment. Your one-hour guided tour (English and Italian) finishes with a tutored tasting of three Antinori wines beside the family museum. (0552 35 97 00; www.antinorichianticlassico.it; Via Cassia per Siena 133, Località Bargino; tour & tasting €25-50, bookings essential; 10am-6pm summer, to 5pm winter)

Badia a Passignano
It doesn't get much more atmospheric: an 11th-century abbey, owned by Benedictine monks and set amid vineyards run by the legendary Antinori dynasty. The four-hour 'Antinori at Badia a Passignano' tour (€150, two daily, Monday to Saturday) includes a vineyard and cellar visit and a meal in the estate's restaurant, accompanied by four signature Antinori wines. (www.osteriadipassignano.com; Badia a Passignano)

www.portellenclan.com; Via del Fosso 120; meals €30; 7.30pm-1am Wed-Fri, noon-3pm & 7.30pm-1am Sat & Sun)

INFORMATION

Tourist office (0583 58 31 50; www.luccaitinera.it; Piazzale Verdi; 9am-7pm summer, to 5pm winter) Free hotel reservations, left-luggage service (two bags €2.50/4.50/7 per hour/half-day/day) and guided city tours in English departing daily at 2pm (€10, two hours).

GETTING THERE & AWAY

BUS

From the bus stops around Piazzale Verdi, Vaibus runs services throughout the region, including to Pisa airport (€3.40, 45 minutes to one hour, 30 daily) and Castelnuovo di Garfagnana (€4.20, 1½ hours, eight daily)

TRAIN

The station is south of the city walls: take the path across the moat and through the tunnel under Baluardo San Colombano.

Florence €7.20, 1¼ to 1¾ hours, hourly

Pisa €3.40, 30 minutes, every half-hour

Viareggio €3.40, 25 minutes, hourly

Montalcino

This medieval hill town is known throughout the world for its coveted wine, Brunello, and a remarkable number of *enoteche* line its medieval streets.

SIGHTS

Fortezza Historic Building
This imposing 14th-century structure was expanded under the Medici dukes and now dominates the town's skyline. You can sample and buy local wines in its *enoteca* (tasting of two/three/five Brunellos €9/13/19) and also climb up to the fort's ramparts. Buy a ticket for the ramparts at the bar. (Piazzale Fortezza; courtyard free, ramparts adult/child €4/2; 9am-8pm Apr-Oct, 10am-6pm Nov-Mar)

Museo Civico e Diocesano d'Arte Sacra Museum

Occupying the former convent of the neighbouring **Chiesa di Sant'Agostino**, this collection of religious art from the town and surrounding region includes a triptych by Duccio and a *Madonna and Child* by Simone Martini. Other artists represented include the Lorenzetti brothers, Giovanni di Paolo and Sano di Pietro. (☎0577 84 60 14; Via Ricasoli 31; adult/reduced €4.50/3; ⌚10am-1pm & 2-5.30pm Tue-Sun)

DRINKING & NIGHTLIFE

Osticcio Wine Bar

In a town overflowing with *enoteche*, this is definitely one of the best. A huge selection of Brunello and its more modest sibling Rosso di Montalcino accompanies tempting dishes such as marinated anchovies, *cinta senese* (Tuscan pork) crostini, and pasta with pumpkin and pecorino. The panoramic view, meanwhile, almost upstages it all. (www.osticcio.it; Via Matteotti 23; antipasto plates €7-18, meals €37; ⌚noon-4pm & 7-11pm Fri-Wed, plus noon-7pm Thu summer)

Fiaschetteria Italiana 1888 Cafe

You could take a seat in the slender square outside this atmosphere-laden *enoteca*-cafe, but then you'd miss its remarkable 19th-century decor – all brass, mirrors and ornate lights. It's been serving coffee and glasses of Brunello to locals since 1888 (hence the name) and is still chock-full of charm. (Piazza del Popolo 6; ⌚7.30am-midnight, closed Thu winter)

INFORMATION

Tourist Office (☎0577 84 93 31; www.prolocomontalcino.com; Costa del Municipio 1; ⌚10am-1pm & 2-5.50pm) The tourist office is just off the main square and can book cellar-door visits and accommodation.

GETTING THERE & AWAY

Regular Siena Mobilità buses (€5, 1½ hours, six daily) run to/from Siena.

Fortezza, Montalcino

Piazza Grande, Montepulciano

Montepulciano

Exploring this reclaimed narrow ridge of volcanic rock will push your quadriceps to their failure point. When this happens, self-medicate with a generous pour of the highly reputed Vino Nobile while drinking in the spectacular views over the Val di Chiana and Val d'Orcia.

SIGHTS

Il Corso Street

Montepulciano's main street – called in stages Via di Gracciano, Via di Voltaia, Via dell'Opio and Via d'Poliziano – climbs up the eastern ridge of the town from Porta al Prato and loops to meet Via di Collazzi on the western ridge. To reach the centre of town (Piazza Grande) take a dog-leg turn into Via del Teatro.

Palazzo Comunale Palace

Built in the 14th-century in Gothic style and remodelled in the 15th century by Michelozzo, the Palazzo Comunale still functions as the town hall. Head inside to drink in the extraordinary views from the panoramic terrace and the tower – from the latter you can see as far as Pienza, Montalcino and even, on a clear day, Siena. (Piazza Grande; terrace/tower €3/5; ⏲10am-6pm summer)

Museo Civico Museum, Art Gallery

Montepulciano's modest museum and pinacoteca have recently had a curatorial dream come true: a painting in their collections has been attributed to Caravaggio. The masterpiece is a characteristic *Portrait of a Gentleman*. Worth the entrance fee alone, it's accompanied by high-tech, touch-screen interpretation, which allows you to explore details of the painting, its restoration and diagnostic attribution. (www.museocivicomontepulciano.it; Via Ricci 10; adult/reduced €5/3; ⏲10am-1pm & 3-6pm Tue-Sun summer, Sat & Sun only winter)

EATING

Osteria Acquacheta Tuscan **€€**

Hugely popular with locals and tourists alike, this bustling *osteria* specialises in *bistecca alla fiorentina* (chargrilled T-bone steak), which comes to the table in huge, lightly seared and exceptionally flavoursome slabs (don't even *think* of asking for it to be served otherwise). Book ahead. (☎0578 71 70 86; www.acquacheta.eu; Via del Teatro 2; meals €25; ⏲12.15-4pm & 7.30-10.30pm Wed-Mon)

La Grotta Ristorante **€€€**
The ingredients, and sometimes dishes, may be traditional, but the presentation is full of refined flourishes – artfully arranged Parmesan shavings and sprigs of herbs crown delicate towers of pasta, vegetables and meat. The service is exemplary and the courtyard garden divine. It's just outside town on the road to Chiusi. (☎0578 75 74 79; www.lagrottamontepulciano.it; Via San Biagio 15; meals €44, 6-course tasting menu €48; ⏲12.30-2.30pm & 7.30-10pm Thu-Tue, closed mid-Jan–mid-Mar)

INFORMATION

Strada del Vino Nobile di Montepulciano Information Office (☎0578 71 74 84; www.stradavinonobile.it; Piazza Grande 7; ⏲10am-1pm & 3-6pm Mon-Fri) Books accommodation and arranges courses and tours.

Tourist office (☎0578 75 73 41; www.prolocomontepulciano.it; Piazza Don Minzoni 1; ⏲9.30am-12.30pm & 3-6pm Mon-Sat, 9.30am-12.30pm Sun) Reserves last-minute accommodation (in person only), offers internet access (€3.50 per hour), can advise on mountain-bike and scooter rental (€25 to €50) and sells bus and train tickets (€1 commission applies for train tickets).

GETTING THERE & AROUND

The bus station is next to Car Park No 5. Siena Mobilità runs two buses daily between Siena and Montepulciano (€6.60, 1½ hours) stopping at Pienza (€2.50) en route. There are three services per day to/from Florence (€11.20, 90 minutes).

Regular buses connect with Chiusi-Chianciano Terme (€3.40, 40 minutes), from where you can catch a train to Florence (€12.90, two hours, frequent) via Arezzo (€6.40, 50 minutes).

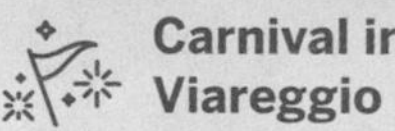

Carnival in Viareggio

For Tuscany's best winter party head to Viareggio, a popular resort near Lucca. From February to early March, the city stages one of Italy's most flamboyant Carnevale celebrations. Festivities involve fireworks and rampant dusk-to-dawn parties, but the headline attraction is the parade of floats carrying giant satirical effigies of politicians and topical celebrities.

ANDREA PUCCI/GETTY IMAGES ©

Arezzo

Arezzo may not be a Tuscan centrefold, but those parts of its historic centre that survived merciless WWII bombing are as compelling as anywhere in the region: the city's central square is as beautiful as it appears in Roberto Benigni's film *La vita è bella* (Life is Beautiful).

For art lovers, Arezzo is the place to see one of Italy's great masterpieces – Piero della Francesca's fresco cycle of the *Legend of the True Cross* adorns the **Cappella Bacci** (☎0575 35 27 27; www.pierodellafrancesca.it; Piazza San Francesco; adult/reduced €8/5; ⏲9am-6.30pm Mon-Fri, to 5.30pm Sat, 1-5.30pm Sun) in the apse of the 14th-century **Basilica di San Francesco**. Painted between 1452 and 1466, it relates the story of the cross on which Christ was crucified. Only 25 people are allowed in every half-hour, making advance booking (by telephone or email) essential in high season.

Riomaggiore (p154)

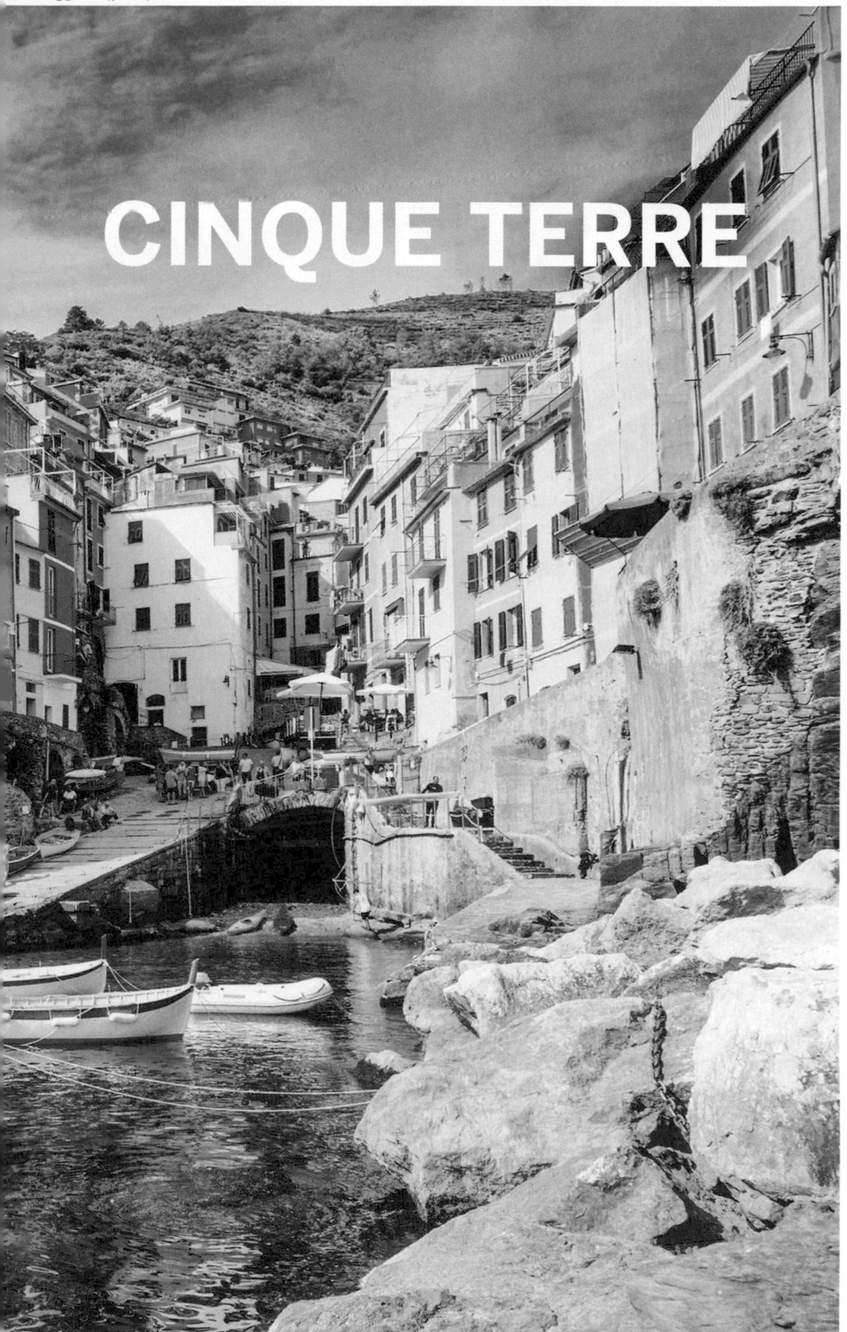

CINQUE TERRE

Cinque Terre

Set amid some of the most dramatic coastal scenery on the planet, these five ingeniously constructed fishing villages, dating from the early medieval period, can bolster the most jaded of spirits. A Unesco World Heritage Site since 1997, Cinque Terre isn't the undiscovered Eden it was 30 years ago, but frankly, who cares? Sinuous paths traverse seemingly impregnable cliffsides, while a 19th-century railway line connects the villages. Thankfully cars were banned over a decade ago.

The region's steeply terraced cliffs are bisected by a unique and complicated system of fields and gardens that have been shaped and layered over the course of nearly two millennia. So marked are these contours that some scholars have compared the extensive muretti *(low stone walls) to the Great Wall of China in their grandeur and scope.*

☑ In This Section

Arriving in the Cinque Terre

The easiest way to access the Cinque Terre is by train from La Spezia to the south or Genoa to the north. Between 6.30am and 10pm, regular trains trundle along the coast, stopping at each of the Cinque Terre's villages.

A more scenic, but slower, approach is by boat – in summer the **Golfo Paradiso SNC** (p155) runs daily boats to the Cinque Terre from Genoa.

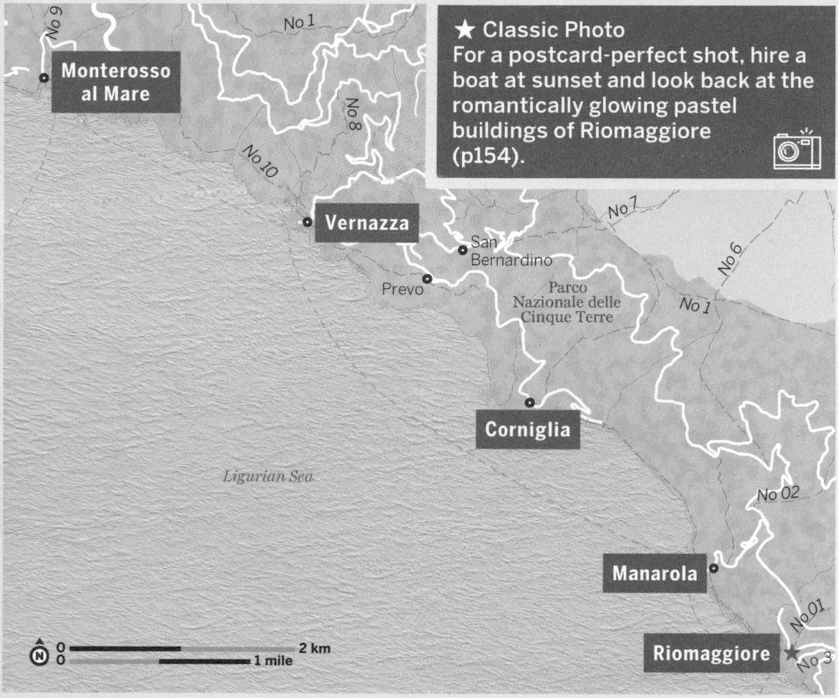

★ Classic Photo

For a postcard-perfect shot, hire a boat at sunset and look back at the romantically glowing pastel buildings of Riomaggiore (p154).

From left: Beach at Monterosso (p152); Train travelling along the Cinque Terre coast; Manarola (p153)

DANIEL SCHOENEN/GETTY IMAGES ©; ALESSANDROCOLLE/GETTY IMAGES ©; GAVIN HELLIER/ROBERTHARDING/GETTY IMAGES ©

Santuario della Madonna delle Grazie

Walking in the Cinque Terre

With its spectacular scenery, terraced slopes and network of ancient trails, the Cinque Terre offers superlative walking. Routes cater to all levels, ranging from simple 20-minute strolls to daunting hillside hikes.

Great For...

☑ Don't Miss

The breathtaking views from the Belvedere di Santa Maria (p153) in Corniglia.

Sanctuary Walks

Each of the Cinque Terre's villages is associated with a sanctuary perched high on the cliffsides above the azure Mediterranean. Reaching these religious retreats used to be part of a hefty Catholic penance, but these days the walks through terraced vineyards and across view-splayed cliffs are a heavenly reward in themselves.

Monterosso to Santuario della Madonna di Soviore From Via Roma, follow trail 9 up through forest and past the ruins of an old hexagonal chapel to an ancient paved mule path that leads to Soviore, Liguria's oldest sanctuary, dating from the 11th century. Here you'll find a bar, a restaurant and views as far as Corsica on a clear day.

Vernazza to Santuario della Madonna di Reggio From underneath Vernazza's

Monterosso

JON ARNOLD/GETTY IMAGES ©

railway bridge, follow trail 8 up numerous flights of steps and past 14 sculpted Stations of the Cross to this 11th-century chapel with a Romanesque facade.

Corniglia to Santuario della Madonna delle Grazie This sanctuary can be approached from either Corniglia (on trail 7b) or Vernazza (trail 7), though the latter is better. Branch off the Sentiero Azzurro and ascend the spectacular Sella Comeneco to the village of San Bernardino, where you'll find the church with its adored image of Madonna and child above the altar.

Manarola to Santuario della Madonna delle Salute The pick of all the sanctuary walks is this breathtaking traverse (trail 6) through Cinque Terre's finest vineyards to a tiny Romanesque-meets-Gothic chapel in the tiny village of Volastra.

Need to Know

Throughout the day trains ply up and down the coast, linking the Cinque Terre villages.

Take a Break

Sit down to seafood at the **Trattoria da Oscar** (p152) in Monterosso's old town.

Top Tip

Check out the Parco Nazionale delle Cinque Terre website (www.parconazionale5terre.it) for trail details and online maps.

Riomaggiore to Santuario della Madonna di Montenero Trail 3 ascends from the top of the village, up steps and past walled gardens to a restored 18th-century chapel with a frescoed ceiling, which sits atop an astounding lookout next to the park's new cycling centre.

Sentiero Rosso

Just a few kilometres shy of a full-blown marathon, the 38km Sentiero Rosso (Red Trail; marked No 1 on maps) – which runs from Porto Venere to Levanto – dangles a tempting challenge to experienced walkers who aim to complete it in nine to 12 hours.

For every 100 people you see on the Sentiero Azzurro (Blue Trail), there are less than a dozen up here plying their way along a route that is mainly flat, tree-covered and punctuated with plenty of shortcuts.

Trail Closures

Since the 2011 floods, many of Cinque Terre's walking paths have been in a delicate state and prone to periodic closure. However, Cinque Terre has a whole network of spectacular trails and you can still plan village-to-village hikes via 30 numbered paths. Check ahead for the most up-to-date trail information at the Parco Nazionale delle Cinque Terre website.

Sentiero Azzurro

The Cinque Terre's best-known path is the Sentiero Azzurro (Blue Trail; marked No 2 on maps), a sinuous 11km trail that follows the precipitous coastline through all five villages. Unfortunately, at the time of writing, the paths between Riomagiorre and Manarola and Manarola and Corniglia were closed, and will possibly remain so until at least 2017. It is, of course, possible to walk the open sections and catch the train to avoid the closed sections.

Distance: 11km

Monterosso

Start Riomaggiore train station

❶ Riomaggiore

The Sentiero can be tackled in both directions, but many people start in Riomaggiore, the easternmost of the five villages. The first leg, popularly known as the Via dell'Amore, starts from near Riomaggiore train station and leads around the cliffsides to Manarola, a leisurely 20 minutes' stroll away. (The name is a nod to the number of marriages the opening of the path engendered between villagers of the once geographically divided hamlets.) Before setting out, take a moment to admire Riomaggiore's colourful houses and snug harbour.

❷ Manarola

One of the busiest of the villages, Manarola tumbles down to the sea in a helter-skelter of pastel-coloured buildings, cafes, trattorias and restaurants. Have a look around – it won't take long – then stop off to admire views from Punta Bonfiglio, a prized viewpoint on a rocky promontory, before pushing on to Corniglia, some 2.9km away.

❸ Corniglia

The only village with no direct sea access, Corniglia is the high point of the coast, quite literally given its lofty position on a towering rock spur. Once you've climbed the 377 steps to the village centre and soaked up the amazing views, rejoin the path, which now becomes more rugged as it wends 3.4km through lush vegetation to Vernazza.

Terreced vineyards

❹ Vernazza

Make it to Vernazza, considered by many the coast's most beautiful village, and you can reward yourself with a swim at the small beach. Next, lap up the atmosphere at the harbour and poke around the ruins of the 11th-century Castello Doria before striking onward. The last leg, the 3.6km stretch to Monterosso, is the toughest on the route, a draining two-hour hike with some pretty hard climbing.

❺ Monterosso

Waiting at the end of the trail is Monterosso, the largest and most developed of the villages, and the only place with a long sandy beach. To celebrate completion of the hike, treat yourself to a slap up seafood dinner at one of the many fish restaurants in town.

Finish Monterosso

Need to Know

To walk the Sentiero you'll need to buy a Cinque Terre Card (p155).

☑ Did You Know

The trail dates back to the early days of the Republic of Genoa in the 12th and 13th centuries and, until the opening of the railway line in 1874, it was the only practical means of getting from village to village.

Monterosso

The most accessible village by car and the only Cinque Terre settlement to sport a proper beach, Monterosso is the furthest west and least quintessential of the quintet. The village, known for its lemon trees and anchovies, is split in two, its new and old halves linked by a tunnel burrowed beneath the blustery San Cristoforo promontory. Monterosso was badly hit by the 2011 floods, but recovered remarkably quickly.

SIGHTS

Convento dei Cappuccini Church
The village's most interesting church and convent complex is set on the hill that divides the old town from the newer Fegina quarter. The striped church, the Chiesa di San Francesco, dates from 1623 and has a painting attributed to Van Dyck (*Crocifissione*) to the left of the altar. Nearby, the ruins of an old castle have been converted into a cemetery.

EATING

Trattoria da Oscar Ligurian **€€**
Behind Piazza Matteoti, in the heart of the old town, this vaulted dining room is run by a young, friendly team. The town's famed anchovies dominate the menu; whether you go for the standard fried-with-lemon, with a white wine sauce or deep fried, they are all good. No credit cards. (Via Vittorio Emanuele 67; meals €33; noon-2pm & 7-10pm)

Miky Seafood **€€€**
If you're looking for something elegant, Miky does a seasonal fish menu in a moody, modern dining room. Booking ahead is advised; if you miss out on a table, it also has casual beach side tables at the *cantina* (wine bar). (0187 81 76 08; www.ristorantemiky.it; Lungomare Fegina 104; meals €45-60; noon-2.30pm & 7-10pm Wed-Mon summer)

Vernazza

Vernazza's small harbour – the only secure landing point on the Cinque Terre coast – guards the quaintest of the five villages.

Vernazza

Lined with little cafes, a main cobbled street, Via Roma, links seaside Piazza Marconi with the train station. Side streets lead to the village's trademark Genoa-style *caruggi* (narrow lanes), where sea views pop at every turn. There's also a tiny sandy beach where swimming is possible.

 SIGHTS & ACTIVITIES

Castello Doria Castle

This castle, the oldest surviving fortification in the Cinque Terre, commands superb views. Dating to around 1000, it's now largely a ruin except for the circular tower in the centre of the esplanade. To get there, head up the steep, narrow staircase by the harbour. (admission €1.50; 10am-7pm summer, to 6pm winter)

Vernazza Winexperience Wine Tasting

Sommelier Alessandro Villa's family have lived in Vernazza for over six generations. Let him take you through the rare, small-yield wines that come from the vineyards that tumble down the surrounding hills. While the wine and stupendous sunset view will be pleasure enough, knowing you're also helping keep a unique landscape and culture alive feels good. (Deck Giani Franzi; 331 3433801; www.cinqueterrewinetasting.com; Via San Giovanni Battista 41; 5-9pm May-Oct)

EATING

Batti Batti Takeaway €

Batti Batti knocks out the best foccacia slices in the village (some would say in the whole Cinque Terre), along with bountifully topped pizza. Its *friggitoria*, a few shops down, turns out *fritto misto* (fried seafood) to take away in paper cones. (Via Visconti 3; focaccia €3-5, seafood €8-12)

Corniglia

Corniglia is the 'quiet' middle village that sits atop a 100m-high rocky promontory surrounded by vineyards. By virtue of its spectacular position, it is the only place you can see all five settlements in the same panorama. This dazzling 180-degree sea view is best enjoyed from the Belvedere di Santa Maria. To find it, follow Via Fieschi through the village until you eventually reach the cliff-top balcony.

Narrow alleys and colourfully painted houses characterise a timeless streetscape that was name checked in Boccaccio's *Decameron*. There is no direct sea access here, only steep steps leading down to a rocky cove. To reach the village from the railway station you must first tackle the Lardarina, a 377-step brick stairway, or jump on a shuttle bus (one-way €2.50).

Wine on the Cinque Terre

Grapes grow abundantly on the the Cinque Terre's terraced plots, especially around the village of Manarola. The area's signature wine is Sciacchetrà, a blend of Bosco, Albarola and Vermentino grapes best sampled with cheese or sweet desserts.

BRUCE YUANYUE BI/GETTY IMAGES ©

Manarola

Bequeathed with more grapevines than any other Cinque Terre village, Manarola is famous for its sweet Sciacchetrà wine. It's also awash with priceless medieval relics, supporting claims that it is the oldest of the five villages. Due to its proximity to Riomaggiore (852m away), the village is heavily trafficked, especially by Italian school parties.

Where to Stay

B&Bs and a handful of hotels are situated in Riomaggiore, along with several room- and apartment-rental agencies. Hostels are situated in Corniglia and Manarola, while Monterosso has quite a good selection of hotels to choose from. The villages also boast a handful of boutique hotels and B&Bs.

La Spezia is an affordable place to stay and Levanto, just west of Monterosso, is another option with excellent train links to the Cinque Terre villages.

SIGHTS

Punta Bonfiglio Lookout

Manarola's prized viewpoint is on a rocky promontory on the path out of town towards Corniglia where walkers stop for classic photos of the village. A rest area, including a kid's playground, has been constructed here and there's also a bar just below. Nearby are the ruins of an old chapel once used as a shelter by local farmers.

Piazzale Papa Innocenzo IV Piazza

At the northern end of Via Discovolo, you'll come upon this small piazza dominated by a bell tower that was once used as a defensive lookout. Opposite, the Chiesa di San Lorenzo dates from 1338 and houses a 15th-century polyptych. If you're geared up for a steep walk, from nearby Via Rollandi you can follow a path that leads through vineyards to the top of the mountain.

Riomaggiore

Cinque Terre's easternmost village, Riomaggiore is the largest of the five and acts as its unofficial HQ (the main park office is based here). Its peeling pastel buildings tumble down a steep ravine to a tiny harbour – the region's favourite postcard view – and glow romantically at sunset. The famous Sentiero Azzurro (p150) coastal path starts here.

SIGHTS

Fossola Beach Beach

This small pebbly beach is immediately southeast of Riomaggiore marina. It's rugged but secluded. Swimmers should be wary of rocks and currents.

Torre Guardiola Nature Reserve

Birdlife and local flora can be seen from a nature-observation and birdwatching centre on a promontory of land just east of Riomaggiore. The building was a naval installation in WWII, known as La Batteria Racchia. It's reachable via a trail that starts just west of Fossola Beach. (admission €1.50; 9am-1pm & 4-7pm Feb-Jul, Sep & Oct, 9am-1pm Aug)

ACTIVITIES

Since 2009 the Cinque Terre national park has allowed mountain bikes on some of its paths, though it's still very much a niche sport. The starting point of most of the paths is the Santuario della Madonna di Montenero, accessible by road or *sentiero* (trail) No 3 above Riomaggiore.

For offshore sport, the **Cooperative Sub 5 Terre** (0187 92 00 11; www.5terrediving.it; Via San Giacomo; seasonal) runs dive and snorkelling trips, aand hires out canoes.

EATING

Dau Cila Modern Italian **€€**

Perched within pebble-lobbing distance of Riomaggiore's wee harbour, Dau Cila is a smart, kitsch-free zone, and specialises in classic seafood and hyper-local wines. Pair the best Cinque Terre whites with cold plates such as smoked tuna with apples and lemon, or lemon-marinated anchovies. (0187 76 00 32; www.ristorantedaucila.com; Via San Giacomo 65; meals €40; 8am-2am Mar-Oct)

INFORMATION

Parco Nazionale (www.parconazionale5terre.it; 7am-8pm) has offices in the train stations of all five villages and La Spezia station; has full info about trail closures.

GETTING THERE & AROUND

Easily the best way to get around the Cinque Terre is with a Cinque Terre Card. Two versions of the card are available: with or without train travel. Both include unlimited use of walking paths and electric village buses, as well as cultural exhibitions. The basic one-/two-day card costs €7.50/14.50. With unlimited train trips between the villages, the card costs €12/23. A one-day family card for two adults and two children (under 12) costs €31.50/19.60 with/without train travel.

All these cards are sold at the Cinque Terre park information offices and at each of the Cinque Terre's train stations. For those not interested in hiking, an all-day train ticket between the villages is also good value at €4.

BOAT

Consorzio Liguria Via Mare (www.liguriaviamare.it)

Consorzio Marittimo Turistico Cinque Terre Golfo dei Poeti (www.navigazionegolfodeipoeti.it) From late March to October, La Spezia–based Consorzio Marittimo Turistico Cinque Terre Golfo dei Poeti runs daily shuttle boats between all of the Cinque Terre villages (except Corniglia), costing €9 one way, including all stops, or €20 for an all-day ticket.

Golfo Paradiso SNC (www.golfoparadiso.it) In summer the Golfo Paradiso runs boats to the Cinque Terre from Genoa (one way/return €18/33).

CAR & MOTORCYCLE

Private vehicles are not allowed beyond village entrances. If you're arriving by car or motorcycle, you'll need to pay to park in designated car parks (€12 to €25 per day). In some villages, minibus shuttles depart from the car parks (one way/return €1.50/2.50); park offices have seasonal schedules.

TRAIN

Between 6.30am and 10pm, one to three trains an hour trundle along the coast between Genoa and La Spezia, stopping at each of the Cinque Terre's villages. Unlimited 2nd-class rail travel between Levanto and La Spezia is covered by the Cinque Terre Card, or you can buy a €4 all-day ticket that allows unlimited travel between the five villages.

Castello Doria (p153)

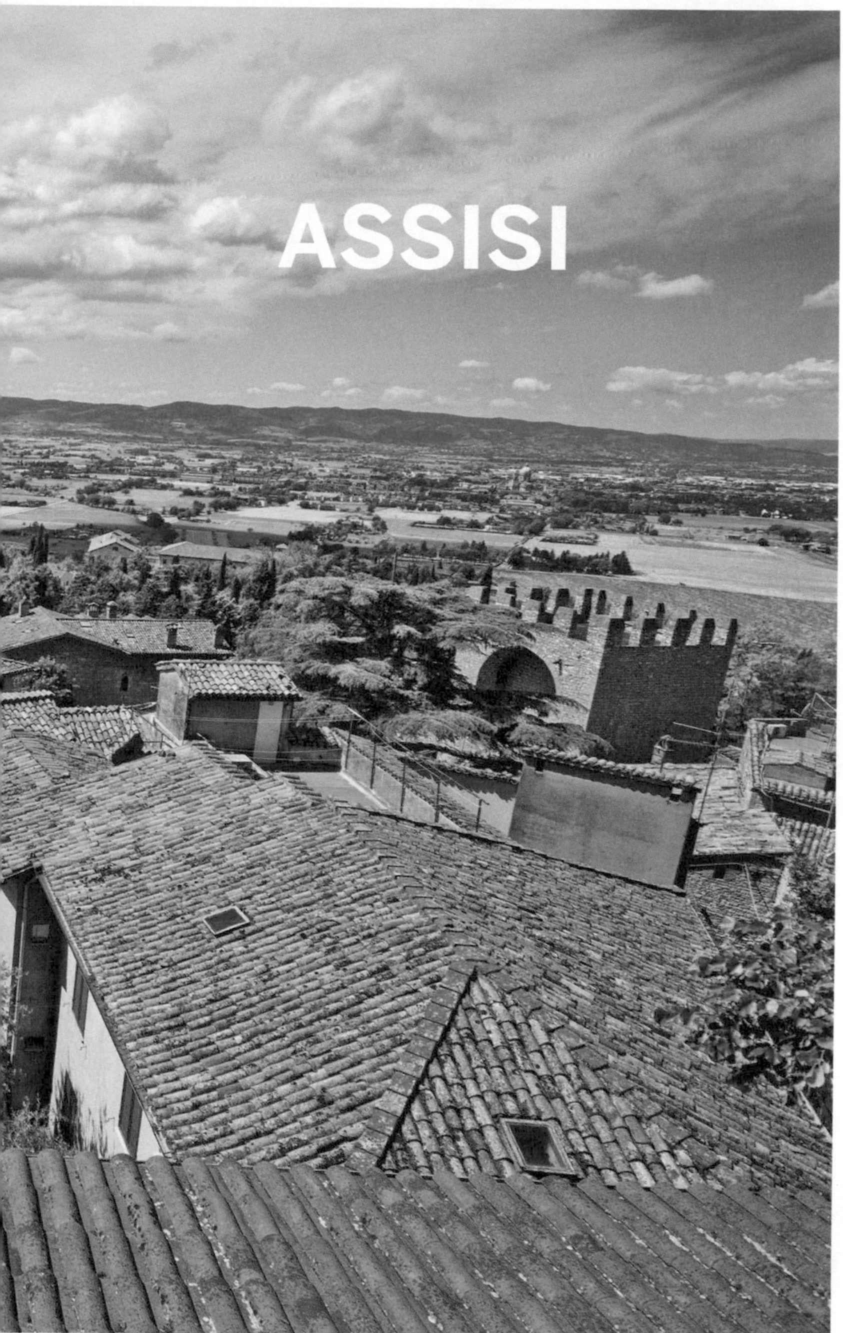

ASSISI

Assisi

As if cupped in celestial hands, with the plains spreading picturesquely below and Monte Subasio rearing steep and wooded above, the mere sight of Assisi in the rosy glow of dusk is enough to send pilgrims' souls spiralling to heaven. It is at this hour, when the pitter-patter of day-tripper footsteps have faded and the town is shrouded in saintly silence, that the true spirit of St Francis of Assisi, born here in 1181, can be felt most keenly.

The hilltop town is centred on Piazza del Comune in the heart of the medieval centro storico *(historic centre). From here, Via San Paolo and Via Portica both head towards the Basilica di San Francesco, the headline sight at the northwestern edge of town.*

☑ In This Section

🛈 Arriving in Assisi

Umbria Mobilità buses arrive at Piazza Matteotti from Perugia and Gubbio. Arriving from further afield, a daily Sulga bus runs to Porta San Pietro from Naples and two daily arrive from Rome's Stazione Tiburtina.

Hourly trains from Perugia (€2.40) stop at Assisi's train station, 4km west of town in Santa Maria degli Angeli. Half-hourly shuttle buses connect the station with Piazza Matteotti.

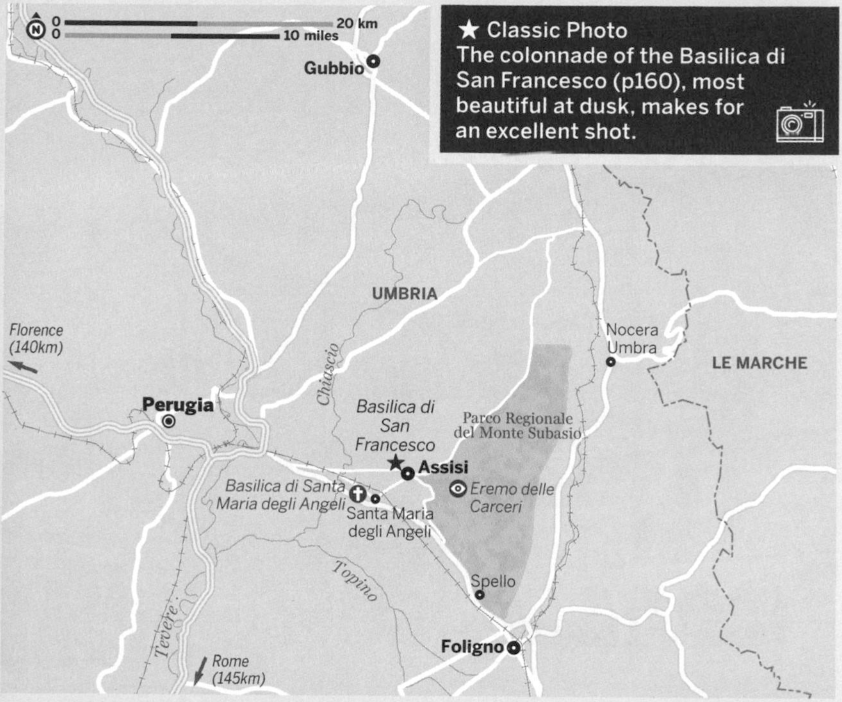

0 20 km
0 10 miles
Gubbio
UMBRIA
Florence (140km)
Perugia
Chiascio
Basilica di San Francesco
Assisi
Basilica di Santa Maria degli Angeli
Santa Maria degli Angeli
Parco Regionale del Monte Subasio
Eremo delle Carceri
Nocera Umbra
LE MARCHE
Topino
Spello
Tevere
Foligno
Rome (145km)

★ Classic Photo
The colonnade of the Basilica di San Francesco (p160), most beautiful at dusk, makes for an excellent shot.

From left: Eremo delle Carceri (p163); Assisi street; Piazza del Comune
JUERGEN RICHTER/GETTY IMAGES ©; BRUCE YUANYUE BI/GETTY IMAGES ©; BRUCE YUANYUE BI/GETTY IMAGES ©

Basilica di San Francesco

Visible for miles around, the Basilica di San Francesco is the crowning glory of Assisi's Unesco World Heritage ensemble. For almost six centuries it has been a beacon to pilgrims, brown-robed friars and saintly sightseers.

Great For...

☑ Don't Miss

An hour-long tour led by a Franciscan friar. Book at http://www.sanfrancescoassisi.org/

The Basilica is divided into two churches: the upper Basilica Superiore, with a celebrated cycle of Giotto frescoes, and beneath, the older Basilica Inferiore, where you'll find frescoes by Cimabue, Pietro Lorenzetti and Simone Martini. Also here, in the crypt, is St Francis' elaborate tomb.

Basilica Superiore

The Basilica Superiore, which was built between 1230 and 1253, is home to one of Italy's most famous works of art: the 28-fresco cycle *Life of St Francis* (1297–1300). This is widely attributed to Florentine master Giotto, though some art historians contest this, claiming that stylistic discrepancies suggest that it was created by several different artists.

Episodes from the life of the poverty-preaching saint are depicted in contemplative, emotive works such as the

Interior of the Basilica Superiore

XPACIFICA/GETTY IMAGES ©

Renunciation of Worldly Goods, *Miracle of the Spring* and *Death and Ascension of St Francis*. Above them, frescoes illustrate scenes from the Old and New Testament, from the *Creation of the World* through to the *Three Marys at the Sepulchre*.

Decay and oxidation have reduced Cimabue's frescoes (1280) in the apse and transepts to ghostly silhouettes, rendering them all the more enigmatic – look out for *The Crucifixion* showing St Francis kneeling below the cross.

Basilica Inferiore

From outside the upper church, steps lead down to the Romanesque Basilica Inferiore. The half-light and architectural restraint of this basilica beautifully embody the ascetic, introspective spirit of Franciscan life.

On entering the church, immediately to your left is the Cappella di San Martino,

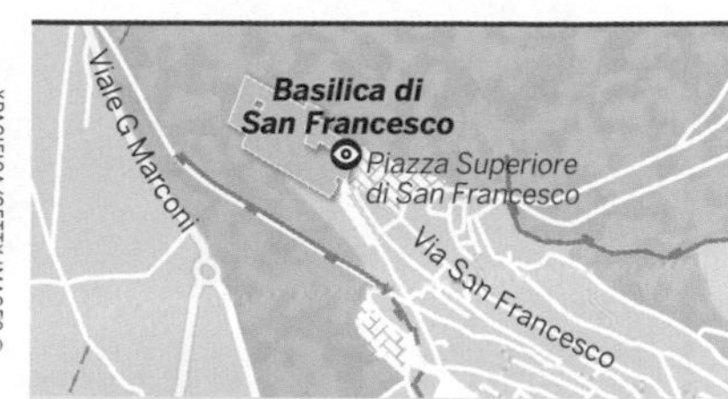

Need to Know

www.sanfrancescoassisi.org; Piazza di San Francesco; upper church 8.30am-6.45pm, lower church & tomb 6am-6.45pm; FREE

Take a Break

Wander back up to the centre for lunch at the **Osteria dei Priori** (p164).

★ Top Tip

The basilica has its own information office where you can schedule an hour-long tour. (Piazza di San Francesco 2; 9am-noon & 2-5.30pm Mon-Sat)

bearing the imprint of Sienese genius Simone Martini, whose 10-piece fresco cycle (1313–1318) spells out the life and deeds of St Martin of Tours. Pietro Lorenzetti's frescoes depicting *The Passion of Christ* (1320) dance across the walls of the left transept, while Cimabue's *Madonna Enthroned with Child, St Francis and Four Angels* (1289) adorns the right transept. The vault above the high altar showcases the quadriptych allegorical marvel of the *Quattro Vele* (1315–20), an ode to St Francis' virtues of poverty, chastity and obedience, alongside a fresco showing the saint's apotheosis.

Crypt

Beneath the church, the crypt is home to the **Tomb of St Francis**. Hidden for almost 600 years, it was discovered in 1818 following a 52-day dig, and painstakingly restored in 2011.

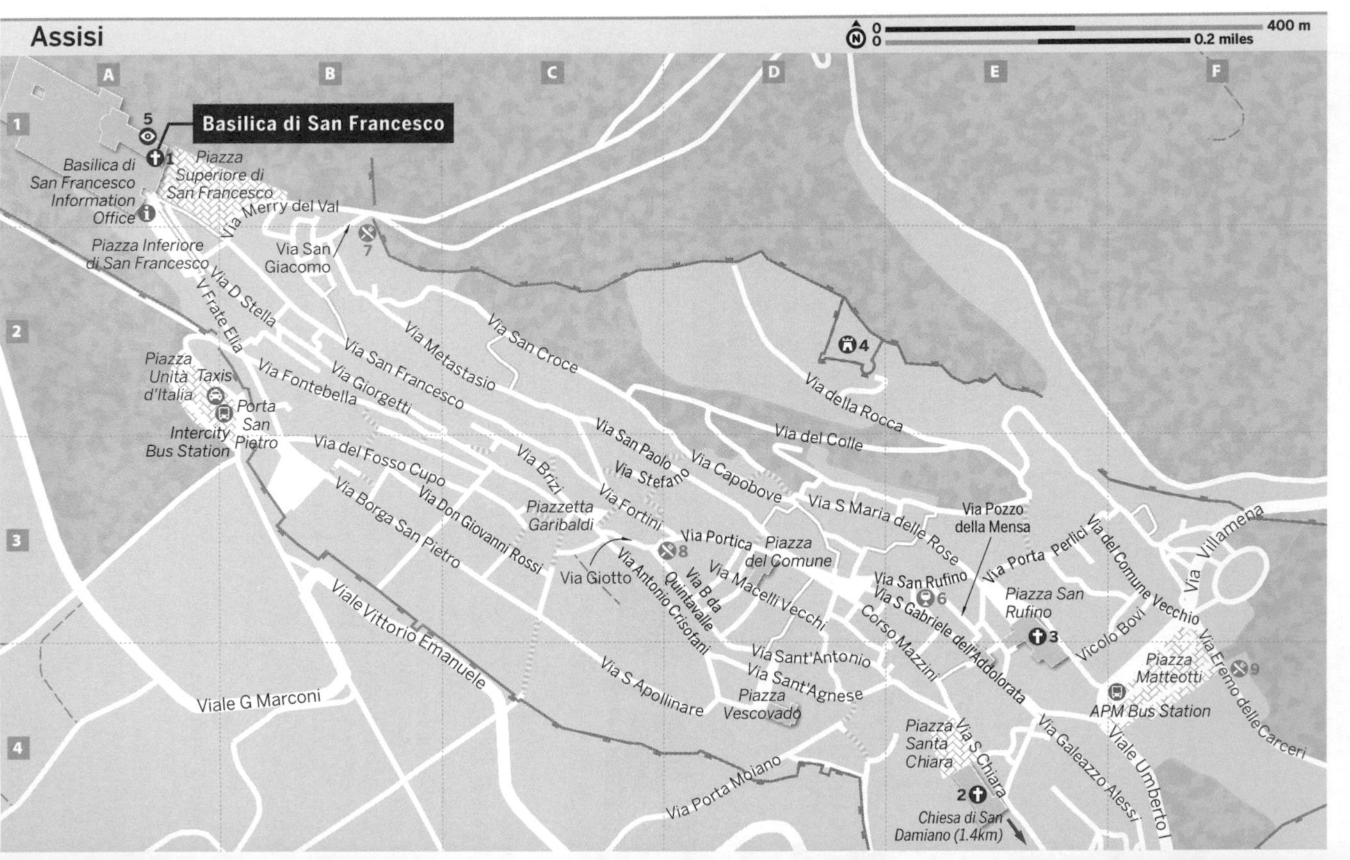
Assisi
0
0
400 m
0.2 miles
A
B
C
D
E
F
1
2
3
4
Basilica di San Francesco
Basilica di San Francesco
Information Office
Piazza Superiore di San Francesco
Via Merry del Val
Via San Giacomo
Piazza Inferiore di San Francesco
Via D Stella
V Frate Elia
Piazza Unità d'Italia
Taxis
Porta San Pietro
Intercity Bus Station
Via Fontebella
Via Giorgetti
Via San Francesco
Via Metastasio
Via San Croce
Via della Rocca
Via del Colle
Via del Fosso Cupo
Via Borga San Pietro
Via Don Giovanni Rossi
Via Brizi
Via San Paolo
Via Stefano
Via Capobove
Via Fortini
Piazzetta Garibaldi
Via Giotto
Via Antonio Crisofani
Via B da Quintavalle
Via Portica
Piazza del Comune
Via Macelli Vecchi
Via S Maria delle Rose
Via Pozzo della Mensa
Via Porta Perlici
Via del Comune Vecchio
Via Villamena
Via San Rufino
Via S Gabriele dell'Addolorata
Piazza San Rufino
Vicolo Bovi
Piazza Matteotti
APM Bus Station
Via Eremo delle Carceri
Corso Mazzini
Via Sant'Antonio
Via Sant'Agnese
Piazza Vescovado
Via S Apollinare
Viale Vittorio Emanuele
Viale G Marconi
Via Porta Moiano
Piazza Santa Chiara
Via S Chiara
Chiesa di San Damiano (1.4km)
Via Galeazzo Alessi
Viale Umberto I
1
2
3
4
5
6
7
8
9

Assisi

Sights

1 Basilica di San Francesco A1
2 Basilica di Santa Chiara E4
3 Duomo di San Rufino E3
4 Rocca Maggiore D2
5 Tomb of St Francis A1

Eating & Drinking

6 Bibenda Assisi E3
7 La Locanda del Podestà B2
8 Osteria dei Priori D3
9 Osteria Eat Out F4

SIGHTS

Rocca Maggiore — Fort

Dominating the city is the massive 14th-century Rocca Maggiore, an often-expanded, pillaged and rebuilt hill-fortress offering 360-degree views of Perugia to the north and the surrounding valleys below. Walk up winding staircases and claustrophobic passageways to reach the archer slots that served Assisians as they went medieval on Perugia. (Via della Rocca; adult/reduced €5.50/3.50; 10am-7pm, shorter hours winter)

Basilica di Santa Chiara — Basilica

Built in a 13th-century Romanesque style, with steep ramparts and a striking pink-and-white facade, this church is dedicated to St Clare, a spiritual contemporary of St Francis and founder of the Sorelle Povere di Santa Chiara (Order of the Poor Ladies), now known as the Poor Clares. She is buried in the church's crypt, alongside the Crocifisso di San Damiano, a Byzantine cross before which St Francis was praying when he heard from God in 1205. (Piazza Santa Chiara; 6.30am-noon & 2-7pm summer, to 6pm winter)

Basilica di Santa Maria degli Angeli — Church

That enormous domed church you can see as you approach Assisi along the Tiber Valley is the 16th-century Basilica di Santa Maria degli Angeli, the seventh-largest church in the world, some 4km west and several hundred metres further down the hill from old Assisi.

Built between 1565 and 1685, its vast ornate confines house the tiny, humble Porziuncola Chapel, where St Francis first took refuge having found his vocation and given up his worldly goods, and which is generally regarded as the place where the Franciscan movement started. St Francis died at the site of the Cappella del Transito on 3 October 1226. (Santa Maria degli Angeli; 6.15am-12.50pm & 2.30-7.30pm)

Eremo delle Carceri — Religious Site

In around 1205 St Francis chose these caves above Assisi as his hermitage where he could retire to contemplate spiritual matters and be at one with nature. The *carceri* (isolated places, or 'prisons') along Monte Subasio's forested slopes are as peaceful today as in St Francis' time, even though they're now surrounded by various religious buildings.

Take a contemplative walk or picnic under the oaks. It's a 4km drive (or walk) east of Assisi, and a dozen nearby hiking trails are well signposted. (6.30am-7pm summer, to 6pm winter) FREE

Chiesa di San Damiano — Church

It's a 1.5km olive-tree-lined stroll southeast of the centre to the church where St Francis first heard the voice of God and where he wrote his *Canticle of the Creatures*. The serene surroundings are popular with pilgrims. (Via San Damiano; 10am-noon & 2-6pm summer, to 4.30pm winter)

Duomo di San Rufino — Church

The 13th-century Romanesque church, remodelled by Galeazzo Alessi in the 16th century, contains the fountain where St Francis and St Clare were baptised. The facade is festooned with grotesque figures and fantastic animals. (Piazza San Rufino; 8am-1pm & 2-7pm summer, to 6pm winter)

ACTIVITIES

To really feel the spirituality of Assisi, do as St Francis did and make the pilgrimage into the surrounding wooded hills. Many make the trek to **Eremo delle Carceri** or **Santuario di San Damiano** on foot. The tourist office has several maps, including a route that follows in St Francis' footsteps to Gubbio (18km). A popular spot for hikers is nearby **Monte Subasio**. Local bookshops sell walking and mountain-biking guides and maps for the area.

EATING & DRINKING

Osteria Eat Out — Umbrian €€

With such astounding views and minimalist-chic interiors, you might expect Nun Assisi's glass-fronted restaurant to prefer style over substance. Not so. Polished service and an exciting wine list are well matched with seasonal Umbrian cuisine flavoured with home-grown herbs. Dishes like *umbricelli* pasta (spaghetti's Umbrian sister) with fresh truffle and fillet of Chianina beef are big on flavour and easy on the eye. (☎075 81 31 63; www.nunassisi.com; Via Eremo delle Carceri 1a; meals €35-50; ⏰12.30-2.30pm & 7.30-10.30pm Tue-Sun)

Osteria dei Priori — Umbrian €€

This wonderfully cosy *osteria* believes wholeheartedly in sourcing the best local ingredients. Tables draped in white linen are gathered under brick vaults. Presuming you've booked ahead, you're in for quite a treat: Umbrian specialities like *norcina* (pasta in a creamy mushroom-sausage sauce) and rich wild-boar stew are brilliantly fresh, full of flavour and beautifully presented. (☎075 81 21 49; Via Giotto 4; meals €25-35, 2-course day menu €18; ⏰12.30-2.30pm & 7.30-10pm Tue-Sun)

La Locanda del Podestà — Umbrian €€

This inviting cubby hole of a restaurant is big on old-world charm, with low arches and stone walls. Distinctly Umbrian dishes such as *torta al testo* with prosciutto and truffle-laced *strangozzi* pasta are expertly matched with regional wines. Friendly service adds to the familiar vibe. (☎075 81 65 53; www.locandadelpodesta.it; Via San Giacomo

Rocca Maggiore (p163)

6; meals €20-30; ⌚noon-2.45pm & 7-9.30pm Thu-Tue)

Bibenda Assisi Wine Bar

Everyone has been singing the praises of this rustic-chic wine bar recently. Here you can try regional *vini* with tasting plates of local *salumi e formaggi* (cured meats and cheeses). Nila will talk you through the wine list. (www.bibendaassisi.it; Via Nepis 9; ⌚11.30am-11pm Wed-Mon; 📶)

WHERE TO STAY

Keep in mind that in peak periods such as Settimana Santa (Easter week), August and September, and during the Festa di San Francesco (3 and 4 October), you will need to book accommodation well in advance. The tourist office has a list of private rooms, religious institutions (of which there are 17), flats and agriturismi (farmstay accommodation) in and around Assisi.

GETTING THERE & AROUND

BUS

Umbria Mobilità (www.umbriamobilita.it) buses run to Perugia (€4.20, 45 minutes, nine daily) and Gubbio (€6.10, 70 minutes, 11 daily) from Piazza Matteotti.

Sulga (www.sulga.it) buses leave from Porta San Pietro for Florence (€12, 2½ hours, one daily at 7am) and Rome's Stazione Tiburtina (€18.50, 3¼ hours, three daily).

TRAIN

Assisi is on the Foligno–Terontola train line with regular services to Perugia (€2.40, 24 minutes, hourly). You can change at Terontola for Florence (€15 to €22.50, two to three hours, 11 daily) and at Foligno for Rome (€10 to €22, two to three hours, 14 daily). Assisi's train station is 4km west in Santa Maria degli Angeli; shuttle bus C (€1.30, 13 minutes) runs between the train station and Piazza Matteotti every 30 minutes. Buy tickets from the station *tabaccaio* or in town.

St Francis

Born the son of a wealthy cloth merchant in 1181, Francis enjoyed a carefree youth, drinking and partying his way around town. But that all changed when he went off to fight against Perugia in his mid-20s and spent a year locked up in an enemy prison. Illness followed and he began to receive visions, culminating in the call from God, which famously came in 1209 at the Chiesa di San Damiano. According to legend, he heard the voice of Jesus on the cross instructing him to 'repair my church'. Taking this at its word, Francis sold his father's entire stock of cloth to pay for the repairs. When his father subsequently admonished him in front of the local bishop, Francis stripped off his clothes and renounced his former life.

He began walking the countryside and preaching the simple virtues of poverty and equal respect for everyone. Over time he developed a following and soon after he founded the Frati Minori, the order that subsequently became known as the Franciscans.

Francis spent the last years of his life embodying the tenets of what would later become the Franciscans' vows of poverty, chastity and obedience. In 1224 he received the stigmata, and two years later he died at the age of 44, lying on the mud floor of his simple Assisi hut.

Statue of St Francis
ROGER COULAM/GETTY IMAGES ©

VENICE

Venice

Imagine the audacity of deciding to build a city of marble palaces on a lagoon. Instead of surrendering to acque alte *(high tides) like reasonable folk might do, Venetians flooded the world with vivid painting, baroque music, modern opera, spice-route cuisine, bohemian-chic fashions and a Grand Canal's worth of spritz: the signature prosecco and Aperol cocktail.*

Today cutting-edge architects and billionaire benefactors are spicing up the art scene, musicians are rocking out 18th-century instruments and backstreet osterie *(taverns) are winning a Slow Food following. Your timing couldn't be better: the people who made walking on water look easy are well into their next act.*

☑ In This Section

Arriving in Venice

Marco Polo airport Located on the mainland 12km from Venice. Alilaguna operates a ferry service (€15) to Venice from the airport ferry dock. Water taxis cost from €110. Half-hourly buses (€6) connect with Piazzale Roma.

Stazione Santa Lucia Venice's train station. Vaporetti (small passenger boats) depart from Ferrovia (Station) docks.

Stazione Venezia Mestre The mainland train station; transfer here to Stazione Santa Lucia.

0 1 km
0 0.5 miles
Marco Polo Airport (8km); Treviso Airport (25km)
Sacca Serenella
Museo del Vetro
Murano
Venetian Islands
Canale delle Sacche
Canale delle Navi
Cimitero
Canale delle Navi
Isola di San Michele
Museo Ebraico
Chiesa della Madonna dell'Orto
Cannaregio
Canale delle Fondamente Nuove
Laguna Veneta
Isola del Tronchetto
Stazione di Santa Lucia (Ferrovia)
Stazione Merci
Santa Croce
Grand Canal
Chiesa di San Francesco della Vigna
Former Stazione Marittima (Merci)
Ponte di Calatrava
San Polo
Rialto
Basilica di San Marco
Grand Canal
Santa Marta
Cattedrale di San Pietro di Castello
Gallerie dell'Accademia
San Marco
Castello
Santa Marta
Old Stazione Marittima
Museo Storico Navale
La Tana
Arsenale
Isola di San Pietro
Palazzo Ducale
Canale di Fusina
Dorsoduro
Magazzini del Sale
Chiesa di San Giorgio Maggiore
Canale di San Marco
Giardini Pubblici
Sacca Fisola
Sacca Fisola
Canale della Giudecca
Sant'Elena
Chiesa delle Zitelle
Giudecca
Isola della Giudecca
Parco delle Rimembranze
Isola di Sant'Elena
San Marco & San Polo Map (p180)

➡ Venice in Two Days

Rise early to get to **Basilica di San Marco** (p172) and **Palazzo Ducale** (p174). Then choose between the **Gallerie dell'Accademia** (p176) or the **Peggy Guggenheim Collection** (p182). On day two, visit the **Ca' Rezzonico** (p183) and **Scuola Grande di San Rocco** (p183) before crossing the Ponte di Rialto to happy hour at **DOK dall'Ava LP26** (p190).

➡ Venice in Four Days

Begin with the **Museo Ebraico** (p183) synagogue tour, followed by Grand Canal views at **Ca' d'Oro** (p184) and the Tintorettos at the **Chiesa della Madonna dell'Orto** (p184). After lunch, cross canals to Castello's many-splendoured **Zanipolo** (p184) and the **Giardini Pubblici** (p185). On the fourth day island-hop to Murano, Burano and Torcello.

From left: Grand Canal (p170); Outside Stazione Santa Lucia; Basilica di San Marco (p172); Chiesa della Madonna dell'Orto (p184) PICAVET/GETTY IMAGES ©; PICAVET/GETTY IMAGES ©; WIBOWO RUSLI/GETTY IMAGES ©; MARCO BRIVIO/GETTY IMAGES ©

Grand Canal

Never was a thoroughfare so aptly named as the Grand Canal. Snaking through the heart of the city, Venice's signature waterway is flanked by a magnificent array of Gothic, Moorish, Renaissance and Rococo palaces.

Great For...

☑ **Don't Miss**

The Ponte di Rialto, the Palazzo Grassi and the iconic Basilica di Santa Maria della Salute

For most people, a trip down the Canal starts near the train station, near the Ponte di Calatrava. Officially known as the Ponte della Costituzione (Constitution Bridge), this contemporary bridge, designed by avant-garde Spanish architect Santiago Calatrava in 2008, is one of the few modern structures you'll see in central Venice.

To the Rialto

Leaving the bridge in your wake, one of the first landmarks you'll pass, on your left, is the arcaded Gothic facade of the Ca' d'Oro (p184), a 15th-century *palazzo* that now houses an art museum.

Ponte di Rialto & Around

A short way on, the **Ponte di Rialto** (Rialto Bridge; Rialto-Mercato) is the oldest of the four bridges that cross the canal. Built in the late 16th century to a monumental

Need to Know

Take *vaporetti* 1 or 2 from the Ferrovia; it takes 35 to 40 minutes to Piazza San Marco.

Take a Break

Jump off at Rialto and search out **Cantina Do Spade** (p194) for a cosy drink.

★ Top Tip

Avoid the crowds and tour the canal in the early evening or at night.

design by Antonio da Ponte, it links the *sestrieri* (districts) of San Marco and San Polo, and forms a popular vantage point for photographers. Nearby, local shoppers crowd to the Rialto market and Pescaria fish market.

Palazzo Grassi

The clean, geometric form of Palazzo Grassi (p186) comes into view on the first bend after the Rialto. A noble 18th-century palace, it now provides the neo-classical setting for show-stopping contemporary art. Over the water, the sumptuous Ca' Rezzonico (p183) is a model of baroque bombast with its lavish furnishings and decor.

Ponte dell'Accademia & Around

A couple of ferry stops further down and you arrive at the wooden Ponte dell'Accademia, a bridge with a simple design that seems strangely out of place amid Venice's fairy-tale architecture. Nearby, the Gallerie dell'Accademia (p176) is Venice's premier art gallery and the Peggy Guggenheim (p182) impresses with its collection of celebrated modern paintings.

Basilica di Santa Maria della Salute

The imperious dome of the Basilica di Santa Maria della Salute (p183) has been overlooking the canal's entrance since the 17th century. Impressive both outside and in, the basilica harbours a number of important works by local painter Titian. Beyond the basilica, the Punta della Dogana is a former customs warehouse that now stages contemporary-art exhibitions.

Piazza San Marco & Palazzo Ducale

You're now at the mouth of the canal, where you can disembark for Piazza San Marco. Dominating the waterside here is Palazzo Ducale (p174), the historic residence of the Venetian doges.

Basilica di San Marco

With its tapering spires, Byzantine domes, lavish marblework and 8500 sq metres of luminous mosaics, the Basilica di San Marco, Venice's signature basilica, is an unforgettable sight.

Great For...

☑ Don't Miss

Loggia dei Cavalli, where reproductions of the four bronze horses gallop off the balcony over Piazza San Marco.

The basilica dates to the 9th century, when, according to legend, two merchants smuggled the corpse of St Mark out of Egypt in a barrel of pork fat. When the original burnt down in 932 Venice rebuilt the basilica in its own cosmopolitan image, with Byzantine domes, a Greek-cross layout and walls clad in marbles from Syria, Egypt and Palestine.

Exterior & Portals

The front of the basilica ripples and crests like a wave, its five niched portals capped with shimmering mosaics and frothy stonework arches. In the far-left portal, lunette mosaics dating from 1270 show St Mark's stolen body arriving at the basilica. Grand entrances are made through the central portal, under an ornate triple arch with Egyptian purple porphyry columns and 13th- to 14th-century reliefs of vines, virtues and astrological signs.

Mosaics inside the Basilica di San Marco

LONELY PLANET/GETTY IMAGES ©

Need to Know

St Mark's Basilica; 041 270 83 11; www.basilicasanmarco.it; Piazza San Marco; 9.45am-5pm Mon-Sat, 2-5pm Sun summer, to 4pm Sun winter; San Marco FREE

Take a Break

Treat yourself to a *bellini* at world-famous **Harry's Bar** (041 528 57 77; Calle Vallaresso 1323; cocktails €12-22; 10.30am-11pm)

Top Tip

Booking your visit online at www.venetoinside.com (€2 booking fee) allows you to skip the queues.

Mosaics

Blinking is natural upon your first glimpse of the basilica's mosaics, many made with 24-carat gold leaf. Just inside the vestibule are the basilica's oldest mosaics: *Apostles with the Madonna*, standing sentry by the main door for more than 950 years. Mystical transfusions occur in the *Dome of the Holy Spirit*, where a dove's blood streams onto the heads of saints. In the central 13th-century *Cupola of the Ascension*, angels swirl overhead while dreamy-eyed St Mark rests on the pendentive. Scenes from St Mark's life unfold over the main altar, in vaults flanking the *Dome of the Prophets*.

Pala d'Oro

The latter mosaic is best seen from the **Pala d'Oro** (admission €2; 9.45am-5pm Mon-Sat, 2-5pm Sun summer, to 4pm winter; San Marco), an altarpiece studded with 2000 emeralds, amethysts, sapphires, rubies and pearls. It houses the sarcophagus of St Mark and is guarded by saints in vibrant cloisonné.

Tesoro & Museum

Holy bones and booty from the Crusades fill the **Tesoro** (Treasury; admission €3; 9.45am-5pm Mon-Sat, 2-5pm Sun summer, to 4pm winter; San Marco); while ducal treasures on show in the **museum** (Basilica di San Marco Museum; admission €5; 9.45am-4.45pm summer, to 3.45pm winter; San Marco) would put a king's ransom to shame. A highlight is the *Quadriga of St Mark's*, a group of four bronze horses originally plundered from Constantinople and later carted off to Paris by Napoleon before being returned to the basilica and installed in the 1st-floor gallery.

Palazzo Ducale

Gothic Palazzo Ducale was the doge's official residence from the 9th century onwards, and seat of the Venetian Republic's government (and prisons) for nearly seven centuries.

Great For...

Don't Miss

At the top of the Scala d'Oro is the face of a grimacing man with his mouth agape. This was a postbox for secret accusations.

After fire gutted the original palace in 1577, Venice considered Palladio's offer to build one of his signature neoclassical temples in its place. Instead, Antonio da Ponte won the commission to restore the palace's Gothic facade with white Istrian stone and Veronese pink marble, creating a marvellous, pink-chequered confection.

First Floor

Inside, climb the Scala dei Censori (Stairs of the Censors) to the Doge's Apartments on the first floor. The 18 roaring lions decorating the doge's Sala degli Stucci are reminders that Venice's most powerful figurehead lived like a caged lion in his gilded suite, which he could not leave without permission. The Sala del Scudo (Shield Room) is covered with world maps that reveal the extents of Venetian power c 1483 and 1762.

Need to Know

041 271 59 11; www.palazzo ducale.visitmuve.it; Piazzetta San Marco 52; incl Museo Correr adult/reduced €18/11; 8.30am-7pm summer, to 5.30pm winter; San Zaccaria

Take a Break

Drink in stunning views over cocktails at the **Bar Terazza Danieli** (041 522 64 80; www.starwoodhotels.com; Riva degli Schiavoni 4196; cocktails €18-22; 3-6.30pm mid-Apr–Oct ; San Zaccaria

Top Tip

Check www.palazzoducale.visitmuve.it for details of Secret Itineraries tours and special openings.

Second Floor

Ascend Sansovino's 24-carat gilt stucco work **Scala d'Oro** (Golden Staircase) and emerge into second-floor rooms covered with gorgeous propaganda. In the Palladio-designed Sala delle Quattro Porte (Hall of the Four Doors), ambassadors awaited ducal audiences under a display of Venice's virtues by Giovanni Cambi, Titian and Tiepolo.

Few were granted an audience in the Palladio-designed Collegio (Council Room), where Veronese's 1575–78 *Virtues of the Republic* ceiling shows Venice as a bewitching blonde waving her sceptre like a wand over Justice and Peace. Father-son team Jacopo and Domenico Tintoretto attempt similar flattery, showing Venice keeping company with Apollo, Mars and Mercury in their *Triumph of Venice* ceiling for the Sala del Senato (Senate Hall).

Government cover-ups were never so appealing as in the Sala Consiglio dei Dieci (Trial Chambers of the Council of Ten), where Venice's star chamber plotted under Veronese's *Juno Bestowing Her Gifts on Venice*. Arcing over the Sala della Bussola (Compass Room) is his *St Mark in Glory* ceiling.

Sala del Maggior Consiglio

The cavernous 1419 Sala del Maggior Consiglio (Grand Council Hall) provides the setting for Domenico Tintoretto's swirling *Paradise*, a work that's more politically correct than pretty: heaven is crammed with 500 prominent Venetians, including several Tintoretto patrons. Veronese's political posturing is more elegant in his oval *Apotheosis of Venice* ceiling, where gods marvel at Venice's coronation by angels, with foreign dignitaries and Venetian blondes rubbernecking on the balcony below.

The Return of the Prodigal Son by Palma Giovane

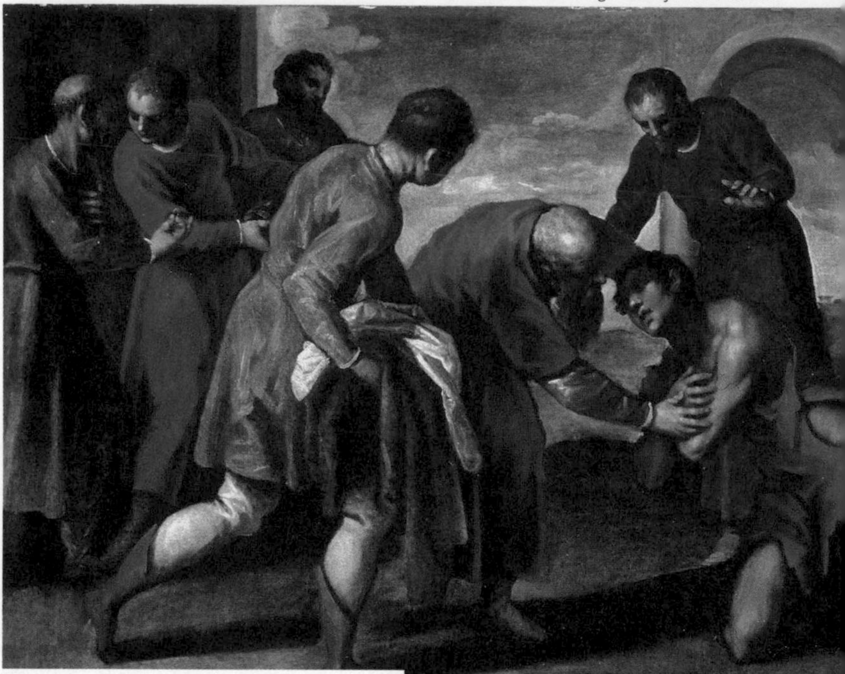

Gallerie dell'Accademia

The Gallerie dell'Accademia traces the development of Venetian art from the 14th to 18th centuries, with works by Bellini, Titian, Tintoretto, Veronese and Canaletto.

Great For...

Don't Miss

The Return of the Prodigal Son by Palma Giovane and Bernardo Strozzi's *Feast in the House of Simon*, in which a rather mischievous cat seems intent on stealing the spotlight from Jesus.

Early Works

The grand gallery you enter upstairs features vivid early works that show Venice's precocious flair for colour and drama. Case in point: Jacobello Alberegno's *Apocalypse* (Room 1) shows the whore of Babylon riding a hydra, babbling rivers of blood from her mouth. At the opposite end of the emotional spectrum is Paolo Veneziano's *Coronation of Mary* (Room 1), where Jesus bestows the crown on his mother with a gentle pat on the head to the tune of an angelic orchestra.

Rooms 2–23

UFO arrivals seem imminent in the eerie, glowing skies of Carpaccio's lively *Crucifixion and Glorification of the Ten Thousand Martyrs of Mount Ararat* (Room 2), which offers an intense contrast to Giovanni Bellini's quietly elegant *Madonna and Child*

Need to Know

041 520 03 45; www.gallerieaccademia.org; Campo della Carità 1050; adult/reduced €11/8 plus supplement during special exhibitions, first Sun of the month free; 8.15am-2pm Mon, to 7.15pm Tue-Sun; Accademia

Take a Break

Join the locals for delicious *cicheti* (bar snacks) at **Cantinone Già Schiavi** (p193).

★Top Tip

To skip ahead of the queues in high season, book tickets online (booking fee €1.50).

between St Catherine and Mary Magdalene (Room 4). Further along, Room 10 features paintings by Tintoretto and Titian, as well as Paolo Veronese's monumental *Feast in the House of Levi*, originally called Last Supper until Inquisition leaders condemned him for showing dogs and drunkards, among others, cavorting with Apostles.

While rooms 12 to 19 are occasionally used for temporary exhibitions, it's in Room 12 that you'll find Giambattista Piazzetta's saucy socialite in *Fortune Teller*. Yet even her lure is no match for the glorious works gracing Room 20. Among them is Gentile Bellini's *Procession in St Mark's Square*, which offers an intriguing view of Venice's iconic piazza before its 16th-century makeover. Room 21 is no less captivating, home to Vittore Carpaccio's *St Ursula Cycle*, a series of nine paintings documenting the saint's ill-fated life

The original convent chapel (Room 23) is a serene show-stopper fronted by a Bellini altarpiece. Sharing the space is Giorgione's highly charged *La Tempesta* (The Storm).

Sala dell'Albergo

The Accademia's grand finale is the newly restored Sala dell'Albergo, with a lavishly carved ceiling, Antonio Vivarini's wraparound 1441–50 masterpiece of fluffy-bearded saints, and Titian's touching 1534–39 *Presentation of the Virgin*. Here, a young, tiny Madonna trudges up an intimidating staircase while a distinctly Venetian crowd of onlookers point to her example – yet few of the velvet- and pearl-clad merchants offer alms to the destitute mother, or even feed the begging dog.

Venetian Islands

Where other cities have suburban sprawl, Venice has a teal blue northern lagoon dotted with small islands: Murano, the historic home of Venetian glass-making; Burano, with its colourful streets; and Torcello, the republic's original island settlement.

Great For...

Don't Miss

The Museo del Vetro in Murano.

Murano

Venetians have been working in crystal and glass since the 10th century, but due to the fire hazards of glass-blowing, the industry was moved to the island of Murano in the 13th century. Woe betide the glass-blower with wanderlust: trade secrets were so jealously guarded that any glass worker who left the city was guilty of treason and subject to assassination. Today, glass artisans ply their trade at workshops along the Fondamenta dei Vetrai marked by *Fornace* (furnace) signs. Tour a factory for a behind-the-scenes look at production or visit the **Museo del Vetro** (Glass Museum; ☎041 527 47 18; www.museovetro.visitmuve.it; Fondamenta Giustinian 8; adult/reduced €10.50/8; ⏰10am-6pm summer, to 5pm winter; Museo) in Palazzo Giustinian near the Museo *vaporetto* stop.

Murano

Vaporetto services 4.1 and 4.2 run to the island every 10 minutes throughout the day.

Burano

Venice's lofty Gothic architecture might leave you feeling slightly loopy, but Burano will bring you back to your senses with a reviving shock of colour. The 50-minute ferry ride (Line 12) from the Fondamente Nove is packed with photographers bounding into Burano's backstreets, snapping away at pea green stockings hung to dry between hot pink, royal blue and caution orange houses.

Burano is famed for its handmade lace, which once graced the décolletage and ruffs of European aristocracy. Some women still maintain the traditions, but few production houses remain – most of the lace for sale in local shops is of the imported, machine-made variety.

Need to Know

Regular *vaporetti* serve the is
from Fondamente Nove and Sa
Zaccaria.

Take a Break

Feast on fresh seafood at **Acquastanca** (041 319 51 25; www.acquastanca.it; Fondamenta Manin 48; meals €30-40; 9am-8pm Tue-Thu & Sat, to 11pm Mon & Fri; Faro) on Murano.

★Top Tip

Hit the outer islands first, then work your way back to Murano for the early evening.

Torcello

On the pastoral island of Torcello, a three-minute ferry-hop from Burano, sheep outnumber the 14 or so human residents. This bucolic backwater was the republic's original island settlement, growing over time to become a Byzantine metropolis of 20,000. Little has survived from this golden age, and of its original nine churches and two abbeys only the striking brick **Chiesa di Santa Fosca** (10am-4.30pm; Torcello) and splendid mosaic-filled **Basilica di Santa Maria Assunta** (041 73 01 19; Piazza Torcello; adult/reduced €5/4, incl museum €8/6, incl campanile €9; 10.30am-6pm summer, 10am-5pm winter; Torcello) remain.

From Fondamente Nuove, Line 12 runs every 15 minutes until midnight. Line 9 connects Torcello with Burano. Follow the path along the canal, Fondamenta Borgognoni, which leads you from the ferry stop to Torcello's basilica.

co & San Polo
B
C
D
2
3
4
5
6
SANTA CROCE
SAN POLO
DORSODURO
Grand Canal
Gallerie dell'Accademia
C Larga dei Bari
C Gallion
C Orsetti
Rio Marin
Rio di San Zan Degola
28
Chiesa di San Giacomo dell'Orio
Campo San Giacomo
C del Tintor
Saliz di San Stae
Fond delle Grue
Rio Pesaro
4
C Corner
C della Rosa
C del Tozzi
41
C d Regina
Rio di San Cassiano
37
C dei Botteri
C Raspi
Corte Canal
C del Tintor
C Filosi
Rio di S Boldo
C di Cristo
C del Scaleter
C d Chiesa
20
Rio di San Zuane
35
C della Vida
C Dona
Campiello Albrizzi
Campo San Stin
Rio di San Stin
C delle Chiovere
C Drio l'Archivio
C Corner
Campo Sant'Aponal
Campo San Polo
Rio di San Polo
Campo S Silvestro
Rio Terà
Rio dei Frari
C Nicoletto
Rio delle Sacchere
Campo San Rocco
7
Campo dei Frari
38
San Silvestro
14
33
C del Scaleter
Campiello Mosca
Campo San Tomà
C Crosera
Rio della Frescada
C Balbi
Campo S Pantalon
Rio di S Luca
C degli Avvocati
Campo S Beneto
Rio di Ca' Foscari
C della Chiesa
Campo Santa Margherita
Campiello dei Squellini
Ramo Lezze
C Crosera
Campiello Nuovo
C d Caffettier
Campo S Anzolo
C Bernardo
10
5
San Samuele
C dei Orbi
Fond Gherardini
25
Campo San Barnaba
24
Rio Malpaga
Rio del Duca
Campo Santo Stefano
Rio del Santissimo
C del Cerchieri
C Vitturi
Campo S Maurizio
Fond Corner Zaguri
22
Rio della Toletta
Campo di S Vidal
Rio dell'Orso
Campo di Santa Maria del Giglio
Ponte dell'Accademia
Palazzo Franchetti
Campo Traghetto
Fond di Borgo
Rio di San Trovaso
C della Chiesa
6
Rio Terà Carità
Grand Canal
Rio di Ognissanti
Campo S Trovaso
32
Piscina Forner
Campo San Vio
39
11
Ca' Dario
Rio della Fornace

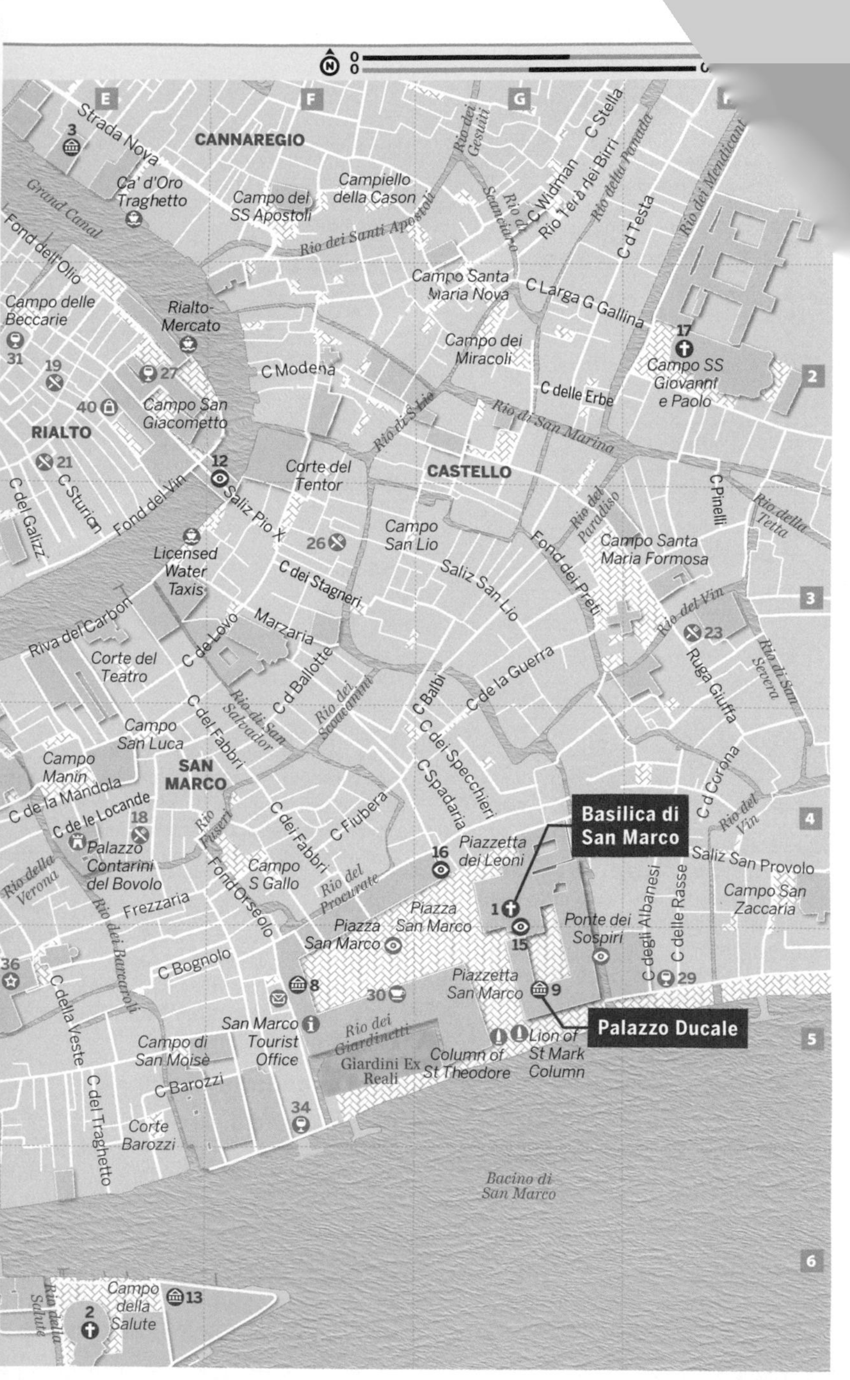

CANNAREGIO
Strada Nova
Ca' d'Oro Traghetto
Grand Canal
Fond dell'Olio
Campo del SS Apostoli
Campiello della Cason
Rio dei Santi Apostoli
Rio dei Gesuiti
C Widman
C Stella
Rio Terà dei Birri
Rio della Panada
C d Testa
Rio dei Mendicanti
Campo Santa Maria Nova
C Larga G Gallina
Campo delle Beccarie
Rialto-Mercato
Campo dei Miracoli
Campo SS Giovanni e Paolo
C Modena
C delle Erbe
Rio di S Lio
Rio di San Marina
Campo San Giacometto
RIALTO
CASTELLO
Corte del Tentor
C Pinelli
Rio della Tetta
C Sturion
C del Galizz
Fond del Vin
Saliz Pio X
Campo San Lio
Rio del Paradiso
Fond dei Preti
Campo Santa Maria Formosa
Licensed Water Taxis
C dei Stagneri
Saliz San Lio
Rio del Vin
Riva del Carbon
Marzaria
C de Lovo
Corte del Teatro
C d Ballotte
C Balbi
C de la Guerra
Ruga Giuffa
Rio di San Severa
Rio di San Salvador
Rio dei Scoacamini
Campo San Luca
C del Fabbri
C dei Specchieri
Campo Manin
SAN MARCO
C Spadaria
C Corona
C de la Mandola
C de le Locande
Rio Fuseri
C dei Fabbri
C Fiubera
Basilica di San Marco
Rio del Vin
Palazzo Contarini del Bovolo
Piazzetta dei Leoni
Saliz San Provolo
Rio della Verona
Campo S Gallo
Rio del Procurate
C degli Albanesi
C delle Rasse
Campo San Zaccaria
Frezzaria
Fond Orseolo
Piazza San Marco
Ponte dei Sospiri
Rio dei Barcaroli
C Bognolo
C della Veste
Piazzetta San Marco
San Marco Tourist Office
Palazzo Ducale
Rio dei Giardinetti
Lion of St Mark Column
Campo di San Moisè
Column of St Theodore
Giardini Ex Reali
C Barozzi
C del Traghetto
Corte Barozzi
Bacino di San Marco
Campo della Salute
Rio della Salute

[illegible]arco & San Polo

[illegible]ts

[illegible] [illegible]asilica di San Marco G4
Basilica di San Marco Museum .... (see 1)
2 Basilica di Santa Maria della Salute E6
3 Ca' d'Oro E1
4 Ca' Pesaro D1
5 Ca' Rezzonico B5
6 Gallerie dell'Accademia C6
7 I Frari B3
8 Museo Correr F5
9 Palazzo Ducale G5
10 Palazzo Grassi B5
11 Peggy Guggenheim Collection D6
12 Ponte di Rialto F2
13 Punta della Dogana E6
14 Scuola Grande di San Rocco A3
15 Tesoro G5
16 Torre dell'Orologio G4
17 Zanipolo H2

Eating

18 Ai Mercanti E4
19 All'Arco E2
20 Antiche Carampane D2
21 Dai Zemei E2
22 Enoteca Ai Artisti A5
23 Osteria Ruga di Jaffa H3
24 Ristorante La Bitta A5
25 Ristoteca Oniga A5
26 Rosticceria Gislon F3

Drinking & Nightlife

27 Al Mercà E2
28 Al Prosecco C1
29 Bar Terazza Danieli H5
30 Caffè Florian F5
31 Cantina Do Spade E2
32 Cantinone Già Schiavi B6
33 Estro A3
34 Harry's Bar F5

Entertainment

35 Palazetto Bru Zane B2
36 Teatro La Fenice E5

Shopping

37 Cárte D2
38 Gilberto Penzo C3
39 Marina e Susanna Sent C6
40 Pied à Terre E2
41 Veneziastampa C2

SIGHTS

Piazza San Marco & Around

Museo Correr — Museum

Napoleon filled his royal digs over Piazza San Marco with the riches of the doges, and took some of Venice's finest heirlooms to France as trophies. But the biggest treasure here couldn't be lifted: Jacopo Sansovino's 16th-century Libreria Nazionale Marciana, covered with larger-than-life philosophers by Veronese, Titian and Tintoretto, and miniature back-flipping sea creatures. (☎041 4273 0892; http://correr.visitmuve.it/; Piazza San Marco 52; incl Palazzo Ducale adult/reduced €18/11; ⏰10am-7pm summer, to 5pm winter; San Marco)

Torre dell'Orologio — Landmark

The two hardest-working men in Venice stand duty on a rooftop around the clock, and wear no pants. No need to file workers' complaints: the *Do Mori* (Two Moors) exposed to the elements atop the Torre dell'Orologio are made of bronze, and their bell-hammering mechanism runs like, well, clockwork. Below the Moors, Venice's gold-leafed 15th-century timepiece tracks lunar phases. (Clock Tower; ☎041 4273 0892; www.museicivicivenezian i.it; Piazza San Marco; adult/reduced with Museum Pass €12.50/7.50; ⏰tours in English 10am & 11am Mon-Wed, 2pm & 3pm Thu-Sun, in Italian noon & 4pm daily, in French 2pm & 3pm Mon-Wed, 10am & 11am Thu-Sun; San Marco)

Dorsoduro

Peggy Guggenheim Collection — Museum

After losing her father on the *Titanic*, heiress Peggy Guggenheim became one of the great collectors of the 20th century. Her palatial canalside home, Palazzo Venier dei Leoni, showcases her stockpile of surrealist, futurist and abstract expressionist art with works by up to 200 artists, including her ex-husband Max Ernst, Jackson Pollock (among her many rumoured lovers), Picasso and Salvador Dalí. (041 240 54 11; www.guggenheim-venice.it; Palazzo Venier dei Leoni 704; adult/reduced €15/9; 10am-6pm Wed-Mon; Accademia)

Ca' Rezzonico Museum

Baroque dreams come true at Baldassare Longhena's Grand Canal palace, where a marble staircase leads to gilded ballrooms, frescoed salons and sumptuous boudoirs. Giambattista Tiepolo's Throne Room ceiling is a masterpiece of elegant social climbing, showing gorgeous Merit ascending to the Temple of Glory clutching the Golden Book of Venetian nobles' names – including Tiepolo's patrons, the Rezzonico family. (Museum of the 18th Century; 041 241 01 00; www.visitmuve.it; Fondamenta Rezzonico 3136; adult/reduced €10.50/8, or Museum Pass; 10am-6pm Wed-Mon summer, to 5pm winter; Ca' Rezzonico)

Basilica di Santa Maria della Salute Basilica

Guarding the entrance to the Grand Canal, this 17th-century domed church was commissioned by Venice's plague survivors as thanks for salvation. Baldassare Longhena's uplifting design is an engineering feat that defies simple logic; in fact the church is said to have mystical curative properties. Titian eluded the plague until age 94, leaving 12 key paintings in the basilica's art-slung sacristy. (La Salute; 041 241 10 18; www.seminariovenezia.it; Campo della Salute 1b; admission free, sacristy adult/reduced €3/1.50; 9am-noon & 3-5.30pm; Salute)

San Polo & Santa Croce

I Frari Church

A soaring Italian-brick Gothic church, I Frari's assets include marquetry choir stalls, Canova's pyramid mausoleum, Bellini's achingly sweet *Madonna with Child* triptych in the sacristy and Longhena's creepy Doge Pesaro funereal monument. Upstaging them all, however, is the small altarpiece. This is Titian's lauded 1518 *Assunta* (Assumption), in which Madonna reaches heavenward, steps ont[illegible] and escapes this mortal coil. Titi[illegible] is buried here near his celebrated [illegible] piece. (Basilica di Santa Maria Gloriosa de[illegible] Campo dei Frari, San Polo 3072; adult/reduc[illegible] €3/1.50; 9am-6pm Mon-Sat, 1-6pm Sun; [illegible] San Tomà)

Scuola Grande di San Rocco Museum

Everyone wanted the commission to paint this building dedicated to the patron saint of the plague-stricken, so Tintoretto cheated: instead of producing sketches like rival Veronese, he gifted a splendid ceiling panel of patron St Roch, knowing it couldn't be refused or matched by other artists. The artist documents Mary's life story in the assembly hall, and both Old and New Testament scenes in the Sala Grande Superiore upstairs. (041 523 48 64; www.scuolagrandesanrocco.it; Campo San Rocco 3052, San Polo; adult/reduced €10/8; 9.30am-5.30pm, Tesoro to 5.15pm; San Tomà)

Ca' Pesaro Museum

Like a Carnevale costume built for two, the stately exterior of this Baldassare Longhena–designed 1710 *palazzo* hides two intriguing museums: Galleria Internazionale d'Arte Moderna and Museo d'Arte Orientale. While the former includes art showcased at the Venice Biennale, the latter holds treasures from Prince Enrico di Borbone's epic 1887–89 art-shopping spree across Asia. (Galleria Internazionale d'Arte Moderna e Museo d'Arte Orientale; 041 72 11 27; www.visitmuve.it; Fondamenta di Ca' Pesaro 2070, Santa Croce; adult/reduced €10.50/8; 10am-6pm Tue-Sun summer, to 5pm winter; San Stae)

Cannaregio

Museo Ebraico Museum

This museum explores the history of Venice's Jewish community through everyday artefacts, and showcases its pivotal contributions to Venetian, Italian and world history. Enquire at the museum for guided synagogue tours (adult/reduced €10/8 incl museum; four tours daily from 10.30am) to see inside three of the ghetto's seven

ues: the 1528 Schola Tedes-
an Synagogue), with a gilded, women's gallery modelled after a balcony; the 1531 Schola Canton ch Synagogue), with eight charm- andscapes taken from the biblical rables; and either the simple, dark-wood Schola Italiana (Italian Synagogue) or the still-active Schola Spagnola (Spanish Synagogue), with interiors attributed to Baldassare Longhena. (041 715 359; www.museoebraico.it; Campo del Ghetto Nuovo 2902b; adult/reduced €4/3; 10am-7pm Sun-Fri except Jewish holidays Jun-Sep, 10am-5.30pm Sun-Fri Oct-May; Guglie)

Chiesa della Madonna dell'Orto Church

This elegantly spare 1365 brick Gothic cathedral dedicated to the patron saint of travellers remains one of Venice's best-kept secrets. It was the parish church of Venetian Renaissance painter Tintoretto, who is buried here in the corner chapel and saved two of his finest works for the apse: *Presentation of the Virgin in the Temple* and his 1546 *Last Judgement*, where lost souls attempt to hold back a teal tidal wave while an angel rescues one last person from the ultimate *acqua alta*. (Campo della Madonna dell'Orto 3520; admission €2.50; 10am-5pm Mon-Sat; Madonna dell'Orto)

Ca' d'Oro Museum

Along the Grand Canal, you can't miss 15th-century Ca' d'Oro's lacy arcaded Gothic facade, resplendent even without the original gold-leaf details that gave the palace its name (Golden House). Baron Franchetti donated to Venice this treasure-box palace packed with masterpieces displayed upstairs in Galleria Franchetti, alongside Renaissance wonders plundered from Veneto churches during Napoleon's Italy conquest. (041 520 03 45; www.cadoro.org; Calle di Ca' d'Oro 3932; adult/reduced €9.50/6.50; 8.15am-2pm Mon, to 7.15pm Tue-Sun; Ca' d'Oro)

Castello

Zanipolo Basilica

When the Dominicans began building Zanipolo in 1333 to rival the Franciscans' I Frari, the church stirred passions more common to Serie A football than archi-

Ca' d'Oro

tecture. Both structures feature red-brick facades with high-contrast detailing in white stone. But since Zanipolo's facade remains unfinished, the Frari won a decisive early decision. Over the centuries, Zanipolo has at least tied the score with its pantheon of ducal funerary monuments and the variety of its masterpieces, including works by Bellini, Lorenzetti and Veronese. (Chiesa dei SS Giovanni e Paolo; ☎041 523 59 13; www.basilicasantigiovanniepaolo.it; Campo Zanipolo; adult/reduced €2.50/1.25; ⏲9am-6pm Mon-Sat, noon-6pm Sun, tours in English 5.30pm Thu; ⛴Ospedale)

Giardini Pubblici Gardens

Begun under Napoleon as the city's first green space, a large portion of these public gardens serves as the main home of the Biennale, with curators and curiosity-seekers swarming the pavilions, from Carlo Scarpa's daring 1954 raw-concrete-and-glass Venezuelan Pavilion to Denton Corker Marshall's 2015 Australian Pavilion in black Zimbabwean granite. Part of the gardens is open to the public all year; sometimes during off years you can wander among the pavilions and admire the facades. (www.labiennale.org; ⛴Giardini, Biennale)

Isola di San Giorgio Maggiore

Chiesa di San Giorgio Maggiore Church

Solar eclipses are only marginally more dazzling than Palladio's white Istrian marble facade. Begun in the 1560s, it owes more to ancient Roman temples than the bombastic baroque of Palladio's day. Inside, ceilings billow over a generous nave, with high windows distributing filtered sunshine. Two of Tintoretto's masterworks flank the altar, and a lift whisks visitors up the 60m-high bell tower for stirring Ventian panoramas – a great alternative to long lines at San Marco's *campanile* (bell tower) (☎041 522 78 27; Isola di San Giorgio Maggiore; bell tower adult/reduced €6/4; ⏲9.30am-12.30pm & 2.30-6.30pm Mon-Sat, 2-6.30pm Sun; ⛴San Giorgio Maggiore)

Making the Most of Your Euro

Civic Museum Pass (adult/reduced €24/18) Valid for single entry to 11 civic museums for six months, or just the five museums around Piazza San Marco (adult/child €17/10). Purchase online or at participating museums.

Chorus Pass (adult/reduced €12/8) Single entry to 16 Venice churches at any time within a year; on sale online or at church ticket booths.

Tourist City Pass (adult/reduced €39.90/29.90) Combines the Museum Pass and Chorus Pass as well as reduced entry to the Guggenheim Collection and the Biennale, plus other discounts. Purchase at tourist offices or at www.veneziaunica.it.

Rolling Venice (14 to 29 years €4) Entitles young visitors to discounted access to monuments and cultural events, plus eligibility for a 72-hour public-transport pass for €18. Identification is required for purchase at tourism offices or at most ACTV public-transport ticket booths.

Fondazione Giorgio Cini Museum

A defunct naval academy has been converted into this shipshape gallery . After escaping the Dachau internment camp with his son Giorgio, Vittorio Cini returned to Venice on a mission to save San Giorgio Maggiore, which was a ramshackle mess in 1949. Cini's foundation restored the island into a cultural centre. In addition to its permanent collection of Old Masters and modern art, the gallery hosts important contemporary works, from Peter Greenaway to Anish Kapoor. (☎041 220 12 15; www.cini.it; Isola di San Giorgio Maggiore; adult/reduced incl guided tour €10/8; ⏲guided tours 10am-5pm Sat & Sun; ⛴San Giorgio Maggiore)

The Lido

Only 15 minutes by *vaporetti* 1, 5.1, 5.2, 6, 10 (summer only) and N from San Marco, the Lido has been the beach and bastion

Contemporary Art

…nta della Dogana Gallery

…nice's long-abandoned customs warehouses reopened in 2009 after a striking reinvention by Tadao Ando. The dramatic space now hosts rotating exhibitions of ambitious, large-scale contemporary artworks from some of the world's most prolific and provocative creative minds. (www.palazzograssi.it; adult/reduced €15/10, incl Palazzo Grassi €20/15; 10am-7pm Wed-Mon; Salute)

Palazzo Grassi Museum

Grand Canal gondola riders gasp at first glimpse of massive sculptures by contemporary artists like Thomas Houseago docked in front of Giorgio Masari's 1749 neoclassical palace. French billionaire François Pinault's provocative art collection overflows Palazzo Grassi, but despite the artistic glamour, Tadao Ando's creatively repurposed interior architecture steals the show. (www.palazzograssi.it; Campo San Samuele 3231; adult/reduced €15/10; 10am-7pm Wed-Mon mid-Apr–Nov; San Samuele)

Magazzini del Sale Gallery

A retrofit designed by Pritzker Prize–winning architect Renzo Piano transformed Venice's historic salt warehouses into Fondazione Vedova art galleries, commemorating pioneering Venetian abstract painter Emilio Vedova. Fondazione Vedova shows are often literally moving and rotating: powered by renewable energy sources, 10 robotic arms move major modern artworks in and out of storage slots. (www.fondazionevedova.org; Fondamenta delle Zattere 266; adult/reduced €8/6; during shows 10.30am-6pm Wed-Mon; Zattere)

of Venice for centuries. In the 19th century, it found a new lease of life as a glamorous bathing resort, attracting monied Europeans to its grand Liberty-style hotels. Thomas Mann's novel *Death in Venice* was set here, and you'll spot plenty of ornate villas that date from those decadent days. Walking itineraries around the most extravagant are available to download at www2.comune.venezia.it/lidoliberty.

Lido beaches, such as the Blue Moon complex, line the southern, seaward side of the island and are easily accessed from the *vaporetto* down the Gran Viale. To head further afield, hire a bike from **Lido on Bike** (041 526 80 19; www.lidoonbike.it; Gran Viale 21b; bikes per hour/day €5/9; 9am-7pm; Lido) and cycle south across the Ponte di Borgo to tiny Malamocco, a miniature version of Venice right down to the lions of St Mark on medieval facades.

ACTIVITIES

A **gondola trip** (041 528 50 75; www.gondolavenezia.it) is anything but pedestrian, with glimpses into *palazzi* courtyards and hidden canals otherwise invisible on foot. Official daytime rates are €80 for 40 minutes (six passengers maximum), and it's €100 between 7pm and 8am, not including songs (negotiated separately) or tips. Additional time is charged in 20-minute increments (day/night €40/50). You may negotiate a price break in low season, overcast weather or around midday, when other travellers get hot and hungry. Agree on a price, time limit and singing in advance to avoid surcharges. Gondolas cluster at *stazi* (stops) along the Grand Canal, at the train station, the Rialto and near major monuments (eg I Frari, Ponte Sospiri and Accademia), but you can also book a pick-up by calling the main number.

TOURS

The tourist office (p195) can set you up with authorised tour guides and can book well-priced tours.

Venice Day Trips Cultural Tour

A fantastic selection of off-the-shelf and customised tours run by the ebullient Mario, Rachel and Silvia. Keen to show you the genuine face of the Veneto, these bite-sized tours range from cooking classes in Cannaregio to cheese-making on Monte Veronese and tutored wine tastings (Mario and Rachel are qualified sommeliers). Pick-up is from the Isola di Tronchetto *vaporetto* stop in Venice. (☎049 60 06 72; www.venicedaytrips.com; Via Saetta 18, Padua; semi-private/private tours per person from €165/275)

Walks Inside Venice Walking Tour

A spirited team runs both private tours (maximum six people) and public group tours (maximum eight people) exploring the city's major monuments and hidden backstreets. Group tours include explorations of the San Marco and San Polo, while private tour options include contemporary art and photography, and Venice's lagoon islands. (☎041 524 17 06; www.walksinsidevenice.com; 2½hr group tours per person €60; 👪)

Terra e Acqua Boat Tour

Eco-friendly Terra e Acqua offers wild rides to the outer edges of the lagoon. Itineraries are customised, and can cover abandoned plague-quarantine islands, fishing a[nd] birdwatching hot spots, Burano and Torcello. Lunch is served on board or a[t a] local trattoria, and trips accommodate u[p] to 12 people on a sunny, sturdy motorise[d] *bragozzo* (a flat-bottomed fishing and cargo vessel typical of the Adriatic), making trips sociable and easygoing for those not accustomed to boats. (☎347 4205004; www.veneziainbarca.it; ⏲day trips incl lunch for 9-12 people €380-460; 👪) 🌿

Row Venice Boat Tour

The next-best thing to walking on water: rowing a traditional *batellina coda di gambero* (shrimp-tailed boat) standing up like gondoliers do. Tours must be pre-booked and commence at the wooden gate of the Sacca Misericordia boat marina at the end of Fondamenta Gasparo Contarini in Cannaregio. (☎347 7250637; www.rowvenice.org; 90min lessons 1-2 people €80, 4 people €120)

> *"a marble staircase leads to gilded ballrooms and sumptuous boudoirs"*

Ca' Rezzonico (p183)

OPPING

Terre Shoes

courtesans and their 30cm-high s are long gone, but Venetian slippers ay stylish. Pied à Terre's colourful *furlane* slippers) are handcrafted with recycled bicycle-tyre treads, ideal for finding your footing on a gondola. Choose from velvet, brocade or raw silk in vibrant shades of lemon and ruby, with optional piping. Don't see your size? Shoes can be custom made and shipped. (041 528 55 13; www.piedaterre-venice.com; Sotoportego degli Oresi 60, San Polo; 10am-12.30pm & 2.30-7.30pm; Rialto)

Cárte Handicrafts

Venice's shimmering lagoon echoes in marbled-paper earrings and artist's portfolios, thanks to the steady hands and restless imagination of *carta marmorizzata* (marbled-paper) *maestra* Rosanna Corrò. After years restoring ancient Venetian books, Rosanna began creating her original, bookish beauties: tubular statement necklaces, op-art jewellery boxes, one-of-a-kind contemporary handbags, even wedding albums. (320 0248776; www.cartevenezia.it; Calle dei Cristi 1731, San Polo; 11am-5.30pm; Rialto-Mercato)

Gilberto Penzo Handicrafts

Yes, you actually can take a gondola home in your pocket. Anyone fascinated by the models at the Museo Storico Navale will go wild here, amid handmade wooden models of all kinds of Venetian boats, including some that are seaworthy (or at least bath-tub worthy). Signor Penzo also creates kits so crafty types and kids can have a crack at it themselves. (041 71 93 72; www.veniceboats.com; Calle 2 dei Saoneri 2681, San Polo; 9am-12.30pm & 3-6pm Mon-Sat; ; San Tomà)

Marina e Susanna Sent Glass

Wearable waterfalls and unpoppable soap-bubble necklaces are Venice style signatures, thanks to the Murano-born Sent sisters. Defying centuries-old beliefs that women can't handle molten glass, their minimalist art-glass statement jewellery is featured in museum stores worldwide, from Palazzo Grassi to MoMA. See new collections at this flagship, their Murano

studio, or the San Marco branch (at Ponte San Moise 2090). (041 520 81 36; www.marinaesusannasent.com; Campo San Vio 669; 10am-1pm & 1.30-6.30pm; Accademia)

ENTERTAINMENT

To find out what's on the calendar in Venice during your visit, check listings in free mags distributed citywide and online: *VeNews* (www.venezianews.it), *Venezia da Vivere* (www.veneziadavivere.com) and *2Venice* (www.2venice.it).

Teatro La Fenice Opera

La Fenice (041 78 65 11, theatre tours 041 78 66 75; www.teatrolafenice.it; Campo San Fantin 1965; theatre visits adult/reduced €9/6, concert/opera tickets from €15/45; tours 9.30am-6pm; Santa Maria dei Giglio), one of Italy's top opera houses, hosts a rich program of opera, ballet and classical music. With advance booking you can tour the theatre, but the best way to see it is with the *loggionisti* (opera buffs in the cheap top-tier seats).

Get tickets at the theatre, online or through **HelloVenezia** (041 24 24; Piazzale Roma; transport tickets 7am-8pm, events tickets 8.30am-6.30pm; Piazzale Roma).

Palazetto Bru Zane Classical Music

Pleasure palaces don't get more romantic than Palazetto Bru Zane on concert nights, when exquisite harmonies tickle Sebastiano Ricci angels tumbling across stucco-frosted ceilings. Multi-year restorations returned the 1695–97 Casino Zane's 100-seat music room to its original function, attracting world-class musicians to enjoy its acoustics from late September to mid-May. (Centre du Musique Romantique Française; 041 521 10 05; www.bru-zane.com; Palazetto Bru Zane 2368, San Polo; adult/reduced €15/5; box office 2.30-5.30pm Mon-Fri, closed late Jul–mid-Aug; San Tomà)

EATING

Piazza San Marco & Around

Rosticceria Gislon Venetian, Deli €

Serving San Marco workers since the 1930s, this no-frills *roticceria* has an ultramarine canteen counter downstairs and a small eat-in restaurant upstairs. Hot to trot you'll find *arancini* (rice balls), deep-fried

★ Top Five for Venetian Food

All'Arco (p191)
Trattoria Corte Sconta (p192)
Antiche Carampane (p191)
Ristoteca Oniga (p190)
Dai Zemei (p191)

From left: Gondolas; Baroque bookcase, Scuola Grande di San Rocco (p183); Venetian glass

zzarella balls, croquettes and fish fry-ps. No one said it was going to be healthy! hose with more time might indulge in surprisingly good seafood risottos, grilled cuttlefish and, of course, the perennially popular roast chicken. (☎0415 22 35 69; Calle de la Bissa 5424; meals €15-25; ⏰9am-9.30pm Tue-Sun, to 3.30pm Mon; ⛴Rialto)

Ai Mercanti Osteria **€€**

With its pumpkin coloured walls, gleaming golden fixtures and jet black tables and chairs, Ai Mercanti effortlessly conjures up a romantic mood. No wonder dates whisper over glasses of Veneto wines from the 300-plus bottles in the wine cellar before ordering contemporary dishes of risotto with mullet and nori. If you fancy something simpler, opt instead for the superb 'smokey' burger and a glass of Barolo. (☎041 523 82 69; www.aimercanti.com; Corte Coppo 4346/A; meals €40-45; ⏰noon-3pm & 7-11pm Tue-Sat, 7-11pm Mon; ⛴Rialto)

> “cicheti *are some of the best culinary finds in Italy*”

Dorsoduro

Ristorante La Bitta Ristorante **€€**

Recalling a cosy, woody bistro, La Bitta keeps punters purring with hearty rustic fare made using the freshest ingredients – the fact that the kitchen has no freezer ensures this. Scan the daily menu for mouthwatering, seasonal options like tagliatelle with artichoke thistle and gorgonzola or juicy pork *salsiccette* (small sausages) served with *verze* (local cabbage) and warming polenta. Reservations essential. Cash only. (☎041 523 05 31; Calle Lunga San Barnaba 2753a; meals €35-40; ⏰6.45-10.45pm Mon-Sat; ⛴Ca' Rezzonico)

Ristoteca Oniga Venetian **€€**

Its menu peppered with organic ingredients, Oniga serves exemplary *sarde in saor* (sardines in tangy onion marinade), seasonal pastas, and the odd Hungarian classic like goulash (a nod to former chef Annika Major). Oenophiles will appreciate the selection of 100-plus wines, handy for toasting to the €19 set lunch menu. Grab a sunny spot in the *campo,* or get cosy in a wood-panelled corner. (☎041 522 44 10;

Dining by the Grand Canal

www.oniga.it; Campo San Barnaba 2852; meals €19-35; noon-2.30pm & 7-10.30pm Wed-Mon; ; Ca' Rezzonico)

Enoteca Ai Artisti Italian **€€€**

Indulgent cheeses, exceptional *nero di seppia* (cuttlefish ink) pasta, and tender *tagliata* (sliced steak) drizzled with aged balsamic vinegar atop arugula are paired with exceptional wines by the glass by your gracious oenophile hosts. Pavement tables for two make great people-watching, but book ahead for indoor tables for groups; space is limited. Note: only turf (no surf) dishes on Mondays. (041 523 89 44; www.enotecaartisti.com; Fondamenta della Toletta 1169a; meals €45; noon-3pm & 7-10pm Mon-Sat; Ca' Rezzonico)

San Polo & Santa Croce

Dai Zemei Venetian, Cicheti **€**

Running this closet-sized *cicheti* counter are *zemei* (twins) Franco and Giovanni, who serve loyal regulars small meals with outsized imagination: gorgonzola lavished with *peperoncino* (chilli) marmalade, duck breast drizzled with truffle oil, or chicory paired with leek and marinated anchovies. A gourmet bargain for inspired bites and impeccable wines – try a crisp Nosiola or invigorating Prosecco Brut. (041 520 85 46; www.ostariadaizemei.it; Ruga Vecchia San Giovanni 1045, San Polo; cicheti from €1.50; 8.30am-8.30pm Mon-Sat, to 7pm Sun; San Silvestro)

All'Arco Venetian **€**

Search out this authentic neighbourhood *osteria* (casual tavern) for some of the best *cicheti* in town. Armed with ingredients from the nearby Rialto market, father-son team Francesco and Matteo serve miniature masterpieces such as *cannocchia* (mantis shrimp) with pumpkin and roe, and *otrega* (butterfish) *crudo* with mint-and-olive-oil marinade. (041 520 56 66; Calle dell'Ochialer 436, San Polo; cicheti from €1.50; 8am-8pm Wed-Fri, to 3pm Mon, Tue & Sat; Rialto-Mercato)

Cicheti, Bar Snacks Venetian-Style

Even in unpretentious Venetian *osterie* and *bacari* most dishes cost a couple of euros more than they might elsewhere in Italy – not a bad mark-up really, considering all that fresh seafood and produce is brought in by boat. But *cicheti* are some of the best culinary finds in Italy, served at lunch and from around 6pm to 8pm with sensational Veneto wines by the glass. *Cicheti* range from basic bar snacks (spicy meatballs, fresh tomato and basil bruschetta) to highly inventive small plates: think white Bassano asparagus and plump lagoon shrimp wrapped in pancetta or pungent gorgonzola paired with sweet, spicy *peperoncino* (chilli).

Prices start at €1 for tasty meatballs and range from €3 to €6 for gourmet fantasias with fancy ingredients, typically devoured standing up or perched atop stools at the bar. Nightly *cicheti* spreads could easily pass as dinner.

Antiche Carampane Venetian **€€**

Hidden in the once-shady lanes behind Ponte delle Tette, this culinary indulgence is a trick to find. Once you do, say goodbye to soggy lasagne and hello to a market-driven menu of silky *crudi* (raw fish/seafood), surprisingly light *fritto misto* (fried seafood) and caramote prawn salad with seasonal vegetables. As it's never short of a smart, convivial crowd, it's a good idea to book ahead. (041 524 01 65; www.antichecarampane.com; Rio Terà delle Carampane 1911, San Polo; meals €30-45; 12.45-2.30pm & 7.30-10.30pm Tue-Sat; San Stae)

Cannaregio

Dalla Marisa Venetian **€€**

At this Cannaregio institution, you'll be seated where there's room and get no menu – you'll have whatever Marisa's

Eating & Drinking Like a Venetian

Venice Urban Adventures Food Tour

Why drink alone? Venice Urban Adventures offers intimate tours of happy-hour hot spots led by knowledgable, enthusiastic, English-speaking local foodies. Tours run €77 per person (with up to 12 participants), covering *ombre* (wine by the glass) and *cicheti* in five (yes, five) *bacari* and a tipsy Rialto gondola ride (weather permitting). Tours depart from Campo della Maddalena in Cannaregio and end at Ponte di Rialto (Rialto Bridge). (348 980 85 66; www.veniceurbanadventures.com; cicheti tour €77; tours 11.30am & 5.30pm Mon-Sat)

Cook in Venice Food Tour, Course

If you want to learn to cook like an Italian mama or eat like a Venetian gondolier look no further than Monica and Arianna's cookery classes and food tours. These two Venetian cooks are a tour de force: welcoming, engaging teachers and connoisseurs of Venetian food and wine. Whipping up polpette or zabaglione in Arianna's country home is a truly memorable experience, while Monica's food tours have earned high praise from Katie Caldesi, Alex Polizzi and numerous well-fed chefs! (www.cookinvenice.com; tours €35-60, courses €140-225)

cooking. And you'll like it. Lunches are a bargain at €15 for a first, main, side, wine, water and coffee – pace yourself through prawn risotto to finish steak and grilled zucchini, or Marisa will jokingly scold you over coffee. (041 72 02 11; Fondamenta di San Giobbe 652b, Cannaregio; set menus lunch/dinner €15/35; noon-3pm daily & 7-11pm Tue & Thu-Sat; Crea)

Da Rioba Modern Italian €€€

Taking the lead with interesting spices and herbs pulled from the family's Sant'Erasmo farm, da Rioba's inventive kitchen turns out exquisite plates as colourful and creative as the artwork on the walls. This is prime date-night territory. In winter enjoy goose carpaccio with dried fruits in the cosy wood-beamed interior, and in summer sit canalside with a plate of pretty fish fillet 'flowers' marinated in aromatic herbs. Reservations recommended. (041 524 43 79; www.darioba.com; Fondamenta della Misericordia 2553; meals €45-60; 12.30-2.30pm & 7.30-11pm Tue-Sun; San Marcuola)

Castello

Osteria Ruga di Jaffa Osteria €

Hiding in plain sight on the busy Ruga Giuffa is this excellent *osteria*. You should be able to spot it by the gondoliers packing out the tables at lunchtime. They may not appreciate the vase of blooming hydrangeas on the bar or the artsy Murano wall lamps, but they thoroughly approve of the select menu of housemade pastas and succulent oven-roast pork soaked in its own savoury juices. (Ruga Giuffa 4864; meals €20-25; 8am-11pm)

Trattoria Corte Sconta Modern Venetian €€€

Well-informed visitors and celebrating locals seek out this vine-covered *corte sconta* (hidden courtyard) for its trademark seafood antipasti and imaginative house-made pasta. Inventive flavour pairings transform the classics: clams zing with the hot, citrus-like taste of ginger; prawn and zucchini linguine is recast with an earthy dash of saffron; and the roast eel loops like the Brenta river in a drizzle of balsamic reduction. (041 522 70 24; Calle del Pestrin 3886; meals €50-65; 12.30-2.30pm & 7-9.30pm Tue-Sat, closed Jan & Aug; Arsenale)

Giudecca

Trattoria Altanella Venetian €€€

In 1920 fisherman Nane Stradella and his wife, Irma, opened a trattoria overlooking the Rio di Ponte Longo. Their fine Venetian cooking was so successful he soon gave up fishing and the restaurant now sustains a fourth generation of family cooks. Inside, the vintage interior is hung with artworks, reflecting the restaurant's popularity with artists, poets and writers, while outside a flower-fringed balcony hangs over the canal. Eat Irma's potato gnocchi with cuttlefish or Nane's enduringly good John Dory fillet. (041 522 77 80; Calle delle Erbe 268; meals €35-45; noon-2.30pm & 7-10.30pm Tue-Sat; Palanca)

The Lido

La Favorita Seafood **€€**

For long, lazy lunches, bottles of fine wine and impeccable service, look no further than La Favorita. The menu is as elegant as the surroundings, including giant *rhombo* (turbot) simmered with capers and olives, spider-crab *gnochetti* (mini-gnocchi) and classic fish risotto. Book ahead for the wisteria-filled garden and well ahead during the film festival, when songbirds are practically out-sung by the ringtones of movie moguls. (041 526 16 26; Via Francesco Duodo 33; meals €35-45; 12.30-2.30pm & 7-10.30pm Fri-Sun, 7-10.30pm Tue-Thu; Lido)

DRINKING & NIGHTLIFE

Piazza San Marco & Around

Caffè Florian Cafe

One of Venice's most famous cafes, Florian maintains rituals (if not prices) established c 1720: white-jacketed waiters serve cappuccino on silver trays, lovers canoodle in plush banquettes and the orchestra strikes up a tango as the sunset illuminates San Marco's mosaics. Piazza seating during concerts costs €6 extra, but dreamy-eyed romantics hardly notice. (041 520 56 41; www.caffeflorian.com; Piazza San Marco 56/59; drinks €10-25; 9am-midnight; San Marco)

Dorsoduro

Cantinone Già Schiavi Bar

Regulars gamely pass along orders to timid newcomers, who might otherwise miss out on smoked swordfish *cicheti* with top-notch house Soave, or *pallottoline* (mini-bottles of beer) with generous *sopressa* (soft salami) *panini*. Chaos cheerfully prevails at this legendary canalside spot, where Accademia

Teatro La Fenice (p189)

Lace souvenirs for sale

art historians rub shoulders with San Trovaso gondola builders without spilling a drop. (☎041 523 95 77; Fondamenta Nani 992; ⏰8.15am-8.30pm Mon-Sat; ⛴Zattere)

Estro Wine Bar

New-entry Estro is anything you want it to be: wine and charcuterie bar, *aperitivo* pit stop, or sit-down degustation restaurant. The 500 *vini* (wines) – many of them natural-process wines – are chosen by young-gun sibling owners Alberto and Dario, whose passion for quality extends to the grub, from *cicheti* topped with house-made *porchetta* (roast pork), to a succulent burger made with asiago cheese and house-made ketchup and mayonnaise. (www.estrovenezia.com; Dorsoduro 3778; ⏰11am-midnight Wed-Mon, kitchen closes 10pm)

San Polo & Santa Croce

Al Mercà Wine Bar

Discerning drinkers throng to this cupboard-sized counter on a Rialto market square to sip on top-notch *prosecco* and DOC wines by the glass (from €2). Edibles usually include meatballs and mini *panini* (from €1), proudly made using super-fresh ingredients. (Campo Cesare Battisti 213, San Polo; ⏰10am-2.30pm & 6-9pm Mon-Thu, to 9.30pm Fri & Sat; ⛴Rialto)

Al Prosecco Wine Bar

The urge to toast sunsets in Venice's loveliest *campo* is only natural – and so is the wine at Al Prosecco. This bar specialises in *vini naturi* (natural-process wines) – organic, biodynamic, wild yeast fermented – from enlightened Italian winemakers like Cinque Campi and Azienda Agricola Barichel. So order a glass of unfiltered 'cloudy' *prosecco* and toast to the good things in life (☎041 524 02 22; www.alprosecco.com; Campo San Giacomo dell'Orio, Santa Croce 1503; ⏰10am-8pm; ⛴San Stae)

Cantina Do Spade Bar

Famously mentioned in Casanova's memoirs, cosy, brick-lined 'Two Spades' continues to keep Venice in good spirits with its bargain Tri-Veneto wines and young, laid-back management. Come early for market-fresh *fritture* (batter-fried seafood) or linger longer with satisfying, sit-down dishes like *bigoli in salsa* (pasta in anchovy and onion sauce). (041 521 05 83; www.cantinadospade.com; Calle delle Do Spade 860, San Polo; 10am-3pm & 6-10pm; ; Rialto)

Cannaregio

Vino Vero Wine Bar

Lining the exposed brick walls of Matteo Bartoli's superior local wine bar are interesting small-production wines, including a great selection of natural and biodynamic labels. The *cicheti*, too, are deliciously varied: wild boar sausage with aubergine, gorgonzola drizzled with honey, or creamy *baba ganoush* topped with prosciutto. (041 275 00 44; Fondamenta della Misericordia 2497; 6pm-midnight Mon, 11am-midnight Tue-Sun; Ca' d'Oro)

Al Timon Wine Bar

Find a spot on the boat moored out front along the canal and watch the motley parade of drinkers and dreamers arrive for seafood crostini and quality organic and DOC wines by the *ombra* (half-glass of wine) or carafe. Folk singers play sets canalside when the weather obliges; when it's cold, regulars scoot over to make room for newcomers at indoor tables. (041 524 60 66; Fondamenta degli Ormesini 2754; 11am-1am Thu-Tue, 6pm-1am Wed; San Marcuola)

Agli Ormesini Pub

While the rest of Venice is awash in wine, Ormesini offers more than 100 brews, including reasonably priced bottles of speciality craft ales and local Birra Venezia. The cheery, beery scene often spills into the street – but keep it down, or the neighbours will get testy. (Da Aldo; 041 71 58 34; Fondamenta degli Ormesini 2710; 8pm-1am Mon-Sat; Madonna dell'Orto)

INFORMATION

Airport Tourist Office (041 529 87 11; www.turismovenezia.it; Arrivals Hall, Marco Polo Airport; 8.30am-7.30pm)

San Marco Tourist Office (041 529 87 11; www.turismovenezia.it; Piazza San Marco 71F; 8.30am-7pm; San Marco)

Venice for Shoppers

To find unique pieces, just wander key artisan areas: San Polo around Calle dei Saoneri, Santa Croce around Calle Lunga and Calle del Tentor, San Marco along Frezzeria, Dorsoduro around the Peggy Guggenheim, and Murano.

Glass Venetians have been working in crystal and glass since the 10th century. Today, along Murano's Fondamenta dei Vetrai, centuries of tradition are upheld by Marina and Susanna Sent. (p188)

Paper Embossing and marbling paper began in the 14th century as part of Venice's burgeoning publishing industry, but these bookbinding techniques and *ebru* (Turkish marbled paper) endpapers have taken on lives of their own. You can still watch a Heidelberg press in action at **Veneziastampa** (041 71 54 55; www.veneziastampa.com; Campo Santa Maria Mater Domini 2173, Santa Croce; 8.15am-1pm & 2.30-7pm Mon-Fri, 9.30am-5pm Sat; San Stae).

Lace Burano lace was a fashion must for centuries. But the modern master of Venetian textiles is Fortuny, whose showroom, **Fortuny Tessuti Artistici** (041 528 76 97; www.fortuny.com; Fondamenta San Biagio 805; 10am-1pm & 2-6pm Mon-Sat; Palanca) on Giudecca features fabrics created using top-secret techniques.

Stazione Santa Lucia Tourist Office (041 529 87 11; www.turismovenezia.it; Stazione Santa Lucia; 8.30am-7pm; Ferrovia Santa Lucia)

GETTING THERE & AWAY

AIR

Most flights arrive at and depart from Marco Polo airport 12km outside Venice, east of Mestre. Ryanair also uses **Treviso airport** (TSF; 0422 31 51 11; www.trevisoairport.it; Via Noalese 63), about 5km southwest of Treviso and a 30km, one-hour drive from Venice.

TRAINS

Trains run frequently to Venice's Stazione Santa Lucia (signed as Ferrovia within Venice). In addition, there are direct InterCity services to major points in France, Germany, Austria and Slovenia.

To	Fare (€)	Journey Time (hr)	Frequency (per hour)
Florence	29-45	2-3	1-2
Milan	20-39	2½-3½	2-3
Naples	55-120	5½-9	1
Padua	4.05-9	½-1	3-4
Rome	40-80	3½-6	1-2
Verona	8.60-23	1¾	3-4

 GETTING AROUND

TO/FROM THE AIRPORT

BOAT

Alilaguna (041 240 17 01; www.alilaguna.it) operates several lines that link the airport with various parts of Venice, including the Linea Blu (Blue Line, with stops at Lido, San Marco, Stazione Marittima and points in between), the Linea Rossa (Red Line, with stops at Murano and Lido) and Linea Arancio (Orange Line, with stops at Stazione Santa Lucia, Rialto and San Marco via the Grand Canal). Boats to Venice cost €15 and leave from the airport ferry dock (an eight-minute walk from the terminal).

BUS

ATVO (ATVO; 0421 59 46 71; www.atvo.it) buses run to the airport from Piazzale Roma (€6, one hour, every 30 minutes 8am to midnight).

WATER TAXI

The standard **water taxi** (Consorzio Motoscafi Venezia; 24hr 041 522 23 03, Marco Polo airport desk 041 541 50 84; www.motoscafivenezia.it) between Marco Polo airport and Venice costs €110 one way and €25 per person in a shared taxi with up to eight passengers, more for night trips, luggage and large groups. Prices can be metered or negotiated in advance.

GETTING AROUND VENICE

VAPORETTO

Venice's main form of public transport; check routes at www.actv.it.

Single rides cost €7; for frequent use, get a pass for unlimited travel within a set period (1-/2-/3-/7-day passes cost €20/30/40/60). Tickets and passes are available dockside from ACTV booths and vending machines, or from tobacconists. Swipe your card every time you board, even if you have already validated it upon initial boarding. You may be charged double with luggage, though this is not always enforced.

From Piazzale Roma or the train station, vaporetto 1 zigzags up the Grand Canal to San Marco and onward to the Lido. If you're not in a rush, it's a great introduction to Venice. Vaporetto 17 carries vehicles from Tronchetto,near Piazzale Roma, to the Lido. Vaporetto 1 runs every 10 minutes throughout most of the day.

GONDOLA

Daytime rates run to €80 for 30 minutes (six passengers maximum) or €100 for 35 minutes from 7pm to 8am.

TRAGHETTO

A daytime public gondola service (€2) to cross the Grand Canal between bridges.

WATER TAXI

Licensed **water taxis** (Consorzio Motoscafi Venezia; 24hr 041 522 23 03; www.motoscafivenezia.it) are a costly way to get around Venice, though they may prove handy. Fares can be metered or negotiated in advance. Official rates start at €15 plus €2 per minute, €6 extra if they're called to your hotel. There's a €10 surcharge for night trips (10pm to 6am), a €5 surcharge for additional luggage (above five pieces) and a €10 surcharge for each extra passenger above the first five.

Where to Stay

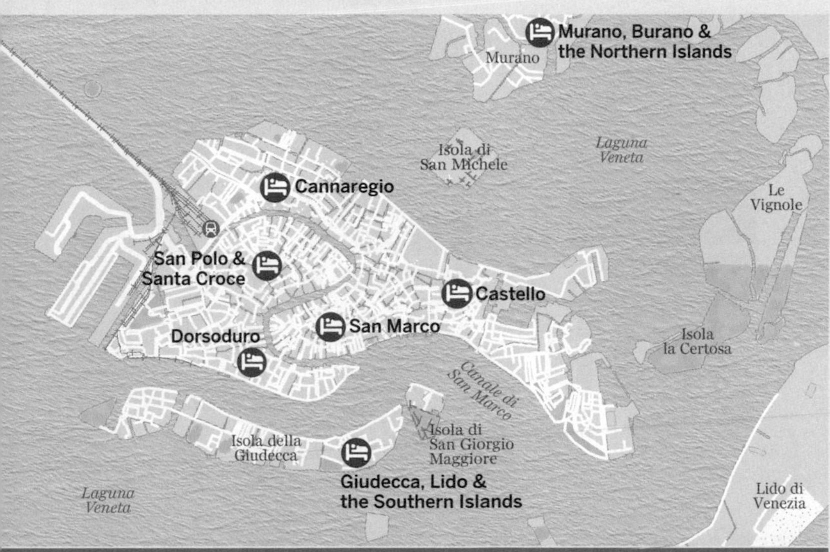

Neighbourhood	Atmosphere
San Marco	Central location, optimal for sightseeing and shopping. Streets noisy in the morning; fewer good restaurants.
Dorsoduro	Lively art and student scenes (so can be noisy), with design hotels near museums and seaside getaways along Zattere.
San Polo & Santa Croce	Prime local dining, Rialto markets, drinking and shopping; convenient to train and bus.
Cannaregio	Venice's best deals on B&Bs and hotels convenient to the train and bus stop. Long walk or vaporetto ride to San Marco sightseeing.
Castello	Fewer tourists as you move away from San Marco; good budget options close to San Marco and the park. Eastern fringes are far away from key sights and services.
Giudecca, Lido & the Southern Islands	Good value for money; beaches within walking distance in summer; fewer tourists. Far from the action; less-frequent public transport at night.
Murano, Burano & the Northern Islands	Murano is a crowd-free, good-value alternative base within 10 minutes of Cannaregio. Limited eating and drinking options; outer islands are far from Venice; very quiet in low season.

PRADA
PRADA
PRADA
S·P·Q·R

Galleria Vittorio Emanuele II (p203)

MILAN

Milan

Milan is Italy's city of the future, a fast-paced metropolis with New World qualities: ambition, aspiration and a highly individualistic streak. The Milanese love beautiful things; indeed, in Milan appearances really do matter and materialism requires no apology.

Many, however, consider Milan to be vain, distant and dull, and it is true that the city makes little effort to seduce visitors. But this superficial lack of charm disguises a city of ancient roots and many treasures, which – unlike in the rest of Italy – you'll often get to experience without the queues. So while the Milanese may not have time to always play nice, jump in and join them in their intoxicating round of pursuits, be that precision shopping, browsing contemporary galleries or loading up a plate with local delicacies.

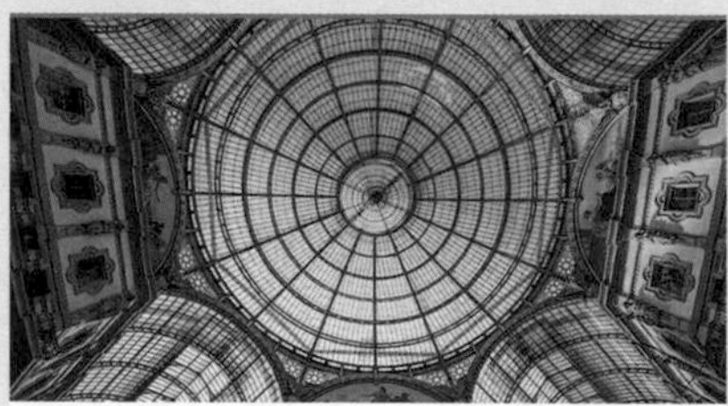

☑ In This Section

From left: Galleria Vittorio Emanuele II; Stazione Centrale; Pinacoteca di Brera; Chiesa di San Maurizio

ℹ Arriving in Milan

Malpensa Airport Northern Italy's main international airport, about 50km northwest of Milan. Regular shuttle buses (€10) run to Stazione Centrale. Also, half-hourly express trains (€10) depart Terminal 1 for Stazione Central.

Linate Airport Located 7km east of the city, serves domestic and European flights. Half-hourly coaches run to Stazione Centrale.

Stazione Centrale A major national and international rail hub.

★ Classic Photo
Head to the highline walkway of the Galleria Vittorio Emanuele II (p203) for beautiful city skyline views.

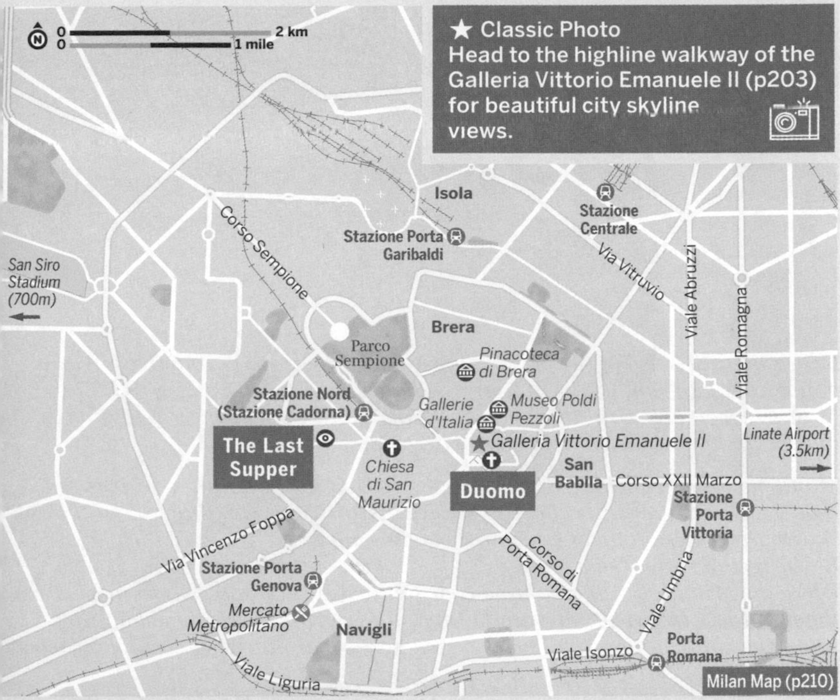

Milan Map (p210)

➡ Milan in Two Days

Start with the blockbuster sights in and around Piazza del Duomo: the **Duomo** (p204), **Galleria Vittorio Emanuele II** (p203) and the **Teatro alla Scala** (p213). Next, immerse yourself in modern art at the **Museo del Novecento** (p208). On day two, stop by Leonardo da Vinci's **The Last Supper** (p206) and the **Pinacoteca di Brera** (p208) before window-shopping in the **Quadrilatero d'Oro** (p202) and an evening canal-side in the Navigli.

➡ Milan in Four Days

Dedicate day three to some lesser-known gems: the **Museo Poldi Pezzoli** (p209) and its cache of Renaissance artworks, the frescoed **Chiesa di San Maurizio** (p209) and the fascinating **Triennale di Milano** (p203). Afterwards, clear your head in **Parco Sempione** (p209) and get in some foodie shopping at legendary deli, **Peck** (p212). On day four, take a tour of the city on the tram before finishing up at **La Teatro alla Scala** (p213).

Quadrilatero d'Oro

Shopping & Design Hot Spots

Milan is a mecca for fashionistas and fans of cutting-edge design. Many of Italy's big-name designers are based here and its streets are lined with flagship stores, showrooms and hip boutiques.

Great For...

☑ Don't Miss

Dress up and join the evening *passeggiata* (stroll) in Galleria Vittorio Emanuele II..

Quadrilatero d'Oro

A stroll around the **Quadrilatero d'Oro** (Golden Quad; M Monte Napoleone), the world's most famous shopping district, is a must. This quaintly cobbled quadrangle of streets – bounded by Via Monte Napoleone, Via Sant'Andrea, Via della Spiga and Via Alessandro Manzoni – has always been synonymous with elegance and money (Via Monte Napoleone was where Napoleon's government managed loans). And even if you don't plan on buying anything, the window displays and people-watching are priceless.

Design Heaven

From 19th-century shopping arcades to cutlery and coffee cups, Milanese design marries form, function and style. Judge for yourself at the following places:

Galleria Vittorio Emanuele II

STEFANO OPPO/GETTY IMAGES ©

Triennale di Milano — Museum

Italy's first Triennale took place in 1923 in Monza. It aimed to promote interest in Italian design and applied arts, from 'the spoon to the city', and its success led to the creation of Giovanni Muzio's Palazzo d'Arte in Milan in 1933. Since then this exhibition space has championed design in all its forms, although the triennale formula has since been replaced by long annual events, with international exhibits as part of the program. (☎02 72 43 41; www.triennaledesignmuseum.it; Viale Emilio Alemanga 6; adult/reduced €8/6.50; ⏰10.30am-8.30pm Tue, Wed, Sat & Sun, to 11pm Thu & Fri; Ⓜ Cadorna)

Galleria Vittorio Emanuele II — Historic Building

So much more than a shopping arcade, the neoclassical Galleria Vittorio Emanuele II is a soaring iron-and-glass structure known

Need to Know

For the Quadrilatero d'Oro, take the metro to Monte Napoleone.

Take a Break

Search out **Bagutta** (p214) for a historic feed.

★ Top Tip

Go bargain hunting in the *saldi* (sales), which start each January and July.

locally as *il salotto bueno*, the city's fine drawing room. Shaped like a crucifix, it also marks the *passeggiata* (evening stroll) route from Piazza del Duomo to Piazza di Marino and the doors of Teatro alla Scala (La Scala). In 2015 a new highline **walkway** (www.highlinegalleria.com; Via Pellico 2; adult/reduced €12/10; ⏰9am-11pm; Ⓜ Duomo) gave access to the Galleria's rooftops for stunning bird's-eye views of the arcade and the city. (Piazza del Duomo; Ⓜ Duomo)

Studio Museo Achille Castiglioni — Museum

Architect, designer and teacher Achille Castiglioni was one of Italy's most influential 20th-century thinkers. This is the studio where he worked daily until his death in 2002, and the hour-long tours vividly illuminate his intelligent but playful creative process. Details abound and await discovery: job folders printed with specially produced numerical stamps; scale models of his Hilly sofa designed for Cassina; and a host of inspirational objects from joke glasses to bicycle seats. (☎02 7243 4231; www.achillecastiglioni.it; Piazza Castello 27; adult/reduced €10/7; ⏰tours 10am, 11am & noon Tue-Fri, 6.30pm, 7.30pm & 8.30pm Thu; Ⓜ Cadorna)

GEORGE FRENCH/GETTY IMAGES ©

Duomo

Milan's extravagant Gothic Duomo is a soul-stirring sight. Its pearly white facade, adorned with 135 spires and 3400 statues, rises like the filigree of a fairy-tale tiara, wowing the crowds with its extravagant detail.

Great For...

☑ Don't Miss

The spectacular view through the marble pinnacles on the roof. On a clear day you can see the Alps.

Commissioned by Giangaleazzo Visconti in 1386 and finished nearly 600 years later, the cathedral boasts a white facade of Candoglia marble and a vast interior punctuated by the largest stained-glass windows in Christendom. Underground, the remains of the saintly Carlo Borromeo are on display in the early Christian baptistry and crypt, while up top the spired roof terraces command stunning views.

Exterior

During his stint as king of Italy, Napoleon offered to fund the Duomo's completion in 1805, in time for his coronation. The architect piled on the neo-Gothic details and almost all the petrified pinnacles, cusps, buttresses, arches and more than 3000 statues were added in the 19th century.

Crypt

DEA/G. CIGOLINI/GETTY IMAGES ©

Need to Know

www.duomomilano.it; Piazza del Duomo; roof terraces adult/reduced via stairs €8/4, lift €13/7, Battistero di San Giovanni €4/2; duomo 7am-6.40pm, roof terraces 9am-6.30pm, battistero 10am-6pm Tue-Sun; M Duomo.

Take a Break

Head to the sun-trap terrace of **Terrazza Aperol** (p216) for a mid-morning *spritz*.

★ Top Tip

It's quicker to walk up the stairs to the roof rather than queue for the tiny elevator.

Roof Terraces

Climb to the roof terraces where you'll be within touching distance of the elaborate 135 spires and their forest of flying buttresses. In the centre of the roof rises the 15th-century octagonal lantern and spire, on top of which is the golden *Madonnina* (erected in 1774). For centuries she was the highest point in the city (108.5m) until the Pirelli skyscraper outdid her in 1958.

Interior

Initially designed to accommodate Milan's then population of around 40,000, the vast interior is divided into five grandiose naves supported by 52 columns. Looking up you'll see a magnificent set of stained-glass windows, whilst underfoot the polychrome marble floor sweeps across 12,000 sq metres. Features to look out for include a 1562 figure of St Bartholomew by Marco d'Agrate, a student of Leonardo da Vinci; the *Altar to the Virgin of the Tree*, the most elaborate of the altars in the transept; and the sculpted 17th-century Choir.

High up in the apse, a red light marks the location of the cathedral's most precious relic: a nail said to be from Christ's cross.

Crypt

From the ambulatory that encircles the choir, stairs lead down to the crypt or Winter Choir. This jewel-like circular chapel with its red porphyry pillars, polychrome marble floor and stucco ceiling contains a casket holding the relics of various saints and martyrs.

Through a gap in the crypt's choir stalls, a dark corridor leads to a chapel housing the remains of Carlo Borromeo, cardinal archbishop of Milan (1564–84).

The Last Supper

One of the world's most iconic images, Leonardo da Vinci's The Last Supper *depicts Christ and his disciples at the dramatic moment when Christ reveals he's aware of his betrayal.*

Great For...

☑ Don't Miss

Don't miss your allotted visiting time. If you're late you will miss out and your ticket will be resold.

The mural, known in Italian as *Il Cenacolo*, is hidden away on a wall of the refectory adjoining the Basilica di Santa Maria delle Grazie. To see it you must book in advance or sign up for a guided city tour.

When Leonardo was at work on the masterpiece, a star-struck monk noted that he would sometimes arrive in the morning, stare at the previous day's efforts, then promptly call it quits for the day. Your visit will be similarly brief (15 minutes to be exact), but the baggage of a thousand dodgy reproductions are quickly shed once standing face to face with the luminous work itself.

Centuries of damage have left the mural in a fragile state despite 22 years of restoration, which was completed in 1999. Da Vinci himself is partly to blame: his experimental mix of oil and tempera

Need to Know

02 9280 0360; www.cenacolovinciano.net; Piazza Santa Maria delle Grazie 2; adult/reduced €8/4.75; 8.15am-7pm Tue-Sun; M Cadorna

Take a Break

Grab an espresso or beer at **Bar Magenta** (http://barmagenta.jimdo.com; Via Giosué Carducci 13; 8am-7.30pm Mon-Wed & Sun, to 10.30pm Thu, to 2am Fri & Sat; M Cadorna).

Top Tip

Reservations for *The Last Supper* must be made weeks, if not months, in advance.

was applied between 1495 and 1498, rather than within a week as is typical of fresco techniques. The Dominicans didn't help matters when in 1652 they raised the refectory floor, hacking off a lower section of the scene, including Jesus' feet. The most damage was caused by restorers in the 19th century, whose use of alcohol and cotton wool removed an entire layer. But the work's condition does little to lessen its astonishing beauty.

Basilica di Santa Maria delle Grazie

Any visit to *The Last Supper* should be accompanied by a tour of the **Basilica di Santa Maria delle Grazie** (www.grazieop.it; Piazza Santa Maria delle Grazie; 7am-noon & 3-7.30pm Mon-Sat, 7.30am-12.30pm & 3.30-9pm Sun; M Cadorna, 16), a Unesco World Heritage Site. Designed by Guiniforte Solari, with later additions by Bramante, the basilica encapsulates the magnificence of the Milanese court of Ludovico 'il Moro' Sforza and Beatrice d'Este. Articulated in fine brickwork and terracotta, the building is robust, but fanciful, its apse topped by Bramante's cupola and its interior lined with frescoes.

Codex Atlanticus

The *Codex Atlanticus* is the largest collection of da Vinci's drawings in the world. More than 1700 of them were gathered by sculptor Pompeo Leoni in 12 volumes, so heavy they threatened the preservation of the drawings themselves. The sheets have now been unbound and are displayed in softly lit glass cases in Bramante's frescoed **Sagrestia Monumentale** (www.leonardo-ambrosiana.it; Via Caradosso 1; adult/reduced €10/8; 8.30am-7pm Tue-Sun, 9am-1pm & 2-6pm Mon; M Cadorna, 16).

SIGHTS

Museo del Novecento — Gallery

Overlooking Piazza del Duomo, with fabulous views of the cathedral, is Mussolini's Arengario, from where he would harangue huge crowds in his heyday. Now it houses Milan's museum of 20th-century art. Built around a futuristic spiral ramp (an ode to the Guggenheim), the lower floors are cramped, but the heady collection, which includes the likes of Umberto Boccioni, Campigli, de Chirico and Marinetti, more than distracts. (☎02 8844 4061; www.museodelnovecento.org; Via Marconi 1; adult/reduced €5/3; ⏰2.30-7.30pm Mon, 9.30am-7.30pm Tue, Wed, Fri & Sun, to 10.30pm Thu & Sat; Ⓜ Duomo)

Il Grande Museo del Duomo — Museum

Stepping through Guido Canali's glowing spaces in the Duomo's new museum is like coming upon the sets for an episode of *Game of Thrones*. Tortured gargoyles leer down through the shadows; shafts of light strike the wings of heraldic angels; and a monstrous godhead glitters awesomely in copper once intended for the high altar. It's an exciting display, masterfully choreographed through 26 rooms, which tell the 600-year story of the cathedral's construction through priceless sculptures, paintings, stained glass, tapestries and bejewelled treasures. (www.museo.duomomilano.it; Piazza del Duomo 12; adult/reduced €6/4; ⏰10am-6pm Tue-Sun; Ⓜ Duomo)

Gallerie d'Italia — Museum

Housed in three fabulously decorated palaces, the enormous art collection ranges from a magnificent sequence of bas-reliefs by Antonio Canova to luminous Romantic masterpieces by Francesco Hayez. The works span 23 rooms and document Milan's significant contribution to the rebirth of Italian sculpture, the patriotic romanticism of the Risorgimento (reunification period) and the birth of futurism at the dawn of the 20th century. (www.gallerieditalia.com; Piazza della Scala 6; adult/reduced €10/8; ⏰9.30am-7.30pm Tue-Sun; Ⓜ Duomo)

Pinacoteca di Brera — Gallery

Located upstairs from the centuries-old Accademia di Belle Arti (still one of Italy's most prestigious art schools), this gallery houses Milan's impressive collection of Old

View over Milan

Masters, much of it 'lifted' from Venice by Napoleon. Rembrandt, Goya and Van Dyck all have a place in the collection, but look for the Italians: Titian, Tintoretto, Veronese and the Bellini brothers. Much of the work has tremendous emotional clout, most notably Mantegna's brutal *Lamentation over the Dead Christ*. (☎02 7226 3264; www.brera.beniculturali.it; Via Brera 28; adult/reduced €10/7; ⏰8.30am-7.15pm Tue-Sun; Ⓜ Lanza, Montenapoleone)

Museo Poldi Pezzoli Museum

Inheriting his fortune at the age of 24, Gian Giacomo Poldi Pezzoli also inherited his mother's love of art. During extensive European travels he was inspired by the 'house museum' that was to become London's Victoria & Albert Museum and had the idea of transforming his apartments into a series of themed rooms based on the great art periods. Crammed with big-ticket Renaissance artworks, these Sala d'Artista are exquisite works of art in their own right. (☎02 79 48 89; www.museopoldipezzoli.it; Via Alessandro Manzoni 12; adult/reduced €10/7; ⏰10am-6pm Wed-Mon; Ⓜ Montenapoleone)

Chiesa di San Maurizio Church

The 16th-century royal chapel and convent of San Maurizio is Milan's hidden crown jewel, every inch of it covered in breathtaking frescoes, several of them executed by Bernardino Luini who worked with Leonardo. Many of the frescoes immortalise Ippolita Sforza, Milanese literary maven, and other members of the powerful Sforza clan. (Corso Magenta 15; ⏰9.30am-5.30pm Tue-Sat, 1.30-5.30pm Sun; Ⓜ Cadorna)

Parco Sempione Park

Situated behind Castello Sforzesco, Parco Sempione was once the preserve of hunting Sforza dukes. Then Napoleon came to town and set about landscaping. First the French carved out orchards; next they mooted the idea in 1891 for a vast public park. It was a resounding success and even today Milanese of all ages come to enjoy its winding paths and ornamental ponds.

DIY Tram Tour

Enjoy your own city tour by hopping on Tram No.1 (€1.50, valid for 75 minutes). This retro orange beauty, complete with wooden seats and original fittings, runs along Via Settembrini before cutting through the historic centre along Via Manzoni, through Piazza Cordusio and back up towards Piazza Cairoli and the Castello Sforzesco.

Tram passing La Scala
LEONID ANDRONOV/GETTY IMAGES ©

TOURS

Ad Artem Cultural Tour

Unusual cultural tours of Milan's museums and monuments with qualified art historians and actors. Highlight tours include a walk around the battlements of Castello Sforzesco; explorations of the castle's subterranean Ghirlanda passageway; and family-friendly tours of the Museo del Novecento, where kids are invited to build and design their own artwork. (☎02 659 77 28; http://adartem.it; Via Melchiorre Gioia 1; tours €8-17.50; ⏰9am-1pm & 2-4pm; 👪; Ⓜ Sondrio)

Autostradale Tour

Autostradale's three-hour city bus tours include admission to *The Last Supper*, Castello Sforzesco and the Teatro alla Scala (La Scala) museum. Tours depart from the taxi rank on the western side of Piazza del Duomo at 9.30am. (www.autostradale.it; Piazza Castello 1; tickets €65; ⏰Tue-Sun)

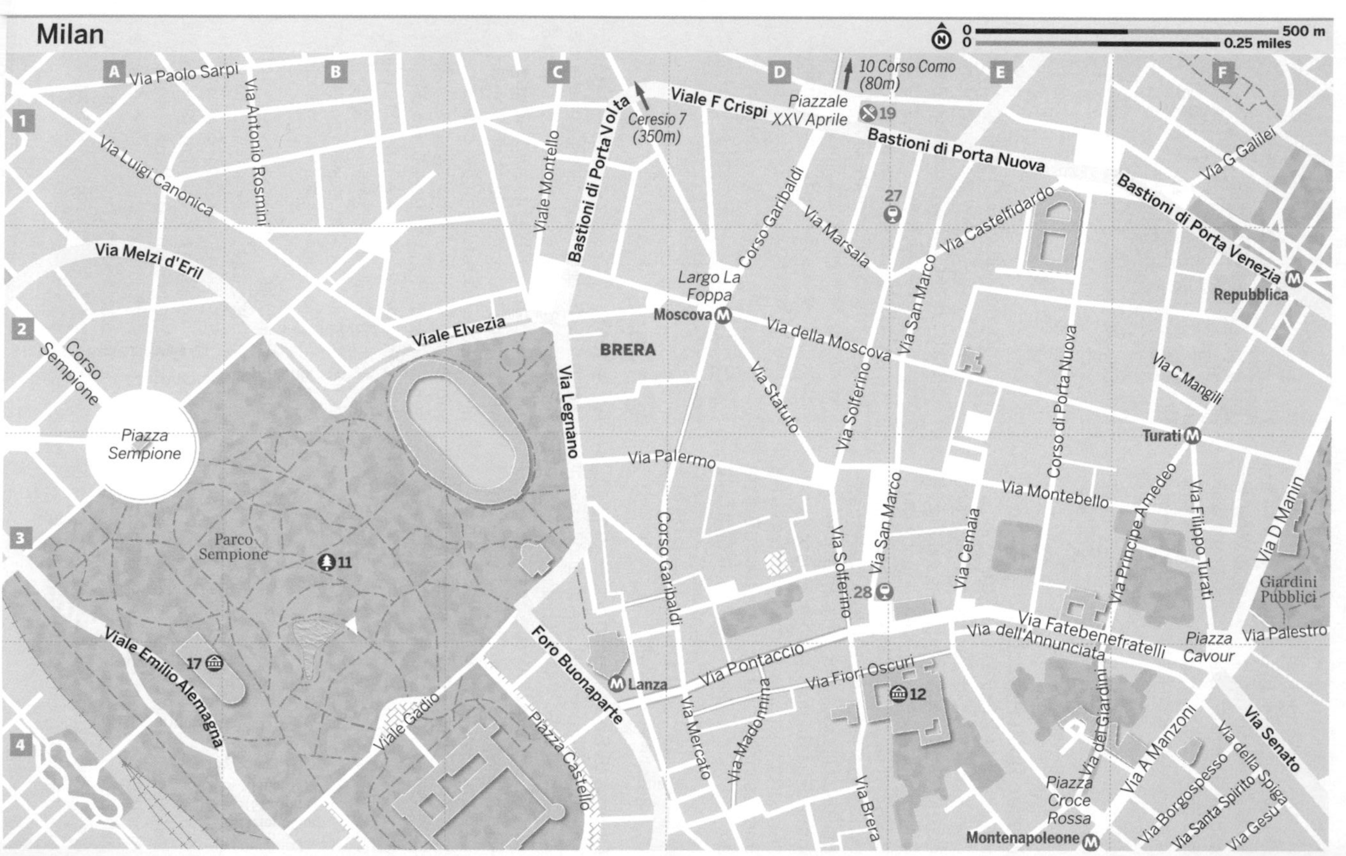

Milan
0
0
500 m
0.25 miles
A
B
C
D
E
F
1
2
3
4
Via Paolo Sarpi
Via Antonio Rosmini
10 Corso Como (80m)
Viale F Crispi
Ceresio 7 (350m)
Piazzale XXV Aprile
19
Bastioni di Porta Volta
Bastioni di Porta Nuova
Bastioni di Porta Venezia
Via G Galilei
Repubblica
Via Luigi Canonica
Viale Montello
Corso Garibaldi
Via Marsala
27
Via Castelfidardo
Via Melzi d'Eril
Largo La Foppa
Moscova
Via San Marco
Viale Elvezia
BRERA
Via della Moscova
Via C Mangili
Corso Sempione
Via Legnano
Via Statuto
Via Solferino
Corso di Porta Nuova
Piazza Sempione
Turati
Via Palermo
Via Montebello
Via Principe Amedeo
Via Filippo Turati
Via D Manin
Corso Garibaldi
Via San Marco
Via Cernaia
Parco Sempione
11
Via Solferino
Giardini Pubblici
28
Via Fatebenefratelli
Via dell'Annunciata
Piazza Cavour
Via Palestro
Viale Emilio Alemagna
Foro Buonaparte
17
Lanza
Via Pontaccio
Via Fiori Oscuri
12
Viale Gadio
Piazza Castello
Via Mercato
Via Madonnina
Via Brera
Via dei Giardini
Via A Manzoni
Via Senato
Via della Spiga
Piazza Croce Rossa
Via Borgospesso
Via Santo Spirito
Via Gesù
Montenapoleone

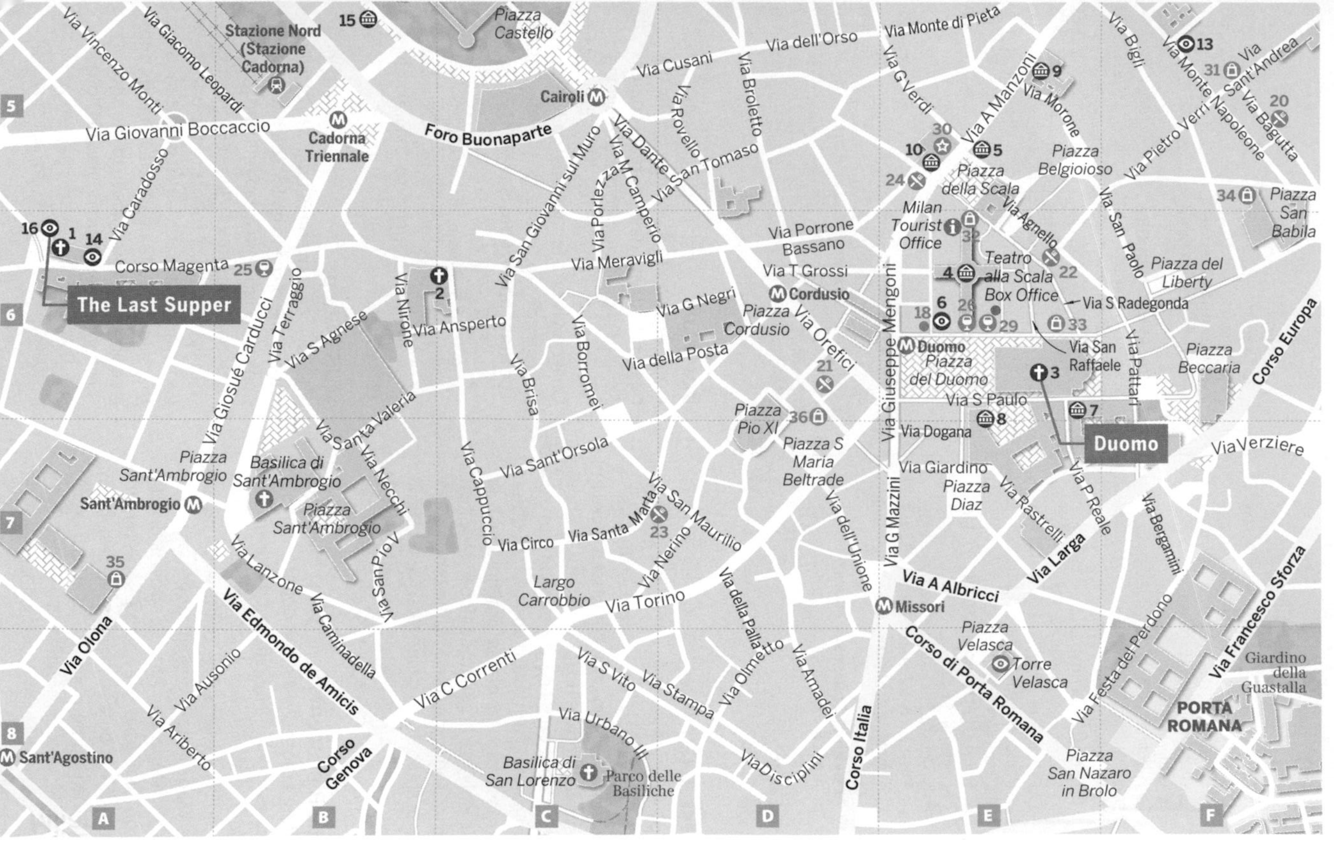

Via Vincenzo Monti
Via Giacomo Leopardi
Stazione Nord (Stazione Cadorna)
15
Piazza Castello
Via Cusani
Via dell'Orso
Via Monte di Pietà
Via Bigli
13
Via Monte Napoleone
Via Sant'Andrea
31
Via Bagutta
20
Cairoli
Foro Buonaparte
Via Giovanni Boccaccio
Cadorna Triennale
Via Rovello
Via Broletto
Via G Verdi
Via A Manzoni
9
Via Morone
30
10
5
Piazza Belgioioso
Via Pietro Verri
24
Piazza della Scala
34
Piazza San Babila
Via Caradosso
16
1
14
Via San Giovanni sul Muro
Via Porlezza
Via M Camperio
Via Dante
Via San Tomaso
Milan Tourist Office
32
Via Agnello
Via San Paolo
Teatro alla Scala Box Office
22
Piazza del Liberty
Corso Magenta
25
Via Meravigli
Via Porrone
Bassano
4
Via T Grossi
Cordusio
Via S Radegonda
The Last Supper
Via Terraggio
Via Nirone
2
Via G Negri
Piazza Cordusio
18
6
26
29
33
Via Ansperto
Via S Agnese
Via Giosuè Carducci
Via Brisa
Via Borromei
Via della Posta
Via Orefici
Via Giuseppe Mengoni
Duomo
Piazza del Duomo
Via San Raffaele
Via Pattari
Piazza Beccaria
Corso Europa
21
3
Via S Paolo
7
Piazza Pio XI
36
Via Santa Valeria
Via Necchi
Via Cappuccio
Via Sant'Orsola
Piazza S Maria Beltrade
Via Dogana
8
Duomo
Via Verziere
Piazza Sant'Ambrogio
Basilica di Sant'Ambrogio
Sant'Ambrogio
Piazza Sant'Ambrogio
Via Giardino
Piazza Diaz
Via Rastrelli
Via P Reale
Via Bergamini
Via Santa Marta
23
Via San Maurilio
Via dell'Unione
Via G Mazzini
Via Circo
Via San Pio V
Via Lanzone
Via Nerino
Via Larga
35
Largo Carrobbio
Via Torino
Via A Albricci
Missori
Via Caminadella
Via della Palla
Via Olmetto
Via Amadei
Piazza Velasca
Torre Velasca
Corso di Porta Romana
Via Festa del Perdono
Via Francesco Sforza
Giardino della Guastalla
Via Olona
Via Edmondo de Amicis
Via Ausonio
Via C Correnti
Via S Vito
Via Stampa
Via Urbano III
Corso Italia
Via Ariberto
Sant'Agostino
Corso Genova
Basilica di San Lorenzo
Parco delle Basiliche
Via Disciplini
Piazza San Nazaro in Brolo
PORTA ROMANA
5
6
7
8
A
B
C
D
E
F

Milan

Sights

1 Basilica di Santa Maria delle Grazie........A6
2 Chiesa di San Maurizio........C6
3 Duomo........E6
4 Galleria Vittorio Emanuele II........E6
5 Gallerie d'Italia........E5
6 Highline Galleria........E6
7 Il Grande Museo del Duomo........E6
8 Museo del Novecento........E6
9 Museo Poldi Pezzoli........E5
10 Museo Teatrale alla Scala........E5
11 Parco Sempione........B3
12 Pinacoteca di Brera........E4
13 Quadrilatero d'Oro........F5
14 Sagrestia Monumentale del Bramante........A6
15 Studio Museo Achille Castiglioni........B5
16 The Last Supper........A6
17 Triennale di Milano........A4

Activities, Courses & Tours

18 Autostradale........E6

Eating

19 Alice Ristorante........D1
20 Bagutta........F5
21 Cracco........D6
22 Luini........E6
23 Trattoria Milanese........D7
24 Trussardi alla Scala........E5

Drinking & Nightlife

25 Bar Magenta........B6
26 Camparino in Galleria........E6
27 Dry........E1
28 N'Ombra de Vin........D3
29 Terrazza Aperol........E6

Entertainment

30 Teatro alla Scala........E5

Shopping

31 Borsalino........F5
32 Borsalino (Galleria Vittoria Emanuele II)........E6
33 La Rinascente........E6
34 Moroni Gomma........F5
35 MUST Shop........A7
36 Peck........D6

SHOPPING

Peck — Food, Wine

Milan's historic deli is smaller than its reputation suggests, but what it lacks in space it makes up for in variety. It's home to a mind-boggling selection of *parmigiano reggiano* (Parmesan) and myriad other treasures: chocolates, pralines, pastries, freshly made gelato, seafood, caviar, pâté, fruit and vegetables, truffle products, olive oils and balsamic vinegars. (02 802 31 61; www.peck.it; Via Spadari 9; 3.30-7.30pm Mon, 9.30am-7.30pm Tue-Sat; M Duomo)

La Rinascente — Department Store

Italy's most prestigious department store doesn't let the fashion capital down – come for Italian diffusion lines, French lovelies and LA upstarts. The basement also hides a 'Made in Italy' design supermarket, and chic hairdresser Aldo Coppola is on the top floor. Take away edible souvenirs from the 7th-floor food market (and peer across to the Duomo while you're at it). (02 8 85 21; www.rinascente.it; Piazza del Duomo; 8.30am-midnight Mon-Sat, 10am-midnight Sun; M Duomo)

Borsalino — Accessories

Iconic Alessandrian milliner Borsalino has worked with design greats such as Achille Castiglioni, who once designed a pudding-bowl bowler hat. This outlet in the Galleria Vittoria Emanuele II (p203) shopping arcade stocks seasonal favourites. The **main showroom** is at Via Sant'Andrea (02 7601 7072; www.borsalino.com; Via Sant'Andrea 5; M Montenapoleone). (02 8901 5436; www.borsalino.com; Galleria Vittorio Emanuele II 92; 3-7pm Mon, 10am-7pm Tue-Sat; M Duomo)

MUST Shop — Museum Shop

The science museum's fabulous concept shop is *the* place to go for science-inspired books, design items, gadgets and games. Personal favourites include submarine bath lights, Corker robots made out of wine corks, and the star theatre planetarium that allows you to beam the heavens onto a ceiling near you. Access to the shop is through the museum or via Via Olona. (02 4855 5340; www.mustshop.it; Via Olona 6; 10am-7pm Tue-Sun; M Sant'Ambrogio)

Moroni Gomma Homewares, Accessories

Stocked with irresistible gadgets and great accessories for the bathroom, kitchen and office, this family-owned design store is a one-stop shop for funky souvenirs and Milanese keepsakes. Who but the strongest willed will be able to resist the cuckoo clock shaped like the Duomo, a retro telephone in pastel colours or classic Italian moccasins in nonslip rubber? (02 79 62 20; www.moronigomma.it; Corso Matteotti 14; 3-7pm Mon, 10am-7pm Tue-Sun; M San Babila)

10 Corso Como Fashion

This might be the world's most hyped 'concept shop', but Carla Sozzani's selection of desirable things (Lanvin ballet flats, Alexander Girard wooden dolls, a demicouture frock by a designer you've not read about *yet*) makes 10 Corso Como a fun window-shopping experience. There's a bookshop upstairs with art and design titles, and a hyperstylish bar and restaurant in the main atrium and picture-perfect courtyard. (02 2900 2674; www.10corsocomo.com; Corso Como 10; 10.30am-7.30pm Tue & Fri-Sun, to 9pm Wed & Thu, 3.30-7.30pm Mon; M Garibaldi)

Bargain hunters take note: the **outlet store** nearby sells last season's stock at a discount. (02 2900 2674; www.10corsocomo.com; Via Tazzoli 3; 1-7pm Fri, 11am-7pm Sat & Sun; M Garibaldi, 3, 4)

ENTERTAINMENT

Teatro alla Scala Opera

One of the most famous opera stages in the world, La Scala's season runs from early December through July. You can also see theatre, ballet and concerts here year-round (except August). (La Scala; 02 8 87 91; www.teatroallascala.org; Piazza della Scala; M Duomo)

Buy tickets online or by phone up to two months before the performance, and then from the **central box office** (02 7200 3744; www.teatroallascala.org; Galleria Vittorio Emanuele II; noon-6pm; M Duomo). On performance days, 140 tickets for the gallery are sold two hours before the show (one ticket per customer). Queue early.

When rehearsals are not in session, you can get a glimpse of the gilt-encrusted interior, or visit the **museum** (Largo Ghiringhelli 1; admission €7; 9am-12.30pm & 1.30-5.30pm; M Duomo) next door.

San Siro Stadium Football

San Siro Stadium wasn't designed to hold the entire population of Milan, but on a Sunday afternoon amid 85,000 football-mad citizens it can certainly feel like it. The city's two clubs, AC Milan and FC Internazionale Milano (aka Inter), play on alternate weeks from October to May. (Stadio Giuseppe Meazza; www.sansiro.net; Piazzale Angelo Moratti, museum & tours gate 14; tickets from €20; M San Siro)

EATING

Mercato Metropolitano Market €

'Good Italian food is not a luxury' is the cry of Milan's new food market located in former railway housings near Porta Genova. Choose from small-producer food stalls selling oysters, DOP Franciacorta, and gourmet *panini* made with 24-year-aged San Daniele ham. Plant stalls, artisanal ice-cream carts, craft beer, cocktail purveyors, and even cooking classes and seminars give it a convivial country-fair feel. (www.mercatometropolitano.com; Porta Genova; meals €10-20; 11am-midnight Mon-Thu, to 2am Fri, 9-2am Sat, 9am-noon Sun; M Porta Genova)

Luini Fast Food €

This historic joint is the go-to place for *panzerotti,* delicious pizza-dough parcels stuffed with a combination of mozzarella, spinach, tomato, ham or spicy salami, and then fried or baked in a wood-fired oven. (www.luini.it; Via Santa Radegonda 16; panzerotti €2.50; 10am-3pm Mon, to 8pm Tue-Sat; M Duomo)

Trattoria Milanese Milanese €€

Like an old friend you haven't seen in years, this true trattoria welcomes you with generous goblets of wine, hearty servings of traditional Milanese fare and convivial

Aperitivo

Milan's nightly *aperitivo* is a two- or three-hour ritual, starting around 6pm, where for €8 to €20, a cocktail, beer or glass of wine comes with an unlimited buffet of bruschetta, foccacia, cured meats, salads, and even seafood and pasta. (Occasionally you'll pay a cover charge up front that includes a drink and buffet fare, but it generally works out the same.) Take a plate and help yourself; snacks are also sometimes brought to your table. Most of the city's bars offer *aperitivi,* in some form or other.

banter over the vegetable buffet. Regulars slide into their favourite spots, barely needing to order as waiters bring them their usual: meatballs wrapped in cabbage, minestrone or the sinfully good *risotto al salto* (refried risotto). (02 8645 1991; Via Santa Marta 11; meals €30-45; 12.30-2.30pm & 7-11.30pm; 2, 14)

Bagutta Milanese **€€€**

The Ministry of Cultural Resources calls Bagutta a historical landmark, but your taste buds will call it fabulous: the tasty lamb chops with sage and the melt-away spinach gnocchi with gorgonzola have kept napkins expectantly tucked under chins here since 1920. (02 7600 2767; www.bagutta.it; Via Bagutta 14; meals €40-50; 12.30-10.30pm Mon-Sat; M San Babila)

Alice Ristorante Modern Italian **€€€**

The restaurant of talented chef Viviana Varese and maître d', sommelier and fish expert Sandra Ciciriello, Alice is the pride of Eataly's new flagship foodstore. The top-floor views are a match for the superlative food on your plate and the menu is full of humour, with dishes such as Polp Fiction (octopus with zucchini trumpets) and That Ball! (truffle ice cream with chocolate, *zabaglione* and cocoa). (02 4949 7340; www.aliceristorante.it; Piazza XXV Aprile , Eataly; meals €40-50; 12.30-2.30pm & 7.30-10.30pm Mon-Sat; ; M Moscova, Garibaldi)

Cracco Modern Italian **€€€**

Star chef Carlo Cracco keeps the Milanese in thrall with his off-the-wall inventiveness. Let the waiters do the thinking by ordering one of the tasting menus (€130 and €160). (02 87 67 74; www.ristorantecracco.it; Via Victor Hugo 4; meals €130-160; 7.30pm-12.30am Mon & Sat, 12.30-2.30pm & 7.30pm-12.30am Tue-Fri; M Duomo)

Ristorante Berton Modern Italian **€€€**

Berton's ultramodern interior, with its gleaming elm wood panelling, provides a sleek environment for chef Andrea Berton's 'evolved' cuisine. As such you can expect traditional ingredients in new, creative guises: Milanese veal enhanced by slow-cooked lemon or the extraordinary rice ravioli. (02 6707 5801; www.ristoranteberton.com; Viale della Liberazione 13; meals €90-120; 8-10.30pm Mon, noon-2.30pm & 8-10.30pm Tue-Fri; M Gioia)

Trussardi alla Scala Modern Italian **€€€**

Luigi Taglienti presides over one of Milan's finest gourmet dining rooms with windows looking out onto La Scala. The food is a mix of French and Italian classics, including an elegantly executed French onion soup alongside more imaginative fare such as violet parsnip tortelli with pine nuts and radicchio. (02 8068 8201; www.trussardiallascala.com; Piazza della Scala 5; menus from €140; 12.30-2.30pm & 8-10.30pm Mon-Fri, 8-10.30pm Sat; M Duomo)

Sadler Modern Italian **€€€**

Get ready for a serious tummy-cramming session in this architecturally elegant space: with combinatorial creativity and reverential respect for ingredients, this two-starred Michelin establishment is one of the most awarded restaurants in Milan. (02 87 67 30; www.sadler.it; Via Ascanio Sforza 77; meals €75-160; 7.30-11pm Mon-Sat; M Romolo, 3)

DRINKING & NIGHTLIFE

Camparino in Galleria Bar, Cafe

Open since the inauguration of the Galleria Vittorio Emanuele II shopping arcade in 1867, this perfectly perserved art nouveau bar has served drinks to the likes of Verdi, Toscanini, Dudovich and Carrà. Cast-iron chandeliers and huge mirrored walls trimmed with wall mosaics of birds and flowers set the tone for a classy Campari-based *aperitivo*. Drinks at the bar are cheaper. (www.camparino.it; Piazza del Duomo 21; drinks €12-24; 7.15am-8.40pm)

Ceresio 7 Bar

Heady views match the heady price of *aperitivo* at Milan's coolest rooftop bar, sitting atop the former 1930s Enel (electricity company) HQ. Two pools, two bars and a restaurant under the guidance of former Bulgari head chef Elio Sironi make this a hit with Milan's beautiful people. In the summer you can book a whole day by the pool from €110. (02 3103 9221; www.ceresio7.com; Via Ceresio 7; aperitivo €15, meals €60-80; 12.30pm-1am; 2, 4)

N'Ombra de Vin Wine Bar

This *enoteca* (wine bar) is set in a one-time Augustine refectory. Tastings can be had all day and you can also indulge in food such as *carpaccio di pesce spade agli agrumi* (swordfish carpaccio prepared with citrus) from a limited menu. (02 659 96 50; www.nombradevin.it; Via San Marco 2; 10am-2am; M Lanza, Moscova)

Dry Cocktail Bar

The brainchild of Michelin-starred chef Andrea Berton, Dry mixes its cocktails with gourmet pizzas. The inventive cocktail list includes the Corpse Reviver (London Dry gin, cointreau, Cocchi Americano and lemon juice) and the Martinez (Boompjes genever, vermouth, Maraschino liqueur and Boker's bitters), the latter inspired by French gold hunters in Martinez, the birthplace of barman Jerry Thomas. (02 6379 3414; www.drymilano.it; Via Solferino 33; cocktails €8-13, meals €20-25; 7pm-midnight; M Moscova)

Teatro alla Scala (p213)

San Siro Stadium (p213)

Terrazza Aperol Bar

With its whacky moulded orange bar, orange bubble lights and low-slung '70s seats, this bar dedicated to the classic Aperol *spritz* cocktail channels a strong Austin Powers vibe. Still, the Duomo's extravagant exterior, which seems within arm's reach from the terrace, is more than a match for a paisley velvet suit. (www.terrazzaaperol.it; Piazza del Duomo; cocktails €12-17; ⏲11am-11pm Sun-Fri, to midnight Sat; Ⓜ Duomo)

INFORMATION

Milan Tourist Office (☎02 8845 6555; www.turismo.milano.it; Galleria Vittorio Emanuele II 11-12; ⏲9am-7pm Mon-Fri, to 6pm Sat, 10am-6pm Sun; Ⓜ Duomo) Centrally located with helpful English-speaking staff and tons of maps and brochures.

GETTING THERE & AWAY

AIR

Linate Airport (LIN; ☎02 23 23 23; www.milanolinate-airport.com) Located 7km east of Milan city centre; domestic and European flights only.

Malpensa Airport (MXP; ☎02 23 23 23; www.milanomalpensa-airport.com) About 50km northwest of Milan city; northern Italy's main international airport.

Orio al Serio (Aeroporto Il Caravaggio; ☎035 32 63 23; www.sacbo.it) Low-cost carriers link Bergamo airport with a wide range of European cities. It has direct transport links to Milan.

BUS

National and international buses depart from **Lampugnano bus station** (Via Giulia Natta), next to the Lampugnano metro stop, 5km west of central Milan. The main national operator is **Autostradale** (www.autostradale.it) Tickets can be purchased at their office or on boarding.

TRAIN

International, high-speed trains from France, Switzerland and Germany arrive in Milan's **Stazione Centrale** (Piazza Duca d'Aosta). The ticketing office and left luggage are located on the ground floor. For regional trips, skip the queue and buy your tickets from the multilingual, touch-screen vending machines, which accept both cash and credit card. Daily international and long-distance destinations include Florence (€35 to €60, 1½ to 3½ hours, hourly), Rome (€85 to €130, three hours, half-hourly) and Venice (€19 to €47; 2½ to 3½ hours, half-hourly).

GETTING AROUND

TO/FROM THE AIRPORT

BUS

Malpensa Shuttle (www.malpensashuttle.it; one way/return €10/16) This Malpensa airport shuttle runs every 20 minutes between 5am and 10.30pm from Stazione Centrale, and hourly throughout the rest of the night. It stops at both terminals and the journey time is 50 minutes.

Orio al Serio Bus Express (02 7200 1304; www.autostradale.it; 1 Piazza Castello; one way/return €5/9) This Autostradale service departs Piazza Luigi di Savoia at Stazione Centrale approximately every half-hour between 2.45am and 11.15pm, and from Orio al Serio airport between 7.45am and 11.15am. The journey takes one hour.

Starfly (02 5858 7237; www.airportbusexpress.it; one way/return €5/9) Departs from Milan's Stazione Centrale for Linate airport every half-hour between 7.45am and 10.45pm, and between 5.30am and 10pm in the other direction. Tickets are sold on board.

TAXI

There is a flat fee of €90 between Malpensa Airport and central Milan. The drive should take 50 minutes outside peak traffic times. For travellers to Terminal 2, this might prove the quickest option. The taxi fare to Linate Airport is between €20 and €30.

TRAIN

Malpensa Express (02 7249 4949; www.malpensaexpress.it; one way €12) From 6.53am to 9.53pm trains run every 30 minutes between Malpensa airport Terminal 1, Cadorna Stazione Nord (35 minutes) and Stazione Centrale (45 minutes). Passengers for Terminal 2 need to take the free shuttle bus to/from Terminal 1.

Where to Stay

Great-value accommodation is hard to come by in Milan, particularly during the Salone del Mobile furniture fair, the fashion shows and other large fairs, at which time you should book months in advance. The tourist office distributes Milano Hotels, which lists more than 350 options.

PUBLIC TRANSPORT

ATM (Azienda Trasporti Milano; 02 4860 7607; www.atm.it) runs the metro, buses and trams. The metro is the most convenient way to get around and consists of four underground lines (red M1, green M2, yellow M3 and lilac M5) and a suburban rail network, the blue Passante Ferroviario. Services run from 6am to 12.30am. A ticket costs €1.50 and is valid for one metro ride or up to 90 minutes' travel on buses and trams. Tickets are sold at metro stations, tobacconists and newspaper stands. Tickets must be validated on trams and buses.

Bus and tram route maps are available at ATM Info points, or download the IATM app. There are several good money-saving passes available for public transport:

One-day ticket Valid 24 hours, €4.50

Three-day ticket Valid 72 hours, €8.25

Carnet of 10 tickets Valid for 90 minutes each, €13.80.

TAXI

Taxis are only available at designated taxi ranks; you cannot flag them down. Alternatively, call 02 40 40, 02 69 69 or 02 85 85. The average short city ride costs €10. Be aware that when you call for a cab, the meter runs from receipt of call, not pick up.

Lago di Como (p228)

ITALIAN LAKES

Italian Lakes

Formed at the end of the last ice age, and a popular holiday spot since Roman times, the Italian Lakes have an enduring, beguiling beauty.

Travellers will be greeted by a Mediterranean burst of colour: gardens filled with rose-red camellias, hot-pink oleanders and luxurious palms surrounding cerulean blue lakes. It's impossible not to be seduced. Fishing boats bob in tiny harbours, palaces float in the Borromean Gulf, rustic churches cling to cliff faces and grand belle époque spas and hotels line the waterfronts.

☑ In This Section

Arriving in the Italian Lakes

For Lago Maggiore, hourly trains leave Milan's Stazione Centrale for Stresa (on the Domodossola line), a convenient base on the lake's western shore.

For Lago di Como, hourly services depart Stazione Centrale and Porta Garibaldi to Como San Giovanni. Trains from Milan's Stazione Nord also serve Como's lakeside Stazione FNM (listed on timetables as Como Nord Lago).

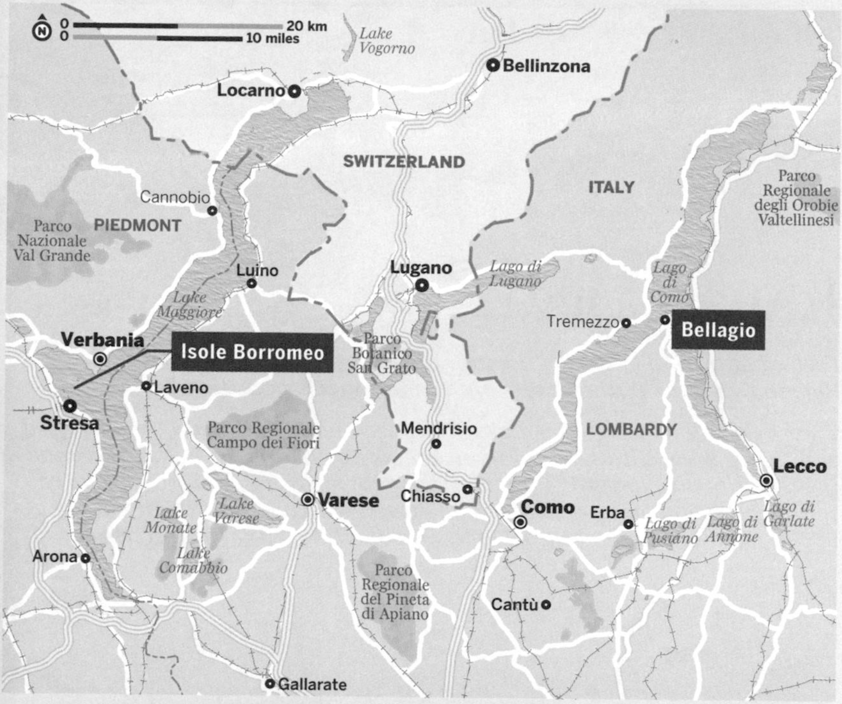

From left: Bellagio (p222); San Giovanni church, near Bellagio; Lago di Como (p228)
JEAN-PIERRE LESCOURRET/GETTY IMAGES ©; DANITA DELIMONT/GETTY IMAGES ©; PANORAMIC IMAGES/ GETTY IMAGES ©

ALEXANDER CHAIKIN/SHUTTERSTOCK ©

Explore Bellagio

It's impossible not to be smitten by Bellagio's waterfront of bobbing boats and its maze of steep stone staircases, red-roofed and green-shuttered buildings, dark cypress groves and rhododendron-filled gardens.

Great For...

☑ Don't Miss

Bellagio's new Lido with sand-scattered decking and diving platforms over the lake.

Bellagio's peerless position on the promontory jutting out into the centre of the inverted Y-shape of Lago di Como made it the object of much squabbling between Milan and Como, hence its ruined fortifications and its Romanesque **Basilica di San Giacomo** (Piazza della Chiesa), built by Como masters between 1075 and 1125. These days, it teems with visitors in summer, but if you turn up out of season, you'll have it almost to yourself.

Villa Serbelloni

Bellagio has been a favoured summer resort since Roman times, when Pliny the Younger holidayed on the promontory where **Villa Serbelloni** (☎031 95 15 55; Piazza della Chiesa 14; adult/child €9/5; ⏲tours 11.30am & 2.30pm Tue-Sun mid-Mar–Oct) now stands. The Romans introduced the olive and laurel trees that dot the villa's 20-hectare gardens,

View from Villa Serbelloni

which took on their Italianate, English and Mediterranean designs at the beginning of the 19th century. The villa, which has hosted Europe's great and good, including Austria's emperor Maximilian I, Ludovico il Moro and Queen Victoria, is now privately owned by the Rockefeller Foundation. The interior is closed to the public, but you can explore the terraced park and gardens by guided tour. Numbers are limited; tickets are sold at the PromoBellagio information office near the church.

Villa Melzi d'Eril

Built in 1808 for Francesco Melzi d'Eril (1753–1816), Napoleon's advisor and vice president of the First Italian Republic, neo-classical **Villa Melzi d'Eril** (www.giardinidivillamelzi.it; Lungo Lario Manzoni; adult/reduced €6.50/4; ⏲9.30am-6.30pm Apr-Oct) is one of the most elegant villas on the lake. The neo-classical temple is where Liszt came over all romantic and composed his 1837 sonata dedicated to Dante and Beatrice.

The walk to Villa Melzi, south along the lake shore from the Bellagio ferry jetties, reveals views of ranks of gracious residencies stacked up on the waterside hills.

Need to Know

Useful information is provided by local businesses at **PromoBellagio** (☎031 95 15 55; www.bellagiolakecomo.com; Piazza della Chiesa 14; ⏲9.30am-1pm Mon, 9-11am & 1.30-3.30pm Tue-Sun Apr-Oct).

Take a Break

For lunch, dine on the terrace at **Albergo Silvio** (www.bellagiosilvio.com; Via Carcano 12, Bellagio; meals €25-30; ⏲noon-3pm & 6.30-10pm Mar–mid-Nov).

★ Top Tip

The gardens are at their finest between March and May when the flowers are in bloom.

Lake Tours

For a touch of Clooney-esque glamour, consider taking a tour of the lake in one of the slick mahogany cigarette boats operated by **Barindelli Taxi Boats** (www.barindellitaxiboats.it; Piazza Mazzini; tours per hour €140). Hour-long sunset tours (€140 for up to 12 people) take you around Bellagio's headland, where you can view the splendour of Villa Serbelloni from the water. Alternatively, DIY it on a kayak tour with **Bellagio Water Sports** (www.bellagiowatersports.com; Pescallo Harbour; rental per 2/4hr €18/30, tours €35), an experienced outfit in Pescallo, on the east side of the Bellagio headland.

Isole Superiore (Pescatori)

MICHAL KRAKOWIAK/GETTY IMAGES ©

Isole Borromee

The Borromean Gulf forms Lago Maggiore's most beautiful corner, and the Isole Borromee (Borromean Islands) harbour its most spectacular sights: the privately owned palaces of the Borromeo family.

Great For...

☑ Don't Miss

The 3000-year-old fossilised boat displayed in the grotto of Palazzo Borromeo.

Isola Bella

The grandest and busiest of the islands – the crowds can get a little overwhelming on weekends – Isola Bella is the centrepiece of the Borromeo Lake Maggiore empire. The island, the closest to Stresa, took the name of Carlo III's wife, Isabella, in the 17th century, when its centrepiece, **Palazzo Borromeo** (www.isoleborromee.it; Isola Bella; adult/child €15/8.50, incl Palazzo Madre €21/10; 9am-5.30pm mid-Mar–mid-Oct), was built for the Borromeo family.

Presiding over 10 tiers of spectacular terraced gardens, this baroque palace is Lago Maggiore's finest building. Wandering its sumptuous interiors reveals guestrooms, studies and reception halls. Particularly striking are the Sala di Napoleone, where the emperor Napoleon stayed with his wife in 1797; the Sala da Ballo (Ballroom);

Gardens of Palazzo Borromeo

the ornate Sala del Trono (Throne Room); and the Sala delle Regine (Queen's Room). Paintings from a 130-strong Borromeo collection hang all around.

Isola Madre

The fabulous **Palazzo Madre** (www.isoleborromee.it; adult/child €12/6.50, incl Palazzo Borromeo €21/10; ⌚9am-5.30pm mid-Mar–mid-Oct) *is* the island of Madre. The 16th- to 18th-century *palazzo* is a wonderfully decadent structure crammed full of all manner of antique furnishings and adornments. Highlights include Countess Borromeo's doll collection, a neoclassical puppet theatre designed by a scenographer from Milan's La Scala, and a 'horror' theatre with a cast of devilish marionettes.

Outside, the palace's gardens are even more lavish than those of Palazzo Borromeo on Isola Bella, although in June 2006 a freak tornado struck the island, uprooting many of the island's prized plants. Nevertheless, this English-style botanic garden remains full of interest, with azaleas, rhododendrons, camellias, eucalypts, banana trees, hibiscus, fruit orchards, an olive grove and much more. Exotic birdlife, including white peacocks and golden pheasants, roam the grounds.

Isola Superiore (Pescatori)

Tiny 'Fishermen's Island,' with a permanent population of around 50, retains much of its original fishing-village atmosphere. Apart from an 11th-century apse and a 16th-century fresco in the charming Chiesa di San Vittore, there are no real sights. Many visitors make it their port of call for lunch, but stay overnight and you'll fall in love with the place. Restaurants cluster around the boat landing, all serving grilled fish fresh from the lake (from around €15). On some days in spring and autumn, abundant rainfalls can lift the lake's level a fraction, causing minor flooding on the island. The houses are built with this in mind, with entrance stairs facing internal streets and situated high enough to prevent water entering the houses.

Baveno
Isola Madre
Isola Superiore (Pescatori)
Isole Borromeo
Lago Maggiore
Isola Bella
Stresa

Need to Know

A combined ticket covers admission to Palazzo Borromeo and Palazzo Madre .

Take a Break

Stop for lunch on Isola Superiore at **Casabella** (p227).

★ Top Tip

Give yourself at least half a day to enjoy each palace.

Lago Maggiore

Even in this region of breathtaking beauty, Lake Maggiore shines. Its wide waters reflect mountains that are often snow-topped; its shores are lined with rich architectural reminders of a grand 19th-century past. And it boasts the beguiling palace-dotted Isole Borromee (p224), which, like a fleet of fine vessels, lie at anchor in the Borromean Gulf.

More than Como and Garda, Lake Maggiore retains the belle époque air of its 19th-century heyday when the European *haute bourgeoisie* flocked to buy and build grand lakeside villas and establish a series of extraordinarily rich gardens.

GETTING THERE & AROUND

BOAT

Navigazione Lago Maggiore (☎800 551801; www.navigazionelaghi.it) operates passenger ferries and hydrofoils around the lake; its ticket booths are next to embarkation quays. Services include those connecting Stresa with Arona (€6, 40 minutes), Angera (€6, 35 minutes) and Verbania Pallanza (often just called Pallanza; €5, 35 minutes). Day passes include a ticket linking Stresa with Isola Superiore, Isola Bella and Isola Madre (€17). Services are drastically reduced in autumn and winter.

The only car ferry connecting the western and eastern shores sails between Verbania Intra (often just called Intra) and Laveno. Ferries run every 20 to 30 minutes; one-way transport costs from €8 to €13 for a car and driver; €5 for a bicycle and cyclist.

BUS

SAF (☎0323 55 21 72; www.safduemila.com) offers a daily service from Stresa to Milan (€9, 1½ hours), and also serves Verbania Pallanza (€3, 20 minutes) and Arona (€3, 20 minutes), departing from the waterfront.

TRAIN

Stresa is 1¼ hours from Milan (from €7.50) on the Domodossola–Milan train line. Domodossola (€3 to €9), 30 minutes northwest, is on the Swiss border, from where the train line leads to Brig and on to Geneva.

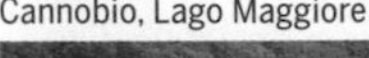

Cannobio, Lago Maggiore

Stresa

Stresa's easy accessibility from Milan has long made it a favourite for artists and writers, and today its sunny lake-front promenades are backed by architectural reminders of its heyday. One of the many high-profile visitors to Stresa, Lake Maggiore's main town, was author Ernest Hemingway; in 1918 he arrived in Stresa to convalesce from a war wound. A couple of pivotal scenes towards the end of his novel *A Farewell to Arms* are set at the Grand Hotel des Iles Borromees, the most palatial of the historic hotels garlanding the lake.

Stresa is also one of the casting-off points for the Isole Borromee (p224). It's well worth catching a ferry across to Isola Bella or Isola Madre to marvel at the baroque wealth of the Borromeo family's extravagant palaces and gardens.

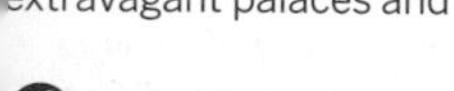

ACTIVITIES

Lake Maggiore Express Tour

The Lago Maggiore Express is a picturesque day trip you can do under your own steam. It includes train travel from Arona or Stresa to Domodossola, from where you get the charming Centovalli (Hundred Valleys) train to Locarno in Switzerland, before hopping on a ferry back to Stresa. Tickets are available from the Navigazione Lago Maggiore ticket booths at each port. (www.lagomaggioreexpress.com; adult/child €30/15)

EATING

Piemontese Piedmontese €€

The name gives a huge clue as to the focus of this refined *ristorante*. Regional delights include gnocchi with gorgonzola and hazelnuts; cold veal with tuna sauce; and risotto made using Piedmont's own Barolo wine. The Lake Menu (€34) features carp, trout, perch and pike, while the set lunch menu is a steal (2/3 courses €23/28). (☎0323 3 02 35; www.ristorantepiemontese.com; Via Mazzini 25; meals €35-45; ⏰12.30-2pm & 6.30-9.30pm)

BUENA VISTA IMAGES/GETTY IMAGES ©

Mountain Biking

Bicicò (☎340 3572189; www.bicico.it; Piazzale della Funivia; half-/full-day rental €25/30; ⏰9.30am-12.30pm & 1.30-5.30pm) rents mountain bikes from its base at the foot of the Stresa–Monte Mottarone cable car. Rates include a helmet and road book detailing an easy 25km, three-hour panoramic descent from the mountain top back to Stresa. Also runs guided trips (half-/full day €80/150) and advises on other mountain- and road-bike routes. Book trips and hire two days in advance.

Casabella Ristorante €€€

The setting is bewitching – right by the shore – and the food is acclaimed. The admirably short menu might feature home-smoked beef with spinach; blanched squid with ricotta, or perfectly cooked lake fish. Leave room for dessert; the pear cake with chocolate fondant is faultless.

If you don't want to leave after dinner (likely) there are two snug bedrooms on-site. (☎0323 3 34 71; www.isola-pescatori.it; Via del Marinaio 1; meals €30-50, 5-course tasting menu €55; ⏰noon-2pm & 6-8.30pm Feb-Nov)

INFORMATION

Stresa Tourist Office (☎0323 3 13 08; www.stresaturismo.it; Piazza Marconi 16; ⏰10am-12.30pm & 3-6.30pm summer, reduced hours winter)

BUENA VISTA IMAGES/GETTY IMAGES ©

Verbania's Villa Taranto

The grounds of late-19th-century **Villa Taranto** (☎0323 55 66 67; www.villataranto.it; Via Vittorio Veneto 111, Verbania Pallanza; adult/reduced €10/5.50; ⏰8.30am-6.30pm mid-Mar–Sep, 9am-4pm Oct; Ⓟ) are one of Lago Maggiore's highlights. A Scottish captain, Neil McEacharn, bought the Normandy-style villa from the Savoy family in 1931 after spotting an ad in the *Times*. He planted some 20,000 plant species over 30 years, and today it's considered one of Europe's finest botanic gardens. Even the main entrance path is a grand affair, bordered by lawns and a cornucopia of colourful flowers. It's a short walk from the Villa Taranto ferry stop.

Lago di Como

Set in the shadow of the snow-covered Rhaetian Alps and hemmed in on both sides by steep, wooded hills, Lago di Como (also known as Lake Lario) is the most spectacular and least visited of the three major lakes. Shaped like an upside-down letter Y, its winding shoreline is scattered with villages, including delightful Bellagio (see p222), which sits at the centre of the two southern branches on a small promontory. Where the southern and western shores converge is the lake's main town, Como.

GETTING THERE & AROUND

BOAT

Navigazione Lago di Como (☎800 551801; www.navigazionelaghi.it) operates year-round lakewide ferries and hydrofoils, which in Como depart from the jetties beside Piazza Cavour. Single fares range between €2.50 (to Cernobbio) and €12.60 (to Lecco). Return fares cost double. The faster hydrofoil services cost €1.40 to €4.90 extra. Car ferries link Menaggio on the west shore of Lago di Como with Varenna on the east and Bellagio to the south.

Ferries operate year-round, but services are reduced in winter. Zonal passes (per day €7 to €28; per six days €10.50 to €84) allow unlimited journeys and can work out cheaper than buying single or return tickets.

BUS

ASF Autolinee (☎031 24 72 47; www.sptlinea.it) operates regular buses around Lago di Como, which in Como depart from the bus station on Piazza Matteotti. Key routes include Como to Colico (€6, two hours, three to five daily), via all the villages on the western shore, and Como to Bellagio (€3.40, 70 minutes, hourly).

CAR

From Milan, take the A9 motorway and turn off at Monte Olimpino for Como. The SP342 leads east to Lecco and west to Varese. The roads around the lake are superbly scenic, but also windy, narrow and busy in summer.

TRAIN

Como's main train station (Como San Giovanni) is served from Milan's Stazione Centrale and Porta Garibaldi station (€4.80 to €13, 30 minutes to one hour, hourly). Trains from Milan's Stazione Nord (€4.10, one hour) use Como's lakeside Stazione FNM (aka Como Nord Lago). Trains from Milan to Lecco continue north along the eastern shore. When heading for Bellagio, it's best to continue on the train to Varenna and take the ferry from there.

Como

With its charming historic centre, 12th-century city walls and self-confident air, Como is an elegant and prosperous town. Built on the wealth of the silk industry, its pedestrianised core is full of bars, restaurants and shops, making the town an ideal lakeside base for the southern half of the lake.

SIGHTS & ACTIVITIES

Duomo Cathedral

Although largely Gothic in style, elements of Romanesque, Renaissance and baroque can also be seen in Como's marble-clad *duomo* (cathedral). The cathedral was built between the 14th and 18th centuries, and is crowned by a high octagonal dome. (Piazza del Duomo; 7.30am-7.30pm Mon-Sat, to 9.30pm Sun)

Basilica di San Fedele Basilica

With three naves and three apses, this evocative basilica is often likened to a clover leaf. Parts of it date from the 6th century while the facade is the result of a 1914 revamp. The 16th-century rose window and 16th- and 17th-century frescoes enhance the appeal. The apses are centuries old and feature some eye-catching sculpture on the right. (Piazza San Fedele; 8am-noon & 3.30-7pm)

Passeggiata Lino Gelpi Waterfront

One of Como's most charming walks is the lakeside stroll west from Piazza Cavour. Passeggiata Lino Gelpi leads past the **Monumento ai Caduti** (Memorial; Viale Puecher 9), a 1931 memorial to Italy's WWI dead and a classic example of Fascist-era architecture. Next you'll pass a series of mansions and villas, including Villa Saporiti and Villa Gallia, both now owned by the provincial government and closed to the

> *the Duomo is Gothic with elements of Romanesque, Renaissance and baroque*

Duomo, Como

public, before arriving at the garden-ringed Villa Olmo.

Villa Olmo Historic Building

Set facing the lake, the grand creamy facade of neoclassical Villa Olmo is one of Como's biggest landmarks. The extravagant structure was built in 1728 by the Odescalchi family, related to Pope Innocent XI. If there's an art exhibition showing, you'll get to admire the sumptuous Liberty-style interiors. Otherwise, you can enjoy the Italianate and English gardens. (031 25 23 52; Via Cantoni 1; gardens free, villa entry varies by exhibition; villa during exhibitions 9am-12.30pm & 2-5pm Mon-Sat, gardens 7.30am-11pm summer, to 7pm winter)

Museo della Seta Museum

Lago di Como's aspiring silk makers still learn their trade in the 1970s-built Istituto Tecnico Industriale di Setificio textile technical school. It's also home to the Museo della Seta, which draws together the threads of the town's silk history. Early dyeing and printing equipment features amid displays that chart the entire fabric-production process. (www.museosetacomo.com; Via Castelnuovo 9; adult/reduced €10/7; 10am-6pm Tue-Fri, to 1pm Sat)

Funicolare Como–Brunate Cable Car

Prepare for some spectacular views. The Como–Brunate cable car (built in 1894) takes seven minutes to trundle up to the quiet hilltop village of Brunate (720m), revealing a memorable panorama of mountains and lakes. From there a steep 30-minute walk along a stony mule track leads to San Maurizio (907m), where 143 steps climb to the top of a lighthouse. (031 30 36 08; www.funicolarecomo.it; Piazza de Gasperi 4; adult one way/return €3/5.50, reduced €2/3.20; half-hourly departures 8am-midnight summer, to 10.30pm winter)

Lido di Villa Olmo Swimming

What a delight: a compact *lido* (beach) where you can plunge into open-air pools, sunbathe beside the lake, rent boats, sip cocktails at the waterfront bar and soak up mountain views. Bliss. (031 57 08 71; www.

Funiculare Como–Brunate

idovillaolmo.it; Via Cernobbio 2; adult/reduced €7/3.50; ⏲9am-7pm mid-May–Sep)

EATING

Natta Café Cafe €

t's almost as if this is an *osteria* for the next generation. Yes, there's a proud focus on superb local ingredients and classic wines, but this laid-back cafe also has a beatnik atmosphere. So you get Chianti on the wine list, risotto with lake perch on the menu and Edith Piaf on the soundtrack. One cool vibe. (☎031 26 91 23; www.nattacafe.com; Via Natta 16; meals €15-20; ⏲12.30-3pm & 6.30-midnight Tue-Sat, 12.30-3pm & 7.30-11.30pm Sun; 📶)

Osteria del Gallo Italian €€

An ageless *osteria* that looks exactly the part. In the wood-lined dining room, wine bottles and other goodies fill the shelves, and diners sit at small timber tables to tuck into traditional local food. The menu is chalked up daily and might include a first course of *zuppa di ceci* (chickpea soup), followed by lightly fried lake fish. (☎031 27 25 91; www.osteriadelgallo-como.it; Via Vitani 16; meals €25-30; ⏲12.30-3pm Mon, to 9pm Tue-Sat)

INFORMATION

Main tourist office (☎031 26 97 12; www.comotourism.it; Piazza Cavour 17; ⏲9am-1pm & 2-5pm Mon-Sat) Como's main tourist office; has walking and cycling information.

Tremezzo

Tremezzo draws a fleet of ferries thanks to its spectacular lake views and 17th-century **Villa Carlotta** (☎034 44 04 05; www.villacarlotta.it; Via Regina 2; adult/reduced €9/7; ⏲9am-7.30pm Apr–mid-Oct). The waterfront villa sits high on Como's must-visit list; its botanic gardens are filled with colour from orange trees interlaced with pergolas, while some of Europe's finest rhododendrons, azaleas and camellias bloom. The villa, strung with paintings, sculptures (some by Antonio Canova) and tapestries, takes its name from the Prussian princess who was given the place in 1847 as a wedding present from her mother.

Situated on a steep hillside with panoramic lake views from its terrace, the excellent **Al Veluu** (☎0344 4 05 10; www.alveluu.com; Via Rogaro 11; meals €40-70; ⏲noon-2.30pm & 7-10pm Wed-Mon; 👪) serves up home-cooked dishes that are prepared with great pride. They also reflect Lago di Como's seasonal produce, so expect butter-soft, milk-fed kid with rosemary at Easter or wild asparagus and polenta in spring.

The restaurant terrace is a great place to view the Ferragosto fireworks on 15 August, while in winter the dining room log fire is lit. Upstairs there are two equally comfortable suites (€150 to €250) each sleeping up to four people. Staff even pick you up from the ferry dock.

Where to Stay

Cannobio on Lake Maggiore, just 5km from the Swiss border, is a dreamy place with some of the best restaurants and hotels on the lake.

Como's pedestrianised core is chock-full of bars, restaurants and places to sleep, making the town an ideal southern Lago di Como base.

Bellagio draws the summer Lake Como crowds – stay overnight for a more authentic feel and the full magical effect.

Seasonal closings (including hotels) are generally from November to February, but this can vary.

JEAN-PIERRE LESCOURRET/GETTY IMAGES ©

NAPLES

Naples

Italy's third-largest city is one of its oldest, most artistic and most delicious. Naples' centro storico *(historic centre) is a Unesco World Heritage Site, its archaeological treasures are among the world's most impressive, and its palaces, castles and churches make Rome look positively provincial.*

Then there's the food. Blessed with rich volcanic soils, a bountiful sea, and centuries of culinary know-how, the Naples region is one of Italy's epicurean heavyweights, serving up the country's best pizza, pasta and coffee, and many of its most celebrated seafood dishes, street snacks and sweet treats.

Certainly, Naples' urban sprawl can feel anarchic and unloved. But look beyond the grime and graffiti and you'll uncover a city of breathtaking frescoes, sculptures and panoramas, of unexpected elegance. Welcome to Italy's most unlikely masterpiece.

☑ In This Section

Left: Naples and Mt Vesuvius; Right: *Sfogliatella*

Arriving in Naples

Naples' Capodichino airport is 7km northeast of the centre. The Alibus shuttle bus connects to Piazza Garibaldi (Stazione Centrale) and Molo Beverello (€3, or €4 on board). Official taxi rates are €23 to a seafront hotel, €19 to Piazza del Municipio or €16 to Stazione Centrale.

Naples is southern Italy's main rail hub, with good connections to other Italian cities and towns.

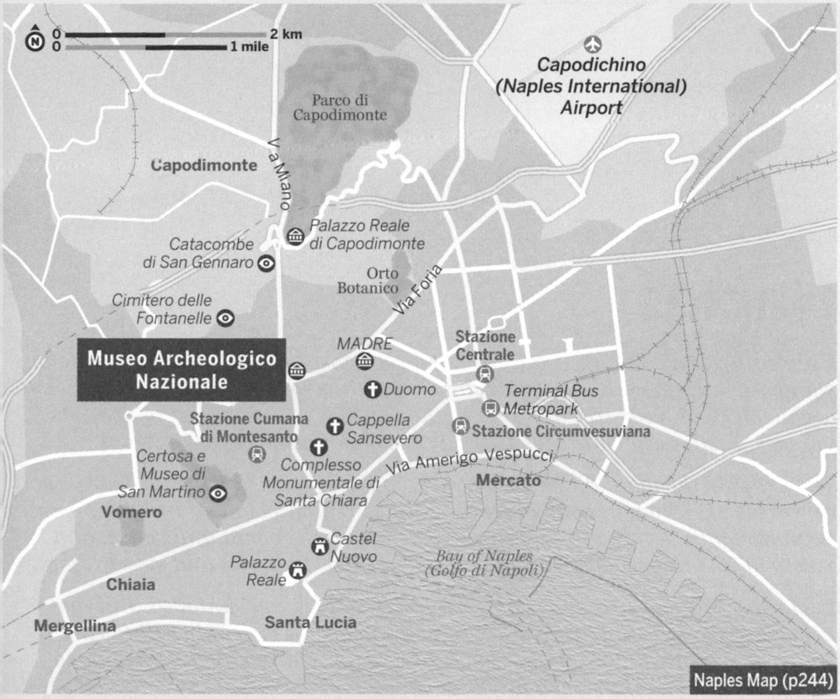

Naples Map (p244)

From left: Naples and Mt Vesuvius; *Sfogliatella;* Castel Nuovo (p247)

Museo Archeologico Nazionale

Naples' premier museum, the Museo Archeologico Nazionale serves up one of the world's finest collections of Graeco-Roman artefacts. The museum was established by the Bourbon king Charles VII in the late 18th century to house the antiquities he inherited from his mother, Elisabetta Farnese, as well as treasures looted from Pompeii and Herculaneum.

Great For...

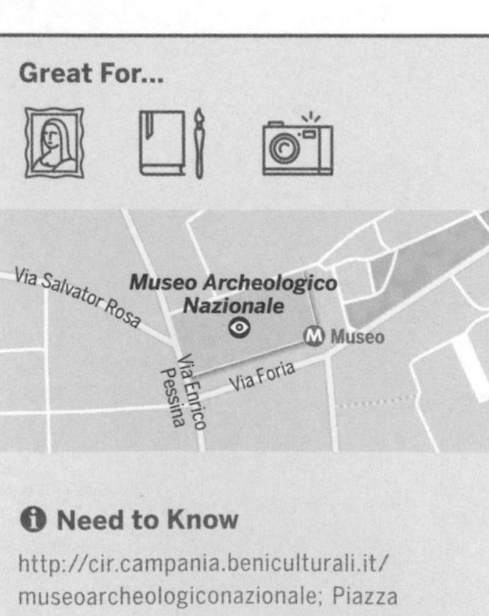

Need to Know

http://cir.campania.beniculturali.it/museoarcheologiconazionale; Piazza Museo Nazionale 19; adult/reduced €8/4; 9am-7.30pm Wed-Mon; M Museo, Piazza Cavour

★ **Top Tip**

You'll need around three hours to cover the museum's greatest hits.

Before tackling the collection, consider investing in the *National Archaeological Museum of Naples* (€12), published by Electa; if you want to concentrate on the highlights, audio guides (€5) are available in English. It's also worth calling ahead to ensure that the galleries you want to see are open, as staff shortages often mean that sections of the museum close for part of the day.

Farnese Collection

The basement houses the Borgia collection of Egyptian relics and epigraphs (closed indefinitely on our last visit). The ground-floor Farnese collection of colossal Greek and Roman sculptures features the celebrated *Toro Farnese* (Farnese Bull) and a muscle-bound *Ercole* (Hercules).

Sculpted in the early 3rd century AD and noted in the writings of Pliny, the *Toro Farnese*, probably a Roman copy of a Greek original, depicts the humiliating death of Dirce, Queen of Thebes. According to Greek mythology she was tied to a wild bull by Zeto and Amphion as punishment for her treatment of their mother Antiope, the first wife of King Lykos of Thebes. Carved from a single colossal block of marble, the sculpture was discovered in 1545 near the Baths of Caracalla in Rome and restored by Michelangelo, before eventually being shipped to Naples in 1787.

Ercole was discovered in the same Roman excavations, albeit without his legs. A pair of substitute limbs was made by Guglielmo della Porta, but when the originals turned up at a later dig, the Bourbons had them fitted onto the torso.

Farnese Atlante sculpture, Sala Meridiana

Mosaics

If you're short on time, take in the *Toro* and *Ercole* before heading straight to the mezzanine floor, home to an exquisite collection of mosaics, mostly from Pompeii. Of the series taken from the Casa del Fauno, it's *La battaglia di Alessandro contro Dario* (The Battle of Alexander against Darius) that really stands out. The best-known depiction of Alexander the Great, the 20-sq-metre mosaic was probably made by Alexandrian craftsmen working in Italy around the end of the 2nd century BC. Other intriguing mosaics include a cat killing a duck and a collection of Nile animals.

★ Top Tip

If you use the metro to get here watch out for snapshots by heavyweight Italian photographers decorating Museo station.

MATTES REN/HEMIS FR/AGE FOTOSTOCK ©

Gabinetto Segreto

Beyond the mosaics, the Gabinetto Segreto (Secret Chamber) contains a small but much-studied collection of ancient erotica. Pan is caught in the act with a nanny goat in the collection's most famous piece – a small and surprisingly sophisticated statue taken from the Villa dei Papiri in Herculaneum. You'll also find a series of nine paintings depicting erotic positions – a menu for brothel patrons.

Sala Meridiana

Originally the royal library, the enormous Sala Meridiana (Great Hall of the Sundial) on the 1st floor is home to the *Farnese Atlante*, a statue of Atlas carrying a globe on his shoulders, as well as various paintings from the Farnese collection. Look up and you'll find Pietro Bardellino's riotously colourful 1781 fresco depicting the (short-lived) triumph of Ferdinand IV of Bourbon and Marie Caroline of Austria in Rome. The rest of the 1st floor is largely devoted to fascinating discoveries from Pompeii, Herculaneum, Boscoreale, Stabiae and Cuma. Among them are whimsical wall frescoes from the Villa di Agrippa Postumus and the Casa di Meleagro, extraordinary bronzes from the Villa dei Papiri, as well as ceramics, glassware, engraved coppers and Greek funerary vases.

Take a Break

Head down to boho Piazza Bellini for drinks at **Spazio Nea** (p250).

☑ Don't Miss

The colossal *Toro Farnese*.

Cimitero delle Fontanelle

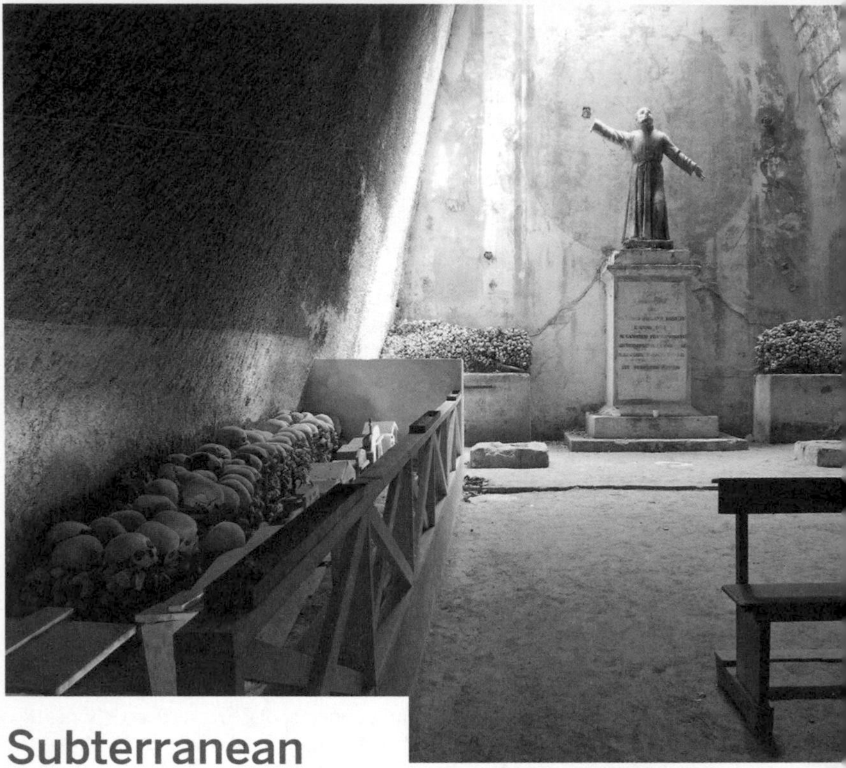

OLIVIERO OLIVIERI/ROBERTHARDING/GETTY IMAGES ©

Subterranean Naples

Lurking beneath Naples' streets is a thrilling urban wonderlands, a silent sprawl of Greek-era grottoes, paleo-Christian burial chambers, catacombs and ancient ruins.

Great For...

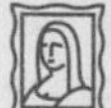

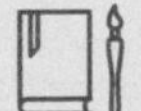

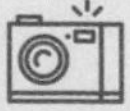

Don't Miss

The skulls in the Cimitero delle Fontanelle.

Search out these places for a glimpse of the city's fascinating *sottosuolo* (underground).

Catacombe di San Gennaro Catacomb

Naples' oldest and most sacred catacomb became a Christian pilgrimage site when San Gennaro's body was interred here in the 5th century. The carefully restored site allows visitors to experience an evocative otherworld of tombs, corridors and broad vestibules, its treasures including 2nd-century Christian frescoes, 5th-century mosaics and the oldest-known portrait of San Gennaro. (081 744 37 14; www.catacombedinapoli.it; Via Capodimonte 13; adult/reduced €8/5; 1hr tours every hour 10am-5pm Mon-Sat, to 1pm Sun; R4, 178 to Via Capodimonte)

Catacombe di San Gennaro

MATHESS/GETTY IMAGES ©

Cimitero delle Fontanelle Cemetery

Holding about eight million human bones, the ghoulish Fontanelle Cemetery was first used during the 1656 plague, before becoming Naples' main burial site during the 1837 cholera epidemic. At the end of the 19th century it became a hot spot for the *anime pezzentelle* (poor souls) cult, in which locals adopted skulls and prayed for their souls. Lack of information at the site makes joining a tour much more rewarding. (081 1970 3197; cimiterofontanelle.com; Via Fontanelle 80; 9am-4pm; C51 to Via Fontanelle) FREE

Tunnel Borbonico Historic Site

Traverse five centuries along Naples' engrossing Bourbon Tunnel. Conceived by Ferdinand II in 1853 to link the Palazzo Reale to the barracks and the sea, the never-completed escape route is part of the 17th-century Carmignano Aqueduct system, itself incorporating 16th-century cisterns. An air-raid shelter and military hospital during WWII, this underground labyrinth rekindles the past with evocative wartime artefacts. The standard tour doesn't require prebooking, though the Adventure Tour and adults-only Speleo Tour do. (366 2484151, 081 764 58 08; www.tunnelborbonico.info; Vico del Grottone 4; 75min standard tour adult/reduced €10/5; standard tour 10am, noon, 3.30pm & 5.30pm Fri-Sun; R2 to Via San Carlo)

Need to Know

For more on Naples' underground wonders check out www.napoliunplugged.com/locations-category/subterranean-naples.

Take a Break

Test the epic reputation of **Da Ettore** (081 764 35 78; Via Gennaro Serra 39; meals €25; 12.30-3pm daily, 7.45-10.15pm Tue-Sat; R2 to Via San Carlo), near the Tunnel Borbonico

★ Top Tip

Tour the Cimitero delle Fontanelle with the Cooperativa Sociale Onlus 'La Paranza' (www.catacombedinapoli.it).

Complesso Monumentale di San Lorenzo Maggiore Archaeological Site

Architecture and history buffs shouldn't miss this richly layered religious complex, its commanding basilica deemed one of Naples' finest medieval buildings. Aside from Ferdinando Sanfelice's petite facade, the Cappella al Rosario and the Cappellone di Sant'Antonio, beneath the basilica a sprawl of extraordinary ruins will transport you back two millennia. (081 211 08 60; www.sanlorenzomaggiorenapoli.it; Via dei Tribunali 316; church admission free, excavations & museum adult/reduced €9/7; 9.30am-5.30pm; C55 to Via Duomo)

…SIGHTS

… Centro Storico

…appella Sansevero Chapel

In this Masonic-inspired baroque chapel you'll find Giuseppe Sanmartino's incredible sculpture *Cristo velato* (Veiled Christ), its marble veil so realistic that it's tempting to try to lift it and view Christ underneath. It's one of several artistic wonders that include Francesco Queirolo's sculpture *Disinganno* (Disillusion), Antonio Corradini's *Pudicizia* (Modesty) and riotously colourful frescoes by Francesco Maria Russo, the latter untouched since their creation in 1749. (☎081 551 84 70; www.museosansevero.it; Via Francesco de Sanctis 19; adult/reduced €7/5; ⏰9.30am-6.30pm Mon & Wed-Sat, to 2pm Sun; Ⓜ Dante)

Complesso Monumentale di Santa Chiara Basilica, Monastery

The vast, Gothic Basilica di Santa Chiara stands at the heart of this tranquil monastery complex. The church was severely damaged in WWII: what you see today is a 20th-century re-creation of Gagliardo Primario's 14th-century original. Adjoining it are the basilica's cloisters, adorned with brightly coloured 17th-century majolica tiles and frescoes. (☎081 551 66 73; www.monasterodisantachiara.eu; Via Santa Chiara 49c; basilica free, Complesso Monumentale adult/reduced €6/4.50; ⏰basilica 7.30am-1pm & 4.30-8pm, Complesso Monumentale 9.30am-5.30pm Mon-Sat, 10am-2.30pm Sun; Ⓜ Dante)

Pio Monte della Misericordia Church, Museum

This octagonal, 17th-century church delivers a small, satisfying collection of Renaissance and baroque art, including works by Francesco de Mura, Giuseppe de Ribera, Andrea Vaccaro and Paul van Somer. It's also home to contemporary artworks by Italian and foreign artists, each inspired by Caravaggio's masterpiece *Le Sette Opere di Misericordia* (The Seven Acts of Mercy). Considered by many to be the most important painting in Naples, it's above the main altar in the ground-floor chapel. (☎081 44 69 44; www.piomontedellamisericordia.it; Via dei Tribunali 253; adult/reduced €7/5; ⏰9am-2pm Thu-Tue; 🚌 C55 to Via Duomo)

Cloisters of the Basilica di Santa Chiara

Duomo Cathedral

Whether you go for Giovanni Lanfranco's fresco in the Cappella di San Gennaro (Chapel of St Janarius), the 4th-century mosaics in the baptistry, or the thrice-annual miracle of San Gennaro, do not miss Naples' cathedral. Kick-started by Charles I of Anjou in 1272 and consecrated in 1315, it was largely destroyed in a 1456 earthquake, with copious nips and tucks over the subsequent centuries. (☎081 44 90 65; Via Duomo 149; baptistry €1.50; ⏰cathedral 8.30am-1.30pm & 2.30-8pm Mon-Sat, 8.30am-1.30pm & 4.30-7.30pm Sun, baptistry 8.30am-1pm Mon-Sat, 8.30am-12.30pm & 5-6.30pm Sun; 🚌C55 to Via Duomo)

MADRE Gallery

When *Madonna and Child* overload hits, reboot at Naples' museum of modern and contemporary art. Start on level three – the setting for temporary exhibitions – before hitting level two's permanent collection of painting, sculpture and installations from prolific 20th- and 21st-century artists. Among these are Olafur Eliasson, Shirin Neshat and Julian Beck, as well as Italian heavyweights Mario Merz and Michelangelo Pistoletto. Specially commissioned installations from the likes of Francesco Clemente, Anish Kapoor and Rebecca Horn cap things off on level one. (Museo d'Arte Contemporanea Donnaregina; ☎081 1931 3016; www.madrenapoli.it; Via Settembrini 79; adult/reduced €7/3.50, Mon free; ⏰10am-7.30pm Mon & Wed-Sat, to 8pm Sun; Ⓜ Piazza Cavour)

Vomero

Certosa e Museo di San Martino Monastery, Museum

The high point of the Neapolitan baroque, this charterhouse-turned-museum was founded as a Carthusian monastery in the 14th century. Centred on one of the most beautiful cloisters in Italy, it has been decorated, adorned and altered over the centuries by some of Italy's finest talent, most importantly Giovanni Antonio Dosio in the 16th century and baroque master Cosimo Fanzago a century later. Nowadays, it's a superb repository of Neapolitan artistry.

The monastery's church and the rooms that flank it contain a feast of frescoes and paintings by some of Naples' greatest 17th-century artists, among them Francesco Solimena, Massimo Stanzione, Giuseppe de Ribera and Battista Caracciolo. In the nave, Cosimo Fanzago's inlaid marble work is simply extraordinary. Adjacent to the church, the Chiostro dei Procuratori is the smaller of the monastery's two cloisters. A grand corridor on the left leads to the larger Chiostro Grande (Great Cloister). Originally designed by Dosio in the late 16th century and added to by Fanzago, it's a sublime composition of Tuscan-Doric porticoes, marble statues and vibrant camellias. The skulls mounted on the balustrade were a light-hearted reminder to the monks of their own mortality.Just off the Chiostro dei Procuratori, the small Sezione Navale documents the history of the Bourbon navy from 1734 to 1860, and features a collection

Museum Discounts

If you're planning to blitz the sight Campania Artecard (www.campania card.it) is an excellent investment. A cumulative ticket that covers museum admission and transport, it comes in various forms. The Naples three-day ticket (adult/reduced €21/12) gives free admission to three participating sites, a 50% discount on others and free use of public transport in the city. Other handy options include a 7-day 'Tutta la Regione' ticket (€34), which offers free admission to five sites and discounted admission to others in areas as far afield as Ravello (on the Amalfi Coast) and Paestum. The latter does not cover transport. Cards can be purchased online, at the dedicated Artecard booth inside the tourist office at Stazione Centrale, or at participating sites and museums.

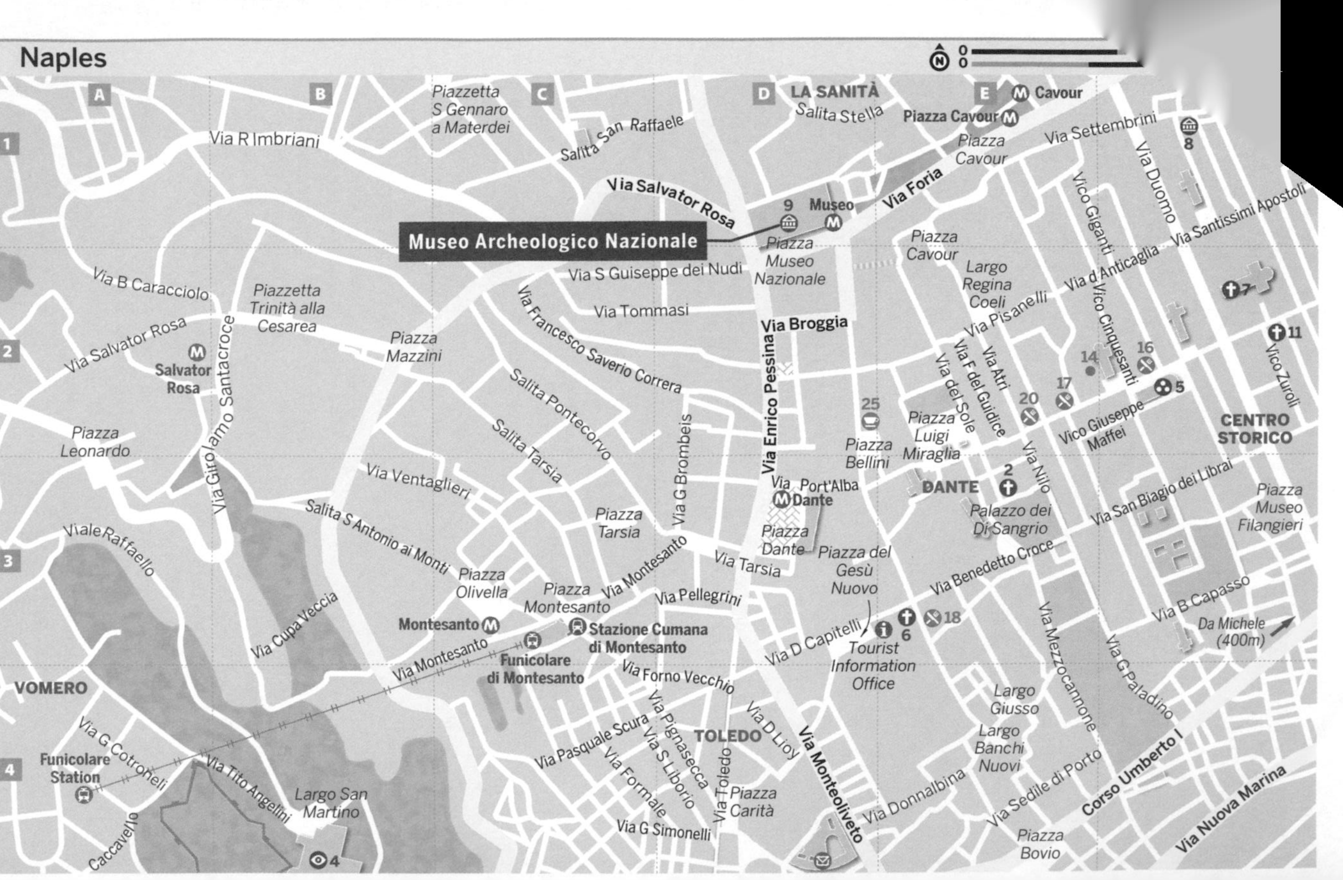
Naples
Museo Archeologico Nazionale
LA SANITÀ
CENTRO STORICO
DANTE
TOLEDO
VOMERO
Via R Imbriani
Piazzetta S Gennaro a Materdei
Salita San Raffaele
Salita Stella
Piazza Cavour
Cavour
Via Settembrini
Via Duomo
Via Salvator Rosa
Museo
Via Foria
Piazza Museo Nazionale
Via S Guiseppe dei Nudi
Via Tommasi
Via B Caracciolo
Piazzetta Trinità alla Cesarea
Via Salvator Rosa
Salvator Rosa
Via Girolamo Santacroce
Piazza Mazzini
Via Francesco Saverio Correra
Salita Pontecorvo
Salita Tarsia
Via G Brombeis
Via Enrico Pessina
Via Broggia
Largo Regina Coeli
Via Pisanelli
Via d'Anticaglia
Via Santissimi Apostoli
Vico Giganti
Vico Cinquesanti
Vico Zuroli
Via Atri
Via F del Guidice
Via del Sole
Via Nilo
Vico Giuseppe Maffei
Piazza Luigi Miraglia
Piazza Bellini
Via Port'Alba
Dante
Piazza Dante
Piazza del Gesù Nuovo
Palazzo dei Di Sangrio
Via San Biagio dei Librai
Piazza Museo Filangieri
Via Benedetto Croce
Via B Capasso
Da Michele (400m)
Piazza Leonardo
Via Ventaglieri
Salita S Antonio ai Monti
Piazza Tarsia
Via Montesanto
Via Tarsia
Piazza Olivella
Piazza Montesanto
Via Pellegrini
Montesanto
Stazione Cumana di Montesanto
Funicolare di Montesanto
Via Montesanto
Viale Raffaello
Via Cupa Veccia
Via D Capitelli
Tourist Information Office
Via Forno Vecchio
Via Pasquale Scura
Via Pignasecca
Via S Liborio
Via Formale
Via G Simonelli
Via Toledo
Piazza Carità
Via D Lioy
Via Monteoliveto
Via Donnalbina
Largo Giusso
Largo Banchi Nuovi
Via Mezzocannone
Via G Paladino
Via Sedile di Porto
Corso Umberto I
Via Nuova Marina
Piazza Bovio
Via G Cotroneli
Funicolare Station
Via Tito Angelini
Largo San Martino
Caccavello
A
B
C
D
E
1
2
3
4
2
4
5
6
7
8
9
11
14
16
17
18
20
25

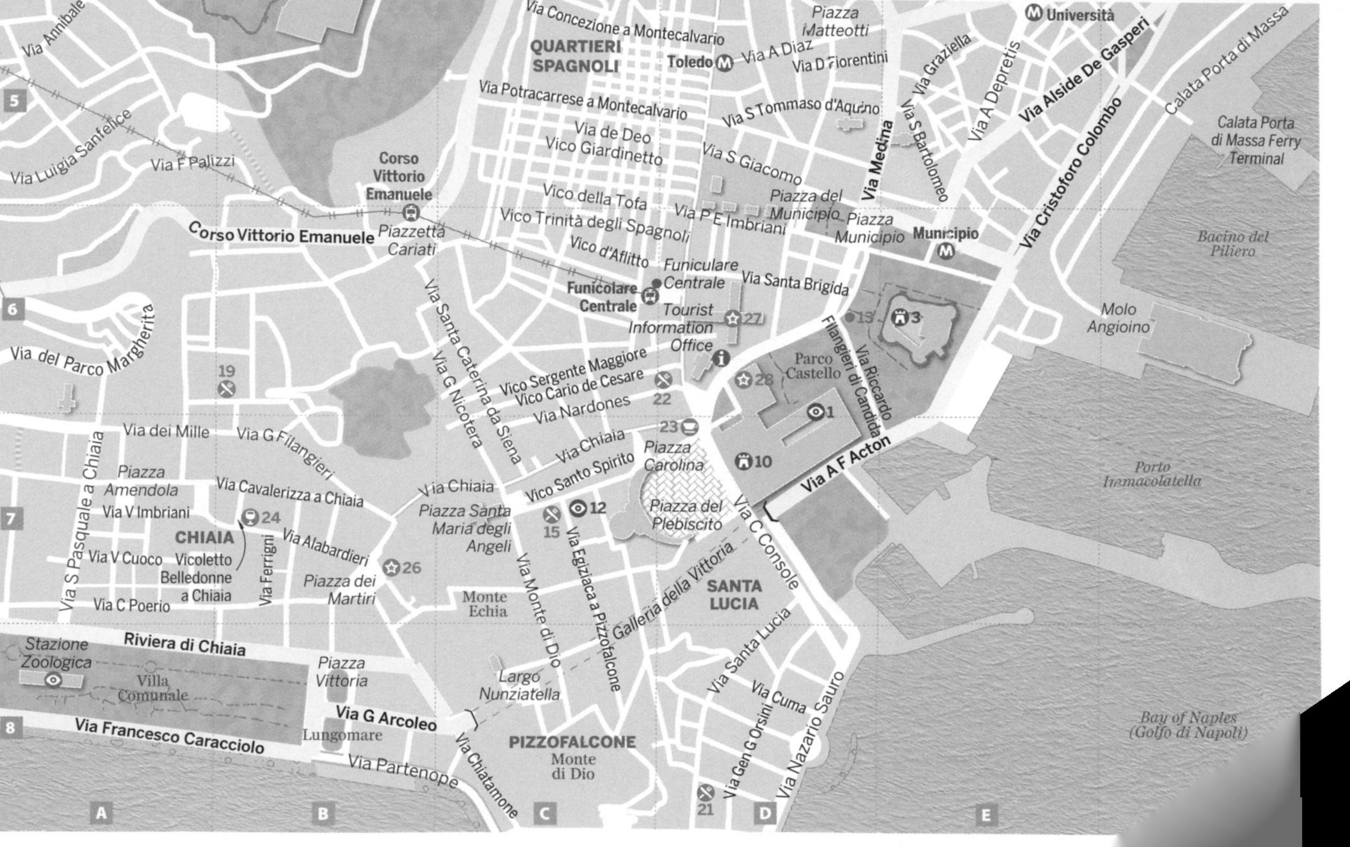
QUARTIERI SPAGNOLI
CHIAIA
SANTA LUCIA
PIZZOFALCONE
Via Annibale
Via Luigia Sanfelice
Via F Palizzi
Corso Vittorio Emanuele
Piazzetta Cariati
Via del Parco Margherita
Via dei Mille
Via G Filangieri
Via S Pasquale a Chiaia
Piazza Amendola
Via V Imbriani
Via V Cuoco
Vicoletto Belledonne a Chiaia
Via C Poerio
Via Cavalerizza a Chiaia
Via Ferrigni
Via Alabardieri
Piazza dei Martiri
Stazione Zoologica
Riviera di Chiaia
Villa Comunale
Piazza Vittoria
Via G Arcoleo
Lungomare
Via Francesco Caracciolo
Via Partenope
Via Chiatamone
Monte di Dio
Largo Nunziatella
Monte Echia
Via Monte di Dio
Via Egiziaca a Pizzofalcone
Galleria della Vittoria
Piazza Santa Maria degli Angeli
Via Chiaia
Vico Santo Spirito
Via Santa Caterina da Siena
Via G Nicotera
Vico Sergente Maggiore
Vico Cario de Cesare
Via Nardones
Piazza Carolina
Piazza del Plebiscito
Via C Console
Via Santa Lucia
Via Cuma
Via Gen G Orsini
Via Nazario Sauro
Bay of Naples (Golfo di Napoli)
Porto Immacolatella
Via A F Acton
Via Riccardo Filangieri di Candida
Parco Castello
Tourist Information Office
Funicolare Centrale
Vico d'Afflitto
Vico Trinità degli Spagnoli
Vico della Tofa
Vico Giardinetto
Via de Deo
Via Potracarrese a Montecalvario
Via Concezione a Montecalvario
Toledo
Via A Diaz
Piazza Matteotti
Via D Fiorentini
Via S Tommaso d'Aquino
Via S Giacomo
Via P E Imbriani
Piazza del Municipio
Piazza Municipio
Municipio
Via Santa Brigida
Via Medina
Via S Bartolomeo
Via Graziella
Via A Depretis
Università
Via Alside De Gasperi
Via Cristoforo Colombo
Calata Porta di Massa
Calata Porta di Massa Ferry Terminal
Bacino del Piliero
Molo Angioino
A
B
C
D
E
5
6
7
8
1
3
10
12
13
15
19
21
22
23
24
26
27
28

ioteca Nazionale D6
appella Sansevero E3
Castel Nuovo E6
4 Certosa e Museo di San Martino B4
5 Complesso Monumentale di San Lorenzo Maggiore F2
6 Complesso Monumentale di Santa Chiara E3
7 Duomo F2
8 MADRE F1
9 Museo Archeologico Nazionale D1
10 Palazzo Reale D7
11 Pio Monte della Misericordia F2
12 Tunnel Borbonico C7

Activities, Courses & Tours
13 City Sightseeing Napoli D6
14 Napoli Sotterranea E2

Eating
15 Da Ettore C7
16 Di Matteo F2
17 La Campagnola E2
18 La Taverna di Santa Chiara E3
19 L'Ebbrezza di Noè B6
20 Pizzeria Gino Sorbillo E2
21 Ristorantino dell'Avvocato D8
22 Trattoria San Ferdinando D6

Drinking & Nightlife
23 Caffè Gambrinus D7
24 Enoteca Belledonne B7
25 Spazio Nea D2

Entertainment
26 Azzurro Service B7
27 Box Office D6
28 Teatro San Carlo D6

of beautiful royal barges. The Sezione Presepiale houses a whimsical collection of rare Neapolitan *presepi* (nativity scenes). The Quarto del Priore has the bulk of the picture collection, as well as one of the museum's most famous pieces, Pietro Bernini's tender *Madonna col Bambino e San Giovannino* (Madonna and Child with the Infant John the Baptist). Room 32 boasts the beautiful *Tavola Strozzi* (Strozzi Table); its fabled depiction of 15th-century maritime Naples is one of the city's most celebrated historical records. You will need to book in advance to access the Certosa's imposing Sotterranei Gotici (Gothic basement), open to the public on Saturday and Sunday at 11.30am (with guided tour in Italian) and 4.30pm (without guided tour). The austere vaulted space is home to about 150 marble sculptures and epigraphs, including a statue of St Francis of Assisi by 18th-century master sculptor Giuseppe Sanmartino. To book a visit, email accoglienza.sanmartino@beniculturali.it at least two weeks in advance. (081 229 45 68; www.polomusealenapoli.beniculturali.it; Largo San Martino 5; adult/reduced €6/3; 8.30am-7.30pm Thu-Tue; M Vanvitelli, Montesanto to Morghen)

Santa Lucia & Chiaia

Palazzo Reale Palace, Museum

Envisaged as a 16th-century monument to Spanish glory (Naples was under Spanish rule at the time), the magnificent Palazzo Reale is home to the Museo del Palazzo Reale, a rich and eclectic collection of baroque and neoclassical furnishings, porcelain, tapestries, sculpture and paintings, spread across the palace's royal apartments.

Among the many highlights is the Teatrino di Corte, a lavish private theatre created by Ferdinando Fuga in 1768 to celebrate the marriage of Ferdinand IV and Marie Caroline of Austria. Incredibly, Angelo Viva's statues of Apollo and the Muses set along the walls are made of papier mâché. The Cappella Reale (Royal Chapel) houses an 18th-century *presepe napoletano* (Neapolitan nativity crib). Fastidiously detailed, its cast of *pastori* (crib figurines) were crafted by a series of celebrated Neapolitan artists, including Giuseppe Sanmartino, creator of the *Cristo velato* (Veiled Christ) sculpture in the Cappella Sansevero. The palace is also home to the **Biblioteca Nazionale** (National Library; 081 781 91 11; www.bnnonline.it; Palazzo Reale, Piazza del Plebiscito; 8.30am-7pm Mon-Fri, to 2pm Sat, papyri exhibition closes 2pm Mon-Sat; R2 to Via San Carlo, M Municipio)

FREE, its own priceless treasures including at least 2000 papyri discovered at Herculaneum and fragments of a 5th-century Coptic Bible. The National Library's beautiful Biblioteca Lucchesi Palli (Lucchesi Palli Library; closed Saturday) – designed by some of Naples' most celebrated 19th-century craftspeople – is home to numerous fascinating artistic artefacts, including letters by composer Giuseppe Verdi. Bring photo ID to enter the Biblioteca Nazionale. (Royal Palace; 081 40 05 47; www.sbapsae.na.it/cms; Piazza del Plebiscito 1; adult/reduced €4/3; 9am-8pm Thu-Tue; R2 to Via San Carlo, M Municipio)

Castel Nuovo Castle, Museum

Locals know this 13th-century castle as the Maschio Angioino (Angevin Keep) and its Cappella Palatina is home to fragments of frescoes by Renaissance maverick Giotto; they're on the splays of the Gothic windows. You'll find Roman ruins under the glass-floored Sala dell'Armeria (Armoury Hall), and a collection of mostly 17th- to early-20th-century Neapolitan paintings on the upper floors. The top floor houses the more interesting works, including landscape paintings by Luigi Crisconio and a watercolour drawing by architect Carlo Vanvitelli. (081 795 77 22; Piazza Municipio; admission €6; 9am-7pm Mon-Sat, last entry 6pm; M Municipio)

Capodimonte & La Sanità

Palazzo Reale di Capodimonte Museum

Originally designed as a hunting lodge for Charles VII of Bourbon, this monumental palace was begun in 1738 and took more than a century to complete. It's now home to the Museo Nazionale di Capodimonte, southern Italy's largest and richest art gallery. Its vast collection ranges from exquisite 12th-century altarpieces to works by Botticelli, Caravaggio, Titian and Andy Warhol.

The gallery is spread over three floors and 160 rooms; for most people, a full morning or afternoon is enough [for an] abridged best-of tour. The 1st floo[r ...] works by greats such as Michelang[elo,] Raphael and Titian, with highlights in[clud]ing Masaccio's *Crocifissione* (Crucifixio[n;] Room 3), Botticelli's *Madonna col Bambi[no] e due angeli* (Madonna with Child and Angels; Room 6), Bellini's *Trasfigurazione* (Transfiguration; Room 8) and Parmigianino's *Antea* (Room 12). Upstairs, the piece that many come to see, is Caravaggio's *Flagellazione* (Flagellation; 1607–10), which hangs in reverential solitude in Room 78. If you have any energy left, the small gallery of modern art on the 3rd floor is worth a quick look, if for nothing else than Andy Warhol's poptastic *Mt Vesuvius*. Once you've finished in the museum, the Parco di Capodimonte – the palace's 130-hectare estate – provides a much-needed breath of fresh air. (081 749 91 11; www.polomusealenapoli.beniculturali.it; Via Miano 2; adult/reduced €7.50/3.75; 8.30am-7.30pm Thu-Tue; R4, 178 to Via Capodimonte)

TOURS

City Sightseeing Napoli Bus Tour

City Sightseeing Napoli operates a hop-on, hop-off bus service with four routes across the city. All depart from Piazza del Municipio Parco Castello, and tickets are available on board. Tour commentaries are provided in English. (081 551 72 79; www.napoli.city-sightseeing.it; adult/reduced €22/11)

Napoli Sotterranea Tour

This evocative guided tour leads you 40m below street level to explore Naples' ancient labyrinth of aqueducts, passages and cisterns. (Underground Naples; 081 29 69 44; www.napolisotterranea.org; Piazza San Gaetano 68; adult/reduced €10/8; English tours 10am, noon, 2pm, 4pm & 6pm; C55 to Via Duomo)

ENTERTAINMENT

Options run the gamut from nail-biting football games to world-class opera. For cultural listings check www.incampania.it.

Naples' Best Pizza

Naples is the spiritual home of pizza and it was already a common street snack when Italian King Umberto I and his wife Queen Margherita visited the city in 1889. Famous *pizzaiola* (pizza maker) Raffaelle Esposito, created a pizza of tomato, mozzarella and basil based on the red, white and green flag of the newly unified Italy. The resulting topping met with the queen's approval and was named in her honour.

Try these legendary pizza hot spots in the *centro storico:*

Pizzeria Gino Sorbillo (☎081 44 66 43; www.accademiadellapizza.it;Via dei Tribunali 32; pizzas from €3.30; ⏰noon-3.30pm & 7pm-1am Mon-Sat; Ⓜ Dante) Day in, day out, this cult-status pizzeria is besieged by hungry hordes. While debate may rage over whether Gino Sorbillo's pizzas are the best in town, there's no doubt that his giant, wood-fired discs – made using organic flour and tomatoes – will have you licking fingertips and whiskers. Head in super early or prepare to queue.

Da Michele (☎081 553 92 04;www.damichele.net; Via Cesare Sersale 1; pizzas from €4; ⏰10.30am-midnight Mon-Sat) Veteran pizzeria Da Michele continues to keep things plain and simple with just two types of pizza: margherita or marinara. Both are delicious. Just show up, take a ticket and wait (patiently) for your turn.

Di Matteo (☎081 45 52 62;www.pizzeriadimatteo.com;Via dei Tribunali 94; snacks from €0.50, pizzas from €3; ⏰9am-midnight Mon-Sat, to 3.30pm Sun; Ⓜ Duomo) One of Naples' hardcore, low-frills pizzerias, Di Matteo is fronted by a popular street-front stall that sells some of the city's best fried snacks, from *pizza fritta* (Neapolitan fried pizza) to nourishing *arancini* (fried rice balls). Inside, expect trademark sallow lighting, surly waiters and gorgeous pizzas.

Tickets for most cultural events are available from ticket agency **Box Office** (☎081 551 91 88; www.boxofficenapoli.it; Galleria Umberto I 17; ⏰9.30am-8pm Mon-Fri, 9.30am-1.30pm & 4.30-8pm Sat; 🚌R2 to Piazza Trieste e Trento) or at **Azzurro Service** inside the Chiaia branch of bookshop Feltrinelli (☎081 032 23 62; www.azzurroservice.net; Piazza dei Martiri 23; ⏰11am-2pm & 3-8pm Mon-Sat; 🚌C24 to Piazza dei Martiri).

Teatro San Carlo — Opera, Ballet

One of Italy's top opera houses, the San Carlo stages opera, ballet and concerts. Bank on €50 for a place in the sixth tier, €100 for a seat in the stalls or – if you're under 30 and can prove it – €30 for a place in a side box. Ballet tickets range from €35 to €80, with €20 tickets for those under 30. (☎081 797 23 31; www.teatrosancarlo.it; Via San Carlo 98; ⏰box office 10am-5.30pm Mon-Sat, to 2pm Sun; 🚌R2 to Via San Carlo)

EATING

La Campagnola — Neapolitan €

Boisterous and affable, this spruced-up Neapolitan stalwart dishes unfussed, soul-coaxing classics. Daily specials include a killer *genovese* (pasta with a slow-cooked lamb, tomato and onion *ragù*) on Thursday, while week-round classics include hearty *salsiccia con friarielli* (pork sausage with Neapolitan bitter greens). If there's still room to move, conclude with the rum-soaked *babà*. (☎081 45 90 34; Via dei Tribunali 47; meals €18; ⏰12.30-4pm & 7-11.30pm; 📶; Ⓜ Dante)

La Taverna di Santa Chiara — Neapolitan €€

Gragnano pasta, Agerola pork, Benevento *latte nobile:* this intimate, two-level eatery is healthily obsessed with small, local producers and Slow Food ingredients. The result is a beautiful, seasonal journey across Campania. For an inspiring overview, order the *antipasto misto* (mixed antipasto), then tuck into lesser-known classics like *zuppa di soffritto* (spicy meat stew) with a glass of smooth house vino. (☎339 8150346;

Via Santa Chiara 6; meals €25; 12.30-3pm & 7-11pm Wed-Mon; ; Dante)

Trattoria San Ferdinando Neapolitan **€€**

Hung with theatre posters, cosy San Ferdinando pulls in well-spoken theatre types and intellectuals. For a Neapolitan taste trip, ask for a rundown of the day's antipasti and choose your favourites for an *antipasto misto*. Seafood standouts include a delicate *seppia ripieno* (stuffed squid), while the homemade desserts make for a satisfying denouement. (081 42 19 64; Via Nardones 117; meals €27; noon-3pm Mon-Sat, 7.30-11pm Tue-Fri; R2 to Via San Carlo, Municipio)

L'Ebbrezza di Noè Neapolitan **€€**

A wine shop by day, 'Noah's Drunkenness' transforms into an intimate culinary hot spot by night. Slip inside for vino and conversation at the bar, or settle into one of the bottle-lined dining rooms for seductive, market-driven dishes like house special *paccheri fritti* (fried pasta stuffed with eggplant and served with fresh basil and a rich tomato sauce). (081 40 01 04; www.lebbrezzadinoe.com; Vico Vetriera 9; me 8.30pm-midnight Tue-Sun; Piazza A

Ristorantino dell' Avvocato Neapolitan **€€**

This elegant yet welcoming restaurant has quickly won the respect of Neapolitan gastronomes. Apple of their eye is affable lawyer turned head chef whose passion for Campania's culinary heritage merges with a knack for subtle, refreshing twists – think gnocchi with fresh mussels, clams, crumbed pistachio, lemon, ginger and garlic. (081 032 00 47; www.ilristorantinodellavvocato.it; Via Santa Lucia 115-117; meals €40; noon-3pm & 7.30-11pm, lunch only Mon & Sun; ; 128 to Via Santa Lucia)

DRINKING & NIGHTLIFE

Caffè Gambrinus Cafe

Grand, chandeliered Caffè Gambrinus is Naples' oldest and most venerable cafe. Oscar Wilde knocked back a few here and Mussolini had some of the rooms shut to keep out left-wing intellectuals. The prices

Pizza margherita

Teatro San Carlo (p248)

may be steep, but the *aperitivo* nibbles are decent, and sipping a spritz or a luscious *cioccolata calda* (hot chocolate) in its belle époque rooms is something worth savouring. (081 41 75 82; www.grancaffegambrinus.com; Via Chiaia 12; 7am-1am Sun-Thu, to 2am Fri, to 3am Sat; R2 to Via San Carlo, M Municipio)

Spazio Nea — Cafe

Aptly skirting bohemian Piazza Bellini, this whitewashed gallery features its own cafe-bar speckled with books, flowers, cultured crowds and alfresco seating at the bottom of a baroque staircase. Eye up exhibitions of contemporary Italian and foreign art, then kick back with a *caffé* or a Cynar *spritz*. Check Nea's Facebook page for readings, live music gigs or DJ sets. (081 45 13 58; www.spazionea.it; Via Constantinopoli 53; 9am-2am; ; M Dante)

Enoteca Belledonne — Bar

Exposed-brick walls, ambient lighting and bottle-lined shelves set a cosy scene at Chiaia's best-loved wine bar – just look for the evening crowd spilling out onto the street. Swill, sniff and eavesdrop over a list of well-chosen, mostly Italian wines, including 30 by the glass. The decent grazing menu includes charcuterie and cheese (€16), crostini (from €6) and *bruschette* (€7). (081 40 31 62; www.enotecabelledonne.com; Vico Belledonne a Chiaia 18; 10am-2pm & 4.30pm-2am Tue-Sat, 6.30pm-1am Mon & Sun; ; C24 to Riviera di Chiaia)

 INFORMATION

Head to the following tourist bureaux for information and a map of the city:

Piazza del Gesù Nuovo (081 551 27 01; Piazza del Gesù Nuovo 7; 9am-5pm Mon-Sat, to 1pm Sun; M Dante) In the *centro storico*.

Stazione Centrale (081 26 87 79; Stazione Centrale; 8.30am-7.30pm; M Garibaldi)

Via San Carlo (081 40 23 94; Via San Carlo 9; 9am-5pm Mon-Sat, to 1pm Sun; R2 to Via San Carlo, M Municipio)

GETTING THERE & AWAY

AIR

Capodichino airport (081 789 61 11; www.aeroportodinapoli.it), 7km northeast of the city centre, is southern Italy's main airport. It's served by a number of major airlines and low-cost carriers, including EasyJet, which operates flights to Naples from London, Paris, Berlin and several other European cities.

BOAT

Molo Beverello Right in front of Castel Nuovo, this terminal services fast ferries and hydrofoils for Capri, Sorrento, Ischia (both Ischia Porto and Forio) and Procida. Some hydrofoils for Capri, Ischia, Procida and Sicily's Aeolian Islands leave from Mergellina, 5km further west.

Molo Angioino Beside Molo Beverello, this terminal services slow ferries for Sicily, the Aeolian Islands and Sardinia.

Calata Porta di Massa Beside Molo Angioino, this terminal services slow ferries to Ischia, Procida and Capri.

BUS

Most national and international buses now leave from **Terminal Bus Metropark** (800 650006; Corso Arnaldo Lucci; M Garibaldi), located on the south side of Stazione Centrale. The bus station is home to **Biglietteria Vecchione** (081 563 03 20; Corso Arnaldo Lucci, Terminal Bus Metropark; 6.30am-7.30pm Mon-Sat; M Garibaldi), a ticket agency selling national and international bus tickets.

Terminal Bus Metropark serves numerous bus companies offering regional services, the most useful of which is **SITA Sud** (www.sitasudtrasporti.it). Connections from Naples include Amalfi and Positano.

At the time of writing CLP and CTP buses departed directly in front of Stazione Centrale on Piazza Garibaldi. This may change as construction work on the piazza nears completion; check the departure point with your bus company.

TRAIN

Naples is southern Italy's main rail hub. Most national trains arrive at or depart from **Stazione Centrale** (081 554 31 88; Piazza Garibaldi) or underneath the main station, from Stazione Garibaldi. Some services also stop at Mergellina station.

National rail company **Trenitalia** (892021; www.trenitalia.com) runs regular services to Rome (2nd class €12 to €43, 70 minutes to 2¾ hours, up to 49 daily). High-speed private rail company **Italo** (06 07 08; www.italotreno.it) also runs daily services to Rome (2nd class €15 to €39, 70 minutes, up to 15 daily). Not all Italo services stop at Roma Termini, with many stopping at Roma Tiburtina instead.

Circumvesuviana (800 211388; www.eavsrl.it) operates frequent train services to Sorrento (€4.50, 66 minutes) via Ercolano (€2.50, 16 minutes), Pompei (€3.20, 35 minutes)

Where to Stay

The *centro storico* (historic centre) is the city's heart and soul, and a convenient spot to slumber. Options span B&Bs, designer dens and converted baroque palazzi.

Mercato, close to the train station, is awash with budget hotels but be warned that the area is bedlam by day and dodgy by night.

Earthy Quartieri Spagnoli (whose reputation for crime is exaggerated) offers an atmospheric mix of razor-thin laneways, lively trattorias and cosy slumber spots spanning homey hotels to a cosy B&Bs.

Chiaia is the place for designer shopping and bar-hopping, so accommodation is chic rather than cheap.

Santa Lucia has some lavish seaside hotels but there are still affordable options, some with stunning bay vistas.

Vomero is not exactly bursting with sights, but the views are divine, the streets are leafy and that heady Neapolitan chaos is a funicular ride away.

La Sanità offers a growing number of atmospheric spots to sleep in an area that's pure old-school Naples.

The Art of the Neapolitan Presepe

Christmas nativity cribs may not be exclusive to Naples, but none match the artistic brilliance of the *presepe napoletano* (Neapolitan nativity crib).

The nobility and bourgeoisie of 18th-century Naples commissioned the finest sculptors to craft their *presepi* and used the finest fabrics. Even the royals got involved: Charles III of Bourbon consulted Dominican monk Padre Rocco, the esteemed *presepe* expert, on the creation of his 5000-*pastore* spectacular, still on show at the Palazzo Reale (p246). Yet even this pales in comparison to the upsized Cuciniello crib on display at the Certosa e Museo di San Martino (p243), considered the world's greatest.

Centuries on, the legacy continues. The craft's epicentre is the *centro storico* street of Via San Gregorio Armeno, its clutter of shops and workshops selling everything from doting donkeys to kitsch celebrity caricatures.

and other towns along the coast, departing from Naples' Porta Nolana and stopping at Piazza Garibaldi station, adjacent to Stazione Centrale.

From late May to October, express tourist train Campania Express runs three times daily between Porta Nolana and Piazza Garibaldi stations in Naples and the town of Sorrento. The only stops en route are Ercolano and Pompei. One-day return tickets (€15, €10 for Artecard holders) can be purchased at the stations, online at www.eavsrl.it or www.campaniartecard/grand-tour, or by phone on 800 600 601.

GETTING AROUND

TO/FROM THE AIRPORT

Airport shuttle bus **Alibus** (800 639525; www.anm.it) connects the airport to Piazza Garibaldi (Stazione Centrale) and Molo Beverello (€3 from selected tobacconists, €4 on board; 45 minutes; every 20 minutes).

Official taxi fares from the airport are €23 to a seafront hotel or to Mergellina hydrofoil terminal, €19 to Piazza Municipio or Molo Beverello ferry terminal, and €16 to Stazione Centrale.

PUBLIC TRANSPORT

If travelling on public transport in Naples and Campania, you will most likely be using Ticket Integrato Campania (TIC) tickets. Readily available from newspaper kiosks and *tabaccaio* (tobacconists), these integrated tickets are valid on bus, tram, funicular, metro and suburban train services in Naples. They are also valid on regional Circumvesuviana and Cumana trains, as well as on EAV and SITA Sud buses across Campania. They are not valid on ferry and hydrofoil services. Ticket types and prices vary depending on where you want to travel.

The cheapest option is a *corsa semplice* (one-trip) ticket, valid for one trip within one travel zone only. The *biglietto orario* (multi-trip ticket) allows for multiple trips within a specified time period and across any number of zones. Daily and multi-day tickets are also available in some areas. Prices listed in this chapter are generally for *biglietto orario* tickets.

The TIC website (www.tic-campania.net) offers a handy ticket calculator covering the entire Campania region: simply click 'Trova la tariffa', type in the town of your departure in the 'Da' box and your destination in the 'A' box, then click 'Cerca'.

TIC tickets aside, many of the region's transport companies offer their own tickets, for use on their own services only. For example, ANM – which runs Naples' city buses, the four funiculars, and metro lines 1 and 6 – offers a €1 single-use ticket. State railway company Ferrovie dello Stato (FS) runs the city's metro line 2, offering a €1.20 single-use ticket for use on that metro line.

BUS

In Naples, city buses are operated by **ANM** (800 639525; www.anm.it). There's no central bus station, but most buses pass through Piazza Garibaldi.

Palazzo Reale (p246)

UNICULAR

ree of Naples' four funicular railways connect e centre with Vomero (the fourth, Funicolare Mergellina, connects the waterfront at Via ergellina with Via Manzoni).

nicolare Centrale Ascends from Via Toledo to azza Fuga.

nicolare di Chiaia From Via del Parco Margh-ita to Via Domenico Cimarosa.

nicolare di Montesanto From Piazza Monte-nto to Via Raffaele Morghen.

ETRO

ne 1 runs from Garibaldi (Stazione Centrale) Vomero and the northern suburbs via the y centre. Useful stops include: Duomo and iversità (southern edge of the *centro storico*), unicipio (hydrofoil and ferry terminals), Toledo a Toledo and Quartieri Spagnoli), Dante estern edge of the *centro storico*) and Museo ational Archaeological Museum).

Line 2 runs from Gianturco to Garibaldi (Stazi-e Centrale) and on to Pozzuoli. Useful stops lude: Piazza Cavour (La Sanità and northern ge of *centro storico*), Piazza Amedeo (Chiaia) d Mergellina (Mergellina ferry terminal).

Change between lines 1 and 2 at Garibaldi or Piazza Cavour (known as Museo on Line 1).

TAXI

Official taxis are white and have meters; always ensure the meter is running. There are taxi stands at most of the city's main piazzas or you can call one of the following taxi cooperatives:

Consortaxi (☎081 22 22; www.consortaxi.com)

Consorzio Taxi Napoli (☎081 88 88; www.consorziotaxinapoli.it)

Radio Taxi Napoli (☎081 556 44 44; www.radiotaxinapoli.it)

The minimum taxi fare is €4.50, of which €3.50 is the starting fare. The minimum charge increases to €6 between 10pm and 7am, on Sundays and on holidays. There is also a baffling range of additional charges, including €1 for a radio taxi call and €0.50 per piece of luggage in the boot.

Official flat rates do exist on some routes, including to/from the airport, Stazione Centrale and the ferry ports. If available, flat-rate fares must be requested at the beginning of your trip.

From Stazione Centrale, fixed-fare routes include Molo Beverello (€11) and Mergellina (€13).

Teatro Grande (p261)

POMPEII

Pompeii

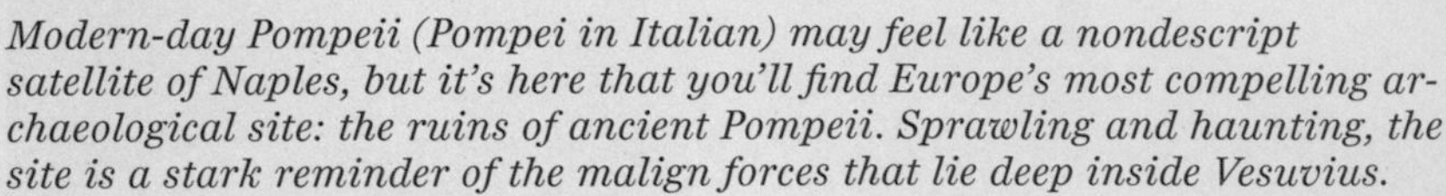

Modern-day Pompeii (Pompei in Italian) may feel like a nondescript satellite of Naples, but it's here that you'll find Europe's most compelling archaeological site: the ruins of ancient Pompeii. Sprawling and haunting, the site is a stark reminder of the malign forces that lie deep inside Vesuvius.

Pompeii's origins are unclear, but it's thought the city was founded in the 7th century BC. Over the next seven centuries it fell to the Greeks and Samnites before becoming a Roman colony in 80 BC.

In AD 62, 17 years before Vesuvius erupted, the city was struck by a major earthquake. Damage was widespread and much of the city's 20,000-strong population was evacuated. Fortunately, many had not returned by the time Vesuvius blew, but still 2000 men, women and children perished.

☑ In This Section

ℹ Arriving in Pompeii

Circumvesuviana trains run to Pompei-Scavi-Villa dei Misteri station from Naples (€3.20, 36 minutes) and Sorrento (€2.80, 30 minutes).

CSTP bus 50 runs from Salerno's Piazza Vittorio Veneto to Pompeii (€2.80, 70 minutes, 15 daily).

If driving, take the A3 from Naples. Use the Pompeii exit and follow signs to Pompeii Scavi. Car parks (approximately €5 per hour) are clearly marked and vigorously touted.

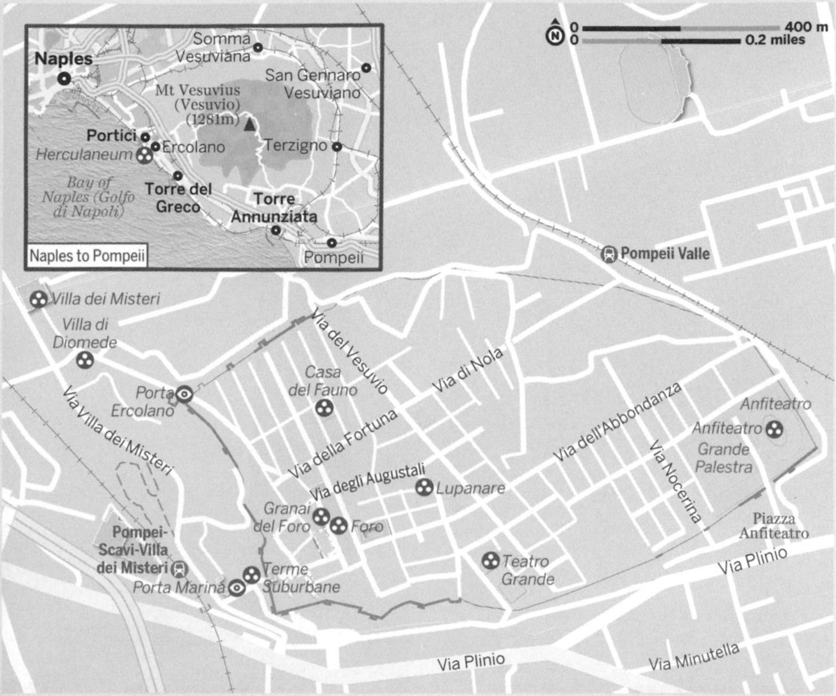

Far left: Wall statues; Pompeii station; Terme del Foro
DAVE G KELLY/GETTY IMAGES ©; PHOTO AND CO/GETTY IMAGES ©; DE AGOSTINI/L.ROMANO/GETTY IMAGES ©

Exploring the Ruins

The ghostly ruins of ancient Pompeii provide a remarkably well-preserved slice of ancient life. Here you can walk down Roman streets and snoop around millennia-old houses, temples, shops, cafes, amphitheatres and even a brothel.

Great For...

Need to Know

Entrances at Porta Marina, Piazza Esedra & Piazza Anfiteatro; www.pompeiisites.org; 8.30am-7.30pm summer, to 5pm winter; adult/reduced €11/5.50, incl Herculaneum €20/10

★ **Top Tip**

The ruins are not well labelled, so an audio guide (€6.50, cash only) will definitely enhance your visit.

Visiting the Site

Much of the site's value lies in the fact that the city wasn't blown away by Vesuvius in AD 79, but buried beneath a layer of *lapilli* (burning fragments of pumice stone). The remains first came to light in 1594, but systematic exploration didn't begin until 1748. Since then 44 of Pompeii's original 66 hectares have been excavated.

Before entering the site through Porta Marina, the gate that originally connected the town with the nearby harbour, duck into the Terme Suburbane. This 1st-century-BC bathhouse is famous for several erotic frescoes that scandalised the Vatican when they were revealed in 2001. The panels decorate what was once the *apodyterium* (changing room). The room leading to the colourfully frescoed *frigidarium* (cold-water bath) features fragments of stuccowork, as well as one of the few original roofs to have survived at Pompeii.

Done in the Terme, continue through the city walls to the main part of the site.

Foro — Archaeological Site

A huge grassy rectangle flanked by limestone columns, the *foro* (forum) once served as ancient Pompeii's main piazza, as well as the site of gladiatoral battles before the Anfiteatro was constructed. The buildings surrounding the forum are testament to its role as the city's hub of civic, commercial, political and religious activity.

Lupanare — Archaeological Site

Ancient Pompeii's only dedicated brothel, Lupanare is a tiny two-storey building with five rooms on each floor. Its collection of raunchy frescoes provided a menu of

Impluvium (rain tank) in a Pompeii house

sorts for clients. The walls in the rooms are carved with graffiti – including declarations of love and hope written by the brothel workers – in various languages.

Teatro Grande Archaeological Site
The 2nd-century-BC Teatro Grande was a huge 5000-seat theatre carved into the lava mass on which Pompeii was originally built.

Anfiteatro Archaeological Site
Gladiatorial battles thrilled up to 20,000 spectators at the grassy *anfiteatro* (amphitheatre). Built in 70 BC, it's the oldest-known Roman amphitheatre in existence.

☑ Don't Miss
It's well worth seeking out the peaceful vineyard outside the *anfiteatro* (amphitheatre).

DE AGOSTINI/L. ROMANO/GETTY IMAGES ©

Casa del Fauno Archaeological Site
Covering an entire *insula* (city block) and boasting two atria at its front end (humbler homes had one), Pompeii's largest private house, the House of the Faun is named after the delicate bronze statue in the *impluvium* (rain tank). It was here that early excavators found Pompeii's greatest mosaics, most of which are now in Naples' Museo Archeologico Nazionale (p236). Valuable on-site survivors include a beautiful, geometrically patterned marble floor.

Body Casts
One of the most haunting sights at Pompeii are the body casts in the **Granai del Foro** (Forum Granary). These were made in the late 19th century by pouring plaster into the hollows left by disintegrated bodies. Among the casts is a pregnant slave; the belt around her waist would have displayed the name of her owner.

Tours of the Site
You'll almost certainly be approached by a guide outside the *scavi* (excavations) ticket office; note that authorised guides wear identification tags.

If considering a guided tour of the ruins, reputable tour operators include **Yellow Sudmarine** (☎329 1010328, 334 1047036; www.yellowsudmarine.com; 2hr Pompeii guided tour €110) and **Walks of Italy** (www.walksofitaly.com; 2½hr Pompeii guided tour per person €52), both of which also offer excursions to other areas of Campania.

☑ **Don't Miss**
Gazing at Mt Vesuvius glowering over the town and imaging the horror of it spewing ash and molten rock.

Take a Break
For a memorable bite, try Michelin-starred **President** (☎081 850 72 45; www.ristorantepresident.it; Piazza Schettini 12; meals €35; ⏰noon-4pm & 7pm-midnight, closed Mon Oct-Apr) in Pompeii town.

Tragedy in Pompeii

24 AUGUST AD 79

8am Buildings including the **Terme Suburbane** ❶ and the **foro** ❷ are still undergoing repair after an earthquake in AD 63 caused significant damage to the city. Despite violent earth tremors overnight, residents have little idea of the catastrophe that lies ahead.

Midday Peckish locals pour into the **Thermopolium di Vetutius Placidus** ❸. The lustful slip into the **Lupanare** ❹, and gladiators practise for the evening's planned games at the **anfiteatro** ❺. A massive boom heralds the eruption. Shocked onlookers witness a dark cloud of volcanic matter shoot some 14km above the crater.

3pm–5pm Lapilli (burning pumice stone) rains down on Pompeii. Terrified locals begin to flee; others take shelter. Within two hours, the plume is 25km high and the sky has darkened. Roofs collapse under the weight of the debris, burying those inside.

25 AUGUST AD 79

Midnight Mudflows bury the town of Herculaneum. Lapilli and ash continue to rain down on Pompeii, bursting through buildings and suffocating those taking refuge within.

4am–8am Ash and gas avalanches hit Herculaneum. Subsequent surges smother Pompeii, killing all remaining residents, including those in the **Orto dei Fuggiaschi** ❻. The volcanic 'blanket' will safeguard frescoed treasures like the **Casa del Menandro** ❼ and **Villa dei Misteri** ❽ for almost two millennia.

TOP TIPS

» Visit in the afternoon
» Allow three hours
» Wear comfortable shoes and a hat
» Bring drinking water
» Don't use flash photography

Terme Suburbane
The *laconicum* (sauna), *caldarium* (hot bath) and large, heated swimming pool weren't the only sources of heat here; scan the walls of this suburban bathhouse for some of the city's raunchiest frescoes.

Foro
An ancient Times Square of sorts, the forum sits at the intersection of Pompeii's main streets and was closed to traffic in the 1st century AD. The plinths on the southern edge featured statues of the imperial family.

ʼilla dei Misteri

ʼome to the world-famous *Dionysiac Frieze* ʼresco. Other highlights at this villa include ʼrompe l'oeil wall decorations in the *cubiculum* ʼbedroom) and Egyptian-themed artwork in the ʼablinum (reception).

Lupanare

The prostitutes at this brothel were often slaves of Greek or Asian origin. Mattresses once covered the stone beds and the names engraved in the walls are possibly those of the workers and their clients.

CRISTIAN BONETTO ©

Thermopolium di Vetutius Placidus

The counter at this ancient snack bar once held urns filled with hot food. The *lararium* (household shrine) on the back wall depicts Dionysus (the god of wine) and Mercury (the god of profit and commerce).

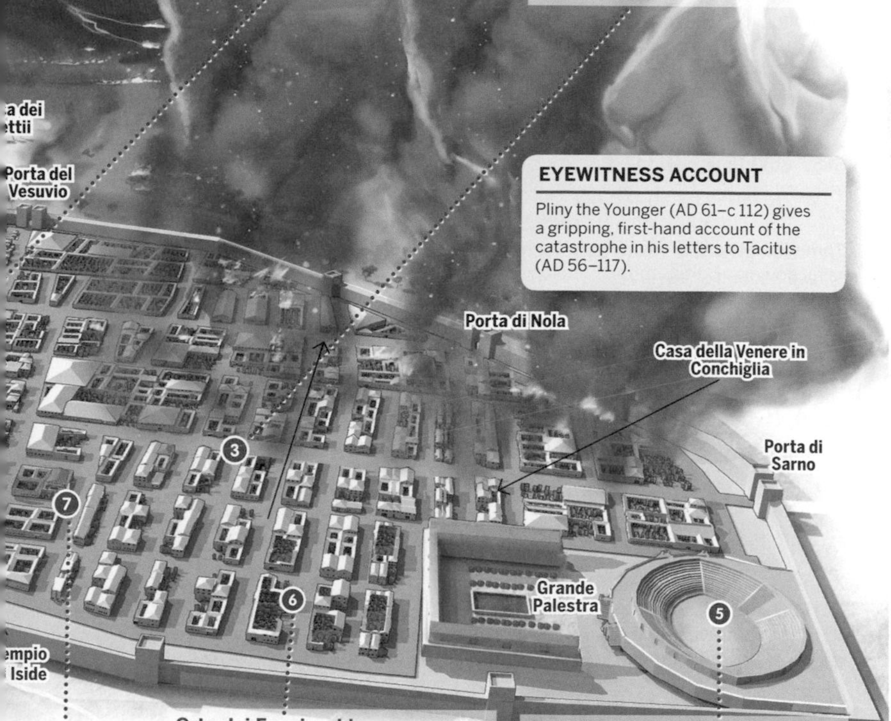

ʼa dei ʼttii

Porta del Vesuvio

EYEWITNESS ACCOUNT

Pliny the Younger (AD 61–c 112) gives a gripping, first-hand account of the catastrophe in his letters to Tacitus (AD 56–117).

Porta di Nola

Casa della Venere in Conchiglia

Porta di Sarno

3

7

6

Grande Palestra

5

ʼempio Iside

Orto dei Fuggiaschi

The Garden of the Fugitives showcases the plaster moulds of 13 locals seeking refuge during Vesuvius' eruption – the largest number of victims found in any one area. The huddled bodies make for a moving scene.

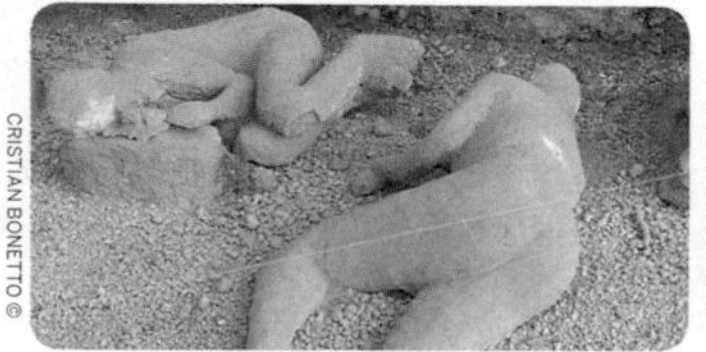

CRISTIAN BONETTO ©

Anfiteatro

Magistrates, local senators and the games' sponsors and organisers enjoyed front-row seating at this veteran amphitheatre, home to gladiatorial battles and the odd riot. The parapet circling the stadium featured paintings of combat, victory celebrations and hunting scenes.

CRISTIAN BONETTO ©

ʼasa del ʼenandro

ʼis dwelling most ʼely belonged to the ʼmily of Poppaea ʼbina, Nero's second ʼfe. A room to the left ʼthe atrium features ʼojan War paintings ʼd a polychrome ʼosaic of pygmies ʼwing down the Nile.

Villa dei Misteri

This recently restored, 90-room villa is one of the most complete structures left standing in Pompeii. The Dionysiac Frieze, the most important fresco still on site, spans the walls of the large dining room. One of the biggest and most arresting paintings from the ancient world, it depicts the initiation of a bride-to-be into the cult of Dionysus, the Greek god of wine.

A farm for much of its life, the villa's *vino*-making area is still visible at the northern end.

Follow Via Consolare out of the town through Porta Ercolano. Continue past Villa di Diomede, turn right, and you'll come to Villa dei Misteri.

OTHER SIGHTS

If you're fascinated by Pompeii or the unearthed Roman artefacts at Museo Archeologico Nazionale (p236), check out these ancient sites.

Herculaneum

Ruins of Herculaneum — Archaeological Site

Upstaged by its larger rival, Pompeii, Herculaneum harbours a wealth of archaeological finds, from ancient advertisements and stylish mosaics to carbonised furniture and terror-struck skeletons. Indeed, this superbly conserved Roman fishing town of 4000 inhabitants is easier to navigate than Pompeii, and can be explored with a map and audio guide (€6.50).

From the site's main gateway on Corso Resina, head down the walkway to the ticket office (at the bottom on your left). Ticket purchased, follow the walkway to the actual entrance to the ruins.Herculaneum's fate runs parallel to that of Pompeii. Destroyed by an earthquake in AD 62, the AD 79 eruption of Mt Vesuvius saw it submerged in a 16m-thick sea of mud that essentially fossilised the city.

This meant that even delicate items, such as furniture and clothing, were discovered remarkably well preserved. Tragically, the inhabitants didn't fare so

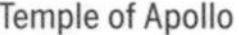

Temple of Apollo

well; thousands of people tried to escape by boat but were suffocated by the volcano's poisonous gases. Indeed, what appears to be a moat around the town is in fact the ancient shoreline. It was here in 1980 that archaeologists discovered some 300 skeletons, the remains of a crowd that had fled to the beach only to be overcome by the terrible heat of clouds surging down from Vesuvius.

The town itself was rediscovered in 1709 and amateur excavations were carried out intermittently until 1874, with many finds carted off to Naples to decorate the houses of the well-to-do or ending up in museums. Serious archaeological work began again in 1927 and continues to this day, although with much of the ancient site buried beneath modern Ercolano it's slow going. Indeed, note that at any given time some houses will invariably be shut for restoration. (☎081 732 43 27; www.pompeiisites.org; Corso Resina 187, Ercolano; adult/reduced €11/5.50, incl Pompeii €20/10; ⏰8.30am-7.30pm summer, to 5pm winter; 🚆Circumvesuviana to Ercolano-Scavi)

MAV Museum

Using high-tech holograms and computer-generated re-creations, this 'virtual archaeological museum' brings ruins like Pompeii's forum and Capri's Villa Jovis back to virtual life. Especially fun for kids, it's a useful place to comprehend just how impressive those crumbling columns once were. The museum is on the main street linking Ercolano-Scavi train station to the ruins of Herculaneum. (Museo Archeologico Virtuale; ☎081 1980 6511; www.museomav.com; Via IV Novembre 44; adult/reduced €7.50/6, optional 3D documentary €4; ⏰9am-5.30pm daily Mar-Sep, reduced hours rest of year; 🚆Circumvesuviana to Ercolano-Scavi)

Where to Stay

There are limited accommodation options around Pompeii itself, but it's a short, easy short train ride from Sorrento and Naples, both of which have ample accommodation options.

Mt Vesuvius

Towering (at 1281m) darkly over Naples and its environs, Mt Vesuvius (Vesuvio, 1281m), is the only active volcano on the European mainland. Since it exploded into history in AD 79, burying Pompeii and Herculaneum and pushing the coastline out several kilometres, it has erupted more than 30 times. The most devastating of these was in 1631, the most recent in 1944.

Established in 1995, the Parco Nazionale del Vesuvio attracts some 400,000 visitors annually. From a car park at the summit, an 860m path leads up to the volcano's **crater** (Vesuvius National Park; www.epnv.it).

From Ercolano, **Vesuvio Express** (☎081 739 36 66; www.vesuvioexpress.it; Piazzale Stazione Circumvesuviana, Ercolano; return incl admission to summit €20; ⏰every 40min, 9.30am to 4pm) runs shuttle buses from outside the train station up to the summit car park. The journey time is 20 minutes each way.

From Pompeii, **Busvia del Vesuvio** (☎340 9352616; www.busviadelvesuvio.com; Via Villa dei Misteri, Pompeii; return incl entry to summit adult/reduced €22/7; ⏰9am-4pm) runs hourly shuttle services between Pompei-Scavi-Villa dei Misteri train station (steps away from the ruins of Pompeii) and Boscoreale Terminal Interchange, from where a 4WD-style bus continues the journey up the slope to the summit car park.

Marina Piccola, Capri (p272)

AMALFI COAST

Amalfi Coast

Stretching about 50km along the southern side of the Sorrento Peninsula, the Amalfi Coast (Costiera Amalfitana) is one of Europe's most breathtaking. Cliffs terraced with scented lemon groves sheer down into sparkling seas; sherbet-hued villas cling precariously to unforgiving slopes; while sea and sky merge in one vast blue horizon.

Yet its stunning topography has not always been a blessing. For centuries after the passing of Amalfi's glory days as a maritime superpower (from the 9th to the 12th centuries), the area was poor and its isolated villages were regular victims of foreign incursions, earthquakes and landslides. But it was this very isolation that first drew visitors in the early 1900s, paving the way for the advent of tourism in the latter half of the century.

☑ In This Section

ℹ Arriving in the Amalfi Coast

Approaching from Naples there are two main routes to the Amalfi Coast. You can either take the Circumvesuviana train to Sorrento and then pick up one of the regular SITA Sud buses to Positano and Amalfi; alternatively, get a train from Naples to Salerno, the Amalfi Coast's main southern gateway, and connect with an onward bus to Amalfi and Positano.

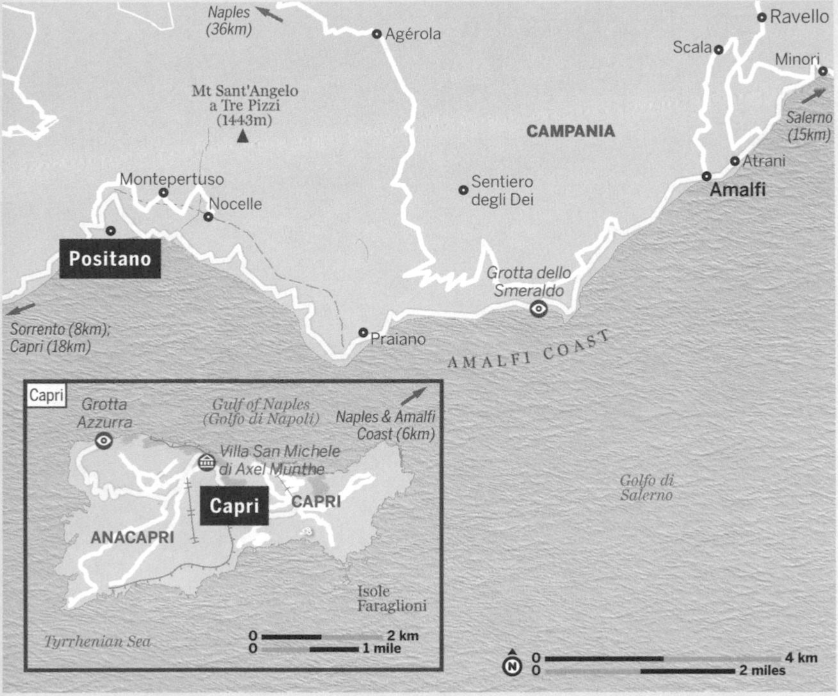

From left: Ravello (p278); Amalfi (p276); Piazza Umberto I, Capri (p274)

ANNHFHUNG/GETTY IMAGES ©

A Day in Positano

Positano's steeply stacked houses are a medley of pastels, and its stepped streets are lined with wisteria-draped hotels, smart restaurants and fashionable boutiques.

Great For...

☑ **Don't Miss**

Wandering aimlessly through the narrow streets.

Positano's Sights

Positano's most memorable sight is its pyramidal townscape, with its vertiginous pastel-coloured houses tumbling down to the seafront. Dominating the skyline is the distinct majolica-tiled dome of the **Chiesa di Santa Maria Assunta** (Piazza Flavio Gioia; 8am-noon & 4-9pm), the town's most famous landmark. Inside is a delightful classical interior, with gold-topped pillars and cherubs peeking from above every arch.

Nestled between the colourful boutiques and lemon-themed ceramics shops on Via dei Mulini, **Franco Senesi** (089 87 52 57; www.francosenesifineart.com; Via dei Mulini 16; 10am-midnight Apr-Nov) is a light and airy exhibition space showcasing life drawings, colourful surrealistic landscapes and edgy abstract sculptures by modern Italian artists and sculptors.

Hikers on the Walk of the Gods

STU SALMON/GETTY IMAGES ©

Beaches & Boating

Positano's main beach, Spiaggia Grande, is nobody's idea of a dream beach, with greyish sand covered by legions of bright umbrellas, but the water is clean and the setting is striking. Hiring a chair and umbrella in the fenced-off areas costs around €20 per person per day, but the crowded public areas are free.

To strike out to sea, **Blue Star** (☎089 81 18 88; www.bluestarpositano.it; Spiaggia Grande; ⊙8.30am-9pm) hires out small motorboats for €60 per hour (€200 for four hours). Consider heading for the archipelago of Li Galli, the four small islands where, according to Homer, the sirens lived. The company also organises popular and fun yacht excursions to Capri and the Grotta dello Smeraldo (€60).

Need to Know

Frequent buses connect with Amalfi (€2.50, 40 to 50 minutes) and Sorrento (€2.50, one hour).

Take a Break

Relax on the flower-draped terrace at **La Zagara** (☎089 812 28 92; www.lazagara.com; Via dei Mulini 8; panini €5, cakes €3; ⊙8am-midnight).

★ Top Tip

Check www.positano.com for information on local sights, activities, accommodation, transport and more.

A gentle walk leads from Spiaggia Grande to Spiaggia di Fornillo, a more laid-back spot than its swanky *spiaggia* (beach) neighbour and home to a handful of summer beach bars, which get spirited after sunset.

Shopping

You can't miss Positano's colourful boutiques – everywhere you look, shop displays scream out at you in a riot of exuberant colour. The humble lemon also enjoys star status; it's not just in limoncello liquer and lemon-infused candles but emblazoned on tea towels, aprons and pottery.

La Bottego di Brunella (☎089 87 52 28; www.brunella.it; Viale Pasitea 72; ⊙9am-9pm) is a chic boutique selling locally designed women's fashions in pure linens and silks. To complete the look, head to **La Botteguccia de Giovanni** (☎089 81 18 24; www.labottegucciapositano.it; Via Regina Giovanni 19; ⊙9.30am-9pm May-Oct) for a pair of handmade leather sandals.

Hiking

For more arduous exercise, hikers can tackle the so-called Walk of the Gods. The three-hour, 12km Sentiero degli Dei follows a ridge through the hills high above Positano to Praiano. The walk starts at Via Chiesa Nuova in the northern part of town.

Capri

The best known of the islands in the Bay of Naples, Capri is the perfect microcosm of Mediterranean appeal – a smooth cocktail of chichi piazzas and cool cafes, Roman ruins, rugged seascapes and holidaying VIPs. The island has three distinct areas: sophisticated and good-looking Capri Town; more rural, low-key Anacapri; and bustling Marina Grande, the harbour where hydrofoils and ferries dock.

Great For...

Need to Know

Ferries and hydrofoils serve Capri from Naples and Sorrento. There are also seasonal connections with Amalfi and Positano.

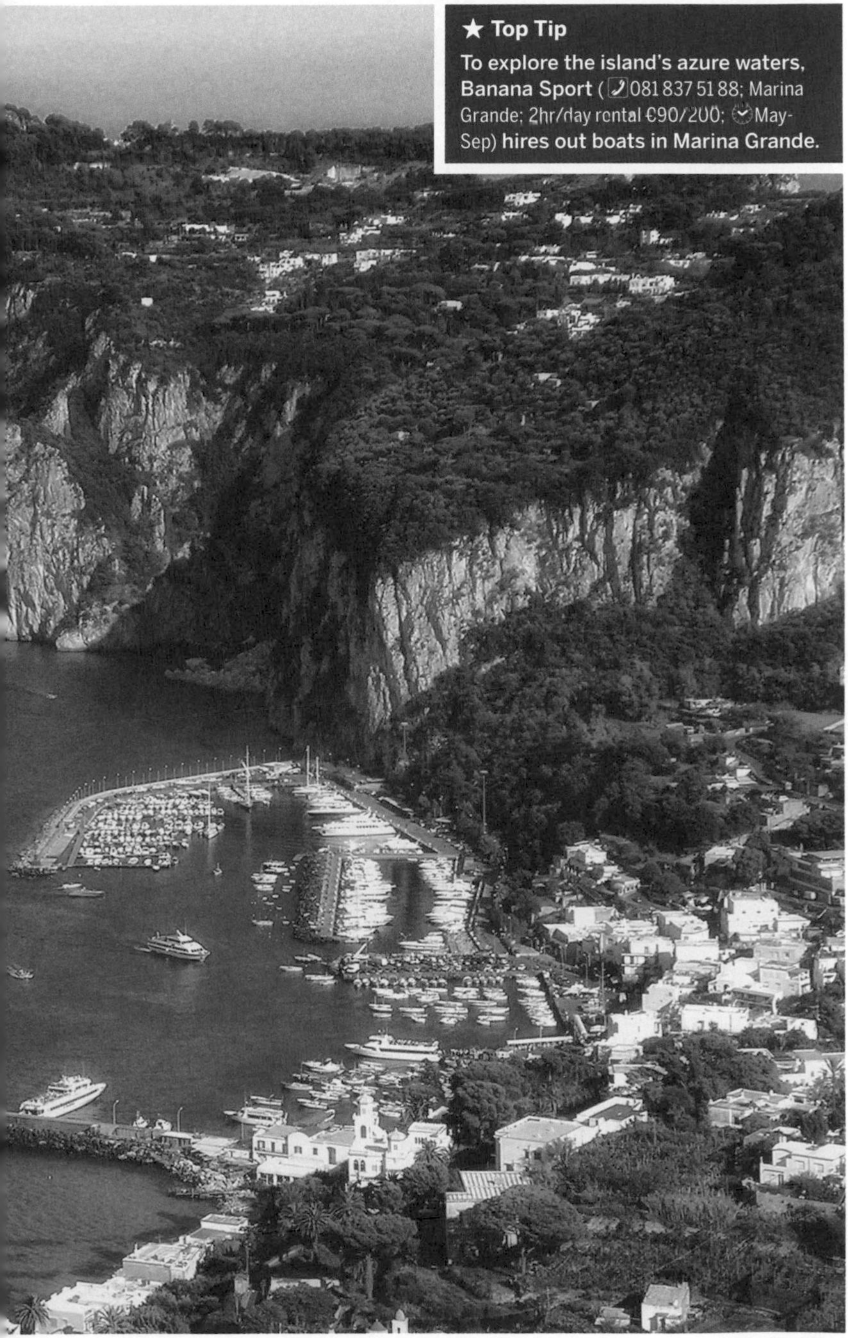

★ **Top Tip**

To explore the island's azure waters, Banana Sport (☎081 837 51 88; Marina Grande; 2hr/day rental €90/200; ⏰May-Sep) **hires out boats in Marina Grande.**

GIUSEPPE ESPOSITO/GETTY IMAGES ©

If time is tight, the island's sights may be visited by funicular, bus and/or taxi.

From Marina Grande, the quickest way up to Capri Town is by funicular, but there are also buses and more costly taxis. On foot, it's a tough 2.3km climb along Via Marina Grande. A further bus ride takes you up the hill to Anacapri.

Capri Town & Around

With its whitewashed stone buildings and tiny, car-free streets, Capri Town feels more film set than real life. Taking centre stage is Piazza Umberto I, aka la Piazzetta, a showy, open-air salon framed by see-and-be-seen cafes. If that's not your scene, head south along Via Vittorio Emanuele to the 14th-century **Certosa di San Giacomo** (081 837 62 18; Viale Certosa 40; admission €4; 9am-2pm Tue-Sun, plus 5-8pm summer), and, beyond that, the **Giardini di Augusto** (Gardens of Augustus; admission €1; 9am-1hr before sunset). Founded by Emperor Augustus, these colourful gardens rise in a series of flowered terraces to a lookout offering breathtaking views over to the Isole Faraglioni, a group of three limestone stacks that rise out of the sea.

A 45-minute walk east of town along Via Tiberio, **Villa Jovis** (Jupiter's Villa; Via A Maiuri; admission €2; 11am-3pm, closed Tue 1st-15th of month, closed Sun rest of month) was the largest and most sumptuous of the island's 12 Roman villas and Tiberius' main Capri residence. A vast pleasure complex, now reduced to ruins, it famously pandered to the emperor's debauched tastes, and included imperial quarters and extensive bathing areas set in dense gardens and woodland.

Villa San Michele di Axel Munthe

Anacapri & Around

A thrilling bus ride from Capri Town, Anacapri is smaller and quieter than its traditional rival. Attention here is largely focussed on **Villa San Michele di Axel Munthe** (www.villasanmichele.eu; Via Axel Munthe 34; admission €7; ⌚9am-6pm summer, reduced hours rest of year), the former home of a Swedish doctor, psychiatrist and animal-rights advocate. Built over the ruins of a Roman villa, the gardens provide stunning views and a beautiful setting for a tranquil stroll.

For more sweeping views, jump on the **Seggiovia del Monte Solaro** (www.capriseggiovia.it; single/return €7.50/10; ⌚9.30am-5pm summer, to 3.30pm winter), a chairlift that whisks you up to Capri's highest peak in a tranquil 12-minute ride. On a clear day you can see the entire Bay of Naples, Amalfi Coast and the islands of Ischia and Procida.

☑ Don't Miss

The great short walks leading through areas that are all but deserted, even in the height of summer. The tourist offices can provide you with maps.

DEA/L.ROMANO/GETTY IMAGES ©

Grotta Azzurra

Capri's single most famous attraction is the **Grotta Azzurra** (Blue Grotto; admission €13; ⌚9am-1hr before sunset), a stunning sea cave illuminated by an other-worldly blue light.

Measuring 54m by 30m and rising to a height of 15m, the grotto is said to have sunk by up to 20m in prehistoric times, blocking every opening except the 1.3m-high entrance. And this is the key to the magical blue light. Sunlight enters through a small underwater aperture and is refracted through the water; this, combined with the reflection of the light off the white sandy seafloor, produces the vivid blue effect to which the cave owes its name.

The easiest way to visit is to take a **tour** (☎081 837 56 46; www.motoscafisticapri.com; Private Pier 0, Marina Grande; online €12, in person €14) from Marina Grande; tickets include the return boat trip and a rowing boat into the cave, with the admission fee paid separately. Allow a good hour.

The grotto is closed if the sea is too choppy and swimming in it is forbidden, although you can swim outside the entrance; get a bus to Grotta Azzurra and take the stairs down to the right.

Bay Islands

Capri is one of three islands in the Bay of Naples. The other two, both of which can be reached from Naples, are picturesque Procida, the smallest and quietest of the trio, and Ischia, famous for its thermal waters and spa resorts.

✕ Take a Break

Search out **È Divino** (☎081 837 83 64; Vico Sella Orta; meals €20; ⌚1-3pm & 7.30pm-midnight Tue-Sun) for tasty, market-fresh food in Capri Town.

Amalfi

Believe it or not, pretty little Amalfi, with its sun-filled piazzas and small beach, was once a maritime superpower with a population of more than 70,000. For one thing, it's not a big place – you can easily walk from one end to the other in about 20 minutes. For another, there are very few historical buildings of note. The explanation is chilling – most of the old city, and its populace, simply slid into the sea during an earthquake in 1343.

SIGHTS

Cattedrale di Sant'Andrea Cathedral

A melange of architectural styles, Amalfi's cathedral, one of the few relics of the town's past as an 11th-century maritime superpower, makes a striking impression at the top of its sweeping flight of stairs. Between 10am and 5pm entrance is through the adjacent **Chiostro del Paradiso** (☎089 87 13 24; Piazza del Duomo; adult/reduced €3/1; ⊙9am-7pm), a 13th-century cloister. (☎089 87 10 59; Piazza del Duomo; ⊙7.30am-7.45pm)

Museo della Carta Museum

Amalfi's paper museum is housed in a rugged, cavelike 13th-century paper mill (the oldest in Europe). It lovingly preserves the original paper presses, which are still in full working order, as you'll see during the 15-minute guided tour (in English), which explains the original cotton-based paper production and the later wood-pulp manufacturing. Afterwards you may well be inspired to pick up some of the stationery sold in the gift shop, alongside calligraphy sets and paper pressed with flowers. (☎089 830 45 61; www.museodellacarta.it; Via delle Cartiere 23; admission €4; ⊙10am-6.30pm daily Mar-Oct, 10am-3.30pm Tue, Wed & Fri-Sun Nov-Feb)

Grotta dello Smeraldo Cave

Four kilometres west of Amalfi, this grotto is named after the eerie emerald colour that emanates from the water. Stalactites hang down from the 24m-high ceiling, while stalagmites grow up to 10m tall. Buses regularly pass the car park above the cave entrance (from where you take a lift or stairs down to the rowing boats). Alterna-

Grotta Azzurra (p274)

tively, **Coop Sant'Andrea** (089 87 29 50; www.coopsantandrea.com; Lungomare dei Cavalieri 1) runs boats from Amalfi (€10 return, plus cave admission). Allow 1½ hours for the return trip. (admission €5; 9.30am-4pm)

EATING

La Pansa — Cafe €

A marbled and mirrored 1830 cafe on Piazza del Duomo where black-bow-tied waiters serve a great Italian breakfast: freshly made *cornetti* (croissants) and deliciously frothy cappuccino. (089 87 10 65; www.pasticceriapansa.it; Piazza del Duomo 40; cornetti & pastries from €1.50; 8am-10pm Wed-Mon)

Il Teatro — Trattoria €€

Superb no-fuss trattoria tucked away in the atmospheric backstreets of the *centro storico* (Via E Marini is reached via Salita delgi Orafi). Seafood specialities include *pesce spada il teatro* (swordfish in a tomato, caper and olive-oil sauce), plus there are good vegetarian options, including *scialatielli al teatro* (pasta with tomatoes and aubergines). (089 87 24 73; Via E Marini 19; meals €25; 11.30am-3pm & 6.30-11pm, closed Wed;)

Le Arcate — Italian €€

On a sunny day, it's hard to beat the dreamy location: at the far eastern point of the harbour overlooking the beach, with Atrani's ancient rooftops and church tower behind you. Huge white parasols shade the sprawl of tables, while the dining room is a stone-walled natural cave. Pizzas are served at night; daytime fare includes risotto with seafood and grilled swordfish. (089 87 13 67; www.learcate.net; Largo Orlando Buonocore, Atrani; pizzas from €6, meals €25; 12.30-3pm & 7.30-11.30pm Tue-Sun Sep-Jun, daily Jul & Aug)

Ristorante La Caravella — Italian €€€

The regional food here recently earned the restaurant a Michelin star, with dishes that offer *nouvelle* zap, like black ravioli with cuttlefish ink, scampi and ricotta, or that are unabashedly simple, like the catch of the day served grilled on lemon leaves. Wine aficionados are likely to find something to try on the 15,000-label list. Reservations are essential. (089 87 10 29; www.ristorantelacaravella.it; Via Matteo Camera 12; tasting menus €50-120; noon-2.30pm & 7.30-11pm Wed-Mon)

Paestum

The Unesco World Heritage temples at **Paestum** (0828 81 10 23; incl museum adult/reduced €10/5; 8.45am-7.45pm, last entry 7pm Jun & Jul, as early as 3.35pm Nov) are among the best-preserved monuments of Magna Graecia, the Greek colony that once covered much of southern Italy. The city of Paestum, originally called Poseidonia, was founded in the 6th century BC and fell under Roman control in 273 BC.

The first temple you come to after the northern entrance is the 6th-century-BC Tempio di Cerere. Originally dedicated to Athena, it served as a Christian church in medieval times.

The Tempio di Nettuno, dating from about 450 BC, is the largest and best preserved of Paestum's three temples; only parts of its inside walls and roof are missing. Almost next door, the so-called basilica (in fact, a temple to the goddess Hera) is Paestum's oldest surviving monument, dating from the mid-6th century BC.

Save time for the **museum** (0828 81 10 23; 8.30am-7.30pm, last entry 6.45pm, closed 1st & 3rd Mon of month), which houses a collection of fascinating *metopes* (bas-relief friezes). The star exhibit here is the 5th-century-BC fresco *Tomba del Truffatore* (Tomb of the Diver), thought to represent the passage from life to death with its depiction of a diver in midair.

The best way to get to Paestum by public transport is to take CSTP bus 34 from Piazza della Concordia in Salerno (€3.80, 1¼ hours, 12 daily).

Where to Stay

If you are planning to explore beyond the coast, Sorrento has the best transport connections and is a good base. Positano, Amalfi and Ravello feature some of the classiest accommodation in Italy, ranging from sumptuous *palazzi* to exquisite B&Bs. Book ahead in summer and remember that most hotels close over the winter. On Capri accommodation is strictly seasonal, which means bed space is tight and, in general, costly.

Marina Grande Seafood **€€€**

Run by the third generation of the same family, this beachfront restaurant serves fish so fresh it's almost flapping. Marina Grande prides itself on its use of locally sourced and organic produce, which, in Amalfi, means high-quality seafood. Reservations are recommended. (089 87 11 29; www.ristorantemarinagrande.com; Viale Delle Regioni 4; tasting menu lunch/dinner €25/60, meals €45; noon-3pm & 6.30-11pm Tue-Sun Mar-Oct)

INFORMATION

Tourist office (089 87 11 07; www.amalfi touristoffice.it; Corso delle Repubbliche Marinare 33; 9am-1pm & 2-6pm Mon-Sat)

GETTING THERE & AWAY

BOAT

Between April and October there are daily sailings to/from Amalfi.

Alicost (089 87 14 83; www.alicost.it) Operates three daily services to Positano (€8, 20 minutes), with two stopping in Capri (€21, 80 minutes) and Sorrento (€17, 60 minutes).

NLG (081 552 07 63; www.navlib.it) Sails once daily to Positano (€8, 15 minutes) and Capri (€21, 80 minutes).

TraVelMar (089 87 29 50; www.travelmar.it) Runs ferries to Positano (€8, 25 minutes, seven daily), Minori (€3, 10 minutes, six daily), Maiori (€3, 15 minutes, six daily) and Salerno (€8, 35 minutes, seven daily).

BUS

SITA Sud (089 40 51 45; www.sitasudtraspor ti.it) runs frequent daily services from Piazza Flavio Gioia in Amalfi to Sorrento (€3.40, 100 minutes) via Positano (€2.20, 50 minutes), as well as to Ravello (€1.60, 25 minutes) and Salerno (€2.80, 1¼ hours). Buy tickets and check current schedules at Bar Il Giardino delle Palme, opposite the bus stop.

Ravello

Sitting high in the hills above Amalfi, refined Ravello is a polished town almost entirely dedicated to tourism. Boasting impeccable bohemian credentials – Wagner, DH Lawrence and Virginia Woolf all lounged here – it's today known for its ravishing gardens and stupendous views, the best in the world according to former resident Gore Vidal.

SIGHTS

Villa Rufolo Gardens

To the south of Ravello's cathedral, a 14th-century tower marks the entrance to this villa, famed for its beautiful cascading gardens. Created by a Scotsman, Scott Neville Reid, in 1853, they are truly magnificent, commanding divine panoramic views packed with exotic colours, artistically crumbling towers and luxurious blooms. Note that the gardens are at their best from May till October; they don't merit the entrance fee outside those times. (089 85 76 21; www.villarufolo.it; Piazza Duomo; adult/reduced €5/3; 9am-5pm)

Cathedral Cathedral

Forming the eastern flank of Piazza Duomo, the cathedral was built in 1086 but has since undergone various makeovers. The facade is 16th century, but the central bronze door, one of only about two dozen in the country, dates from 1179; the interior is a late-20th-century interpretation of what the original must once have looked like.

Villa Rufolo

(Piazza Duomo; museum €3; 8.30am-noon & 5.30-8.30pm)

Villa Cimbrone Gardens

Some 600m south of Piazza Duomo, the Villa Cimbrone is worth a wander, if not for the 11th-century villa itself (now an upmarket hotel), then for the fabulous views from the delightful gardens. They're best admired from the Belvedere of Infinity, an awe-inspiring terrace lined with classical-style statues and busts. (089 85 80 72; www.villacimbrone.com; Via Santa Chiara 26; adult/reduced €7/4; 9am-7.30pm summer, to sunset winter)

EATING

Babel Cafe **€€**

A cool little white-painted deli-cafe, Babel serves high-quality, affordable salads, bruschetta, cheese and meat boards and an excellent range of local wines. There's also a jazz soundtrack, and a little gallery that sells unusually stylish ceramic tiles. (089 85 86 215; Via Trinità 13; meals €20; 11am-11pm)

Da Salvatore Italian **€€**

Located just before the bus stop, Da Salvatore has nothing special by way of decor, but the view – from both the dining room and the large terrace – is very special indeed. Dishes include creative options like tender squid on a bed of pureed chickpeas with spicy *peperoncino*.

In the evening part of the restaurant is transformed into an informal pizzeria, serving some of the best wood-fired pizza you will taste anywhere this side of Naples. (089 85 72 27; www.salvatoreravello.com; Via della Republicca 2; meals €28; noon-3pm & 7.30-10pm Tue-Sun)

INFORMATION

Tourist office (089 85 70 96; www.ravellotime.it; Via Roma 18; 9am-7pm) has info on the town and a handy map with walking trails.

GETTING THERE & AWAY

SITA Sud operates regular daily buses from Piazza Flavio Gioia in Amalfi (€1.60, 25 minutes).

Mondello beach, Palermo (p288)

SICILY

Sicily

Eternal meeting point between East and West, Africa and Europe, Sicily is one of Europe's most alluring destinations. Everything about the Mediterranean's largest island is extreme, from the beauty of its rugged scenery to its hybrid cuisine and flamboyant architecture. After 25 centuries of foreign domination, the island is heir to an impressive cultural legacy, and in a short walk around the regional capital, Palermo, you can see Arab domes, Byzantine mosaics, baroque stuccowork and Norman walls.

This cultural richness is matched by its startlingly diverse landscape, encompassing everything from bucolic farmlands to smouldering volcanoes, sun-baked hills and island-studded seas.The island's cuisine is also a major draw. Marrying Moorish influences with Italian staples, its recipes are steeped in tradition and based on a supply of fabulous local ingredients.

☑ In This Section

ℹ Arriving in Sicily

Flights from mainland Italian cities and an increasing number of European destinations serve Sicily's two main airports: Catania's Fontanarossa and Palermo's Falcone-Borsellino.

If you're not flying, arriving in Sicily involves a ferry crossing. Regular car/passenger ferries cross the Strait of Messina between Villa San Giovanni and Messina, or Reggio di Calabria and Messina. Ferries also sail to Palermo from Genoa, Civitavecchia and Naples.

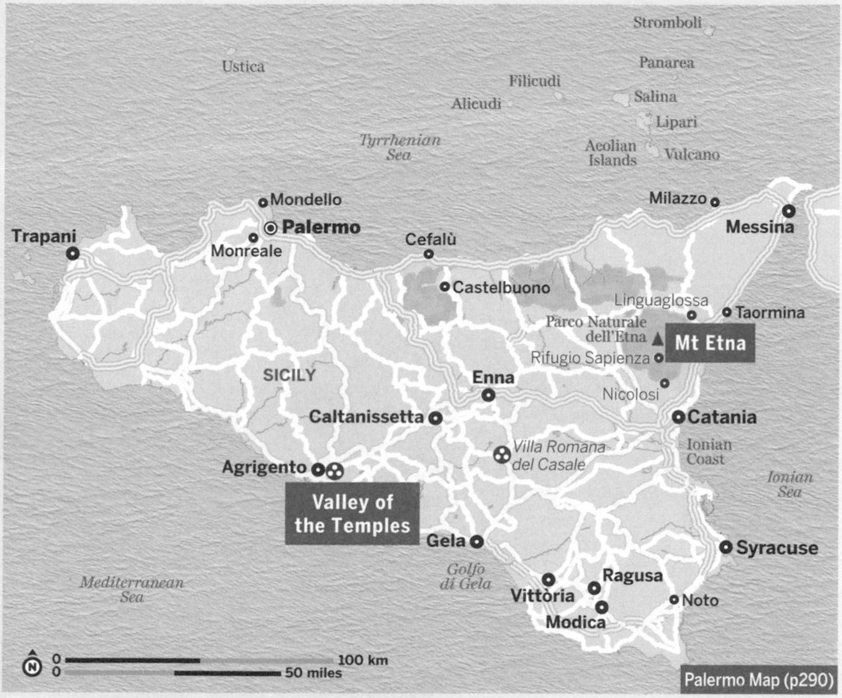

Palermo Map (p290)

From left: Via Giuseppe Garibaldi, Catania (p296); Fontane Bianche beach, Syracuse (p300); Fruit market, Palermo

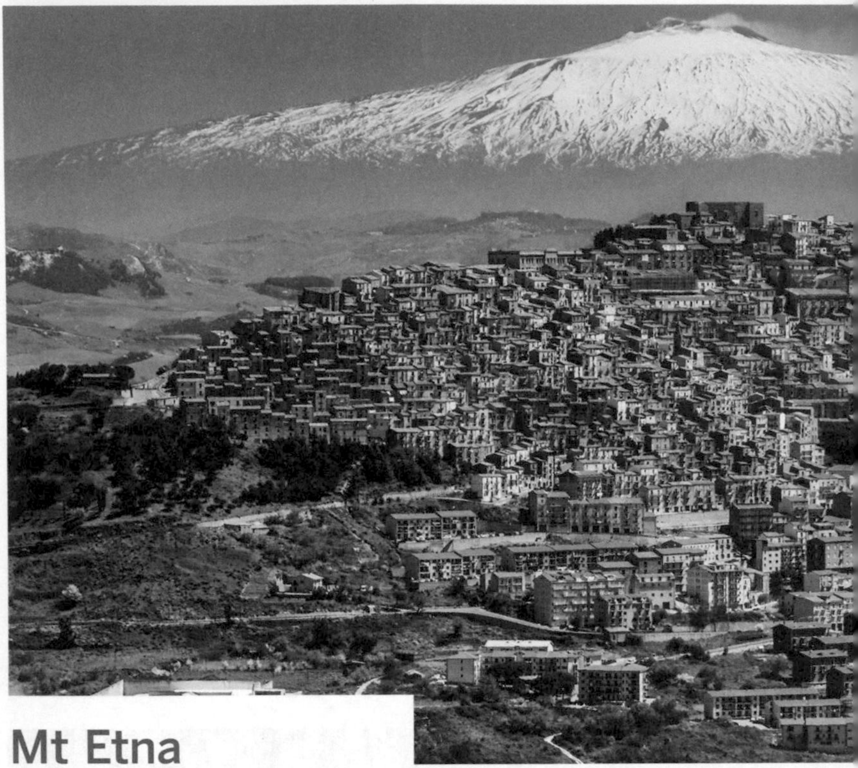

Mt Etna

Dominating the landscape of eastern Sicily, Mt Etna is a massive brooding presence. At 3329m, it's Italy's highest mountain south of the Alps and the largest active volcano in Europe.

Great For...

☑ Don't Miss

The crater zone: how close you can get will depend on the level of volcanic activity.

Mt Etna is in an almost constant state of activity and locals understandably keep a watchful eye on the smouldering peak. Its most devastating eruptions occurred in 1669 and lasted 122 days. A huge river of lava poured down its southern slope, engulfing a good part of Catania and dramatically altering the landscape. Less destructive eruptions continue to occur frequently, both from its four summit craters and from the fissures and old craters on its flanks.

The volcano is surrounded by the Parco Naturale dell'Etna, Sicily's largest remaining unspoilt wilderness, which encompasses a fascinatingly varied natural environment, from the severe, almost surreal summit to the deserts of lava and alpine forests.

The two main approaches to Etna are from the south and north.

Need to Know

The best time for walking is between April and May, and September and October. It gets very busy, and very hot, in high summer.

Take a Break

Round off a day in the mountains at **Antico Orto Dei Limoni** (☎095 91 08 08; www.ortolimoni.it; Via Grotte 4; set menu €26; ⏰Wed-Mon) in Nicolosi.

★ Top Tip

Bring the right kit – it's usually windy up top and temperatures can fall below freezing.

Southern Approach

The southern approach presents the easier ascent to the craters. If driving, follow signs for Etna Sud and head up to Rifugio Sapienza (1923m), 18km beyond Nicolosi; if reliant on public transport, a daily **AST** (☎095 723 05 35; www.aziendasicilianatrasporti.it) bus runs to Rifugio Sapienza (€6.60 return) from Piazza Giovanni XXIII in Catania.

At the Rifugio, take the **Funivia dell'Etna cable car** (☎095 91 41 41; www.funiviaetna.com; return €35, incl bus & guide €65; ⏰9am-5.45pm Apr-Nov, to 3.45pm Dec-Mar) to the upper station at 2500m. Fom here it's a 3½- to four-hour return walk up the winding track to the authorised crater zone (2920m). Make sure you leave enough time to get up *and* down before the last cable car leaves. Alternatively, you can pay an extra €30 for a guided 4WD tour to the crater zone.

Northern Approach

The northern route ascends from Piano Provenzano (1800m), 16km southwest of Linguaglossa. This area was severely damaged during the 2002 eruptions, as still evidenced by the bleached skeletons of the surrounding pine trees. To reach Piano Provenzano you'll need a car, as there's no public transport beyond Linguaglossa.

Guides

There are many operators offering guided tours up to the craters, and even if your natural inclination is to avoid them, they are well worth considering. Tours typically involve some walking and 4WD transport.

Gruppo Guide Alpine Etna Sud (☎095 791 47 55; www.etnaguide.com) is the official guide service on Etna's southern flank, with an office just below Rifugio Sapiena.

Gruppo Guide Alpine Etna (☎095 777 45 02; www.guidetnanord.com) offers a similar service from Linguaglossa.

Tempio di Hera

RODKARV/SHUTTERSTOCK ©

Valley of the Temples

The Unesco-listed Valley of the Temples is one of Italy's most mesmerising archaeological sites. Encompassing the ruins of ancient Akragas, it boasts some of the best-preserved Doric temples outside of Greece.

Great For...

☑ Don't Miss

Tempio della Concordia, which was built on a ridge to act as a beacon for homecoming sailors.

Situated 3km from modern-day Agrigento, the 1300-hectare park is split into eastern and western zones. Ticket offices with car parks are at the park's eastern edge and on the main road dividing the eastern and western zones. For public transport, take bus 1, 2 or 3 from Piazza Rosselli in Agrigento.

If you only have time for part of the park, make it the eastern zone, where you'll find the park's three best-preserved temples.

Eastern Zone

Near the eastern ticket office, the **Tempio di Hera** (Temple of Hera), also known as the Tempio di Giunone (Temple of Juno), is perched on the ridgetop. Built in the 5th-century-BC but partly destroyed by an earthquake, the colonnade remains largely intact as does a long sacrificial altar. Traces of red are the result of fire damage, most

Reconstructed *telamon* (a pillar in the form of a figure)

likely during the Carthaginian invasion of 406 BC.

From here, the path descends past a gnarled 500-year-old olive tree and a series of Byzantine tombs to the **Tempio della Concordia** (Temple of Concord). This remarkable edifice, the model for Unesco's logo, has survived almost entirely intact since its construction in 430 BC, partly due to its conversion into a Christian basilica in the 6th century, and partly thanks to the shock-absorbing, earthquake-dampening qualities of the soft clay underlying its hard rock foundation.

Further downhill, the **Tempio di Ercole** (Temple of Hercules) is Agrigento's oldest, dating from the end of the 6th century BC. Down from the main temples, the miniature **Tomba di Terone** (Tomb of Theron) dates to 75 BC.

Need to Know

Valle dei Templi; www.parcovalledeitempli.it; adult/reduced €10/5, incl Museo Archeologico €13.50/7; 8.30am-7pm year-round, plus 8-10pm Mon-Fri, 8-11pm Sat & Sun mid-Jul–mid-Sep

Take a Break

In Agrigento's historic centre, **Trattoria Concordia** (0922 2 26 68; Via Porcello 8; meals €18-30; noon-3pm & 7-10.30pm Mon-Fri, 7-11pm Sat) serves abundant, flavoursome meals.

★ Top Tip

The temples' magical aura is enhanced at night, when they're brilliantly floodlit. On summer evenings, don't miss the chance to walk among the temples of the Eastern Zone after dark, an experience not to be had at any other Sicilian ancient site.

Western Zone

The main feature of the western zone is the ruin of the **Tempio di Giove** (Temple of Olympian Zeus). This would have been the world's largest Doric temple had its construction not been interrupted by the Carthaginian sacking of Akragas. A later earthquake reduced it to the crumbled ruin you see today. Lying amid the rubble is an 8m-tall *telamon* (a sculpted figure of a man with arms raised, used as a pillar to support the temple), originally intended to support the temple's weight. It's actually a copy – the original is in the Museo Archeologico. A short hop away, you'll find the ruined 5th-century-BC **Tempio dei Dioscuri** (Temple of the Dioscuri, or Temple of Castor and Pollux) and a 6th-century complex of altars and small buildings belonging to the Santuario delle Divine Chtoniche (Sanctuary of the Chthonic Deities).

Palermo

Palermo is a city of decay and of splendour and – provided you can handle its raw energy, deranged driving and chaos – has plenty of appeal. Unlike Florence or Rome, many of the city's treasures are hidden, rather than scrubbed up for endless streams of tourists. The Quattro Canti is the centre of the oldest part of town.

At one time an Arab emirate and seat of a Norman kingdom, Palermo became Europe's grandest city in the 12th century, then underwent another round of aesthetic transformations during 500 years of Spanish rule. The resulting treasure trove of palaces, castles and churches has a unique architectural fusion of Byzantine, Arab, Norman, Renaissance and baroque gems.

SIGHTS

Around the Quattro Canti

Fontana Pretoria Fountain

This huge and ornate fountain, with tiered basins and sculptures rippling in concentric circles, forms the centrepiece of Piazza Pretoria, a spacious square just south of the Quattro Canti. The city bought the fountain in 1573; however, the flagrant nudity of the provocative nymphs proved too much for Sicilian church-goers attending Mass next door, and they prudishly dubbed it the Fountain of Shame.

La Martorana Church

On the southern side of Piazza Bellini, this luminously beautiful 12th-century church was endowed by King Roger's Syrian emir, George of Antioch, and was originally planned as a mosque. Delicate Fatimid pillars support a domed cupola depicting Christ enthroned amid his archangels. The interior is best appreciated in the morning, when sunlight illuminates magnificent Byzantine mosaics. (Chiesa di Santa Maria dell'Ammiraglio; Piazza Bellini 3; adult/reduced €2/1; ⌚9.30am-1pm & 3.30-5.30pm Mon-Sat, 9-10.30am Sun)

Chiesa Capitolare di San Cataldo Church

This 12th-century church in Arab-Norman style is one of Palermo's most striking buildings. With its dusky-pink bijou domes,

Fontana Pretoria

solid square shape, blind arcading and delicate tracery, it illustrates perfectly the synthesis of Arab and Norman architectural styles. The interior, while more austere, is still beautiful, with its inlaid floor and lovely stone-and-brickwork in the arches and domes. (Piazza Bellini 3; admission €2.50; 9.30am-12.30pm & 3-6pm)

Albergheria

Palazzo dei Normanni & Cappella Palatina — Palace, Chapel

This venerable palace dates to the 9th century but owes its current look to a major 12th-century Norman makeover, during which spectacular mosaics were added to its Royal Apartments and priceless jewel of a chapel, the Cappella Palatina. Designed by Roger II in 1130, the chapel glitters with gold mosaics, its aesthetic harmony further enhanced by the inlaid marble floors and wooden *muqarnas* ceiling, a masterpiece of Arabic-style honeycomb carving that reflects Norman Sicily's cultural complexity.

Queues are likely, and that you'll be refused entry if you're wearing shorts, a short skirt or a low-cut top. The top level of the palace's three-tiered loggia houses Sicily's regional parliament and the Royal Apartments, including the mosaic-lined Sala dei Venti, and Sala di Ruggero II, King Roger's magnificent 12th-century bedroom. These latter attractions are only open to visitors Friday through Monday. (www.fondazionefedericosecondo.it; Piazza Indipendenza 1; adult/reduced Fri-Mon €8.50/6.50, Tue-Thu €7/5; 8.15am-5.40pm Mon-Sat, to 1pm Sun, Royal Apartments closed Tue-Thu, chapel closed 9.45-11.15am Sun)

Mercato di Ballarò — Market

Snaking for several city blocks southeast of Palazzo dei Normanni is Palermo's busiest street market, which throbs with activity well into the early evening. It's a fascinating mix of noises, smells and street life, and the cheapest place for everything from Chinese padded bras to fresh produce, fish, meat, olives and cheese – smile nicely for a taste. (7am-7pm Mon-Sat, to 1pm Sun)

Sicilian Cuisine

Eating is one of the great joys of a trip to Sicily. In addition to the island's ubiquitous street food, you'll encounter countless specialities.

Pasta alla Norma Named in honour of the opera by Vincenzo Bellini, Catania's signature pasta dish features aubergines, tomatoes, basil and salty ricotta.

Involtini di pesce spada Thinly sliced swordfish rolled up and filled with breadcrumbs, capers, tomatoes and olives.

Couscous di pesce alla trapanese Savour Sicily's North African influence with fish couscous, seasoned with cinnamon, saffron, parsley and garlic.

Bucatini con le sarde A Palermitan staple: tube-shaped pasta with sardines, wild fennel, pine nuts and raisins.

Caponata A kind of Sicilian ratatouille of aubergine, tomatoes, olives and capers.

Arancino (or *arancina* if you're from Palermo) A plump golden rice ball, stuffed with meat or cheese, coated with breadcrumbs and deep-fried.

Crocché Fried potato dumplings flavoured with cheese, parsley and eggs.

Panelle Fried chickpea-flour fritters, often served in sesame rolls.

Pane con la milza A Palermo favourite consisting of a bread roll with boiled calf's spleen and lemon juice.

Cassata siciliana A rich mix of ricotta, sugar, vanilla, candied fruit and diced chocolate, encased by sponge and topped with green icing.

Capo

Cattedrale di Palermo — Cathedral

A feast of geometric patterns, ziggurat crenellations, maiolica cupolas and blind arches, Palermo's cathedral has suffered aesthetically from multiple reworkings over the centuries, but remains a prime example of Sicily's unique Arab-Norman

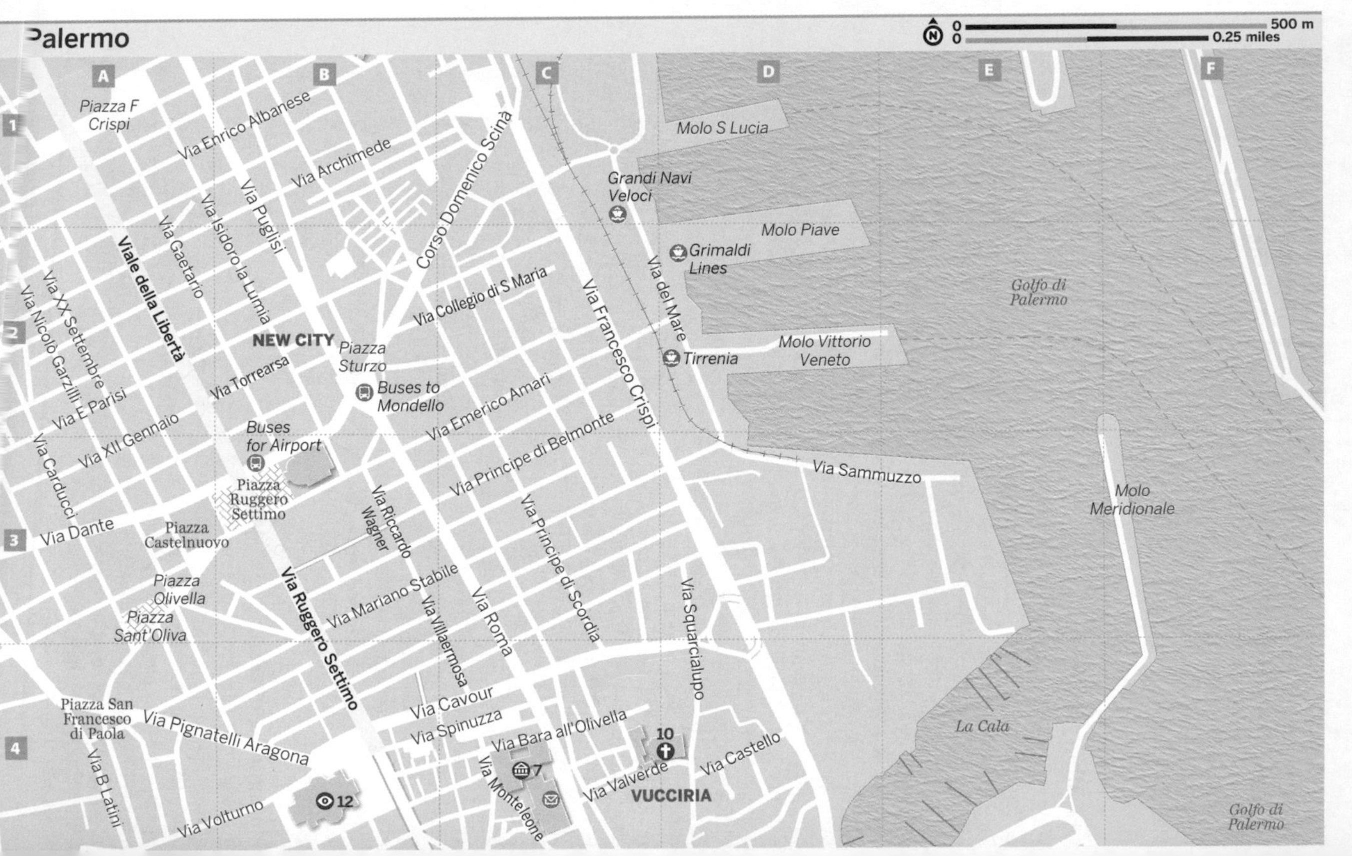

Palermo
0
0
500 m
0.25 miles
A
B
C
D
E
F
1
2
3
4
Piazza F Crispi
Via Enrico Albanese
Via Archimede
Corso Domenico Scinà
Molo S Lucia
Grandi Navi Veloci
Molo Piave
Grimaldi Lines
Via Puglisi
Via Isidoro la Lumia
Via Gaetario
Viale della Libertà
Via XX Settembre
Via Nicolò Garzilli
Via Collegio di S Maria
Via Francesco Crispi
Via del Mare
Golfo di Palermo
NEW CITY
Piazza Sturzo
Molo Vittorio Veneto
Tirrenia
Via Torrearsa
Buses to Mondello
Via E Parisi
Via Emerico Amari
Via XII Gennaio
Buses for Airport
Via Principe di Belmonte
Via Sammuzzo
Via Carducci
Piazza Ruggero Settimo
Molo Meridionale
Via Dante
Piazza Castelnuovo
Via Riccardo Wagner
Via Principe di Scordia
Via Squarcialupo
Via Ruggero Settimo
Piazza Olivella
Via Mariano Stabile
Via Villaermosa
Via Roma
Piazza Sant'Oliva
Via Cavour
La Cala
Piazza San Francesco di Paola
Via Pignatelli Aragona
Via Spinuzza
Via Bara all'Olivella
10
Via Castello
7
Via Valverde
Via B Latini
12
Via Monteleone
VUCCIRIA
Via Volturno
Golfo di Palermo

Via Mura di S Vito
CAPO
Via Trabia
9
Piazza Giovanni Meli
Piazza San Domenico
Via Bandiera
Via della Cala
Corso Vittorio Emanuele
8
Foro Italico Umberto I
Via G Battista
Via Sant'Oliva
Via Sant'Agostino
Via Maqueda
Via Cassari
Via Butera
Villa a Mare
5
Via degli Scalini
Piazza Sant'Onofrio
Via Venezia
Via Roma
Piazza Caracciolo
Giardino Garibaldi
Via IV Aprile
Via Judica
QUATTRO CANTI
13
15
Piazza San Francesco d'Assisi
Giardino Garibaldi
Piazza Marina
Via delle Cappuccinelle
Via Matteo Bonello
Via del Candelai
Via del Celso
Via Merlo
Via Alloro
5
Via Torremuzza
Piazza della Kalsa
Piazza Pretoria
14
Via Lungarini
Piazza dello Spasimo
3
4
LA KALSA
16
Via Papireto
Piazza Bellini
Via Sant'Anna
6
Via Sant'Oliva
Piazza Sett'Angeli
Municipal Tourist Office
2
1
Corso Vittorio Emanuele
Via Cagliari
Via Schiavuzzo
Via C Filippo
Piazza Santa Chiara
Rua Formaggi
Via del Ponticelo
Villa Giulia
Via Novelli
Via Garibaldi
Via Magione
Via Abramo Lincoln
Piazza della Vittoria
Via G M Puglia
Via Roma
6
Via Maqueda
ALBERGHERIA
Orto Botanico di Palermo
7
AMAT Bus to Monreale
BALLARÒ
Via Ballarò
Via Archifari
Via Antonio Ugo
11
Via Porta di Castro
AST Bus to Monreale
Bus to Airport & Local Buses
Cuffaro
Piazza Indipendenza
Via A Mongitore
Via Carmine
Intercity Bus Stop
Via Santa Rosalia
Local Buses Ticket Kiosk
Segesta
Via dei Benedettini
Via Albergheria
Piazzetta Cairoli
Bus Terminal
Parco D'Orleans
Corso Re Ruggero
Palermo Centrale
Via Michele Cipolla
Via Giorgio Arcoleo
Via Antonia Marinuzzi
Via Paolo Emiliano
Via Paolo Francesco
SAIS Autolinee
Corso dei Mille
Via Tiro A Segno
8
Corso Tukory
Via Carlo Pisacane
Via Oreto
Viale delle Scienze
A
B
C
D
E
F

Palermo

Sights

1 Cattedrale di Palermo B6
2 Chiesa Capitolare di San Cataldo C6
3 Fontana Pretoria C6
4 Galleria d'Arte Moderna D6
5 Galleria Regionale della Sicilia E5
La Martorana .... (see 2)
6 Mercato di Ballarò C7
7 Museo Archeologico Regionale C4
8 Museo Internazionale delle Marionette E5
9 Oratorio di San Domenico D5
10 Oratorio di Santa Cita D4
11 Palazzo dei Normanni & Cappella Palatina A7
12 Teatro Massimo B4

Eating

13 Ferro di Cavallo C5
14 Osteria Ballarò D6
15 Trattoria Il Maestro del Brodo D5

Drinking & Nightlife

16 Kursaal Kalhesa F6

architectural style. The interior, while impressive in scale, is essentially a marble shell, the most interesting features of which are the royal Norman tombs (to the left as you enter) and treasury, home to Constance of Aragon's gem-encrusted 13th-century crown. For panoramic city views, climb to the cathedral's roof. (www.cattedrale.palermo.it; Corso Vittorio Emanuele; cathedral free, tombs €1.50, treasury €2, roof €5, all-inclusive ticket €7; royal tombs, treasury & roof 9am-4pm Mon-Sat, tombs only 9am-1pm Sun)

Vucciria

Museo Archeologico Regionale — Museum

This splendid, wheelchair-accessible museum has been undergoing renovations since 2010, with no dependable reopening date in sight. Situated in a Renaissance monastery surrounding a gracious courtyard, it houses some of Sicily's most valuable Greek and Roman artefacts, including the museum's crown jewel, a series of original decorative friezes from the temples at Selinunte. (091 611 68 05; www.regione.sicilia.it/beniculturali/salinas; Piazza Olivella 24)

Oratorio di Santa Cita — Chapel

This 17th-century chapel showcases the breathtaking stuccowork of Giacomo Serpotta, who famously introduced rococo to Sicilian churches. Note the elaborate *Battle of Lepanto* on the entrance wall. Depicting the Christian victory over the Turks, it's framed by stucco drapes held by hundreds of naughty cherubs modelled on Palermo's street urchins. Serpotta's virtuosity also dominates the side walls, where sculpted white stucco figures hold gilded swords, shields and a lute, and a golden snake (Serpotta's symbol) curls around a picture frame. (www.ilgeniodipalermo.com; Via Valverde; admission €4, joint ticket incl Oratorio di San Domenico €6; 9am-2pm Mon-Sat Nov-Mar, to 6pm Apr-Oct)

Oratorio di San Domenico — Chapel

Dominating this small chapel is Anthony Van Dyck's fantastic blue-and-red altarpiece, *The Virgin of the Rosary with St Dominic and the Patronesses of Palermo*. Van Dyck completed the work in Genoa in 1628, after leaving Palermo in fear of the plague. Also gracing the chapel are Giacomo Serpotta's amazingly elaborate stuccoes (1710–17), vivacious and whirling with figures. Serpotta's name meant 'lizard' or 'small snake', and he often included these signature reptiles in his work; see if you can find one! (www.ilgeniodipalermo.com; Via dei Bambinai 2; admission €4, joint ticket incl Oratorio di Santa Cita €6; 9am-2pm Mon-Sat Nov-Mar, to 6pm Apr-Oct)

La Kalsa

Galleria Regionale della Sicilia — Museum

Housed in the stately 15th-century Palazzo Abatellis, this fine museum features works by Sicilian artists from the Middle Ages to the 18th century. Its greatest treasure is *Triunfo della Morte* (Triumph of Death), a magnificent fresco in which Death is represented as a demonic skeleton mounted on a wasted horse, brandishing a wicked-looking scythe while leaping over his hapless victims. (Palazzo Abatellis; 091 623 00 11; www.regione.sicilia.it/beniculturali/palazzo abatellis; Via Alloro 4; adult/reduced €8/4; 9am-6.30pm Tue-Fri, to 1pm Sat & Sun)

Galleria d'Arte Moderna Museum

This lovely, wheelchair-accessible museum is housed in a sleekly renovated 15th-century *palazzo*, which metamorphosed into a convent in the 17th century. Divided over three floors, the wide-ranging collection of 19th- and 20th-century Sicilian art is beautifully displayed. There's a regular program of modern-art exhibitions here, as well as an excellent bookshop and gift shop. English-language audio guides cost €4. (091 843 16 05; www.galleria dartemodernapalermo.it; Via Sant'Anna 21; adult/reduced €7/5; 9.30am-6.30pm Tue-Sun)

Museo Internazionale delle Marionette Museum

This whimsical museum houses over 3500 marionettes, puppets, glove puppets and shadow figures from Palermo, Catania and Naples, as well as from further-flung places such as Japan, Southeast Asia, Africa, China and India. Occasional puppet shows (adult/child €10/5) are staged on the museum's top floor in a beautifully decorated traditional theatre complete with hand-cranked music machine. (091 32 80 60; www.museomarionettepalermo.it; Piazzetta Antonio Pasqualino 5; adult/reduced €5/3; 9am-1pm & 2.30-6.30pm Mon-Sat)

New City

Teatro Massimo Theatre

Palermo's grand neoclassical opera house took over 20 years to complete and has become one of the city's iconic landmarks. The closing scene of *The Godfather: Part III*, with its visually stunning juxtaposition of high culture, crime, drama and death, was filmed here. Guided 25-minute tours are offered throughout the day in English, Spanish, French and Italian. (tour reservations 091 605 32 67; www.teatromassimo.it; Piazza Giuseppe Verdi; guided tours adult/reduced €8; 9.30am-5.30pm)

Around Palermo

Cattedrale di Monreale Cathedral

In the hills 8km southwest of Palermo is the finest example of Norman architecture in Sicily, incorporating Norman, Arab, Byzantine and classical elements. Inspired by a vision of the Virgin, it was built by William II in an effort to outdo his grandfather Roger II, who was responsible for the cathedral in Cefalù and the Cappella Palatina in Palermo. The breathtaking interior, completed in 1184 and executed in shimmering mosaics, depicts 42 Old Testament stories. The **cloister** (adult/reduced €6/3; 9am-6.30pm Mon-Sat, to 1pm Sun) is a tranquil courtyard with a tangible oriental feel.

To reach Monreale, take AMAT bus 389 (€1.40, 35 minutes, every 1¼ hours) from Piazza Indipendenza in Palermo, or AST's Monreale bus (one way/return €1.90/3, 40 minutes, hourly Monday to Saturday) from in front of Palermo Centrale train station. (091 640 44 03; Piazza del Duomo; admission to cathedral free, north transept €2, terrace €2; 8.30am-12.45pm & 2.30-5pm Mon-Sat, 8-10am & 2.30-5pm Sun)

EATING & DRINKING

Ferro di Cavallo Trattoria €

Tables line the footpath and caricatures of the owners beam down from bright-red walls at this cheerful family-run trattoria near the Quattro Canti, in business since 1944. Nothing costs more than €8 on the straightforward à la carte menu. It's a great place to try Sicilian classics like *pasta con le sarde* (pasta with sardines, pine nuts, raisins and wild fennel); save room for the excellent *cannoli* (€2). (091 33 18 35; www.ferrodicavallopalermo.it; Via Venezia 20; meals €15-17; 11.30am-3.30pm Mon-Sat, plus 7.45-11.30pm Wed-Sat)

Aeolian Islands

The Aeolian Islands are a little piece of paradise. Stunning cobalt sea, splendid beaches, some of Italy's best hiking, and an awe-inspiring volcanic landscape are just part of the appeal. The islands also have a fascinating human and mythological history that goes back several millennia; the Aeolians figured prominently in Homer's *Odyssey*, and evidence of the distant past can be seen everywhere, most notably in Lipari's excellent archaeological museum.

The seven islands of Lipari, Vulcano, Salina, Panarea, Stromboli, Alicudi and Filicudi are part of a huge 200km volcanic ridge that runs between the smoking stack of Mt Etna and the threatening mass of Vesuvius above Naples. Collectively, the islands exhibit a unique range of volcanic characteristics, which earned them a place on Unesco's World Heritage list in 2000. Highlights include the spectacular volcanic fireworks of Stromboli, the picturesque vineyards and dormant twin cones of Salina and the therapeutic mud baths of Vulcano.

Both **Ustica Lines** (www.usticalines.it) and **Siremar** (www.siremar.it) run hydrofoils year-round from Milazzo, the mainland city closest to the islands. Regular hydrofoil and ferry services operate between the islands. Ticket offices with posted timetables can be found close to the docks on all islands.

The island of Vulcano

Trattoria Il Maestro del Brodo Trattoria €€

This no-frills trattoria in the Vucciria offers delicious soups, an array of ultrafresh seafood and a sensational antipasto buffet (€8) featuring a dozen-plus homemade delicacies: *sarde a beccafico* (stuffed sardines), eggplant *involtini* (roulades), smoked fish, artichokes with parsley, sun-dried tomatoes, olives and more. (☎091 32 95 23; Via Pannieri 7; meals €22-31; ⊙12.30-3.30pm Tue-Sun, plus 8-11pm Fri & Sat)

Osteria Ballarò Sicilian €€

A hot new foodie address, this classy restaurant-cum-wine bar marries an atmospheric setting with fantastic island cooking. Bare stone columns, exposed brick walls and vaulted ceilings set the stage for delicious seafood *primi*, local wines and memorable Sicilian *dolci*. For a faster eat, you can snack on street food at the bar or take away from the hole-in-the-wall counter outside. (☎091 791 01 84; www.osteriaballaro.it; Via Calascibetta 25; meals €30-45; ⊙12.15-3.15pm & 7-11.30pm)

Kursaal Kalhesa Bar

Kursaal Kalhesa has long been a noted city nightspot. A restaurant, wine bar and jazz club, it draws a cool crowd who come to hang out over *aperitivi*, dine alfresco or catch a gig under the high vaulted ceilings. It's in a 15th-century *palazzo* on the city's massive sea walls. (☎091 616 00 50; www.facebook.com/kursaalkalhesa; Foro Umberto I 21; ⊙6.30pm-1am Tue-Sun)

INFORMATION

Municipal Tourist Office (☎091 740 80 21; promozioneturismo@comune.palermo.it; Piazza Bellini; ⊙8.30am-6.30pm Mon-Sat) The most reliable of Palermo's city-run information booths. Others at Piazza Castelnuovo, the Port of Palermo and Mondello are only intermittently staffed, with unpredictable hours.

Tourist Information – Falcone-Borsellino Airport (☎091 59 16 98; ⊙8.30am-7.30pm Mon-Fri, to 6pm Sat) Downstairs in the arrivals hall.

Caponata, a Sicilian vegetable dish

GETTING THERE & AWAY

AIR

Palermo's airport **Falcone-Borsellino** (☎091 702 02 73; www.gesap.it) is at Punta Raisi, 31km west of Palermo. Alitalia, Easyjet, Ryanair and several other airlines operate between major European cities and Palermo.

BOAT

The ferry terminal is located just east of the corner of Via Francesco Crispi and Via Emerico Amari.

Grandi Navi Veloci (☎091 58 74 04, 010 209 45 91; www.gnv.it; Calata Marinai d'Italia) Runs ferries from Palermo to Civitavecchia, Genoa, Naples and Tunis.

Grimaldi Lines (☎081 49 64 44, 091 611 36 91; www.grimaldi-lines.com; Via del Mare) Twice-weekly ferries from Palermo to Salerno (from €55, 10 to 12 hours) and Tunis (from €42, 11 to 14 hours).

Tirrenia (☎344 0920924; www.tirrenia.it; Calata Marinai d'Italia) Ferries to Cagliari (from €49, 12 hours, Saturday only) and Naples (from €52, 10 hours, daily).

BUS

The two main departure points are the brand-new Piazzetta Cairoli bus terminal, just south of the train station's eastern entrance, and the intercity bus stop on Via Paolo Balsamo, due east of the train station.

Cuffaro (☎091 616 15 10; www.cuffaro.info; Via Paolo Balsamo 13) Services to Agrigento (€9, two hours, three to eight daily).

SAIS Autolinee (☎091 616 60 28; www.saisautolinee.it; Piazza Cairoli) To/from Catania (€15, 2¾ hours, eight to 10 daily) and Messina (€16, 2¾ hours, three to six daily).

Segesta (☎091 616 79 19; www.segesta.it; Piazza Cairoli) Services to Trapani (€8.60, two hours, at least 10 daily). Also sells Interbus tickets to Syracuse (€12, 3¼ hours, two to three daily).

TRAIN

From Palermo Centrale station, just south of the centre at the foot of Via Roma, direct trains leave for Catania (€12.50, 2¾ hours, two to five daily), Agrigento (€8.30, 2¼ hours, eight to 10 daily) and Cefalù (€5.15, one hour, hourly). For Syracuse, the bus is a more efficient option.

GETTING AROUND

/FROM THE AIRPORT

restia e Comandè (091 58 63 51; www.prestiaecomande.it) runs a half-hourly bus service from the airport to the centre of town (one way/return €6.30/11), with stops outside Teatro Politeama Garibaldi (35 minutes) and Palermo Centrale train station (50 minutes).

A slower option is the twice-hourly Trinacria Express train (€5.80, one hour) from Punta Raisi station (just downstairs from the arrivals hall) to Palermo Centrale.

A taxi from the airport to downtown Palermo costs €45.

Catania

Catania is a true city of the volcano. Much of it is constructed from the lava that engulfed the city during Mt Etna's massive 1669 eruption. The city is lava-black in colour, as if a fine dusting of soot permanently covers its elegant buildings, most of which are the work of baroque master Giovanni Vaccarini.

SIGHTS

Piazza del Duomo Square

A Unesco World Heritage Site, Catania's central piazza is a set piece of contrasting lava and limestone, surrounded by buildings in the unique local baroque style and crowned by the grand Cattedrale di Sant'Agata. At its centre stands Fontana dell'Elefante (1736), a naive, smiling black-lava elephant dating from Roman times, surmounted by an improbable Egyptian obelisk. Another fountain at the piazza's southwest corner, Fontana dell'Amenano, marks the entrance to Catania's fish market.

Cattedrale di Sant'Agata Cathedral

Inside the vaulted interior of this cathedral, beyond its impressive marble facade sporting two orders of columns taken from the Roman amphitheatre, lie the relics of the city's patron saint. Consider visiting the **Museo Diocesano** (www.museodiocesanocatania.com; Piazza del Duomo; adult/reduced museum only €7/4, museum & baths €10/6; 9am-2pm Mon, Wed & Fri, 9am-2pm & 3-6pm

Tue & Thu, 9am-1pm Sat) next door for access to the Roman baths directly underneath the church and fine views from the roof terrace beneath the cathedral's dome. (095 32 00 44; Piazza del Duomo; 8am-noon & 4-7pm)

La Pescheria Market
Catania's raucous fish market, which takes over the streets behind Piazza del Duomo every workday morning, is street theatre at its most thrilling. Tables groan under the weight of decapitated swordfish, ruby-pink prawns and trays full of clams, mussels, sea urchins. Fishmongers gut silvery fish and high-heeled housewives step daintily over pools of blood-stained water. Surrounding the market are a number of good seafood restaurants. (Via Pardo; 7am-2pm Mon-Sat)

Graeco-Roman Theatre & Odeon Ruin
These twin theatres west of Piazza del Duomo are Catania's most impressive Graeco-Roman remains. Both are picturesquely sited in the thick of a crumbling residential neighbourhood, with laundry occasionally flapping on the rooftops of vine-covere buildings that appear to have sprouted organically from the half-submerged stag Adjacent to the main theatre is the Casa Liberti, an elegantly restored 19th-century *palazzo* with tiled floors and red wallpaper that now houses two millennia worth of artefacts discovered during excavation of the theatres. (Via Vittorio Emanuele II 262; adult/reduced incl Casa Liberti €6/3; 9am-7pm Mon-Sat, to 1.30pm Sun)

ENTERTAINMENT

Teatro Massimo Bellini Theatre
Catania's premier theatre is named after the city's most famous son, composer Vincenzo Bellini. Sporting the full red-and-gold-gilt look, it stages a year-round season of opera and an eight-month program of classical music from November to June. Tickets, which are available online, start at around €13 and rise to €84 for a first-night front-row seat. (095 730 61 11; www.teatromassimobellini.it; Via Perrotta 12)

ROBERTHARDING/GETTY IMAGES ©

★ Top Five for Mosaics

- Cappella Palatina (p289)
- Cattedrale di Monreale (p293)
- Villa Romana del Casale (p298)
- La Martorana (p288)
- Palazzo dei Normanni (p289)

From left: Capella Palatina; Cattedrale di Monreale; La Martorana

Villa Romana del Casale

The Unesco-listed **Villa Romana del Casale** (0935 68 00 36; www.villaromanadelcasale.it; adult/reduced €10/5; 9am-6pm Apr-Oct, to 4pm Nov-Mar) is central Sicily's biggest attraction, having reopened after years of reconstruction. It is decorated with the finest Roman floor mosaics in existence. The mosaics cover almost the entire floor of the villa and are considered unique for their natural, narrative style, the range of their subject matter and the variety of colour.

Situated in a wooded valley 5km southwest of Piazza Amerina, the villa, sumptuous even by decadent Roman standards, is thought to have been the country retreat of Marcus Aurelius Maximianus, Rome's co-emperor during the reign of Diocletian (AD 286–305). Certainly, the size of the complex – four interconnected groups of buildings spread over the hillside – and the 3535 sq metres of multicoloured floor mosaics suggests a palace of imperial standing. Following a landslide in the 12th century, the villa lay protected under 10m of mud for some 700 years. It was only when excavation work began in the 1950s that the mosaics were brought to light. Recent restorations covered most of the complex with a wooden roof, to protect the mosaics from the elements. An elevated walkway allows visitors to view the mosaics and the structure in its entirety.

EATING & DRINKING

Da Antonio — Trattoria €

This humble hideaway offers the quintessential trattoria experience: reasonably priced, delicious food served by hard-working, unpretentious waitstaff. Despite having made inroads onto the tourist radar, it's still the kind of place where local families come for Sunday lunch. The menu revolves around local fish, homemade pasta and classic Sicilian desserts featuring ricotta, pistachios, almonds and wild strawberries. (347 8330636; www.facebook.com/TrattoriaDaAntonio; Via Castello Ursino 59; meals €19-25; 12.30-2.30pm & 7.30-10pm Tue-Sun)

Me Cumpari Turridu — Sicilian €€

A quirky little spot that mixes tradition and modernity both in food and decor, this place is a real discovery. Try the ricotta and marjoram ravioli in a pork sauce; the cannellini with donkey-meat *ragù* (meat and tomato sauce), or the Ustica lentil stew, with broad beans and fennel. (095 715 01 42; Via Ventimiglia 15; meals €27-40; 1-2.30pm daily, plus 8-11.30pm Mon-Sat)

Osteria Antica Marina — Seafood €€

With a front terrace directly overlooking the fishmongers' stalls in the piazza below, this classy trattoria is *the* place to come for seafood. A variety of tasting menus ranging from €25 to €45 showcase everything from swordfish to scampi, cuttlefish to calamari. (095 34 81 97; www.anticamarina.it; Via Pardo 29; meals €30-50; 1-3pm & 8-11pm Thu-Tue)

Razmataz — Bar

Wines by the glass, draught and bottled beer and an ample cocktail list are offered at this delightful wine bar with tables spread out across a tree-shaded sweet backstreet square. It doubles as a cafe in the morning, but gets packed with locals from *aperitivo* time onward. (095 31 18 93; Via Montesano 17; 8.30am-late)

INFORMATION

Tourist office (095 742 55 73; www.comune.catania.it; Via Vittorio Emanuele 172; 8am-7.15pm Mon-Sat) Very helpful.

GETTING THERE & AWAY

AIR

Catania's airport, **Fontanarossa** (095 723 91 11; www.aeroporto.catania.it), is 7km southwest of the city centre. To get there, take the special Alibus 457 (€4, 30 minutes, every 25 minutes from 4.40am to midnight) from outside the train station. **Etna Transporti/Interbus** (☎095 53 03 96; www.interbus.it; Via d'Amico 187) also runs regular buses from the airport to Taormina (€8, 1½ hours, hourly 7.45am to 8.45pm).

BOAT

The ferry terminal is located southwest of the train station along Via VI Aprile.

TTT Lines (☎800 627414, 095 34 85 86; www.tttlines.info) runs nightly ferries from Catania to Naples (from €42, 11 hours).

BUS

Iintercity buses leave from a terminal one block north of Catania's train station; ticket offices are diagonally across the street on Via d'Amico.

Interbus (☎095 53 03 96; www.interbus.it; Via d'Amico 187) runs buses to Syracuse (€6.20, 1½ hours, hourly Monday to Friday, fewer on weekends) and Taormina (€5, 1¼ hours, hourly)

SAIS Trasporti (☎095 53 61 68; www.saisautolinee.it; Via d'Amico 183) goes to Agrigento (€13.40, three hours, nine to 14 daily). Its sister company **SAIS Autolinee** (☎095 53 61 68; www.saisautolinee.it; Via d'Amico 183) also runs services to Palermo (€12, 2¾ hours, eight to 10 daily).

TRAIN

From Catania Centrale station on Piazza Papa Giovanni XXIII there are frequent trains to Syracuse (€6.35 to €10, 1¼ hours, ten Monday to Saturday, four on Sunday) and Palermo (€12.50, three hours, three to six direct daily).

GETTING AROUND

City buses run by **AMT** (☎095 751 91 11; www.amt.ct.it) terminate in front of the train station, including buses 1-4 and 4-7 (both running hourly from the station to Via Etnea) and Alibus 457 (station to airport every 25 minutes). Also useful is bus D, which runs from Piazza Borsellino (just south of the Duomo) to the local beaches. A 90-minute ticket costs €1 for regular buses, €4 for Alibus airport service.

For a taxi, call **Radio Taxi Catania** (☎095 33 09 66; www.radiotaxicatania.org).

Teatro Massimo Bellini (p297)

Syracuse

A dense tapestry of overlapping cultures and civilisations, Syracuse is one of Sicily's most appealing cities. Settled by colonists from Corinth in 734 BC, this was considered to be the most beautiful city of the ancient world, rivalling Athens in power and prestige.

Today, the ancient island neighbourhood of Ortygia continues to seduce visitors with its atmospheric squares, narrow alleyways and lovely waterfront, while the Parco Archaeologico della Neapolis, 2km across town, remains one of Sicily's great classical treasures. Add to this the city's enlightened moves toward pedestrian-friendliness and environmental sustainability (including the 2014 launch of a fleet of electric minibuses), and you'll soon understand why this has become Sicily's number-one tourist destination.

SIGHTS

Ortygia

Duomo Cathedral

Built on the skeleton of a 5th-century BC Greek temple to Athena (note the Doric columns still visible inside and out), Syracuse's cathedral became a church when the island was evangelised by St Paul. Its most striking feature is the columned baroque facade (1728–53) added by Andrea Palma after the 1693 earthquake. A statue of the Virgin Mary crowns the rooftop, in the same spot where a golden statue of Athena once served as a beacon to homecoming Greek sailors. (Piazza del Duomo; adult/reduced €2/1; 9am-6.30pm Mon-Sat Apr-Oct, to 5.30pm Nov-Mar)

Fontana Aretusa Fountain

Down the winding main street from the cathedral is this ancient spring, where fresh water still bubbles up just as it did in ancient times when it was the city's main water supply. Legend has it that the goddess Artemis transformed her beautiful handmaiden Aretusa into the spring to

> *a golden statue of Athena once stood as a beacon to homecoming Greek sailors*

Duomo, Syracuse

protect her from the unwelcome attention of the river god Alpheus.

La Giudecca Area

Simply walking through Ortygia's tangled maze of alleys is an atmospheric experience, especially down the narrow lanes of Via Maestranza, the heart of the old guild quarter, and the crumbling Jewish ghetto of Via della Giudecca. At the Alla Giudecca hotel you can visit an ancient Jewish miqwe (ritual bath; ☎0931 2 22 55; Via Alagona 52; tours in English & Italian €5; ⏲ tours hourly 9am-7pm mid-May–Sep, 11am, noon, 4pm, 5pm & 6pm Oct–mid-May) some 20m below ground level. Blocked up in 1492 when the Jewish community was expelled from Ortygia, the baths were rediscovered during renovation work at the hotel.

Mainland Syracuse

Parco Archeologico della Neapolis Archaeological Site

For the classicist, Syracuse's real attraction is this archaeological park, with its pearly white 5th-century-BC **Teatro Greco**. Hewn out of the rocky hillside, this 16,000-capacity amphitheatre staged the last tragedies of Aeschylus (including *The Persians*), which were first performed here in his presence. In late spring it's brought to life with an annual season of classical theatre.

Beside the theatre is the mysterious **Latomia del Paradiso** (Garden of Paradise) a deep, precipitous limestone quarry out of which stone for the ancient city was extracted. Riddled with catacombs and filled with citrus and magnolia trees, it's also where the 7000 survivors of the war between Syracuse and Athens in 413 BC were imprisoned. The **Orecchio di Dionisio** (Ear of Dionysius), a 23m-high grotto extending 65m back into the cliffside, was named by Caravaggio after the tyrant Dionysius, who is said to have used the almost perfect acoustics of the quarry to eavesdrop on his prisoners. To reach the park, take Sd'A Trasporti minibus 2 (€0.50, 15 minutes) from Molo Sant'Antonio, on the west side of the main bridge into Ortygia. Alternatively, walking from Ortygia will take about 30 minutes. If driving, park on Viale Augusto (tickets are available at the nearby souvenir kiosks). (☎0931 6 62 06; Viale Paradiso 14; adult/reduced €10/5, incl Museo Archeologico €13.50/7; ⏲9am-6.30pm)

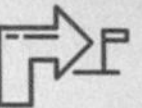

Sicily's Baroque Triangle

With a car and a little extra time on your hands, you can explore the so-called 'baroque triangle'. This remote, rocky corner of southeastern Sicily is home to a series of Unesco-listed towns famous for their lavish baroque architecture.

Just over 35km south of Syracuse, **Noto** can lay claim to what is arguably Sicily's most beautiful street: Corso Vittorio Emanuele, a pedestrianised boulevard lined with golden baroque *palazzi*. West of Noto, and further inland, **Modica** is a bustling town set in a deep rocky gorge. The headline here is the Chiesa di San Giorgio in Modica Alta, the high part of town. From Modica, it's a short, twisting, up-and-down drive through rock-littered hills to **Ragusa**, one of Sicily's nine provincial capitals. The town is divided in two, but it's Ragusa Ibla that you want, a claustrophobic warren of grey stone houses and elegant *palazzi* that opens up onto Piazza Duomo, a superb example of 18th-century town planning.

Chiesa San Giorgio, Modica
WESTEND61/GETTY IMAGES ©

Teatro Greco (p301)

Museo Archeologico Paolo Orsi Museum

About 500m east of the archaeological park, this modern museum contains one of Sicily's largest and most interesting archaeological collections. Allow plenty of time to visit the four sectors charting the area's prehistory, as well as Syracuse's development from foundation to the late Roman period. (☎0931 48 95 11; www.regione.sicilia.it/beniculturali/museopaoloorsi; Viale Teocrito 66; adult/reduced €8/4, incl Parco Archeologico €13.50/7; ⏰9am-6pm Tue-Sat, to 1pm Sun)

ENTERTAINMENT

Piccolo Teatro dei Pupi Theatre

Syracuse's beloved puppet theatre hosts regular performances; see its website for a calendar. You can also buy puppets at its workshop next door and visit the affiliated puppet museum. (☎328 5326600; www.pupari.com; Via della Giudecca 17; ⏰shows 4.30pm, 6 times weekly Apr-Oct, fewer Nov-Mar)

EATING & DRINKING

Le Vin De L'Assassin Bistrot Mediterranean **€€**

This stylish restaurant takes an original French twist on Sicilian ingredients. The friendly Sicilian owner, Saro, spent years in Paris and is generous with advice on the plethora of offerings scrawled on the chalkboard nightly, including Breton oysters, impeccably dressed salads, a host of meat and fish mains, and creamy, chocolatey desserts. (☎0931 6 61 59; Via Roma 115; meals €30-45; ⏰7.30-11pm Tue-Sun year-round, plus 12.30-2.30pm Sun Oct-May)

A Putia delle Cose Buone Sicilian **€€**

From the garden gnomes greeting you at the door to the benches draped in colourful pillows, this lovely place feels welcoming from the word go. Then there's the food: creative, reasonably priced Sicilian dishes that make ample use of local ingredients. Salads, vegan and vegetarian options also abound. (☎0931 44 92 79; www.aputiadellecosebuone.it; Via Roma 8; meals €21-33; ⏰1-3pm & 7-11pm)

Don Camillo Modern Sicilian **€€€**
One of Ortygia's most elegant restaurants, Don Camillo specialises in top service, a classy atmosphere and innovative Sicilian cuisine. Try the starter of mixed shellfish in a thick soup of Noto almonds, lick your lips over the swordfish with orange blossom honey and sweet-and-sour vegetables, or savour the divine *tagliata di tonno* (tuna steak) with red pepper 'marmalade'. (☎0931 6 71 33; www.ristorantedoncamillo-siracusa.it; Via Maestranza 96; meals €35-50; ⏰12.30-2.30pm & 7.30-10.30pm Mon-Sat)

Biblios Cafè Cafe
This beloved bookshop-cafe organises a whole range of cultural activities, including wine tasting, literary readings, art classes and language courses. It's a great place to drop in any time of day, for coffee, *aperitivi* or just to mingle. (www.biblioscafe.it; Via del Consiglio Reginale 11; ⏰11am-3pm & 6pm-midnight Wed-Mon)

Barcollo Bar
Hidden away in a historic courtyard, this seductive bar has outdoor deck seating and serves *aperitivi* from 7pm to 10pm. (Via Pompeo Picherali 10; ⏰7pm-3am)

INFORMATION

Tourist office (☎800 055500, 0931 46 29 46; infoturismo@provsr.it; Via Roma 31; ⏰9am-6.30pm) City maps and lots of good information.

GETTING THERE & AWAY

BUS

Long-distance buses operate from the bus stop along Corso Umberto, just east of Syracuse's train station. **Interbus** (☎093 16 67 10; www.interbus.it) runs buses hourly on weekdays (less frequently on weekends) to Catania (€6.20, 1½ hours) via Fontanarossa airport (€6.20, 1¼ hours). Other Interbus destinations include Noto (€3.60, 55 minutes, two to five daily) and Palermo (€13.50, 3¾ hours, two to three daily).

Where to Stay

There's no shortage of alluring accommodation options in Sicily. At the budget end of the price spectrum you can opt for a pensione (guesthouse) or a B&B. *Alberghi* (hotels), which may range from one star to five stars, are more expensive. *Locande* (inns) and *affittacamere* (rooms for rent) are usually the cheapest options on offer, although in some areas (such as the Aeolian Islands) the standard can be very high and prices are adjusted accordingly. Around Etna and Piano Battaglia in the Parco Naturale Regionale delle Madonie there are a number of *rifugi* (mountain chalets), most of which are open all year. Many are operated by Club Alpino Siciliano. *Agriturismi* (working farms and country houses that offer accommodation) are well worth considering, as is the small but slowly growing number of boutique hotels.

TRAIN

From Syracuse's train station (Via Francesco Crispi), several trains depart daily for Messina (regional/InterCity train €9.70/19.50, 2½ to 3¼ hours) via Catania (€6.35/10, 1¼ hours). For Palermo, the bus is a better option. There are also local trains from Syracuse to Noto (€3.45, 30 minutes, eight daily except Sunday) and Ragusa (€7.65, two to 2½ hours, two daily except Sunday).

GETTING AROUND

Sd'A Trasporti (www.siracusadamare.it; single ticket/day pass/week pass €0.50/2/7) serves Syracuse and Ortygia with a fleet of inexpensive electric minibuses. To reach Ortygia from Syracuse's bus and train stations, hop aboard bus 1, which loops around the island every half-hour or so. To reach Parco Archeologico della Neapolis, take minibus 2 from Molo Sant'Antonio (just west of the bridge to Ortygia).

Positano (p270), Amalfi Coast

In Focus

Ponte di Rialto (p170), Venice

Italy Today

While Italy is the 'beautiful country', under the exquisite surface are some serious problems of corruption and unstable governments. But Italy's youngest ever leader, Matteo Renzi, is effecting dramatic political changes, Pope Francis is reinvigorating the Vatican and Italians are using their ingenuity to address such issues as the cost of maintaining their illustrious heritage.

The Economy

Over the last 15 years, the Italian economy has stagnated. In Europe, Italy's public debt ranks among the highest while its economic growth is among the lowest.

Things are especially difficult for the young. Youth unemployment rose over 44% in 2015. The same year, it was calculated that the cost to the Italian economy of graduates fleeing the country in search of better opportunities elsewhere was around €23 billion.

Nepotism and corruption don't help. In 2014 alone, three major transgressions were exposed: alleged corruption in awarding contracts for the Milan Expo; the 'Mafia Capitale' scandal, in which politicians were discovered to have liaised with criminals to steal funds from the Roman municipality; and corruption relating to the construction of the MOSE flood-defence system that led to the resignation of the mayor of Venice.

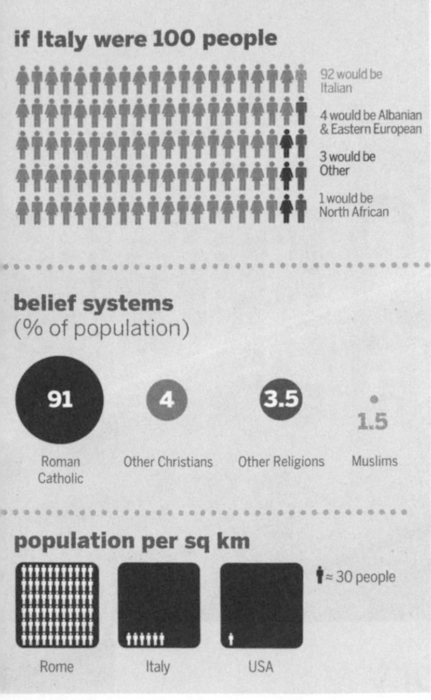

At the Helm

The downfall of former prime minister Silvio Berlusconi, who was convicted of tax fraud in 2013, ushered in a new era in Italian politics. The 39-year-old Matteo Renzi, previously mayor of Florence, took over as leader of a right-left coalition in 2014, making him the third unelected prime minister since Berlusconi's fall (following Mario Monti and Enrico Letta). Renzi's cabinet is the youngest in Italian history and the first with an even gender balance.

Even before taking the role of prime minister, Renzi was known as '*il rottamatore*' (the scrapper), a name he continues to embrace as he attempts to change Italy's political landscape with a package of employment and electoral reforms.

At the spiritual helm, Pope Francis, the popular Argentinian pontiff elected in 2013, goes from strength to strength. Noted for his humble, less formal approach and concern for the poor, he has done much to restore the Church's image, attracting over 7 million pilgrims to the Vatican in 2014.

The Migration Frontline

Even as young people leave Italy (over 94,000 in 2013), many migrants are risking their lives to enter the country. The number of people attempting the dangerous journey from North Africa rose by a third in 2015, with 62,000 migrants arriving by sea in the first half of the year.

Most migrants arrive in Italy on the tiny island of Lampedusa, which is just 113km from the North African coast. Few stay in Italy, however; most travel onward to northern Europe where opportunities are greater.

Saving Italy's Heritage

Italy has 51 Unesco World Heritage Sites, more than any other country, and looking after such a wealth of heritage is expensive. In recent years, walls have collapsed at Pompeii and a Raphael painting at Rome's Borghese Gallery warped due to a broken air-conditioning system.

In answer to such problems, municipalities have been working on attracting private investment, a controversial but successful process. Completed projects include luxury brand Tod's €25-million clean-up of the Colosseum, and a €5-million restoration of Venice's Rialto Bridge by Renzo Rossi's OTB group.

Arco di Settimio Severo (p54) and the Tempio di Saturno (p55), Rome

History

Italy has seen it all: imperial domination, quarrelling city-states, international exploration, crushing poverty and postwar booms. This operatic story features a colourful cast of perverted emperors, ambitious invaders, Machiavellian masterminds and ordinary Italians who have repeatedly performed extraordinary, history-changing feats.

c 700,000 BC

Primitive tribes lived in caves and hunted elephants and other hefty beasts on the Italian peninsula.

2000 BC

The Bronze Age reaches Italy. Copper and bronze are used to fashion tools and arms.

264–241 BC

War rages between Rome and the Carthage empire, across North Africa and into Spain, Sicily and Sardinia.

San Gimignano (p130), Tuscany

…N SCICLUNA/GETTY IMAGES ©

Etruscans, Greeks & Ancient Rome

Long before Renaissance *palazzi* (mansions) and baroque churches, the Italian peninsula was riddled with caves and hill towns built by the Etruscans, who dominated the land by the 7th century BC. Little is known about them, since they spoke a language that today has barely been deciphered. Though impressive as seafarers, warriors and farmers, they lacked cohesion.

Greek traders set up a series of independent city-states along the coast and in Sicily in the 8th century BC, collectively known as Magna Graecia. These Greek settlements flourished until the 3rd century BC, and the remains of magnificent Doric temples still stand in Italy's south (at Paestum) and on Sicily (at Agrigento, Selinunte and Segesta).

The Etruscans tried and failed to conquer the Greek settlements, but the real threat to both civilisations came from an unexpected source – the grubby but growing Latin town of Rome.

AD 79

Mt Vesuvius showers molten rock and ash upon Pompeii and Herculaneum.

312

Constantine becomes the Roman Empire's first Christian leader.

962

Otto I is crowned Holy Roman Emperor in Rome, the first in a long line of Germanic rulers.

★ Best for Archaeological Booty

Vatican Museums (p38), Vatican

Capitoline Museums (p62), Rome

Museo Archeologico Nazionale (p236), Naples

Museo Archeologico Paolo Orsi (p302), Syracuse

Capitoline Museums (p62), Rome

According to legend, Italy's future capital was founded by twins Romulus and Remus on 21 April 753 BC, on the site where they had been suckled by a she-wolf as orphan infants. Romulus later killed Remus and the settlement was named Rome after him. Over the following centuries, this fearless and often ruthless town become Italy's major power, sweeping aside the Etruscans by the 2nd century AD.

The Roman Republic

Although Roman monuments were emblazoned with the initials SPQR (Senatus Popu lusque Romanus, or the Senate and People of Rome), the Roman people initially had precious little say in their republic. Known as plebeians (literally 'the many'), the disenfranchised majority slowly wrested concessions from the patrician class by 280 BC, though only a small political class qualified for positions of power in government.

Slowly at first, Roman armies conquered the Italian peninsula. Defeated city-states were not taken over directly, but were obliged to become allies, providing troops on demand for the Roman army. Wars with rivals such as Carthage in the east gave Rome control of Sardinia, Sicily, Corsica, mainland Greece, Spain, most of North Africa and part of Asia Minor by 133 BC.

Beware the Ides of March

Born in 100 BC, Gaius Julius Caesar would become one of Rome's most masterful generals, lenient conquerors and capable administrators. After quelling revolts in Spain, Caesar received a Roman mandate in 59 BC to govern Gallia Narbonensis, today's southern France. Caesar raised troops to hold off an invasion of Helvetic tribes from Switzerland, and in 52 to 51 BC stamped out Gaul's last great revolt under the leader Vercingetorix. Diplomatic Caesar was generous to defeated enemies, and the Gauls became his staunchest supporters.

1309

Pope Clement V shifts the papacy to Avignon in France (for almost 70 years).

1321

Dante Alighieri completes his epic poem *La divina commedia* (The Divine Comedy); he dies the same year.

1452

Leonardo da Vinci is born 15 April in Vinci, near Florence.

Jealous of the growing power of his one-time protégé, Gnaeus Pompeius Magnus (Pompey) severed his political alliance with Caesar, and convinced the Senate to outlaw Caesar in 49 BC. On 7 January, Caesar crossed the Rubicon River into Italy, sparking civil war. Caesar's three-year campaign ended in decisive victory, and upon his return to Rome in 46 BC, he assumed dictatorial powers.

Caesar launched a series of reforms, overhauled the Senate and embarked on a building program, but by 44 BC, it was clear Caesar had no plans to restore the republic. Dissent grew in the Senate, and on the Ides (15th) of March 44 BC a band of conspirators stabbed Caesar to death in a Senate meeting.

In the years following Caesar's death, his lieutenant, Mark Antony (Marcus Antonius), and nominated heir, great-nephew Octavian, plunged into civil war against Caesar's assassins. Octavian took control of the western half of the empire and Antony headed to the east – but when Antony fell head over heels for Cleopatra VII in 31 BC, Octavian and Antony turned on one another. Octavian claimed victory over Antony and Cleopatra in Greece, and when he invaded Egypt, Antony and Cleopatra committed suicide and Egypt became a province of Rome.

Imperial Insanity

Tiberius (14–37) A steady governing hand but prone to depression, Tiberius had a difficult relationship with the Senate and withdrew in his later years to Capri, devoting himself to drinking, orgies and fits of paranoia.

Gaius (Caligula; 37–41) Sex with his sisters and violence were Caligula's idea of entertainment. He emptied the state's coffers and suggested naming a horse consul before being assassinated.

Claudius (41–54) Apparently timid as a child, he was ruthless with enemies and relished watching their executions. According to English historian Edward Gibbon, he was the only one of the first 15 emperors not to take male lovers.

Nero (54–68) Nero had his mum murdered, his first wife's veins slashed, and his second wife kicked to death. The people accused him of fiddling while Rome burned to the ground in 64; Nero blamed the disaster on the Christians. He executed the evangelists Peter and Paul, and had others thrown to wild beasts.

Augustus & the Glories of Empire

By 27 BC Octavian was renamed Augustus (Your Eminence) and conceded virtually unlimited power by the Senate, effectively becoming Rome's emperor. Under Augustus, the arts flourished and buildings were restored and constructed, including the Pantheon.

Over 1.5 million inhabitants thronged the capital's marble temples, public baths, theatres, circuses and libraries. Poverty was rife, and Augustus created Rome's first police force

1506

Work starts on St Peter's Basilica in Rome, to a design by Donato Bramante.

1508–12

Pope Julius II commissions Michelangelo to paint the ceiling frescoes in the restored Sistine Chapel.

1582

Pope Gregory XIII replaces the Julian calendar (introduced by Caesar) with the modern-day Gregorian calendar.

★ Best for Ancient Awe

Pantheon (p44), Rome

Colosseum (p46), Rome

Pompeii (p255), Campania

Valley of the Temples (p286), Sicily

Colosseum (p46), Rome

under a city prefect *(praefectus urbi)* to curb mob violence and quell dissent among the poor, politically underrepresented masses.

Under Hadrian (76–138), the empire reached its greatest extent, including Britain and most of the modern-day Middle East, from Turkey to northern Morocco. But by the time Diocletian (245–305) became emperor, the empire was faced with attacks from outside and revolts from within. Diocletian's response to the rise of Christianity was persecution, a policy reversed in 313 under Christian Constantine I (c 272–337).

The empire was later divided in two, with the second capital in Constantinople (modern-day Istanbul) founded by Constantine in 330. The Byzantine eastern empire survived, while Italy and Rome were overrun.

Papal Power & Family Feuds

In a historic twist, the minority religion Emperor Diocletian tried so hard to stamp out preserved Rome's glory. While most of Italy succumbed to invasion from Germanic tribes, Byzantine reconquest and Lombards in the north, the papacy established itself in Rome as a spiritual and secular force.

In return for formal recognition of the pope's control of Rome and surrounding Papal States, the Carolingian Franks were granted a powerful position in Italy and their king, Charlemagne, was given the title of Holy Roman Emperor. The bond between the papacy and the Byzantine Empire was broken, and political power shifted north of the Alps, where it remained for more than 1000 years.

Meanwhile, Rome's aristocratic families battled to control the papacy and the right to appoint politically powerful bishops.

The Wonder of the World

Marriage was the ultimate merger between Henry VI, son of Holy Roman Emperor Frederick I (Barbarossa), and Constance de Hauteville, heir to Sicily's Norman throne. The power

1600

Naples is Europe's biggest city, boasting a population of over 300,000.

1805

Napoleon is proclaimed king of the newly constituted Kingdom of Italy, comprising most of the north of the country.

1861

By the end of the 1859–61 Franco-Austrian War, Vittorio Emanuele II is proclaimed king of a newly united Italy.

couple's son, Frederick II (1194–1250), became one of the most colourful figures of medieval Europe. Frederick was a German who grew up in southern Italy and called Sicily home and, as Holy Roman Emperor, allowed freedom of worship to Muslims and Jews. A warrior and scholar, Frederick was nicknamed Stupor Mundi (the Wonder of the World) for his talents as a poet, linguist, mathematician, philosopher and military strategist.

After reluctantly carrying out a (largely diplomatic) Holy Land crusade in 1228–29 under threat of excommunication, Frederick returned to Italy to find papal troops invading Neapolitan territory. Frederick soon had them on the run, and expanded his influence to city-states in central and northern Italy. Battles ensued, which continued after Frederick's death in 1250.

Florence's Trials by Fire

In 1481 Dominican friar Girolamo Savonarola began prophesying apocalyptic days ahead for Florence unless the city changed its wayward habits. With the horrors of war fresh in their minds and vivid accounts of Florentine plague, Savonarola's blood-curdling predictions struck fear in many Florentine hearts. To appease Savonarola's demands, books, clothes, jewellery, fancy furnishings and art were torched on 'bonfires of the vanities'. Drinking, whoring, partying, gambling, flashy fashion and other sinful behaviours were banned. Florentines soon tired of this fundamentalism. To test Savonarola's commitment to his own methods, the Franciscans invited him to submit to trial by fire. Savonarola sent an emissary instead, but the hapless youth was saved when the trial was cancelled on account of rain. Finally the city government had the fiery friar arrested. He was hanged and burned at the stake as a heretic alongside two supporters on 22 May 1498.

Rise of the City-States

While the south of Italy tended to centralised rule, the north did not. Port cities such as Genoa, Pisa and especially Venice increasingly ignored edicts from Rome, and Florence, Milan, Parma, Bologna, Padua, Verona and Modena resisted Roman meddling in their affairs.

Between the 12th and 14th centuries, these cities developed new forms of government. Venice adopted an oligarchic 'parliamentary' system in a limited democracy. Tuscan and Umbrian city-states created a *comune* (town council), a form of republican government dominated initially by aristocrats, then by wealthy middle classes. Family dynasties shaped their home towns, such as the Medici in Florence. War between the city-states was constant, and Florence, Milan and Venice absorbed their neighbours. Italy's dynamic, independent-minded city-states led a sea change in thinking known as the Renaissance, ushering in the modern era with scientific discoveries, publishing houses and compelling new visions for the world in art.

1915

Italy enters WWI on the side of the Allies to win Italian territories still in Austrian hands.

1922

A fearful King Vittorio Emanuele III entrusts Mussolini and his Fascists with the formation of a government.

1929

Catholicism is declared Italy's sole religion and the Vatican an independent state.

★ Best for Renaissance Elegance

Duomo (p98), Florence

Galleria degli Uffizi (p104), Florence

Da Vinci's The Last Supper (p206), Milan

St Peter's Basilica (p42), Rome

Galleria degli Uffizi (p104), Florence

SYLVAIN SONNET/GETTY IMAGES ©

A Nation Is Born

Centuries of war, plague and occasional religious purges took their toll on Italy's divided city-states, whose role on the world stage was largely reduced by the 18th century to a vacation playground. Napoleon marched into Venice in 1797 without much of a fight, ending 1000 years of Venetian independence and creating the so-called Kingdom of Italy in 1805. But just 10 years later, the reactionary Congress of Vienna restored all the foreign rulers to their places in Italy.

Inspired by the French Revolution and outraged by their subjugation to Napoleon and Austria, Italians began to agitate for an independent, unified nationhood. Count Camillo Benso di Cavour (1810–61) of Turin, prime minister of the Savoy monarchy, became the diplomatic brains behind the Italian unification movement. He won British support for the creation of an independent Italian state and negotiated with the French in 1858 to create a northern Italian kingdom, in exchange for parts of Savoy and Nice.

The bloody 1859–61 Franco-Austrian War ensued, and is now better known as the war for Italian Independence. Pro-Independence forces took over Lombardy and forced the Austrians to relinquish the Veneto. Revolutionary Giuseppe Garibaldi claimed Sicily and southern Italy in the name of Savoy King Vittorio Emanuele II in 1860, and Cavour and the king claimed parts of central Italy (including Umbria and Le Marche). The unified Italian state was founded in 1861, with Tuscany, the Veneto and Rome incorporated into the fledgling kingdom by 1870 and parliament established in Rome in 1871.

Mussolini & World Wars

When war broke out in Europe in July 1914, Italy chose to remain neutral, despite being a member of the Triple Alliance with Austria and Germany. Under the terms of the Alliance, Austria was due to hand over northern Italian territory – but Austria refused.

After Austria's deal-breaker, Italy joined the Allies, and plunged into a nightmarish 3½-year war with Austria. When the Austro-Hungarian forces collapsed in November 1918, the

1940
Italy enters WWII on Nazi Germany's side and invades Greece, which quickly proves to be a mistake.

1944
Mt Vesuvius explodes back into action on 18 March.

1946
Italians vote in a national referendum to abolish the monarchy and create a republic.

Italians marched into Trieste and Trento – but the postwar Treaty of Versailles failed to award Italy the remaining territories it sought.

This humiliation added insult to injury. Italy had lost 600,000 men in the war and, while a few war profiteers had benefitted, the majority of the populace was reduced to abject poverty. From this despair rose a demagogue: Benito Mussolini (1883–1945).

A former socialist newspaper editor and one-time draft dodger, Mussolini volunteered for the front and returned wounded in 1917. Frustrated at Italy's treatment in Versailles, Mussolini formed an extremist Italian right-wing militant political group. By 1921 the Fascist Party was feared and admired for its black-shirted street brawlers, Roman salute and its self-anointed Duce (Leader), Mussolini. After his march on Rome in 1922 and victory in the 1924 elections, Mussolini took full control of the country by 1926, banning other political parties, independent trade unions and free press.

As the first step to creating a 'new Roman empire', Mussolini invaded Abyssinia (Ethiopia) in 1935–36. Condemned by the League of Nations for his invasion, Mussolini allied with Nazi Germany to back Fascist rebel General Franco in Spain. Yet Italy remained aloof from WWII battles until June 1940, when Germany's blitz of Norway, Denmark and much of France made it look like a winning campaign. Instead, allying with Italy caused Germany setbacks in the Balkans and North Africa.

By the time the Allies landed in Sicily in 1943, the Italians had had enough of Mussolini and his war, and the king had the dictator arrested. Italy surrendered in September – but the Germans rescued Mussolini, occupied the northern two-thirds of the country and reinstalled the dictator.

The painfully slow Allied campaign up the peninsula was aided by the Italian Resistance sabotage of German forces, until northern Italy was finally liberated in April 1945.

Going the Distance for the Resistance

In 1943–44 the Assisi Underground hid hundreds of Jewish Italians in Umbrian convents and monasteries, while the Tuscan Resistance forged travel documents for them. The refugees needed the documents fast, before they were deported to concentration camps by Fascist officials. Enter the fastest man in Italy: Gino Bartali, world-famous Tuscan cyclist, Tour de France winner and three-time champion of the Giro d'Italia. After his death in 2003, documents revealed that during his 'training rides' throughout the war years, Bartali had carried Resistance intelligence and falsified documents to transport Jewish refugees to safe locations. Bartali was interrogated at the dreaded Villa Triste in Florence, where suspected anti-Fascists were routinely tortured – but he revealed nothing. Until his death, the long-distance hero downplayed his efforts to rescue Jewish refugees, saying, 'One does these things, and then that's that'.

1957

Italy joins France, West Germany and the Benelux countries to sign the Treaty of Rome.

1960

Rome hosts the Games of the XVII Olympiad.

1980

On 25 November, a 6.8-Richter-scale earthquake strikes Campania, killing almost 3000 people.

★ Best for Medieval Mystique

Siena (p132), Tuscany

San Gimignano (p130), Tuscany

Assisi (p157), Umbria

Montalcino (p140), Tuscany

Piazza del Campo (p132),Siena

Resistance fighters shot Mussolini and his lover, Clara Petacci, and strung up their corpses in Milan's Piazzale Lotto.

The Grey & the Red Years

In the aftermath of war, the left-wing Resistance was disarmed and Italy's political forces scrambled to regroup. The USA, through the economic largesse of the Marshall Plan, wielded considerable political influence and used this to keep the left in check. Immediately after the war, three coalition governments succeeded one another. The third, which came to power in December 1945, was dominated by the newly formed right-wing Democrazia Cristiana (DC; Christian Democrats), led by Alcide De Gasperi, who remained prime minister until 1953. Italy became a republic in 1946 and De Gasperi's DC won the first elections under the new constitution in 1948.

Until the 1980s, the Partito Comunista Italiano (PCI; Communist Party) played a crucial role in Italy's social and political development, in spite of being systematically kept out of government. The very popularity of the party led to a grey period in the country's history, the *anni di piombo* (years of lead) in the 1970s. Just as the Italian economy was booming, Europe-wide paranoia about the power of the Communists in Italy fuelled a secretive reaction that, it is said, was largely directed by the CIA and NATO.

The 1970s were thus dominated by the spectre of terrorism and considerable social unrest. Neo-Fascist terrorists struck with a bomb blast in Milan in 1969. In 1978 the Brigate Rosse (Red Brigades, a group of young left-wing militants responsible for several bomb blasts and assassinations) claimed their most important victim – former DC prime minister Aldo Moro. His kidnap and murder some 54 days later (the subject of the 2003 film *Buongiorno, notte*) shook the country.

Despite the disquiet, the 1970s also saw positive change. Divorce became legal, legislation allowed women to keep their own names after marriage, and abortion was legalised.

1995

Maurizio Gucci, heir to the Gucci fashion empire, is gunned down outside his Milan offices.

2001

Silvio Berlusconi's right-wing Casa delle Libertà coalition wins an absolute majority in national polls.

2005

Pope John Paul II dies aged 84, prompting a wave of sorrow.

Clean Hands, Berlusconi & Five Star

A growth spurt in the aftermath of WWII saw Italy become one of the world's leading economies, but by the 1970s the economy had begun to stagnate, and by the mid-1990s a new and prolonged period of crisis had set in. Economic crisis was coupled with the Tangentopoli (Kickback City) scandal. Led by a pool of Milanese magistrates, investigations known as Mani Pulite (Clean Hands) implicated thousands of public figures in corruption scandals.

The old centre-right political parties collapsed in the wake of these trials, and from the ashes rose what many Italians hoped might be a breath of fresh political air. Media magnate Silvio Berlusconi's Forza Italia (Go Italy) party swept to power in 2001 and again in April 2008. Berlusconi's blend of charisma, confidence, irreverence and promises of tax cuts appealed to many Italian voters.

However, Berlusconi's tenure saw the economic situation go from bad to worse, while a series of laws were passed that protected his extensive business interests; for example, granting the prime minister immunity from prosecution while in office. In 2011 Berlusconi was finally forced to resign due to the deepening debt crisis. A government of technocrats, headed by economist Mario Monti, took over until the inconclusive elections of February 2013. After lengthy postelectoral negotiations, Enrico Letta, a member of the Partito Democratico (PD), was named prime minister, steering a precarious right-left coalition. In 2014 he was toppled by the former mayor of Florence, Matteo Renzi, from the same party. Italy's youngest-ever leader, Renzi became the third unelected PM since Berlusconi's fall.

Despite the change of leadership and Renzi's dynamic style, whoever steers this hard-to-govern country has a tough job on their hands. Italy's problems remain the same, including the mafia, corruption, nepotism, the brain drain, lack of growth, unemployment (particularly among the young) and the low birth rate, coupled with an ageing population.

2009

Italy's Constitutional Court overturns a law giving Berlusconi immunity from prosecution while in office.

2011

After a string of vice and corruption scandals, Berlusconi resigns to restore confidence in the ailing Italian economy.

2014

Matteo Renzi becomes Italy's youngest ever prime minister, heading a shaky right-left coalition.

Floor details, Duomo (p133), Siena

Art & Architecture

With more Unesco World Heritage Sites than any other country, Italy is one place you can hardly throw a stone without hitting a masterpiece. Italian architecture is more than just a wall to hang the art on, with geniuses like Michelangelo creating spaces that alternately give a sense of intimacy and inclusion, steadfastness and momentum.

Classical Era

Ancient Romans initially took their cue from the Greeks – only what the Greeks did first, the Romans made bigger. The Greeks invented Doric, Ionic and Corinthian orders of columns, but Romans installed them in the Colosseum.

Harmonious proportions were key to Roman designs, including the Pantheon's carefully balanced, coffered dome showcasing a Roman innovation: concrete. Unlike the Greeks, Roman sculptors created accurate, brutally honest busts. You'll recognise Emperors Pompey, Titus and Augustus across the rooms at the Palatine Museum from their respective facial features: bulbous nose, square head, sunken eyes.

Museo e Galleria Borghese (p50), Rome

MOVEMENTWAY/ROBERT HARDING ©

Roman emperors such as Augustus used art as a PR tool, employing it to celebrate great military victories – the Colonna di Traiano (Trajan's Column) and the Ara Pacis Augustae (Altar of Peace) in Rome are especially gorgeous propaganda.

Byzantine Glitz

After Constantine became Christianity's star convert, the empire's architects turned their talents to Byzantine churches: domed brick basilicas, plain on the outside, with mosaic-encrusted interiors. One early example is Cattedrale Santa Maria Assunta in Torcello. Instead of classical realism, Torcello's *Last Judgment* mosaic conveys a clear message in compelling cartoon shorthand: repent, or snickering devils will drag you off by the hair. Torcello's golden Byzantine mosaics are echoed in Venice's Basilica di San Marco and as far away as Palermo's Cappella Palatina (Palatine Chapel).

Medieval Graces

Italians didn't appreciate over-the-top French Gothic cathedrals; instead, they took Gothic further over the top. A signature Moorish Gothic style graced Venice's *palazzi* (mansions), including the Ca' d'Oro. Milan took Gothic to extremes in its flamboyant Duomo, and the Sienese came up with a novelty for Siena's cathedral: storytelling scenes inlaid in the church floor.

Florentine painter Giotto di Bondone (1266–1337) added another twist. Instead of Byzantine golden cartoon saints, Giotto featured furry donkeys in the life story of St Francis

★ Best Churches

St Peter's Basilica (p42), Vatican City

Basilica di San Marco (p172), Venice

Duomo (p204), Milan

Basilica di San Francesco (p160), Assisi

Duomo (p98), Florence

Basilica di San Marco (p172) and the Palazzo Ducale (p174), Venice

in the Basilica di San Francesco di Assisi. Pot-bellied pack animals dot Giotto's frescoed Assisi landscape, and when the donkey weeps at the death of the patron saint of animals, it's hard not to well up with him.

Meanwhile, in Siena, Ambrogio Lorenzetti (1290–1348) set a trend for secular painting with his *Allegories of Good and Bad Government* (1337–40), using convincing perspective to make good government seem perfectly achievable, with Peace, Prudence, happy merchants and a wedding party – it's like a medieval Jane Austen novel illustration.

The Renaissance

Plague cut short the talents of many artists and architects in the 14th century, and survivors regrouped. Floating, wide-eyed Byzantine saints seemed far removed from reality, where city-state wars and natural disasters loomed large. Florentine sculptors such as Lorenzo Ghiberti (1378–1455) and Donatello (1386–1466) brought Byzantine ideals down to earth, creating anatomically accurate figures with classical principles of perspective and scale.

Architect Filippo Brunelleschi (1377–1446) also looked to the classics as inspiration for Florence's Duomo – specifically Rome's Pantheon – and created a vast dome of mathematically exacting proportions to distribute its massive weight. Critics were sure it would collapse; it still hasn't. But if Brunelleschi studied the classics, neoclassist Palladio pillaged them, borrowing architectural elements of temples, villas and forums for Venice's San Giorgio Maggiore. The idea of creative repurposing wasn't new – the art of reusing old buildings, *spolia,* had been practised in Italy for centuries – but Palladio's conceptual *spolia* was accomplished with easy grace.

Classical laws of harmonious proportions had not been mastered in Roman painting, so Sandro Botticelli (1444–1510) took on the task. Though his early works seem stiff, his *Birth of Venus* (1485) in Florence's Uffizi is a model of poise. Instead of classicism, Leonardo da Vinci (1452–1519) smudged the contours of his lines – a technique called *sfumato,* still visible in his faded *The Last Supper* in Milan. Michelangelo applied the same chiselled perfection to his *David* at Florence's Galleria dell'Accademia and to his image of Adam brought to life by God on the ceiling of the Sistine Chapel.

Mannerism

By 1520, artists such as Michelangelo and Raphael had mastered naturalism, and discovered its expressive limitations – to make a point, the mannerists decided, sometimes you had to exaggerate for effect. One glorious example is *Assunta* (Ascension, 1516–18) by Titian (1490–1576) in Venice's I Frari, where the glowing Madonna rises to heaven in a swirl of red drapery.

Milanese-born Michelangelo Merisi da Caravaggio (1573–1610) had no interest in classical conventions of ideal beauty. Instead he concentrated on revealing and concealing truth through skilful contrasts of light and shadow – or *chiaroscuro* – in his *Conversion of St Paul* and the *Crucifixion of St Peter*, both in Rome's Chiesa di Santa Maria del Popolo.

Italy's Top Museums

It's hard to choose in a country that's stuffed with jaw-dropping museums, but here are a few standouts:

Vatican Museums (p38), Vatican City

Gallerie dell'Accademia (p176), Venice

Museo del Novecento (p208), Milan

Museo e Galleria Borghese (p50), Rome

Baroque

The Renaissance's insistence on restraint and pure form led to an exuberant backlash. Baroque religious art served as a kind of spiritual cattle prod, with works by sculptor Gianlorenzo Bernini (1598–1680) simulating religious ecstasy with frantic urgency.

With sculptural flourishes, baroque architecture was well suited to the showplace piazzas of Rome and shimmering reflections in Venice's Grand Canal. But in high-density Naples, the only place to go for baroque was indoors – hence the kaleidoscope of coloured, inlaid marbles inside Naples' Certosa di San Martino.

Italian Export Art

By the 18th century, Italy was chafing under foreign domination by Napoleon and Austria. Dependent on foreign admirers, impoverished Italy turned out landscapes for European dandies as 'Grand Tour' souvenirs. The best-known *vedutisti* (landscapists) are Francesco Guardi (1712–93) and Giovanni Antonio Canaletto (1697–1768). Neoclassical sculptor Antonio Canova (1757–1822) took a more daring approach, with a nude sculpture of Napoleon's sister, Pauline Bonaparte Borghese, as a reclining *Venere Vincitrice* (Conquering Venus) in Rome's Museo e Galleria Borghese.

Modern & Contemporary

Stilted by convention and bedraggled by industrialisation, Italy found a creative outlet in European art nouveau, called 'Liberty' in Italian. But some found the style decadent and frivolous. Led by poet Filippo Tommaso Marinetti (1876–1944) and painter Umberto Boccioni (1882–1916), the 1909 *Futurist Manifesto* declared, 'Everything is in movement, everything rushes forward, everything is in constant swift change.' Though the look of futurism was co-opted by Fascism, its impulse could not have been more different: Fascism was an extreme nostalgia for a heroic Italian empire that wasn't exclusively Italian or heroic. Today, futurism is highlighted at Milan's Museo del Novecento. In the 1960s radical Arte Povera (Poor Art) used simple and found materials to trigger associations, and the impact is still palpable at Turin's Galleria Civica d'arte Moderna e Contemporanea (GAM).

In architecture, one of the few midcentury high points is the 1956 Pirelli Tower, designed by architect Giò Ponti and engineer Pier Luigi Nervi. Today, Italian architecture is back on the world stage, ranging from Massimiliano Fuksas' whimsical glass sailboat Fiera Milano to Renzo Piano's Turin Fiat factory creatively repurposed into Slow Food showcase, Eataly.

The Italian Table

Sit back, enjoy: you're in for a host of treats. Just don't go expecting the stock-standards served at your local Italian back home. In reality, Italian cuisine is a handy umbrella term for the country's diverse regional cuisines. Has anything ever tasted this good? Probably not. Will it ever again? Probably tomorrow. Buon appetito.

Regional Cuisine

Italian city-state rivalries once settled with castle sieges and boiling oil poured on enemies are now settled through considerably friendlier culinary competition – though there may still be some boiling oil involved. In this stiff regional competition for gourmet affections, there is a clear winner: travellers, who get to sample regional variations on Italy's seasonal speciality produce, seafood and meats.

Rome

Italy's capital offers more than just Viagra-strength espresso at La Casa del Caffè Tazza d'Oro and glorious gelato. Must-try menu items include thin-crust pizza, *saltimbocca* (literally 'leap in the mouth': veal sautéed with prosciutto and sage) and calorific pasta classics *spaghetti carbonara* (with egg, cheese and *guanciale* – pigs' cheeks,) and *bucatini all'amatriciana* (tube pasta with tomato, *pecorino romano* and *guanciale*). Rome is the spiritual home of nose-to-tail noshing, where staples such as *trippa alla Romana* (tripe with tomato and mint) and *pajata* (a pasta dish of milk-fed calf's intestines in tomato sauce) beckon brave gourmands.

Liguria & Milan

Milan specialises in *risotto alla milanese con ossobucco* (Milanese-style veal shank and marrow with saffron rice) and *bresaola* (air-dried salted beef), and the latest culinary trend is *latterie* (milk bars), comfort-food restaurants emphasising cheese, vegetables and simple homemade pasta.

The Ligurian coast south of Turin is famed for pesto and focaccia, best enjoyed with staggering seaside views in the coves of Cinque Terre.

Bologna to Venice

Culinary culture shock may occur between lunch and dinner in the northeast, where you can lunch on Bologna's namesake *pasta alla bolognese* (a rich beef and pork belly *ragú* usually served with tagliatelle pasta; spaghetti bolognese is a foreign adaptation) and then dine on Venetian polenta with *sarde in saor* (marinated sardines with onions, pine nuts and sultanas).

Venice celebrates its lagoon location and spice-trading past in dishes such as squid-ink risotto and *granseole* (spider crab) graced with star anise. Venetian dandies kicked off the European trend for hot chocolate at cafes ringing Piazza San Marco, and you can still enjoy a decadent, gooey cup in baroque splendour.

Central Italy

The Tuscans have a special way with meat, herbs and olive oil – think whole boar, pheasant, rabbit on a spit, or pampered Maremma beef in *spiedino toscano* (mixed grill). Another must for carnivores is the tender, hulking *bistecca alla fiorentina,* the bone-in steak served in slabs 'three fingers thick' at Florence's Trattoria Mario. Peasant soup (*acquacotta,* literally 'cooked water') becomes a royal feast in the Tuscan town of Lucca, with the addition of farm-fresh eggs, local *pecorino* cheese, toasted bread and Lucca's prized golden olive oil.

Naples, Pompeii & the Amalfi Coast

Sun-soaked Mediterranean flavours sparkle in Naples and its coastal turf, where hot capsicums (peppers), citrus and prized San Marzano tomatoes thrive in the volcanic soils that buried Pompeii. Local buffalo-milk mozzarella with basil and tomato sauce piled on pizza dough makes Naples' most famous export: pizza *margherita*. In Naples' *centro storico* (historic centre) you'll find sublime street food in historic *friggitorie* (fast-food kiosks), from *arancini* (mozzarella-filled rice balls) to tempura-style eggplant. Naples was the playground of French conquerors and Spanish royalty, whose influence is savoured in *sfogliatelle* (pastries filled with cinnamon-laced ricotta) and *rum babà,* French rum cake made Neapolitan with Vesuvius-like eruptions of cream.

South of Naples, you'll know you're approaching the Amalfi Coast when you get a whiff of perfumed Amalfi lemons. The local citrus stars alongside the day's seafood catch and in *limoncello,* Amalfi's sweet lemon digestive.

★ **Best Wine & Food Courses**

Decugnano dei Barbi (www.decugnanodeibarbi.com)

Italian Food Artisans (www.foodartisans.com/workshops)

International Wine Academy of Roma (www.wineacademyroma.com)

Sicily & Southern Italy

Ancient Arab influences make Sicily's pasta dishes velvety and complex, and make this one of the best places in Italy to eat dessert. Wild-caught tuna baked in a salt crust, local-anchovy-studded *fiori di zucca ripieni* (cheese-stuffed squash blossoms) and *arancini siciliani* (risotto balls) may forever spoil you for lesser versions.

Begin southern food adventures at Catania's La Pescheria (p297), the legendary fish market, and look out for Sicilian *dolci* (sweets) that include pistachio gelato and sculpted marzipan.

Menu Decoder

Tutti a tavola! (Everyone to the table!) This is one command every Italian heeds without question. To disobey would be unthinkable – what, you're going to eat your pasta cold? And insult the cook? Even anarchists wouldn't dream of it. You're not obliged to eat three courses – or even two – but here is a rundown of your menu options.

Antipasti (Appetiser)

Tantalising offerings on the antipasti menu may include the house bruschetta (grilled bread with a variety of toppings, from chopped tomato and garlic to black-truffle spread), seasonal treats such as *prosciutto e melone* (cured ham and cantaloupe) and regional delights including *friarelle con peperoncino* (Neapolitan broccoli with chilli). At this stage, bread (and sometimes *grissini* – Turin-style breadsticks) are deposited on the table as part of your €1 to €4 *pane e coperto* (bread and 'cover', or table service).

Primo (First Course)

Starch is the star in Italian first courses, including pasta and gnocchi (especially in south and central Italy), risotto and polenta (northern Italian specialities). *Primi* menus usually include ostensibly vegetarian or vegan options, such as pasta *con pesto* (the classic north-western pasta with basil, *parmigiano reggiano* (Parmesan) and pine nuts) or *alla Norma* (with eggplant and tomato, Sicilian-style), or the extravagant *risotto al Barolo* (Piedmont risotto cooked in high-end Barolo wine). But even if a dish sounds vegetarian in theory, ask about the stock used in that risotto or polenta, or the ingredients in that suspiciously rich tomato sauce – there may be beef, ham or ground anchovies involved.

Secondo (Second Course)

Light lunchers usually call it a day after the *primo*, or skip the primo and just opt for a *secondo*. But if you're up for a long meal, you can follow the *primo* with meat, fish or *con-*

torni (side dishes) in the second course. Options may range from ambitious meats (especially in Tuscany and Rome) and elegant seafood (notably in Venice and Sicily) to lightly grilled vegetables such as *radicchio di Treviso* (feathery red rocket). A less inspiring option is *insalata mista* (mixed green salad), typically unadorned greens with vinegar and oil on the side – croutons, cheeses, nuts and other ingredients have no business in classic Italian salads.

Frutti e Dolci

'Siamo arrivati alla frutta' ('We've arrived at the fruit') is an idiom roughly meaning 'we've hit rock bottom' – but hey, not until you've had one last tasty morsel. Your best bets on the fruit menu are local and seasonal. *Formaggi* (cheeses) are an excellent option in Piedmont, but in the south, do the *dolci* (sweets). *Biscotti* (twice-baked biscuits) are divine dunked in wine, and consider *zabaglione* (egg and Marsala custard), tiramisu (literally 'pick me up', combining eggs, marscapone, coffee and Marsala wine), cream-stuffed profiteroles or Sicily's cream-stuffed shell pastries immortalised in *The Godfather*.

Caffè (Coffee)

Snoozing rather than sightseeing will be most attractive after a proper Italian lunch, so if you want to get things done, it's advisable to administer espresso as a final flourish. *Cappuccino* (named after the colour of Capuchin monks' habits) is usually only drunk in the morning, before around 11am, but later in the day you could indulge in an espresso with a tiny stain of milk in a *caffè macchiato*. On the hottest days of summer, a *granita di caffè* (coffee with shaved ice and whipped cream) is just the ticket.

Quale Vino? Which Wine?

Which one of Italy's hundreds of speciality wines will best complement the cuisine? When in doubt, keep it local: below are wines to watch for in each region.

Rome & Around Est! Est!! Est!!! (dry herbal/mineral white).

Venice & Verona Prosecco (Italy's most popular sparkling white), Amarone (dark, brooding red with velvety tannins), Soave (crisp, minerally white), Tocai (unctuous, fruity/floral white), Valpolicella (versatile, medium-bodied red).

Milan & Lakes Franciacorta (Italy's top-quality sparkling white), Bardolino (light, satiny red).

Piedmont & Around Barolo (Italy's favourite red; elegant and structured), Asti (aka Asti Spumante; sparkling white), Cinque Terre (minerally/grassy white), Gavi (dry, aromatic white), Barbera d'Alba (pleasantly acidic, tomato-friendly red), Dolcetto (light-hearted, aromatic red), Sciacchetrá (Cinque Terre's aromatic dessert wine).

Tuscany Chianti Classico (big-hearted red, earthy character), Brunello di Montalcino (Italy's biggest, most complex vintage red), Super Tuscan IGT (bombastic, Sangiovese-based reds), Morellino di Scansano (floral, medium-weight red).

Naples & Amalfi Coast Falanghina (dry, minerally white).

Sicily Marsala (sweet fortified wine), Nero d'Avola (volcanic, mineral red).

Fans of AC Milan at a football game

Lifestyle

Imagine you wake up and discover you're Italian. It's not that obvious at first – your pyjamas just have a subtly more elegant cut. But when you open your wardrobe, there's the dead giveaway: the shoes. What might it be like walking in those butter-soft, richly coloured shoes for the day, and what could you discover about Italy?

A Day in the Life of Italy

Sveglia! You're woken not by an alarm but by the burble and clatter of the *caffetiera,* the ubiquitous stovetop espresso maker. If you're between the ages of 18 and 34, there's a 60% chance that's not a room-mate making your morning coffee: it's *mamma* or *papá*. This is not because Italy is a nation of pampered *mammoni* (mama's boys) and spoilt *figlie di papá* (daddy's girls) – at least, not entirely. With youth unemployment hitting 44% and many university graduates underemployed in short-term contracts, what's the hurry to leave home?

Running late, you bolt down your coffee scalding hot (an acquired Italian talent) then get your morning paper from Bucharest-born Nicolae – your favourite news vendor and (as a Romanian) part of Italy's largest migrant community.

Serving cappuchino

MARK HORN/GETTY IMAGES ©

On your way to work you scan the headlines: another boat of asylum seekers land on Sicilian shores, more coalition-government infighting and an announcement of new EU regulations on cheese. Outrageous! The cheese regulations, that is; the rest is to be expected. At work, you're buried in paperwork until noon, when it's a relief to join friends for lunch and a glass of wine.

Afterwards you toss back another scorching espresso at your favourite bar, and find out how your barista's latest audition went – turns out you went to school with the sister of the director of the play, so you promise to put in a good word. This isn't just a nice gesture, but an essential career boost. About 30% of Italians have landed a job through personal family connections, and in highly paid professions, that number rises as high as 40% to 50%. In Europe's most ancient, entrenched bureaucracy, social networks are also essential to get things done: on average, Italians spend the equivalent of two weeks annually on bureaucratic procedures required of working Italian citizens.

Back at work by 2pm, you surreptitiously check *l'Internet* for employment listings – your work contract will expire soon. After a busy day like this, *aperitivi* are definitely in order, so at 6.30pm you head directly to the latest happy-hour hot spot. The decor is very stylish, the vibe very cool and the DJ extra hot, until suddenly it's time for your English class – everyone's learning it these days, if only for the slang.

The People

Who are the people you'd encounter every day as an Italian? On average, about half your co-workers will be women – quite a change from 10 years ago, when women represented

★ Best Books About Italians, by Italians

The Italians (Luigi Barzini)

History of the Italian People (Giuliano Procacci)

La Bella Figura: A Field Guide to the Italian Mind (Beppe Severgnini)

just a quarter of the workforce. But a growing proportion of the people you'll meet are already retired: one out of five Italians is over 65. You might also notice a striking absence of children. Italy's birth rate is the lowest in Europe, at 1.4 children per woman.

Like Nicolae the news vendor, 8.2% of Italy's population today are non-EU immigrants. Though this is a relatively small number in global terms, it's a reversal of a historical trend: From 1876 to 1976, Italy was a country of net emigration. With some 30 million Italian emigrants dispersed throughout Europe, the Americas and Australia, remittances from Italians abroad helped keep Italy's economy afloat during economic crises after Independence and WWII.

The tables have since turned. Political and economic upheavals in the 1980s brought new arrivals from central Europe, Latin America and North Africa, including Italy's former colonies in Tunisia, Somalia and Ethiopia. More recently, waves of Chinese and Filipino immigrants have given Italian streetscapes a Far Eastern twist. While immigrants account for just over 8% of Italy's population today, the number is growing. In 2001 the country's foreign population (a number that excludes foreign-born people who take Italian citizenship) was 1.3 million. By 2015, that number had almost quadrupled to 5 million.

From a purely economic angle, these new arrivals are vital for the country's economic health. While most Italians today choose to live and work within Italy, fewer are entering blue-collar agricultural and industrial fields. Without immigrant workers to fill the gaps, Italy would be sorely lacking in tomato sauce and shoes. From kitchen hands to hotel maids, it is often immigrants who take the low-paid service jobs that keep Italy's tourism economy afloat.

Despite this, not everyone is dusting down the welcome mat. In 2010 the shooting of an immigrant worker in the town of Rosarno, Calabria, sparked Italy's worst race riots in years. In October 2014 reports of an attempted rape by a group of immigrants sparked three days of protests outside an immigration centre in suburban Rome. The ferocity of the protests saw a number of Africans housed at the complex moved to another area. In March 2015 the troubled neighbourhood hit the headlines once more as protestors set fire to dumpsters near the complex.

High unemployment, economic sluggishness and inadequate infrastructure continue to play significant roles in the rise of anti-immigration sentiment, with many Italians feeling that the country's economic woes are being exacerbated by the growing number of new arrivals.

Religion, Loosely Speaking

While almost 80% of Italians identify as Catholics, only around 15% of Italy's population regularly attends Sunday Mass. That said, the Church continues to exert considerable influence on public policy and political parties, especially those of the center- and far-right.

But in the land of the double park, even God's rules are up for interpretation. Sure, *mamma* still serves fish on Good Friday, but while she might consult la Madonna for guidance, chances are she'll get a second opinion from the *maga* (fortune-teller) on channel 32. It's estimated that around 13 million Italians use the services of psychics, astrologers and fortune-tellers.

Italy's Other Religion: Calcio

Catholicism may be your official faith, but as an Italian your true religion is likely to be *calcio* (football). On any given weekend from September to May, chances are that you and your fellow *tifosi* (football fans) are at the *stadio* (stadium), glued to the TV or checking the score on your mobile phone. Come Monday, you'll be dissecting the match by the office water cooler.

Politics and football sometimes converge; Silvio Berlusconi first found fame as the owner of AC Milan and cleverly named his political party after a football chant.

Nothing quite stirs Italian blood like a good (or a bad) game. Nine months after Italy's 2006 World Cup victory against France, hospitals in northern Italy reported a baby boom. In February the following year, rioting at a Palermo-Catania match in Catania left one policeman dead and around 100 injured. Blamed on the Ultras (a minority group of hard-core football fans), the violence shocked both Italy and the world, leading to a temporary ban of all matches in Italy and increased stadium security. A year earlier, the match-fixing 'Calciopoli' scandals resulted in revoked championship titles and temporary demotion of Serie A (top-tier national) teams, including the mighty Juventus.

Yet, the same game that divides also unites. You might be a Lazio-loathing, AS Roma supporter on any given day, but when the national Azzurri (The Blues) swag the World Cup, you are nothing but a heart-on-your-sleeve italiano (Italian). In his book *The 100 Things Everyone Needs to Know About Italy,* Australian journalist David Dale writes that Italy's 1982 World Cup win 'finally united twenty regions which, until then, had barely acknowledged that they were part of the one country.'

Gender Inequality

It might string straight As in fashion, food and design, but Italy's performance in the gender-equality stakes leaves much room for improvement. Despite the fact that half of Italy's current cabinet ministers are women (a conscious effort on the part of Prime Minister Matteo Renzi to redress the country's male-dominated parliament), sexism remains deeply entrenched in Italian society.

According to the Organisation for Economic Co-operation and Development (OECD), only 47% of Italian women are in the workforce, compared to 72% in Sweden, 69% in Germany and 60% in France. Statistics released by Italy's national bureau of statistics (Istat) indicate that the potential earnings of Italian women is half that of their male counterparts, reflecting both lower employment rates and pay. Though successful Italian businesswomen do exist (among them Poste Italiane chairperson Luisa Todini and Eni president Emma Marcegaglia), almost 95% of public company board members in Italy remain male, and of these, approximately 80% of them are older than 55.

Italian women fare no better on the domestic front. OECD figures reveal that Italian men spend 103 minutes per day cooking, cleaning or caring, less than a third as long as Italian women, who spend an average of 326 minutes per day on unpaid work.

Interestingly, the tables are turned in education. According to the OECD's 2014 Gender Gap Index, entry rates into higher education for women were 74%, compared to 52% for men.

Vintage Vespa

ANDREAROAD/GETTY IMAGES ©

Fashion & Design

Better living by design: what could be more Italian? Though the country could get by on its striking good looks, Italy is ever-mindful of design details. They are everywhere you look, and many places you don't: the yellow silk lining inside a sober grey suit, the glove compartment of a Fiat 500 car, the toy duck hidden inside your chocolate uova di pasqua *(Easter egg).*

Italian Fashion

Italians have strong opinions about aesthetics and aren't afraid to share them. A common refrain is *Che brutta!* (How hideous!), which may strike visitors as tactless. But consider it from an Italian point of view – everyone is rooting for you to look good, and who are you to disappoint? The shop assistant who tells you with brutal honesty that yellow is not your colour is doing a public service, and will consider it a personal triumph to see you outfitted in orange instead. After all, Italy's centuries-old reputation for style is at stake.

Jeweller's shops on Ponte Vecchio (p115), Florence

Trendsetters & Fashion Victims

Italians have been style trendsetters since the Middle Ages, when Venetian merchants imported dyes and silks from the East, and Florence's wool guild rose to political prominence and funded a Renaissance. Clothes became markers of social status, and not only nobles set trends: courtesans and trophy wives were so widely imitated that sumptuary laws were passed restricting low necklines and growing train lengths. Italy's local fashions went global through the dissemination of Florentine art and illustrated pamphlets from Venice's publishing houses – predecessors of billboards and Italian *Vogue*. The Venetian innovation of eyeglasses was initially mocked by monocle-sporting English dandies, who eventually saw the light – and their descendants now pay impressive sums for Italian designer sunglasses.

Italy has also had its share of fashion victims over the centuries. After political crusader Savonarola demanded Florentines surrender their extravagant statement jewellery under pain of flagellation, he was burned at the stake. So many Venetian noblewomen were hobbled emulating courtesans in their staggering platform heels that 1430 sumptuary laws set maximum shoe heights of around 2ft. Siena was more practical, requiring its prostitutes to wear flat shoes. Today, staggering platforms and chic flats still make the rounds of Milan runways.

Italy's Fashion Powerhouses

Cobblers and tailors in Florence who once made only made-to-measure designs began to present seasonal lines in the 1950s to '60s, launching the empires of psychedelic-print

★ Italian Design Icons

Bialetti *caffetiera*

Cinzano vermouth

Acqua di Parma cologne

Piaggio Vespa

Olivetti 'Valentine' typewriter

maestro Emilio Pucci, logoed leather-goods magnate Guccio Gucci and shoe maven Salvatore Ferragamo. But Milan literally stole the show from Florence in 1958, hosting Italy's first Fashion Week. With its ready factories, cosmopolitan workforce and long-established media, Milan created ready-to-wear fashion for global markets from Armani, Missoni, Versace, Dolce & Gabbana and Prada. Rome remains Italy's political capitol and the home of Valentino and his signature red dress, but Milan is Italy's fashion centre, and a key stop on the international design circuit.

Today, Italian fashionistas are combining mass fashion with artisan-made style signatures. This trend is recession friendly: artisan-made items are made to last and singular, hence less trend-sensitive. Fashion-forward artisan hot spots include Florence (cobblers and jewellers), Naples (tailors) and Venice (eyewear, fashion and accessories).

Modern Italian Design

During centuries of domination by Napoleon and other foreign powers, Italy ceded ground as global taste-maker to French and Austrian art nouveau and English Arts and Crafts – until the industrial era. Italian futurism inspired radical, neoclassical streamlining more suited to Italian manufacturers than French decorators or English craftspeople. The dynamic deco style of futurist paintings was co-opted in Fascist propaganda posters, architecture, furniture and design, like cogs in a political machine.

The rise of Fascism required modern factories for the war industry, and after WWII, repurposed military industrial complexes in Turin and Milan became centrepieces of a new global, consumer-centric economy. Turin's strength was industrial design, from Lavazza espresso machines to the Fiat 500 car; Milan focused on fashion and home decor. As seen in Italian film and pioneering Italian lifestyle magazines such as *Domus,* Italy's mass-produced design objects seemed both aspirational and attainable.

Design Showcases

Though Italian design is distributed globally, seeing it in its home context offers fresh appreciation – and critical perspective. While the Vatican Museums showcase pre-20th-century objects of power, from saints' reliquaries to papal thrones, Milan's Triennale Museum focuses on 20th-century secular talismans, including midcentury Vespas to 1980s Memphis Group chairs. Like churches, Italian designer showcases are carefully curated to offer beauty and belonging, from the 1950s Scarpa-designed Olivetti showroom in Venice's Piazza San Marco to Alessi's new flagship store in Milan – but this fully branded lifestyle can seem impersonal. Milan's Salone del Mobile is the world's largest design fair, with 2500 companies represented – yet differences in corporate design can seem slight, and easily outshone by 700 independent designers in the satellite fair.

Survival Guide

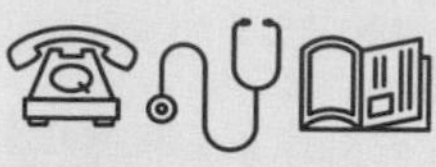

Directory

Accommodation

- It pays to book ahead in high season, especially in popular coastal areas in the summer and popular ski resorts in the winter. In the urban centres you can usually find something if you leave it to luck, though reserving a room is essential during key events (such as the furniture and fashion fairs in Milan) when demand is extremely high.
- Accommodation rates can fluctuate enormously depending on the season, with Easter, summer and the Christmas/New Year period being the typical peak tourist times. Seasonality also varies according to location. Expect to pay top prices in the mountains during the ski season (December to March) or along the coast in summer (July and August). Conversely, summer in the parched cities can equal low season; in August especially, many city hotels charge as little as half price.
- Price also depends greatly on location. A bottom-end budget choice in Venice or Milan will set you back the price of a decent midrange option in, say, rural Campania. Where possible, we present the high-season rates for each accommodation option. Half board equals breakfast and either lunch or dinner; full board includes breakfast, lunch and dinner.
- Most hotels offer breakfast, though this can vary from bountiful buffets to more modest offerings of pastries, packaged yoghurt and fruit.
- Hotels usually require that reservations be confirmed with a credit-card number. No-shows will be docked a night's accommodation.

The Slumber Tax

Italy's *tassa di soggiorno* (accommodation tax) sees visitors charged an extra €1 to €7 per night 'room occupancy tax'.

Exactly how much you're charged depends on several factors, including the type of accommodation, a hotel's star rating and the number of people under your booking. Children may pay a discounted rate or be completely exempt from the tax.

Most of our listings do not include the hotel tax, although it's always a good idea to confirm whether taxes are included when booking.

Bed & Breakfasts

B&Bs can be found throughout the country in both urban and rural settings. Options include everything from restored farmhouses, city *palazzi* (mansions) and seaside bungalows to rooms in family houses. Tariffs for a double room cover a wide range, from around €60 to €140.

Lists of B&Bs across the country are available online at the following sites:

BBItalia.it (www.bbitalia.it)

Bed-and-Breakfast.it (www.bed-and-breakfast.it)

Convents & Monasteries

Some Italian convents and monasteries let out cells or rooms as a modest revenue-making exercise and happily take in tourists, while others only take in pilgrims or people who are on a spiritual retreat. Many impose a fairly early curfew, but prices tend to be quite reasonable.

A useful if ageing publication is Eileen Barish's *The Guide to Lodging in Italy's Monasteries*. A more recent book on the same subject is Charles M Shelton's *Beds and Blessings in Italy: A Guide to Religious Hospitality*. Other resources can assist you in your search:

Chiesa di Santa Susana (www.santasusanna.org/comingToRome/convents.html) This American Catholic church in Rome lists convent and monastery accommodation options around the country on its website. Note that some places are just residential accommodation run by religious orders and not necessarily big on monastic atmosphere. The church doesn't handle bookings; to request a spot, you'll need to contact each individual institution directly.

In Italy Online (www.initaly.com/agri/convents.htm)

MonasteryStays.com (www.monasterystays.com)

Farmhouse Holidays

Live out your bucolic fantasies at one of Italy's growing number of *agriturismi* (farmstays). All *agriturismi* are required to grow at least one of their own products and the farmstays themselves range from rustic country houses with a handful of olive trees to elegant country estates with sparkling pools or fully functioning farms where guests can pitch in.

To find lists of *agriturismi*, ask at any tourist office or check online at one of the following sites:

Agriturist (www.agriturist.com)

Agriturismo.it (www.agriturismo.it)

Agriturismo.net (www.agriturismo.net)

Hotels & Pensioni

While the difference between an *albergo* (hotel) and a *pensione* is often minimal, a *pensione* will generally be of one- to three-star quality while an *albergo* can be awarded up to five stars. *Locande* (inns) long fell into much the same category as *pensioni*, but the term has become a trendy one in some parts and reveals little about the quality of a place. *Affittacamere* are rooms for rent in private houses. They are generally simple affairs.

Quality can vary enormously and the official star system gives limited clues. One-star hotels/*pensioni* tend to be basic and usually do not offer private bathrooms. Two-star places are similar but rooms will generally have a private bathroom. Three-star options usually offer reasonable standards. Four- and five-star hotels offer facilities such as room service, laundry and dry-cleaning.

Prices are highest in major tourist destinations. They also tend to be higher in northern Italy. A *camera singola* (single room) costs from €30. A *camera doppia* (twin beds) or *camera matrimoniale* (double room with

Climate

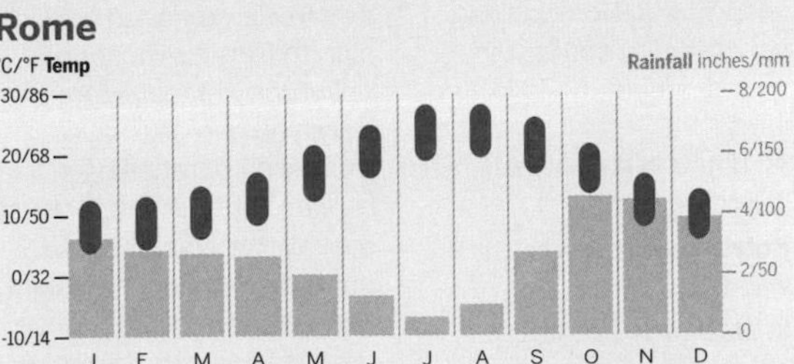

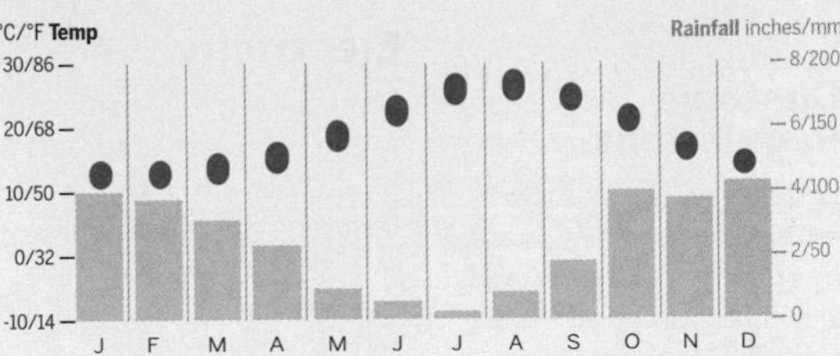

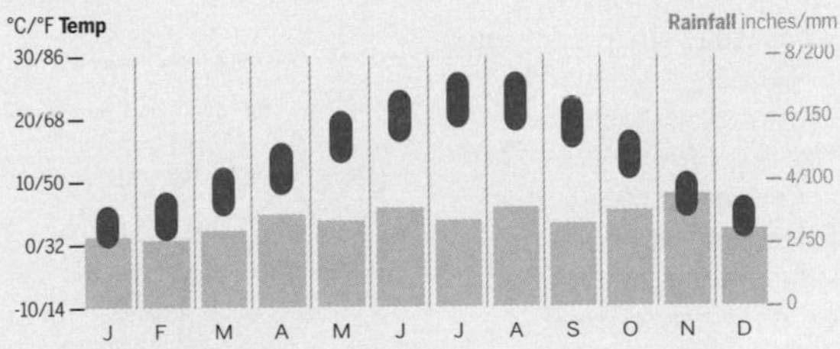

Book Your Stay Online

For more accommodation reviews by Lonely Planet authors, check out lonelyplanet.com/hotels. You'll find independent reviews, as well as recommendations on the best places to stay. Best of all, you can book online.

a double bed) will cost from around €50.

Many hotels use online accommodation-booking services. You could start your searchat the following sites:

All Hotels in Italy (www.hotelsitalyonline.com)

Hotels web.it (www.hotelsweb.it)

In Italia (www.initalia.it)

Customs Regulations

Within the EU you are entitled to tax-free prices on fragrances, cosmetics and skincare; photographic and electrical goods; fashion and accessories; and gifts, jewellery and souvenirs where they are available and if there are no longer any allowance restrictions on these tax-free items.

On leaving the EU, non-EU residents can reclaim value-added tax (VAT) on expensive purchases.

Discount Cards

Free admission to many galleries and cultural sites is available to those under 18 and over 65 years old; and visitors aged between 18 and 25 often qualify for a discount. In some cases, these discounts only apply to EU citizens.

Some cities or regions offer their own discount passes, such as Roma Pass (3 days €36), which offers free use of public transport and free or reduced admission to Rome's museums.

In many places around Italy, you can also save money by purchasing a *biglietto cumulativo*, a ticket that allows admission to a number of associated sights for less than the combined cost of separate admission fees.

Electricity

Electricity in Italy conforms to the European standard of 220V to 230V, with a frequency of 50Hz. Wall outlets typically accommodate plugs with two or three round pins (the latter are grounded, the former are not).

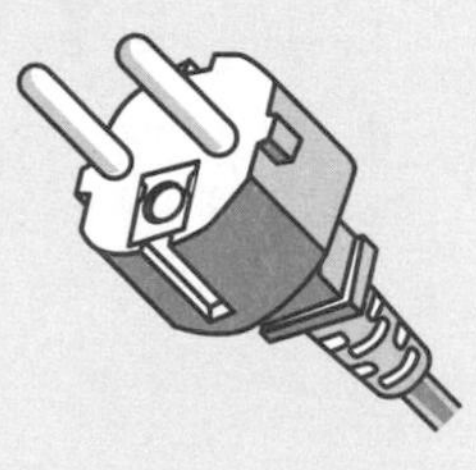

230V/50Hz

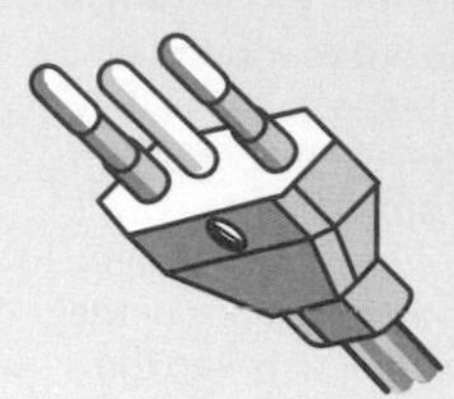

230V/50Hz

Food

For detailed information on eating in Italy see p322. Throughout this guide the following price ranges refer to a meal of two courses (antipasto/*primo* and *secondo*), a glass of house wine, and coperto (cover charge) for one person.

$ less than €25

$$ €25–45

$$$ over €45

Health

Required Vaccinations

No jabs are required to travel to Italy, though the World Health Organization (WHO) recommends that all travellers should be covered for diphtheria, tetanus, the measles, mumps, rubella, polio and hepatitis B.

Health Insurance

Italy has a public-health system that is legally bound to provide emergency care to everyone. EU nationals are entitled to reduced-cost, sometimes free, medical care with a European Health Insurance Card (EHIC), available from your home health authority; non-EU citizens should take out medical insurance.

If you do need health insurance, make sure you get a policy that covers you for the worst possible scenario, such as an accident requiring an emergency flight home. Find out in advance if your insurance plan will make payments directly to providers or reimburse you later for overseas health expenditures.

It's also worth finding out if there is a reciprocal arrangement between your country and Italy. If so, you may be covered for essential medical treatment and some subsidised medications while in Italy. Australia, for instance, has such an agreement; carry your Medicare card.

Availability of Health Care

Health care is readily available throughout Italy, but standards can vary significantly. Public hospitals tend to be less impressive the further south you travel. Pharmacists can give you valuable advice and sell over-the-counter medication for minor illnesses. They can also advise you when more-specialised help is required and point you in the right direction. In major cities you are likely to find English-speaking doctors or a translator service available.

If you need an ambulance anywhere in Italy, call ☎118. For emergency treatment, head straight to the *pronto soccorso* (casualty) section of a public hospital, where you can also get emergency dental treatment.

Insurance

A travel-insurance policy to cover theft, loss and medical problems is a very good idea. It may also cover you for cancellation or delays to your travel arrangements. Paying for your ticket with a credit card can often provide limited travel accident insurance and you may be able to reclaim the payment if the operator doesn't deliver. Ask your credit-card company what it will cover.

Worldwide travel insurance is available at www.lonelyplanet.com/travel-insurance. You can buy, extend and claim online anytime – even if you're already on the road.

Internet Access

Numerous Italian cities and towns offer public wi-fi hot spots, including Rome and Venice. To use them, you will generally need to register online using a credit card or an Italian mobile number. An easier option (no need for a local mobile number) is to head to a cafe or bar offering free wi-fi.

Most hotels, B&Bs, hostels and *agriturismi* offer free wi-fi to guests, though signals can vary in quality. There will usually be at least one fixed computer for guest use.

Legal Matters

Italy is generally a safe country to travel in. The average tourist will only have a brush with the law if robbed by a bag-snatcher or pickpocket.

Police

If you do run into trouble in Italy, you're likely to end up dealing with the *polizia statale* or the *carabinieri*. The former wear powder blue trousers with a fuchsia stripe and a navy blue jacket, the latter wear black uniforms with a red stripe and drive dark-blue cars with a red stripe.

To contact the police in an emergency, dial ☎113.

Drugs & Alcohol

- If you're caught with what the police deem to be a dealable quantity of hard or soft drugs, you risk prison sentences of between six and 20 years.
- Possession for personal use may result in a fine, depending on the type of drug and quantity possessed.

- The legal limit for blood-alcohol when driving is 0.05% and random breath tests do occur.

LGBT Travellers

Homosexuality is legal (over the age of 16) and even widely accepted, but Italy is notably conservative in its attitudes, largely keeping in line with those of the Vatican. Overt displays of affection by homosexual couples can attract a negative response, especially in smaller towns.

There are gay venues in Rome and Milan and a handful in places such as Florence and Naples. Some coastal towns and resorts (such as the Tuscan town of Viareggio or Taormina in Sicily) have much more action in summer.

Online resources include the following Italian-language websites:

Arcigay (www.arcigay.it) Bologna-based national organisation for the LGBTIQ community.

Circolo Mario Mieli (www.mariomieli.org) Rome-based cultural centre that organises debates, cultural events and social functions, including Gay Pride.

Coordinamento Lesbiche Italiano (CLR; www.clrbp.it) The national organisation for lesbians, holding regular conferences and literary evenings.

Gay.it (www.gay.it) Website featuring LGBTIQ news, feature articles and gossip.

Pride (www.prideonline.it) National monthly magazine of art, music, politics and gay culture.

Money

Italy's currency is the euro. The seven euro notes come in denominations of €500, €200, €100, €50, €20, €10 and €5. The eight euro coins are in denominations of €2 and €1, and 50, 20, 10, five, two and one cents.

ATMs & Credit Cards

- ATMs (known as 'Bancomat' in Italy) are widely available throughout Italy and most will accept cards tied into the Visa, MasterCard, Cirrus and Maestro systems.
- Credit cards are good for payment in most hotels, restaurants, shops, supermarkets and tollbooths. Major cards such as Visa, MasterCard, Eurocard, Cirrus and Eurocheques are widely accepted. Amex is also recognised, though less common.
- Let your bank know when you are going abroad, in case it blocks your card when payments from unusual locations appear.
- Check any charges with your bank. Most banks charge a foreign-exchange fee (usually around 1% to 3%) as well as a transaction charge of around 1%.

If your card is lost, stolen or swallowed by an ATM, you can telephone toll-free to have an immediate stop put on its use:

Amex (800 928391)

Diners Club (800 393939)

MasterCard (800 789525)

Visa (800 819014)

Changing Money

You can change money in banks, at post offices or in a *cambio* (exchange office). Post offices and banks tend to offer the best rates; exchange offices keep longer hours, but watch for high commissions and inferior rates.

Have your passport or some form of photo ID available when exchanging money.

Taxes & Refunds

A value-added tax of 22%, known as IVA (Imposta di Valore Aggiunto), is slapped onto just about everything in Italy. If you are a non-EU resident and spend more than €155 (€154.94 to be exact!) on a purchase, you can claim a refund when you leave. The refund only applies to purchases from affiliated retail outlets that display a 'Tax Free' sign. When you make your purchase, ask for a tax-refund voucher, to be filled in with the date of your purchase and its value. When you leave the EU, get this voucher stamped at customs and take it to the nearest tax-refund counter, where you'll get an immediate refund, either in cash or to your credit card. For more information, see www.taxrefund.it.

Tipping

Tipping is not generally expected nor demanded in Italy as it is in some other countries. This said, a discretionary tip for good service is appreciated in some circumstances.

Practicalities

Smoking Banned in enclosed public spaces, which includes restaurants, bars, shops and public transport.

Newspapers The major national dailies are centre-left; try Rome-based *La Repubblica*, and the conservative-liberal, Milan-based *Corriere della Sera*.

Weights and measures Metric

Public Holidays

Most Italians take their annual holiday in August, with the busiest period occurring around 15 August, known locally as Ferragosto. As a result, many businesses and shops close for at least part of that month. Settimana Santa (Easter Holy Week) is another busy holiday period for Italians.

Capodanno (New Year's Day) 1 January

Epifania (Epiphany) 6 January

Pasquetta (Easter Monday) March/April

Giorno della Liberazione (Liberation Day) 25 April

Festa del Lavoro (Labour Day) 1 May

Festa della Repubblica (Republic Day) 2 June

Ferragosto (Feast of the Assumption) 15 August

Festa di Ognisanti (All Saints' Day) 1 November

Festa dell'Immacolata Concezione (Feast of the Immaculate Conception) 8 December

Natale (Christmas Day) 25 December

Festa di Santo Stefano (Boxing Day) 26 December

Telephone

Directory Enquiries

National and international phone numbers can be requested at ☎1254 (or online at 1254.virgilio.it).

Domestic Calls

- Italian telephone area codes all begin with 0 and consist of up to four digits. The area code is followed by anything from four to eight digits. The area code is an integral part of the telephone number and must always be dialled, even when calling from next door.
- Mobile-phone numbers begin with a three-digit prefix such as ☎330.
- Toll-free (free-phone) numbers are known as numeri verdi and usually start with ☎800.
- Nongeographical numbers start with ☎840, 841, 848, 892, 899, 163, 166 or 199.
- Some six-digit national rate numbers are also in use (such as those for Alitalia, rail and postal information).
- As elsewhere in Europe, Italians choose from a host of providers of phone plans and rates, making it difficult to make generalisations about costs.

International Calls

- To call Italy from abroad, call your international access number, then Italy's country code (☎39) and then the area code of the location you want, including the leading 0.
- A cheap option is to call from a private call centre, or from a payphone with an international calling card. These are commonly sold at newsstands and tobacconists.
- To call abroad from Italy dial ☎00, then the country and area codes, followed by the telephone number.
- To make a reverse-charge (collect) international call from a public telephone, dial ☎170. All phone operators speak English.

Mobile Phones

- Italian mobile phones operate on the GSM 900/1800 network, which is compatible with the rest of Europe and Australia but not always with the North American GSM or CDMA systems ; check with your service provider.
- Most smartphones are multiband, meaning that they are compatible with a variety of international networks. Before bringing your own phone to Italy, check with your service provider to make sure it is compatible,

and beware of calls being routed internationally (very expensive for a 'local' call).

- If you have a GSM dual-, tri- or quad-band phone that you can unlock (check with your service provider), it can cost as little as €10 to activate a prepaid (*prepagato*) SIM card in Italy. TIM (Telecom Italia Mobile; www.tim.it), Wind (www.wind.it) and Vodafone (www.vodafone.it) all offer SIM cards and have retail outlets across town. All SIM cards must be registered in Italy, so make sure you have a passport or ID card with you when you buy one.
- You can easily top up your Italian SIM with a recharge card (*ricarica*), available from most tobacconists, some bars, supermarkets and banks.

Payphones & Phonecards

You can still find public payphones around Italy. Most work and most take phonecards (*schede telefoniche*), although you'll still find some that accept coins or credit cards. You can buy phonecards (€5, €10 or €20) at post offices, tobacconists and newsstands.

Time

- Italy is one hour ahead of GMT. When it is noon in London, it is 1pm in Italy.
- Daylight-saving time (when clocks are moved forward one hour) starts on the last Sunday in March and ends on the last Sunday in October.
- Italy operates on a 24-hour clock.

Travellers with Disabilities

Italy is not an easy country for travellers with disabilities and getting around can be a problem for wheelchair users. Although many buildings have lifts, they are not always wide enough for wheelchairs. Not an awful lot has been done to make life for the hearing/vision impaired easier.

The Italian National Tourist Office in your country may be able to provide advice on Italian associations for travellers with disabilities and information on what help is available.

If travelling by train, ring the national helpline ☎199 303060 to arrange assistance (⏰6.45am to 9.30pm daily). Airline companies should be able to arrange assistance at airports if you notify them of your needs in advance. Alternatively, contact ADR Assistance (www.adrassistance.it) for assistance at Fiumicino or Ciampino airports. Some taxis are equipped to carry passengers in wheelchairs; ask for a taxi for a *sedia a rotelle* (wheelchair).

Italy's official tourism website (www.italia.it) offers a number of links for travellers with disabilities. Another online resource is Lonely Planet's Travel for All community on Google+, worth joining for information sharing and networking.

Accessible Italy (www.accessibleitaly.com) A San Marino–based company that specialises in holiday services for people with disabilities. This is the best first port of call.

Sage Traveling (www.sagetraveling.com) A US-based agency offering advice and tailor-made tours to assist mobility-impaired travellers in Europe.

Visas

- Italy is one of the 15 signatories of the Schengen Convention, an agreement whereby participating countries abolished customs checks at common borders. EU citizens do not need a Schengen tourist visa to enter Italy. Nationals of some other countries, including Australia, Canada, Israel, Japan, New Zealand, Switzerland and the USA, do not need a tourist visa for stays of up to 90 days. To check the visa requirements for your country, see www.schengenvisainfo.com/tourist-schengen-visa.
- All non-EU and non-Schengen nationals entering Italy for more than 90 days or for any reason other than tourism (such as study or work) may need a specific visa. See vistoperitalia.esteri.it or contact an Italian consulate for details.

Permesso di Soggiorno

- Non-EU citizens planning to stay at the same address for more than one week are supposed to report to the police station to receive a permesso di soggiorno (a permit to remain in the country). Tourists staying in hotels are not required to do this.

- EU citizens do not require a permesso di soggiorno.

Transport

Getting There & Away

A plethora of airlines link Italy with the rest of the world, and cut-rate carriers have significantly driven down the cost of flights from other European countries. Excellent rail and bus connections, especially with northern Italy, offer efficient overland transport, while car and passenger ferries operate to ports throughout the Mediterranean.

Entering the Country

- European Union and Swiss citizens can travel to Italy with their national identity card alone. All other nationalities must have a valid passport and may be required to fill out a landing card (at airports).
- By law you are supposed to have your passport or ID card with you at all times. You'll need one of these documents for police registration every time you check into a hotel.
- In theory there are no passport checks at land crossings from neighbouring countries, but random customs controls do occasionally still take place between Italy and Switzerland.

Air

Airports & Airlines

Italy's main intercontinental gateways are Rome's Leonardo da Vinci airport (www.adr.it/fiumicino) and Milan's Malpensa airport (www.milanomalpensa-airport.com). Both are served by nonstop flights from around the world. Venice's Marco Polo airport (www.veniceairport.it) is also served by a handful of intercontinental flights.

Dozens of international airlines compete with the country's revamped national carrier, Alitalia, rated a three-star airline by UK aviation research company Skytrax. If you're flying from Africa or Oceania, you'll generally need to change planes at least once en route to Italy.

Intra-European flights serve plenty of other Italian cities; the leading mainstream carriers include Alitalia, Air France, British Airways, Lufthansa and KLM.

Cut-rate airlines, led by Ryanair and easyJet, fly from a growing number of European cities to more than two dozen Italian destinations, typically landing at smaller airports such as Rome's Ciampino (www.adr.it/ciampino).

Land

There are plenty of options for entering Italy by train, bus or private vehicle.

Border Crossings

Aside from the coast roads linking Italy with France and Slovenia, border crossings into Italy mostly involve tunnels through the Alps (open year-round) or mountain passes (seasonally closed or requiring snow chains). The list below outlines the major points of entry.

Austria From Innsbruck to Bolzano via A22/E45 (Brenner Pass); Villach to Tarvisio via A23/E55.

France From Nice to Ventimiglia via A10/E80; Modane to Turin via A32/E70 (Fréjus Tunnel); Chamonix to Courmayeur via A5/E25 (Mont Blanc Tunnel).

Slovenia From Sežana to Trieste via SR58/E70.

Switzerland From Martigny to Aosta via SS27/E27 (Grand St Bernard Tunnel); Lugano to Como via A9/E35.

Car & Motorcycle

- Every vehicle travelling across an international border should display a nationality plate of its country of registration.
- Always carry proof of vehicle ownership and evidence of third-party insurance. If driving an EU-registered vehicle, your home country insurance is sufficient. Ask your insurer for a European Accident Statement (EAS) form, which can simplify matters in the event of an accident. The form can also be downloaded online at http://cartraveldocs.com/european-accident-statement.

- A European breakdown assistance policy is a good investment and can be obtained through the Automobile Club d'Italia.
- Italy's scenic roads are tailor-made for motorcycle touring, and motorcyclists swarm into the country every summer. With a motorcycle you rarely have to book ahead for ferries and can enter restricted-traffic areas in cities. Crash helmets and a motorcycle licence are compulsory.

Train

Regular trains on two western lines connect Italy with France (one along the coast and the other from Turin into the French Alps). Trains from Milan head north into Switzerland and on towards the Benelux countries. Further east, two main lines head for the main cities in central and Eastern Europe. Those crossing the Brenner Pass go to Innsbruck, Stuttgart and Munich. Those crossing at Tarvisio proceed to Vienna, Salzburg and Prague. The main international train line to Slovenia crosses near Trieste.

Depending on distances covered, rail can be highly competitive with air travel. Those travelling from neighbouring countries to northern Italy will find it is frequently more comfortable, less expensive and only marginally more time-consuming than flying.

Those travelling longer distances (say, from London, Spain, northern Germany or Eastern Europe) will doubtless find flying cheaper and quicker.

The comprehensive European Rail Timetable (UK£15.99), updated monthly, is available for purchase online at www.europeanrailtimetable.co.uk, as well as at a handful of bookshops in the UK and continental Europe (see the website for details).

Reservations on international trains to/from Italy are always advisable, and sometimes compulsory.

Some international services include transport for private cars.

Consider taking long journeys overnight, as the supplemental fare for a sleeper costs substantially less than Italian hotels.

Getting Around

Italy's network of train, bus, ferry and domestic-air transport allows you to reach most destinations efficiently and relatively affordably.

Air

Italy offers an extensive network of internal flights. The privatised national airline, Alitalia, is the main domestic carrier, with numerous low-cost airlines also operating across the country. Useful search engines for comparing multiple carriers' fares (including those of cut-price airlines) are www.skyscanner.com, www.kayak.com and www.azfly.it. Airport taxes are factored into the price of your ticket.

Alitalia (☎89 20 10; www.alitalia.com)

Blu-express (☎06 9895 6666; www.blu-express.com)

easyJet (www.easyjet.com)

Etihad Regional (☎06 8997 0422; www.etihadregional.com)

Meridiana (☎89 29 28; www.meridiana.it)

Ryanair (☎895 5895509; www.ryanair.com)

Volotea (☎895 8954404; www.volotea.com)

Boat

Craft *Navi* (large ferries) service Sicily while *traghetti* (smaller ferries) and *aliscafi* (hydrofoils) service the smaller islands. Most ferries carry vehicles; hydrofoils do not.

Routes Main embarkation points for Sicily are Genoa, Livorno, Civitavecchia and Naples. Ferries for Sicily also leave from Villa San Giovanni and Reggio Calabria. Main arrival points in Sicily are Palermo, Catania, Trapani and Messina.

Timetables and tickets Comprehensive website Direct Ferries (www.directferries.co.uk) allows you to search routes, compare prices and book tickets for ferry routes in Italy.

Overnight ferries Travellers can book a two- to four-person cabin or a *poltrona,* which is an airline-type armchair. Deck class (which allows you to sit/sleep in lounge areas or on deck) is available only on some ferries.

Bus & Metro

Routes Bus routes cover everything from meandering local routes to fast, reliable

InterCity connections provided by numerous bus companies.

Cities and towns of any size have an efficient urbano (urban) and extraurbano (suburban) bus system. Services are generally limited on Sundays and holidays.

Extensive metropolitane (metros) exist in Rome, Milan and Naples with a smaller metro in Catania.

Timetables and tickets Intercity bus tickets are available on bus-company websites and from local tourist offices. Buses are generally competitively priced with the train and are often the only way to get to smaller towns. In larger cities most of the InterCity bus companies have ticket offices or sell tickets through agencies. In villages and even some good-sized towns, tickets are sold in bars or on the bus.

For local buses and metro purchase tickets before boarding and validate them once on board. Passengers with unvalidated tickets are subject to a fine (between €50 and €110). Buy tickets from a tabaccaio (tobacconist's shop), news-stands, ticket booths or dispensing machines at bus and metro stations. Tickets usually cost around €1.20 to €2. Many cities offer good-value 24-hour or daily tourist tickets.

Advance booking Generally not required, but advisable for overnight or long-haul bus trips in high season.

Car & Motorcycle

With your own vehicle, you'll enjoy greater freedom, but *benzina* (petrol) and *autostrada* (motorway) tolls are expensive and Italian drivers have a style all their own. For many, the stress of driving and parking in urban areas may outweigh the delights of puttering about the countryside. One solution is to take public transport between large cities and rent a car only to reach more-remote rural destinations.

Italy's extensive network of roads spans numerous categories. The main ones include the following:

- Autostradas – An extensive, privatised network of motorways, represented on road signs by a white 'A' followed by a number on a green background. The main north–south link is the A1. Also known as the Autostrada del Sole (the 'Motorway of the Sun'), it extends from Milan to Naples (called the A1). The main link from Naples south to Reggio di Calabria is the A3. There are tolls on most motorways, payable by cash or credit card as you exit.
- Strade statali (state highways) – Represented on maps by 'S' or 'SS'. Vary from toll-free, four-lane highways to two-lane main roads. The latter can be extremely slow, especially in mountainous regions.
- Strade regionali (regional highways connecting small villages) – Coded 'SR' or 'R'.
- Strade provinciali (provincial highways) – Coded 'SP' or 'P'.
- Strade locali – Often not even paved or mapped.

For information in English about distances, driving times and fuel costs, see en.mappy.com. Additional information, including traffic conditions and toll costs, is available at www.autostrade.it.

Automobile Associations

The **Automobile Club d'Italia** (ACI; ☎803 116, from a foreign mobile ☎800 116 800; www.aci.it) is a driver's best resource in Italy. Foreigners do not have to join to get 24-hour roadside emergency service but instead pay a per-incident fee.

Driving Licences

All EU driving licences are recognised in Italy. Travellers from other countries should obtain an International Driving Permit (IDP) through their national automobile association.

Fuel & Spare Parts

Italy's petrol prices vary from one service station *(benzinaio, stazione di servizio)* to another. At the time of writing, lead-free gasoline (*senza piombo;* 95 octane) averaged €1.57 per litre, with diesel *(gasolio)* costing €1.37 per litre.

Spare parts are available at many garages or via the 24-hour ACI motorist assistance number ☎803 116 (or ☎800 116800 if calling with a non-Italian mobile phone).

Hire

- Prebooking via the internet often costs less than hiring a car in Italy. Online booking agency Rentalcars.com (www.rentalcars.com) compares the rates of numerous car-rental companies.
- Renters must generally be aged 21 or over, with a credit card and home-country driving licence or IDP.

- Consider hiring a small car, which will reduce your fuel expenses and help you negotiate narrow city lanes and tight parking spaces.
- Check with your credit-card company to see if it offers a Collision Damage Waiver, which covers you for additional damage if you use that card to pay for the car.

The following companies have pick-up locations throughout Italy:

Auto Europe (www.autoeurope.com)
Avis (www.avis.com)
Budget (www.budget.com)
Europcar (www.europcar.com)
Hertz (www.hertz.it)
Italy by Car (www.italybycar.it)
Maggiore (www.maggiore.it)
Sixt (www.sixt.com)

Road Rules

- Cars drive on the right side of the road and overtake on the left. Unless otherwise indicated, always give way to cars entering an intersection from a road on your right.
- Seatbelt use (front and rear) is required by law; violators are subject to an on-the-spot fine. Helmets are required on all two-wheeled vehicles.
- Day and night, it is compulsory to drive with your headlights on outside built-up areas.
- It's obligatory to carry a warning triangle and fluorescent waistcoat in case of breakdown. Recommended accessories include a first-aid kit, spare-bulb kit and fire extinguisher.
- A licence is required to ride a scooter – a car licence will do for bikes up to 125cc; for anything over 125cc you'll need a motorcycle licence.
- Motorbikes can enter most restricted traffic areas in Italian cities, and traffic police generally turn a blind eye to motorcycles or scooters parked on footpaths.
- The blood-alcohol limit is 0.05%; for drivers under 21 and those who have had their licence for less than three years it's zero.

Unless otherwise indicated, speed limits are as follows:

- 130km/h on autostradas
- 110km/h on all main, non-urban roads
- 90km/h on secondary, non-urban roads
- 50km/h in built-up areas

Taxi

- You can catch a taxi at the ranks outside most train and bus stations, or simply telephone for a radio taxi. Radio taxi meters start running from when you've called rather than when you're picked up.
- Charges vary from one region to another. Most short city journeys cost between €10 and €15. Generally, no more than four people are allowed in one taxi.

Train

Trains in Italy are convenient and relatively cheap compared with other European countries.

Trenitalia (☎892021; www.trenitalia.com) is the national train system that runs most services. Its privately owned competitor **Italo** (☎060708; www.italotreno.it) runs high-velocity trains on two lines, one between Turin and Salerno, and one between Venice and Salerno.

Train tickets must be stamped in the green machines (usually found at the head of rail platforms) just before boarding. Failure to do so usually results in fines.

Italy operates several types of trains:

Regionale/interregionale Slow and cheap, stopping at all or most stations.

InterCity (IC) Faster services operating between major cities. Their international counterparts are called Eurocity (EC).

Alta Velocità (AV) State-of-the-art, high-velocity trains, including Frecciarossa, Frecciargento, Frecciabianca and Italo trains. with speeds of up to 300km/h and connections to the major cities. More expensive

TRAINS: HIGH-VELOCITY VS INTERCITY

From	To	High-Velocity Duration (hr)	Price (€)	InterCity Duration (hr)	Price (€)
Milan	Rome	3	79	7	38
Rome	Naples	1¼	39	2¼	26
Venice	Florence	2	45	2¾	28.50

than InterCity express trains, but journey times are cut by almost half.

Classes & Costs

Prices vary according to the class of service, time of travel and how far in advance you book. Most Italian trains have 1st- and 2nd-class seating; a 1st-class ticket typically costs from a third to half more than 2nd class.

Travel on Trenitalia's InterCity and Alta Velocità (Frecciarossa, Frecciargento, Frecciabianca) trains means paying a supplement, included in the ticket price, determined by the distance you are travelling. If you have a standard ticket for a slower train and end up hopping on an IC train, you'll have to pay the difference on board. (You can only board an Alta Velocità train if you have a booking, so the problem does not arise in those cases.)

Climate Change & Travel

Every form of transport that relies on carbon-based fuel generates CO_2, the main cause of human-induced climate change. Modern travel is dependent on aeroplanes, which might use less fuel per kilometre per person than most cars but travel much greater distances. The altitude at which aircraft emit gases (including CO_2) and particles also contributes to their climate change impact. Many websites offer 'carbon calculators' that allow people to estimate the carbon emissions generated by their journey and, for those who wish to do so, to offset the impact of the greenhouse gases emitted with contributions to portfolios of climate-friendly initiatives throughout the world. Lonely Planet offsets the carbon footprint of all staff and author travel.

Reservations

- Reservations are obligatory on AV trains. On other services they're not and, outside of peak holiday periods, you should be fine without them.
- Reservations can be made on the Trenitalia and Italo websites, at railway station counters and self-service ticketing machines, or through travel agents.
- Both Trenitalia and Italo offer a variety of advance purchase discounts. Basically, the earlier you book, the greater the saving. Discounted tickets are limited, and refunds and changes are highly restricted.

Language

Italian pronunciation isn't difficult as most sounds are also found in English. The pronunciation of some consonants depends on which vowel follows, but if you read our pronunciation guides below as if they were English, you'll be understood just fine. Just remember to pronounce double consonants as a longer, more forceful sound than single ones. The stressed syllables in words are in italics in our pronunciation guides.

To enhance your trip with a phrasebook, visit **lonelyplanet.com**. Lonely Planet iPhone phrasebooks are available through the Apple App store.

Basics

Hello.
Buongiorno./Ciao. (pol/inf) — bwon·*jor*·no/chow

How are you?
Come sta? — *ko*·me sta

I'm fine, thanks.
Bene, grazie. — *be*·ne *gra*·tsye

Excuse me.
Mi scusi. — mee *skoo*·zee

Yes./No.
Sì./No. — see/no

Please. (when asking)
Per favore. — per fa·*vo*·re

Thank you.
Grazie. — *gra*·tsye

Goodbye.
Arrivederci./Ciao. (pol/inf) — a·ree·ve·*der*·chee/chow

Do you speak English?
Parla inglese? — *par*·la een·*gle*·ze

I don't understand.
Non capisco. — non ka·*pee*·sko

How much is this?
Quanto costa? — *kwan*·to *ko*·sta

Accommodation

I'd like to book a room.
Vorrei prenotare una camera. — vo·*ray* pre·no·*ta*·re *oo*·na *ka*·me·ra

How much is it per night?
Quanto costa per una notte? — *kwan*·to *kos*·ta per *oo*·na *no*·te

Eating & Drinking

I'd like ..., please.
Vorrei . . ., per favore. — vo·*ray* . . . per fa·*vo*·re

What would you recommend?
Cosa mi consiglia? — *ko*·za mee kon·*see*·lya

That was delicious!
Era squisito! — *e*·ra skwee·*zee*·to

Bring the bill/check, please.
Mi porta il conto, per favore. — mee *por*·ta eel *kon*·to per fa·*vo*·re

I'm allergic (to peanuts).
Sono allergico/a (alle arachidi). (m/f) — *so*·no a·*ler*·jee·ko/a (*a*·le a·*ra*·kee·dee)

I don't eat ...
Non mangio . . . — non *man*·jo . . .

fish	*pesce*	*pe*·she
meat	*carne*	*kar*·ne
poultry	*pollame*	po·*la*·me

Emergencies

I'm ill.
Mi sento male. — mee *sen*·to *ma*·le

Help!
Aiuto! — a·*yoo*·to

Call a doctor!
Chiami un medico! — *kya*·mee oon *me*·dee·ko

Call the police!
Chiami la polizia! — *kya*·mee la po·lee·*tsee*·a

Directions

I'm looking for (a/the) ...
Cerco . . . — *cher*·ko . . .

bank
la banca — la *ban*·ka

... embassy
la ambasciata de . . . — la am·ba·*sha*·ta de . . .

market
il mercato — eel mer·*ka*·to

museum
il museo — eel moo·*ze*·o

restaurant
un ristorante — oon rees·to·*ran*·te

toilet
un gabinetto — oon ga·bee·*ne*·to

tourist office
l'ufficio del turismo — loo·*fee*·cho del too·*reez*·mo

Behind the Scenes

Acknowledgements

Climate map data adapted from Peel MC, Finlayson BL & McMahon TA (2007) 'Updated World Map of the Koppen-Geiger Climate Classification', *Hydrology and Earth System Sciences*, 11, 163344

Illustrations pp56–57, pp262–263 by Javier Martinez Zarracina

Send Us Your Feedback

We love to hear from travellers – your comments keep us on our toes and help make our books better. Our well-travelled team reads every word on what you loved or loathed about this book. Although we cannot reply individually to postal submissions, we always guarantee that your feedback goes straight to the appropriate authors, in time for the next edition. Each person who sends us information is thanked in the next edition, the most useful submissions are rewarded with a selection of digital PDF chapters.

Visit lonelyplanet.com/contact to submit your updates and suggestions or to ask for help. Our award-winning website also features inspirational travel stories, news and discussions.

Note: We may edit, reproduce and incorporate your comments in Lonely Planet products such as guidebooks, websites and digital products, so let us know if you don't want your comments reproduced or your name acknowledged. For a copy of our privacy policy visit lonelyplanet.com/privacy.

This Book

This book was curated by Duncan Garwood and researched and written by Cristian Bonetto, Abigail Blasi, Kerry Christiani, Gregor Clark, Belinda Dixon, Paula Hardy, Brendan Sainsbury, Donna Wheeler and Nicola Williams. Helena Smith was a contributing author.
This guidebook was commissioned in Lonely Planet's Melbourne office, and produced by the following:
Destination Editor Anna Tyler
Series Designer Campbell McKenzie
Cartographic Series Designer Wayne Murphy
Product Editor Tracy Whitmey
Senior Cartographers Corey Hutchison, Anthony Phelan
Book Designer Wibowo Rusli
Cartographers Julie Dodkins, Gabriel Lindquist
Assisting Editors Charlotte Orr, Saralinda Turner
Cover Researcher Naomi Parker
Associate Product Director Liz Heynes
Thanks to Sasha Baskett, Andrew Bigger, Katie Coffee, Daniel Corbett, Ruth Cosgrove, Laura Crawford, Brendan Dempsey-Spencer, Elizabeth Jones, James Hardy, Anna Harris, Victoria Harrison, Indra Kilfoyle, Georgina Leslie, Kate Mathews, Dan Moore, Darren O'Connell, Katie O'Connell, Kirsten Rawlings, Diana Saengkham, Dianne Schallmeiner, Ellie Simpson, Luna Soo, Lyahna Spencer, John Taufa, Angela Tinson, Lauren Wellicome, Juan Winata

Index

000 Map pages

L

M

N

O

P

000 Map pages

Symbols & Map Key

Look for these symbols to quickly identify listings:

- Sights
- Activities
- Courses
- Tours
- Festivals & Events
- Eating
- Drinking
- Entertainment
- Shopping
- Information & Transport

These symbols and abbreviations give vital information for each listing:

- Sustainable or green recommendation
- FREE No payment required

- Telephone number
- Opening hours
- Parking
- Nonsmoking
- Air-conditioning
- Internet access
- Wi-fi access
- Swimming pool
- Bus
- Ferry
- Tram
- Train
- English-language menu
- Vegetarian selection
- Family-friendly

Find your best experiences with these Great For... icons.

 Budget

 Food & Drink

Drinking

 Cycling

 Shopping

Sport

 Art & Culture

 Events

Photo Op

Scenery

Family Travel

 Short Trip

 Detour

Walking

Local Life

History

 Entertainment

 Beaches

 Winter Travel

 Cafe/Coffee

 Nature & Wildlife

Sights

- Beach
- Bird Sanctuary
- Buddhist
- Castle/Palace
- Christian
- Confucian
- Hindu
- Islamic
- Jain
- Jewish
- Monument
- Museum/Gallery/Historic Building
- Ruin
- Shinto
- Sikh
- Taoist
- Winery/Vineyard
- Zoo/Wildlife Sanctuary
- Other Sight

Points of Interest

- Bodysurfing
- Camping
- Cafe
- Canoeing/Kayaking
- Course/Tour
- Diving
- Drinking & Nightlife
- Eating
- Entertainment
- Sento Hot Baths/Onsen
- Shopping
- Skiing
- Sleeping
- Snorkelling
- Surfing
- Swimming/Pool
- Walking
- Windsurfing
- Other Activity

Information

- Bank
- Embassy/Consulate
- Hospital/Medical
- Internet
- Police
- Post Office
- Telephone
- Toilet
- Tourist Information
- Other Information

Geographic

- Beach
- Gate
- Hut/Shelter
- Lighthouse
- Lookout
- Mountain/Volcano
- Oasis
- Park
- Pass
- Picnic Area
- Waterfall

Transport

- Airport
- BART station
- Border crossing
- Boston T station
- Bus
- Cable car/Funicular
- Cycling
- Ferry
- Metro/MRT station
- Monorail
- Parking
- Petrol station
- Subway/S-Bahn/Skytrain station
- Taxi
- Train station/Railway
- Tram
- Tube Station
- Underground/U-Bahn station
- Other Transport

Kerry Christiani

Kerry has been drawn back to Italy again and again ever since she toured the country one hazy postgraduation summer in a 1960s bubble caravan. An award-winning travel writer, Kerry authors a number of Lonely Planet guidebooks, including *Sardinia*, and contributes regularly to magazines, newspapers and blog sites. She tweets @kerrychristiani.

Gregor Clark

Gregor caught the Italy bug at age 14 while living in Florence with his professor dad, who took him to see every fresco, mosaic and museum within a 1000km radius. He's lived in Florence and Le Marche and huffed and puffed across the Dolomites while researching Lonely Planet's *Cycling Italy*. A lifelong polyglot with a Romance Languages degree, Gregor has written for Lonely Planet since 2000, with an emphasis on Mediterranean Europe and Latin America.

Belinda Dixon

Having cut her travel teeth on Italy's ferries and trains, rarely has a year passed when Belinda hasn't been back. Research highlights include gazing at mountains while ferry-hopping those gorgeous lakes, encountering Mantua's extraordinary art, tasting olive oil in Malcesine and Bardolino in, well, Bardolino – and always delighting in this, the *bel paese*.

Paula Hardy

From Lido beaches to annual Biennales and spritz-fuelled aperitivo bars, Paula has contributed to Lonely Planet Italian guides for over 15 years, including previous editions of *Venice & the Veneto, Pocket Milan, The Italian Lakes, Sicily, Sardinia* and *Puglia & Basilicata*. When she's not scooting around the *bel paese*, she writes for a variety of travel publications and websites. Currently she divides her time between London, Italy and Morocco, and tweets her finds @paula6hardy.

Brendan Sainsbury

An expat Brit from Hampshire, England, now living near Vancouver, Canada, Brendan has covered Italy five times for Lonely Planet, reporting on 16 of its 20 regions. When not scribbling research notes for Lonely Planet in countries such as Cuba, Peru, Spain and Canada, Brendan likes to run up mountains, strum his flamenco guitar, and experience the pain and occasional pleasure of following Southampton Football Club.

Donna Wheeler

Italy's border regions are Donna Wheeler's dream assignment: Alps, the sea, complex histories, plus spectacular wine and food. Donna has lived in Turin's Quadrilatero Romano and Genova's *centro storico* and been an Italian-by-marriage for almost two decades. A former commissioning editor and content strategist, she's written guidebooks to Italy, France, Tunisia, Algeria, Norway and Belgium and publishes on art, architecture, history and food for LonelyPlanet.com, BBC.com Travel, National Geographic Traveler and My Art Guides; she is also the creative director of travel magazine *She Came to Stay*.

Nicola Williams

British writer Nicola Williams lives on the southern shore of Lake Geneva. Thankfully for her Italianate soul, it is an easy hop through the Mont Blanc Tunnel to Italy where she has spent years eating her way around and revelling in its extraordinary art, architecture, cuisine and landscape. Hunting Tuscan white truffles in October is an annual family ritual. Nicola has worked on numerous titles for Lonely Planet, including *Italy, Milan, Turin & Genoa*, and *Piedmont*. She shares her travels on Twitter at @Tripalong.

Our Story

A beat-up old car, a few dollars in the pocket and a sense of adventure. In 1972 that's all Tony and Maureen Wheeler needed for the trip of a lifetime – across Europe and Asia overland to Australia. It took several months, and at the end – broke but inspired – they sat at their kitchen table writing and stapling together their first travel guide, *Across Asia on the Cheap*. Within a week they'd sold 1500 copies. Lonely Planet was born. Melbourne, London, Oakland, Franklin, Delhi and Beijing, with more than 600 staff and writers. We share Tony's belief that 'a great guidebook should do three things: inform, educate and amuse'.

Our Writers

Duncan Garwood

A Brit travel writer based in the Castelli Romani hills just outside Rome, Duncan has clocked up endless kilometres walking around the Italian capital and exploring the far-flung reaches of the surrounding Lazio region. He's co-author of Lonely Planet's *Rome* city guide and has worked on the past six editions of Lonely Planet's *Italy* guide as well as guides to Piedmont, Sicily, Sardinia, and Naples and the Amalfi Coast. He has also written on Italy for newspapers and magazines.

Abigail Blasi

Abigail moved to Rome in 2003 and lived there for three years; she got married alongside Lago Bracciano and her first son was born in Rome. Nowadays she divides her time between Rome, Puglia and London. She has worked on four editions of Lonely Planet's *Italy* and *Rome* guides and written the 1st edition of *Puglia & Basilicata*. She also regularly writes about Italy for various publications, including the *Independent*, the *Guardian*, and *Lonely Planet Traveller*.

Cristian Bonetto

Thanks to his Italo-Australian heritage, Cristian gets to experience the *bel paese* (beautiful country) as both a local and an outsider. His musings on Italian cuisine, culture and style have appeared in media across the globe and his contributions for Lonely Planet include more than 30 travel guide editions, including *Naples & the Amalfi Coast*, *Venice & the Veneto*, *Denmark*, *New York City* and *Singapore*. Follow Cristian on Twitter (@CristianBonetto) and Instagram (rexcat75).

More Writers

STAY IN TOUCH lonelyplanet.com/contact

AUSTRALIA Levels 2 & 3, 551 Swanston St, Carlton, Victoria 3053 ☎ 03 8379 8000, fax 03 8379 8111

USA 150 Linden Street, Oakland, CA 94607 ☎ 510 250 6400, toll free 800 275 8555, fax 510 893 8572

UK 240 Blackfriars Road, London SE1 8NW ☎ 020 3771 5100, fax 020 3771 5101

twitter.com/lonelyplanet

facebook.com/lonelyplanet

instagram.com/lonelyplanet

youtube.com/lonelyplanet

lonelyplanet.com/newsletter